The Republican Party and Black America

From McKinley to Hoover

1896–1933

The Republican Party and Black America

From McKinley to Hoover

1896-1933

Richard B. Sherman

The College of William and Mary

University Press of Virginia

Charlottesville

For Hanni, Alan, and Linda

THE UNIVERSITY PRESS OF VIRGINIA

First published 1973

ISBN: 0-8139-0467-6
Library of Congress Catalog Card Number: 72-96714
Printed in the United States of America

The Republican Party is the deck, all else is the sea.

—Frederick Douglass, at New Orleans convention of Negro workers, April 1872

Preface

THE devotion of Republicans to democratic and equalitarian principles has always, and inevitably, been tempered by their understanding of the demands of practical politics. During the Reconstruction period after the Civil War the Radicals hoped that their program would promote both these ideals and their party's political fortunes. The granting of the vote and other rights to the freedmen was also a means of gaining and maintaining Republican control in the South. Ultimately, this approach failed on both counts. The rights of the freedmen were sharply curtailed, and the South became Democratic. To be sure, the end of Reconstruction did not mean that Republicans immediately and finally abandoned all efforts to protect Negroes, or to regain a political hold on the South, for during the two decades after 1876 the GOP was in a precarious position in national politics. Neither Hayes, Garfield, nor Harrison was elected by a popular majority, and more often than not the Democrats controlled the House of Representatives and, for two Congresses, even the Senate. Hence some Republicans looked to black voters as a base for a southern revival or even for a strengthening of their position in parts of the North. But such attempts were sporadic and ineffective. In the mid-1890's political conditions changed significantly. At that time the GOP finally emerged as the majority party in the United States, a position it enjoyed, with the exception of a few years of the Wilson administration, until the early 1930's. The new status of the Republican party had important implications for black Americans. On the one hand, it appeared that their votes were not needed to elect Republican presidents or to maintain Republican control of Congress, and they could be safely ignored. On the other, it seemed possible that the GOP might at last have the power to enact and enforce measures to protect and advance Negro rights. The reaction of national Republican leaders to this challenge, the attitudes and actions they took in regard to black Americans during the period of GOP ascendancy from McKinley through Hoover, is the subject of this book.

In preparing this study I have inevitably become indebted to a number of institutions and individuals. For assistance in the early stages of my research I am grateful to The College of William and Mary for grants from the Committee on Faculty Research and for being selected as a recipient of one of the Howard L. Willett Prize Awards. My research was also supported by two grants from the Penrose Fund of the American Philosophical Society. A year spent in Sweden as a Fulbright Lecturer relieved me of all but the lightest teaching duties and afforded me an opportunity to prepare a first draft of the book.

I have received the cheerful assistance from the librarians of a number of institutions and would particularly like to acknowledge my indebtedness to the staff of the Collis P. Huntington Memorial Library at Hampton Institute, Widener Library at Harvard University, the Manuscript Division of the Library of Congress, the Ohio Historical Society, the Herbert C. Hoover Presidential Library, and the Swem Library of The College of William and Mary.

I should also like to thank my colleagues at The College of William and Mary, particularly Ludwell H. Johnson and Helen C. Walker, for suggestions and for the opportunity to discuss with them some aspects of this work. I am also grateful to many of my students with whom I had a chance to talk about a number of the problems and results of my research.

My wife deserves more than the usual word of thanks for her patience and for her assistance in innumerable ways throughout all stages of this project.

The author gratefully acknowledges permission to quote from Elting E. Morison, ed., *The Letters of Theodore Roosevelt* (Cambridge, Mass.: Harvard University Press, 1951–54). The brief quotations from *Along This Way: The Autobiography of James Weldon Johnson,* copyright 1933 by James Weldon Johnson, renewed © 1961 by Grace Nail Johnson, are reprinted by permission of The Viking Press, Inc. A few passages of this study were first published in a somewhat different form in my article "The Harding Administration and the Negro: An Opportunity Lost," © The Association for the Study of Negro Life and History, Inc., published in *The Journal of Negro History,* XLIX (July 1964), and are included with the Association's permission.

Contents

The Republican Party and Black America

From McKinley to Hoover

1896–1933

CHAPTER I

The Price of Unity

On inaugural day, March 4, 1897, William McKinley had reason to feel proud and hopeful. The presidential campaign had been long, bitter, and divisive, but he had led the Republican party to its greatest victory in a generation, and he was confident that his administration could heal the wounds of that contest, oversee the restoration of prosperity, maintain peace, and promote national unity. The election, he asserted in his inaugural address, was "not the triumph of one section, nor wholly of one party, but of all sections and all the people." Black Americans could not help harboring some doubts whether McKinley was including them. Encouraged by his pledge that "equality of rights must prevail," they nevertheless wondered what this would mean in practice. They had suffered too many disappointments since Reconstruction to allow the thoughtful among them to be optimistic. Despite the GOP's traditional commitment to the Negro, it was far from certain that the return of the Republicans to power would be accompanied by a meaningful concern for the problems of black America.

Such doubts stemmed from the very nature of the party, for from the start Republicans had been divided by conflicting attitudes toward Negroes. Abolitionist fervor had contrasted with indifference, equalitarianism with racism, reformism with neglect, and high idealism with crass political expediency. Nevertheless, with the Civil War, emancipation, and enfranchisement, the historic bond of Negroes to the Republican party was firmly established. Although that association became increasingly unhappy in the post-Reconstruction period, neither side could easily cast it aside.

Basic to the calculations of Republican politicians was the fact that from the mid-1870's to the mid-1890's their party was, nationally, in a precarious position. The GOP controlled both the Senate and the House of Representatives in only two Congresses during those years, and in two elections it lost the presidency to the Democrats. Even the successful presidential candidates failed to win a majority of the popular vote. The Republican party's position had to be strengthened, and until this was done it was risky to ignore black voters entirely. In close elections, even their votes in the North, although not very numerous, could be significant, and their support in the border states and the South was even more important.

Because some 90 percent of the Negro population in the United States then lived in the South, the key to the Republican party's relations with black America was its southern policy. Between Hayes and McKinley, however, the party followed no consistent approach. After the initial attempt to construct a Republican South had collapsed in 1877, some Republicans continued to hope that a successful GOP, based largely on black voters, could still be created, or that at the very least their party could win a few congressional seats. But the party actually took few steps to maintain Negro support. In each presidential election during the 1880's and early 1890's the GOP adopted a platform renewing its promises to the black community and reminding the faithful of the wrongs perpetrated by the Democratic South. In addition Republican presidents made occasional showcase appointments, which may have helped to keep some Negro politicians in line. Such devices probably helped as much to encourage black voters in the North as in the South. They did nothing to enlarge the Republican electorate or to protect the Negro's right to the franchise.

Other Republicans argued that the best hope of cracking the solid South was to turn away from the Negro and to court the independent white voter, an approach adopted by President Arthur during the early 1880's. Some wanted to construct a new lily-white Republican party, a strategy that became increasingly popular during the 1890's. An opposite point of view was still represented, at least until the early 1890's, by those Republicans who proposed a return to the harsher methods of Reconstruction in order to guarantee the Negro's right to vote. The last serious effort of this sort was the Lodge Federal Elections bill, passed by the House in July 1890. It was a short-lived victory, for the measure was soon abandoned by Senate Republicans who sought Democratic support for high tariff and silver legislation. Thus ended the last possibility for a Republican revival in the South in which Negroes might play a major role, and thus was maintained the practice of favoring business or other interests at the expense of civil rights.

The events of the two decades before McKinley's election showed how tenuous was the Republican party's commitment to equalitarian ideals. Nevertheless, few Negroes severed their connection with it. Many, of course, felt an emotional attachment to the party of Lincoln and emancipation. Party positions and federal jobs attracted a limited but influential number of black politicians. Beyond such considerations, the simple fact was that most Negroes had nowhere else to go. By the 1880's some dissidents began to recommend political independence, but not many were willing to follow a course that seemed so uncertain in leadership and unpromising in results, and others feared that it might endanger the small influence that Negroes still had in the Republican party. Most Negroes remained loyal to this political organization that was increasingly uninterested in their welfare and that took their support largely for granted.[1]

While Negroes generally welcomed the Republican victory in 1896, they could not be certain about its significance. McKinley was the first president since Grant to have been elected by a majority of the voters, and his party controlled both houses of Congress for only the third time since 1874. As a result the Republicans had a political advantage such as they had not enjoyed in two decades and, in theory at least, had greater power to act. Yet this new majority status also meant that one of the principal reasons for courting the black vote—the party's precarious position—had disappeared. Not previously united on the race question, Republicans were unlikely to become so in 1896.

McKinley both reflected and encouraged a conservative mood that hardly seemed compatible with a rededication to the GOP's equalitarian ideals. With the defeat of the radical reformers in 1896 and with clear signs of recovery from the severe economic depression, he had no interest in disturbing the confidence of businessmen by embarking on idealistic adventures. His reputation as an amiable and decent man helped to sanctify the country's dominant materialist ethic. McKinley had no intention of rocking the boat on the race question. During his early years in politics after the Civil War he had consistently supported the Republican party's goal of civil rights for the freedmen, but he had not been a crusader or a calculated waver of the bloody shirt. By 1896 he had come to prefer ap-

[1] Vincent P. DeSantis, *Republicans Face the Southern Question: The New Departure Years, 1877–1897* (Baltimore, 1959); Stanley P. Hirshon, *Farewell to the Bloody Shirt: Northern Republicans and the Southern Negro, 1877–1893* (Bloomington, Ind., 1962); Rayford W. Logan, *The Betrayal of the Negro, from Rutherford B. Hayes to Woodrow Wilson* (enl. ed., New York, 1965); Leslie H. Fishel, Jr., "The Negro in Northern Politics, 1870–1900," *Mississippi Valley Historical Review*, 42 (Dec. 1955), 466–89; Leslie H. Fishel, Jr., "The North and the Negro, 1865–1900: A Study in Race Discrimination" (Ph.D. diss., Harvard University, 1953); Elsie M. Lewis, "The Political Mind of the Negro, 1865–1900," *Journal of Southern History*, 21 (May 1955), 189–202. On the Republican party and presidential politics, see also Robert D. Marcus, *Grand Old Party: Political Structure in the Gilded Age, 1880–1896* (New York, 1971); H. Wayne Morgan, *From Hayes to McKinley: National Party Politics, 1877–1896* (Syracuse, N.Y., 1969); Carl N. Degler, "The Great Reversal: The Republican Party's First Century," *South Atlantic Quarterly*, 65 (Winter 1966), 1–11.

peals to national unity to positions that might arouse sectional discord. Neither political necessity nor personal inclination was likely to prompt him to confront the South in defense of black Americans. Rather, he concluded that he could best serve his country and his party by avoiding conflict and championing a patriotic nationalism.

McKinley's attitude toward the South caused uneasiness in the minds of some Negroes. His first interest in the region had been directed toward obtaining delegates to the 1896 Republican national convention. In early 1895 his friend Mark Hanna launched a drive to win southern support by purchasing a home in Thomasville, Georgia, which was used as a base of operations in presenting McKinley to important southerners. Numerous whites responded favorably to his personality and economic ideas. McKinley's views on tariff protection for local products were popular among a growing number of southern businessmen. As his support increased, politicians were naturally impressed not only by his charm and dignity but by the fact that he appeared to be a winner.[2]

Although Hanna and McKinley were primarily interested in gaining the support of white leaders, they also invited some Negroes to their Thomasville headquarters. They could ill afford to ignore the fact that black politicians held many important places in the Republican party organizations in the South. Nevertheless, the word spread that they intended to abandon blacks in favor of a lily-white party. Somewhat alarmed, McKinley denounced the rumor as a "base charge" and an insinuation that was "utterly without foundation," and he pledged that he favored "according to every Republican, black or white, the fullest privileges and greatest opportunities."[3]

Thanks to the efforts of Hanna and his assistants, McKinley was able to go to St. Louis with a commanding lead, including the support of all the regular southern delegations except the one from Texas. Since nearly half of the votes needed for nomination came from southern and border states, McKinley's first concern was whether these delegates were loyal to him. At that point race was a secondary matter. The McKinley forces sought the support of Negro politicians whenever it seemed desirable. Both sets of contesting delegations

[2] Herbert Croly, *Marcus Alonzo Hanna: His Life and Work* (New York, 1919), pp. 175–80; Margaret Leech, *In the Days of McKinley* (New York, 1959), pp. 62–64; H. Wayne Morgan, *William McKinley and His America* (Syracuse, N.Y., 1963), pp. 192–94; Morgan, *From Hayes to McKinley*, p. 490; Charles S. Olcott, *The Life of William McKinley* (Boston, 1916), I, 298–305; Olive H. Shadgett, *The Republican Party in Georgia, from Reconstruction through 1900* (Athens, Ga., 1964), pp. 123–29.

[3] McKinley to A. E. Buck, Jan. 8, 1896, McKinley to Walter H. Johnson, Jan. 8, 1896, McKinley Papers, Manuscript Division, Library of Congress.

from Alabama, Georgia, Mississippi, and Tennessee included some Negroes, and in drawing up the roll the national committee seems to have been primarily guided by whether the prospective delegates favored McKinley.[4] The same was true for other states. The regular, if ineffective, black-and-tan delegation from South Carolina was seated over an opposing group of lily-whites.[5] The situation in Louisiana was much more complicated. On the one hand were the lily-white National Republicans, a faction formed in 1894 by protectionist sugar planters, and on the other were the regular black-and-tans. Both sides favored McKinley. The national committee played it safe and favored the latter in selecting delegates-at-large and some of the district delegates.[6] Texas was the only southern state in which the regular party organization, led by a Negro, Norris Wright Cuney, did not support McKinley. Not surprisingly, a contesting delegation committed to the Ohioan was finally seated. This incident marked the end of Cuney's long period of control over the Republican party in Texas and provided the principal support for the charge that McKinley favored a lily-white party in the South.[7]

If the decisions on the contested delegations provided no conclusive evidence about McKinley's intentions for the southern GOP, the precarious position of Negroes was illustrated in other ways at the national convention. Black delegates, for example, were discriminated against by some St. Louis hotels. The fact that the national committee had selected a border-state city as the site of the convention for the first time in the party's history suggested a lessened concern for the welfare of the blacks and made more probable the

[4] Mark Hanna to J. C. Napier, April 15, April 20, 1896, McKinley to R. R. Wright, Jan. 4, 1896, McKinley to A. E. Buck, Jan. 4, 1896, McKinley Papers; New York *Times*, June 11–14, 1896; Shadgett, pp. 131–34. On Hanna's use of Ohio Negroes to keep southern black delegates in line, see Jere A. Brown to Hanna, April 11, 1896, Brown to George A. Myers, April 18, 1896, George A. Myers Papers, Ohio Historical Society. See also Marcus, pp. 224–25.

[5] New York *Times*, June 14, 1896.

[6] F. N. Wicker to C. S. Kelsey, May 20, 22, and 23, 1896, McKinley Papers; New York *Times*, June 13, 1896; De Santis, pp. 251–58; Philip D. Uzee, "The Republican Party in the Louisiana Election of 1896," *Louisiana History*, 2 (Summer 1961), 332–44.

[7] New York *Times*, June 14, June 18, 1896; *Official Proceedings of the Eleventh Republican National Convention Held in the City of Saint Louis, Mo., June 16, 17 and 18, 1896*, pp. 48, 61; Paul Casdorph, *A History of the Republican Party in Texas, 1865–1965* (Austin, Tex., 1965), pp. 64–69; Maud Cuney Hare, *Norris Wright Cuney: A Tribune of the Black People* (New York, 1913), p. 195; Lawrence D. Rice, *The Negro in Texas, 1874–1900* (Baton Rouge, La., 1971), pp. 48–50; Jack Abramowitz, "The Negro in the Populist Movement," *Journal of Negro History*, 38 (July 1953), 269.

likelihood of trouble. At all previous conventions Negro delegates encountered no color bar in obtaining public accommodations, and in choosing St. Louis the national committee had been satisfied with a promise that they would continue to be properly received. Unfortunately, a number of hotels ignored this pledge. Two Negro alternates from Massachusetts obtained their rooms only after the entire state delegation threatened to move elsewhere; other delegates simply were denied promised accommodations. The unpleasantness was alleviated to some extent when the New York State McKinley League placed its special train of sleeping and dining cars at the disposal of the Negro delegates. Nevertheless, some Negroes blamed McKinley for their troubles.[8]

More significant was the Republicans' lack of interest in the pressing problems of black Americans. The liveliest debates over the platform concerned money and the tariff, not civil rights. Some Negroes attempted to get the delegates to take a stand on their behalf, but when the convention finally adopted a Negro plank it was the shortest since Reconstruction. It merely demanded that every citizen "be allowed to cast one free and unrestricted ballot" which should "be counted and returned as cast," and it condemned lynching. But it failed to recommend any legislation or other actions to deal with civil rights problems.

During the campaign McKinley made a serious effort to strengthen Republicanism among southern whites. A number of observers foresaw the impending breakup of the solid South.[9] One basis for this prediction was the increasing sympathy being expressed for Republican economic doctrines by such groups as the National Republicans in Louisiana. Another was the fact that McKinley undercut a principal justification for the Democratic control of the South by carefully avoiding any hint that he might interfere in domestic racial matters. In his letters accepting the party's nomination he did not mention black Americans. Instead he stressed the spirit of forbearance between North and South and the obliteration of sectional lines. "The era of reconciliation . . . has happily come," he asserted, "and the feeling of distrust and hostility between the sections is everywhere vanishing."[10]

Despite this emphasis on national unity, the election returns showed that the predicted demise of the solid South had been pre-

8 New York *Times*, June 8–12. 1896; Hare, pp. 193–94.

9 See, for example, the editorials in the New York *Times*, July 31, Aug. 4, 1896; B. J. Ramage, "The Dissolution of the 'Solid South,'" *Sewanee Review*, 4 (Aug. 1896), 493–510.

10 *Proc. 11th Rep. Nat. Conv.*, p. 159.

mature. All eleven southern states remained Democratic. While the Republican vote generally increased over that received in 1892, when the Populists had split the electorate, McKinley's proportion of the total vote was less than Harrison's in 1888, except in Georgia and Texas. Indeed, in the South as a whole the Republican percentage of the popular vote fell below that received in any presidential election since Reconstruction.[11] Still, the picture was not entirely bad for the Republicans. Among the border states, which had all gone Democratic in 1892, McKinley carried Delaware, Kentucky, Maryland, and West Virginia. Except for Kentucky these states remained Republican in nearly every presidential election through 1928. Moreover, the increased vote in Georgia, the improved showing in several cities of the South, and the gains over 1892 were enough to keep alive the talk about the coming dissolution of the solid South.[12] The returns did not seem to contradict McKinley's opinion that the best course of action was to stress sectional harmony while leaving the South alone to work out its racial problems.

At the very beginning of his administration McKinley made it clear that the promotion of national unity, the final reconciliation of North and South, was to be a major objective of his presidency. In his inaugural address he asserted:

> The recent election not only fortunately demonstrated the obliteration of sectional or geographical lines, but to some extent also the prejudices which for years have distracted our country and marred our true greatness as a nation. . . . The North and South no longer divide on the old lines, but upon principles and policies. . . . It will be my constant aim to do nothing, and permit nothing to be done, that will arrest or disturb his growing sentiment of unity and co-operation, this revival of esteem and affiliation which now animates so many thousands in both the old antagonistic sections, but I shall cheerfully do everything possible to promote and increase it.[13]

Despite this enthusiastic declaration, Negroes had reason to view McKinley's commitment to national unity with considerable apprehension. In view of the mounting Negrophobia in the South, sectional harmony was likely to be achieved only by the North's acquiescence in the South's repression of its black minority.

In June 1897 McKinley made the first of two presidential tours of the South. He was warmly received by southerners who found him

[11] See Appendix A.

[12] New York *Times*, Nov. 4, Nov. 10, 1896; Edward P. Clark, "The 'Solid South' Dissolving," *Forum*, 22 (Nov. 1896), 263–74; Marion L. Dawson, "Will the South Be Solid Again?" *North American Review*, 164 (Feb. 1897), 192–98.

[13] James D. Richardson, ed., *A Compilation of the Messages and Papers of the Presidents, 1789–1904* (rev. and enl. ed., n.p., 1905), X, 18.

personally attractive and who were flattered by the unaccustomed attention he was granting to their section. They were also highly receptive to McKinley's repeated emphasis on national unity. The success of the trip seemed to some observers to indicate a widespread sympathy for McKinley's economic principles of sound money and protectionism, and thus that there was an economic basis for the growth of southern Republicanism among whites.[14] The obstacles to the obliteration of sectional lines remained very formidable, however. Once McKinley went beyond vague rhetoric and attempted to deal with concrete problems, he found that his goodwill gestures had not granted him or his party immunity from attack by sensitive white southerners.

One such source of difficulty was the question of Negro appointments. Since Hayes, Republican presidents had regularly named a few Negroes to positions in the federal government. Some were in the diplomatic and consular services; others were in the departments in Washington, D.C.; and a larger number were in the South, primarily as postmasters or collectors of customs. These appointments were useful politically in helping to keep Negro leaders faithful to the GOP, and they probably provided some vicarious satisfaction for rank-and-file black Republicans. Despite McKinley's desire to placate the white South, he believed that he could not afford to ignore the wishes of all the Negro politicians who had contributed to his nomination in 1896, for their services might be again needed in 1900. Hence, he appointed a few Negroes to positions in the South and elsewhere.[15] Southern whites did not vigorously oppose all of these appointments, but some led to acrimonious controversies that damaged McKinley and his party in the South.

Such a situation arose in North Carolina. The Republican party in that state was one of the strongest in the South, and it had the support not only of Negroes, who were concentrated in the eastern counties, but of many whites, especially in the Piedmont and mountain sections. Leaders came from both races. In 1894 the Republicans had cooperated with the Populists to elect a so-called fusion legisla-

[14] For material on this southern trip, see the McKinley Papers, microfilm, ser. 12, reel 94.

[15] For lists of Negro appointees, see *Republican Campaign Text-Book: 1900*, p. 149; Republican National Committee, *What Has McKinley Done for the Colored Man?*, doc. no. 118 (n.p., 1900), copy in file of Republican National Committee Documents, Widener Library, Harvard University; T. H. R. Clarke and Sergeant B. McKay, eds., *A Republican Text-Book for Colored Voters* (n.p., 1900?), pp. 11–12; Lawrence J. W. Hayes, *The Negro Federal Government Worker: A Study of His Classification in the District of Columbia, 1883–1938* (Washington, D.C., 1941), p. 29.

ture, which in 1895 revised the election laws, making it easier for Negroes to register and vote. Negroes were also appointed to several state jobs and elected to some local offices. In 1896 George H. White, a Negro, was elected to Congress for the first of two successive terms.[16] As a result, Democrats raised the cry of Negro domination in their effort to regain power. In the midst of this growing racial tension McKinley appointed, among others, John C. Dancy as collector of customs at Wilmington in 1897. Long active in politics, Dancy had held the same post under President Harrison and was considered to be a conservative on race questions. But his $4,000 salary, higher than that of the state's governor, aroused considerable jealousy, and the Democrats demanded his removal. He finally left in 1901, when he was made recorder of deeds in Washington, D.C.[17] In the meantime racial tensions reached the explosive stage, culminating in a bloody riot in Wilmington in November 1898. Although McKinley's Negro appointments were not the basic cause of the deterioration in race relations, in such an explosive atmosphere he had little room to maneuver. By the end of his administration the once-promising growth of the Republican party in North Carolina based on the cooperation of Negroes and whites had been checked. Campaigning for white supremacy, the Democrats regained control of the state legislature in the November 1898 election.[18]

Another problem area was Louisiana, where the GOP was torn by the struggle between the powerful lily-white National Republicans and the regular black-and-tans. Although the National Republicans did not control the state organization, Negro politicians blamed them for the poor showing of the party in the 1896 election. Their actions encouraged the Democrats "to resort to all kinds of robbery," complained Walter L. Cohen, a black leader. "If the success of the republican party in this State meant the elevation in any respect of the negro they would rather see the republican party defeated."[19] This hostility to blacks came out clearly in 1897 when McKinley appointed Henry Demas, a Negro who had been active in Louisiana politics for twenty-five years, to be naval officer at New Orleans.

16 Helen G. Edmonds, *The Negro and Fusion Politics in North Carolina, 1894–1901* (Chapel Hill, N.C., 1951); Frenise A. Logan, *The Negro in North Carolina, 1876–1894* (Chapel Hill, N.C., 1964); William A. Mabry, *The Negro in North Carolina Politics since Reconstruction* (Durham, N.C., 1940); William A. Mabry, "Negro Suffrage and Fusion Rule in North Carolina," *North Carolina Historical Review*, 12 (April 1935), 79–102; Samuel D. Smith, *The Negro in Congress, 1870–1901* (Chapel Hill, N.C., 1940), pp. 125–29.

17 Edmonds, pp. 89–92.

18 *Ibid.*, pp. 136–214; Mabry, *Negro in N.C. Politics*, pp. 45–71.

19 Cohen to George A. Myers, Dec. 5, 1896, Myers Papers.

Whites raised a storm of protest. One member of the state committee predicted that "the appointment of Demas destroys any hope for a Republican party worthy of the name in Louisiana or the South for a long time to come."[20] Although such an appointment was hardly so significant, the GOP in Louisiana continued to be torn by the conflict between the regulars and the National Republicans. After the suffrage provisions of the new state constitution of 1898 wiped out a large proportion of the black electorate, the party's strength diminished even further.

McKinley's most serious trouble arose in Georgia. The strong Republican showing in 1896, when the GOP won 36.82 percent of the popular vote in the presidential race, the highest since 1872, merely increased the demands of hungry politicians for patronage. After proposing Judson W. Lyons, a prominent Negro lawyer, for the Augusta postmastership, McKinley was inundated with complaints. Until that time Lyons had been fairly well regarded by whites, and many had no objection to his appointment to a position outside of Georgia. But some were incensed by his impertinence in seeking the Augusta post. McKinley finally decided that the best interests of the party would be served if Lyons took a different federal job. First he offered him a post as superintendent in the Post Office Department at Washington, but Lyons declined it. In December 1897 Lyons finally agreed to give up interest in the Augusta postmastership. Somewhat later he accepted an appointment as register of the Treasury.[21]

In another Georgia case violence was used to oust a black appointee, I. H. Loftin, who had been named postmaster of the small town of Hogansville. Loftin's appointment infuriated the local whites. The old postmaster even refused to give up his office and continued to transact business for four months. On September 15, 1897, a would-be assassin shot and wounded Loftin. Investigations by postal authorities implicated some prominent businessmen and the former postmaster. Feelings ran very high, and the Georgia House of Representatives passed a resolution condemning McKinley for making the appointment. "All sensible negroes understand well enough," asserted the Atlanta *Constitution*, "that when a negro is appointed to a postoffice in this section it is not the result of Re-

20 "Republicanism in the South," *Nation*, 65 (Sept. 23, 1897), 234. See also *Literary Digest*, 15 (Oct. 9, 1897), 692.

21 New York *Times*, April 27, May 11, 1897; Clarence A. Bacote, "Negro Officeholders in Georgia under President McKinley," *Journal of Negro History*, 44 (July 1959), 220–26; J. W. Gibson and W. H. Crogman, *Progress of a Race, or The Remarkable Advancement of the American Negro* (Atlanta, 1902), pp. 631–32.

publican love for the negro, but the outcome of bargain and sale." Loftin recovered from the shooting, but in February 1898 the building he had been using as a postoffice was destroyed by fire. Finally he left Hogansville and accepted a new appointment in Washington.[22]

The Spanish-American War in 1898 afforded the South an opportunity to demonstrate another mood, its patriotism and loyalty to the nation. McKinley's appeals for national unity took on a new intensity which was demonstrated in mid-December 1898 when he made his second tour of the South. His ostensible purpose was to attend the Peace Jubilee at Atlanta. But he also sought support for the peace treaty, and he could not have been oblivious to the possibilities such a trip might provide for strengthening white Republicanism in the South. On the whole the southern reaction to the news of McKinley's contemplated visit was favorable. Nevertheless, the hostility that had been aroused by the Negro appointments was not completely stilled. The Atlanta *Journal* wrote that while no one doubted that the president was sympathetic to the South, he had made the error of appointing Negroes to office, including "some very vicious characters among them."[23] Feeling in Savannah was so strong that the city council twice rejected a resolution inviting McKinley to visit the city.[24] Such sentiment was not general, however, and as far as his personal reception was concerned, the trip was highly successful.

McKinley's first major speech, an address to the Georgia legislature on December 14, 1898, was his most important, and it set the tone of his tour. His theme was conciliation, the reuniting of North and South. Expressing his hopes more than realities, he declared: "Sectional lines no longer mar the map of the United States. Sectional feeling no longer holds back the love we bear each other." The high point came when he proclaimed that "every soldier's grave made during our unfortunate Civil War is a tribute to American valor. . . . The time has now come, in the evolution of sentiment and feeling under the providence of God, when in the spirit of fraternity we should share with you in the care of the graves of the Confederate soldiers."[25] With that remark the success of his trip was assured. One reporter asserted that "nothing has more deeply stirred a Southern

22 New York *Times*, Sept. 18–20, Oct. 2, 1897; *Literary Digest*, 15 (Oct. 9, 1897), 691; Bacote, pp. 225–33; Alfred Holt Stone, *Studies in the American Race Problem* (New York, 1908), pp. 293–94.

23 Atlanta *Journal*, Nov. 19, 1898, clipping in McKinley Papers.

24 *Ibid.*, Nov. 18?, 1898, clipping in McKinley Papers.

25 Copy of the speech, McKinley Papers, microfilm, ser. 4, reel 82.

audience than the simple words of President McKinley this afternoon."[26] The next day the reception at Atlanta was reported to have been unequaled in the history of the city.[27] It was an auspicious beginning for his tour, and McKinley went on to equally warm and friendly welcomes in Montgomery, Savannah, and several other cities.

McKinley did not limit his appearances to white audiences. Before going to Montgomery to address the Alabama state legislature, he accepted Booker T. Washington's invitation to speak to the students at Tuskegee Institute. In Montgomery he stopped briefly at a black church, and he visited the Georgia State Agricultural and Mechanical College near Savannah.[28] These gestures of interest in the black community did not appear to lessen in any way the warmth with which white southerners received him. Washington concluded that only good would result for both races. "Your visit to Tuskegee," he wrote to the president, "has resulted in bringing about a sympathy and union between the races of this section that is almost marvelous. You have helped every black man and white in the South."[29]

Such strong praise does not seem warranted. Indeed, many aspects of the whole episode—McKinley's emotional appeals to union, the cheering audiences, and Washington's optimism—were remote from the harsher day-to-day realities. His visit had in fact changed nothing. The criticism of some of his Negro appointments had revealed the other, more deeply felt, southern mood. McKinley was able to win the South's applause only by keeping silent on sensitive issues and thus by implicitly accepting the Negro's subservience.

McKinley's neglect of black Americans was shown in a number of ways. Perhaps the most disturbing was the fact that he, as well as other Republican leaders, was unwilling to face up to the very real dangers to the physical safety of Negroes in the South, dangers that had been heightened by the tactics employed in the white supremacy campaigns. McKinley's response to the riot in Wilmington, North Carolina, was a case in point. This disturbance broke out on November 10, 1898, shortly before his second southern trip. At least eleven blacks were killed, and several others, along with a few whites, were injured. McKinley was given detailed accounts of the riot, and it was

26 New York *Times*, Dec. 15, 1898.

27 *Ibid.*, Dec. 16, 1898.

28 For McKinley's speeches, see *Speeches and Addresses of William McKinley from March 1, 1897, to May 30, 1900* (New York, 1900), pp. 158–84. See also Washington to McKinley, Nov. 7, Nov. 27, 1898, Richard R. Wright to McKinley, Nov. 16, 1898, McKinley Papers.

29 Washington to McKinley. Dec. 22, 1898, McKinley Papers.

widely reported, and condemned, in the northern press.[30] Alarmed whites begged the president to do something. Public sentiment had been deeply disturbed by "the crusade against the Negro," argued John E. Milholland of New York. "Make no mistake; we are *not* going back to the Ku Klux times without a row. The Black man must be protected in his rights and the Administration failing in this will make a terrible blunder. Stand by him and the Nation will stand by you."[31] But McKinley decided that silence was the best policy. Neither then nor later did he make any comment on the Wilmington massacre, or other attacks upon Negroes.

McKinley rather than Milholland was probably the better judge of public sentiment, for among whites at least there was no widespread concern about this problem. Many Negroes were deeply alarmed, however, and they did not hesitate to criticize the president. On December 19, 1898, the National Race Protective Association passed a resolution condemning him for his inaction. T. Thomas Fortune, the editor of the influential New York *Age*, denounced his willingness to play up to the sentiments of southern whites at the expense of Negro rights.[32] "McKinley is a man of jelly who would turn us loose on the mob and not say a word," Fortune later told some delegates from the Afro-American Council.[33] Reverdy C. Ransom, a prominent Chicago clergyman, warned McKinley and his political advisers that they were mistaken if they thought that they could get along without the black man, and he predicted that despite its protestations of friendship, the South would line up solidly against McKinley.[34] When it came to the steps that could be taken to stem the outbreak of violence, however, Ransom took a conservative position, admitting that many leading Negroes believed that the president had no constitutional authority to use federal power. Still, Ransom could see no valid reason for McKinley's failure to use at least moral suasion against lawlessness.[35] Other Negroes rejected such constitutional conservatism. For example, on October 3, 1899, the Massachusetts Branch of the Colored National League attacked McKinley's "incomprehensible silence" and reminded him that when the federal

30 On the riot, see Edmonds, pp. 158–74. For reports to McKinley on the riot, see McKinley Papers, microfilm, ser. 3, reel 63.

31 Milholland to McKinley, Nov. 14, 1898, McKinley Papers. Milholland, a successful manufacturer, was active in Republican politics. In 1904 he founded the Constitution League, an interracial civil rights organization.

32 New York *Times*, Dec. 21, 1898.

33 *Ibid.*, May 11, 1898.

34 Ransom to George A. Myers, June 10. 1899, Myers Papers.

35 Ransom to John B. Green, June 27, 1899, McKinley Papers.

government had the will to deal with chronic disturbances which it considered menacing to the nation's interests and to humanity—the intervention in Cuba was one example—it was quite able to devise a constitutional justification for its actions.[36] This argument might not appeal to the legal purist, but it pointed up the perplexing nature of the country's priorities, in which the protection of foreigners ranked above the defense of its own citizens.

In cumulative effect lynchings were the most serious form of anti-Negro violence during this period. In a lynching a group of individuals, often with the connivance of local police officials, assumed the functions of judge, jury, and executioner. The victim was not only denied due process of law; he was often subjected to sadistic tortures as well. The largest number of recorded lynchings occurred in the years just prior to McKinley's presidency, and until after the turn of the century, the death toll was well over one hundred a year. Lynchings took place in nearly every state, and many of the dead were whites. But by the latter 1890's they were becoming primarily a southern phenomenon with Negroes the chief victims.[37] The impact of a lynching was not to be measured simply in terms of the number killed. Long after the cries of the sufferer had ceased, waves of fear were felt throughout entire counties and districts. In the South lynchings and the terror that accompanied them had become significant devices of social control; they provided a crudely effective means of enforcing the caste structure demanded by the racial etiquette that accompanied the successful movement for disfranchisement and segregation.

The federal government's response was negligible. McKinley condemned lynchings in his inaugural address, but he made no suggestions for preventing them, and after this initial statement he said nothing. Congress was also reluctant to consider the problem. The silence was finally broken on January 16, 1900, when Senator Shelby M. Cullom of Illinois presented a petition, addressed to McKinley and signed by more than 3,200 Negroes, asking for protection against lynching. A short debate followed. Senator William E. Chandler, a Republican from New Hampshire, at times a strong advocate of Negro rights, now argued that Congress had no power to punish crimes in the states, except, by virtue of the Fifteenth Amendment,

36 [Archibald H. Grimké], *Open Letter to President McKinley by Colored People of Massachusetts* (Boston, Oct. 3, 1899), pamphlet in George Foster Peabody Collection, Collis P. Huntington Memorial Library, Hampton Institute.

37 National Association for the Advancement of Colored People, *Thirty Years of Lynching in the United States, 1889–1918* (New York, 1919), pp. 29–35.

those that prevented citizens from voting. Cullom, also doubtful of the legitimacy of congressional action, suggested that the Senate Judiciary Committee should look into the matter. During this brief discussion only Senator William V. Allen, a Nebraska Populist, took the position that the federal government could act to protect the lives of its citizens under the authority of the Fourteenth Amendment.[38]

A few days later Congressman White of North Carolina, the last remaining Negro member of Congress, introduced another petition requesting legislation against lynching. He accompanied this with a bill (H.R. 6963) "for the protection of all citizens of the United States against mob violence."[39] White's proposal was the first antilynching measure submitted to Congress that was designed to protect Americans. It declared that the murder of an American citizen was treason against the United States, and as such the federal government had jurisdiction. Anyone convicted under it would be subject to the punishment prescribed by the laws against treason.[40] The bill was crudely drafted and not likely to win over those numerous congressmen who had honest doubts about the constitutionality of federal intervention; it was no surprise that it never emerged from the House Judiciary Committee. Still, it was a revealing reflection on the times that so few congressmen showed any concern about the lynchings, let alone gave serious thought to the question of the government's responsibility for the protection of its citizens against violence.

Republicans showed no more interest in meeting another major threat to black Americans, the disfranchisement movement in the South. By the latter 1890's it had become obvious that only a major federal government effort could check the drive to deprive Negroes of their right to vote by so-called legal means. As early as 1890 Mississippi began the process with a constitutional convention which adopted an amendment requiring, among other things, the payment of a poll tax and the passing of a literacy test as qualifications for suffrage. South Carolina was the next state to act, adopting provisions similar to those of Mississippi at a constitutional convention

38 *Congressional Record*, 56th Cong., 1st sess., vol. 33, pt. 1, pp. 846–48. Cullom's petition is in the file on "Petitions Filed with Senate Judiciary Committee," Record Group 46, National Archives.

39 *Cong. Rec.* 56th Cong., 1st sess., vol. 33, pt. 2, pp. 1017, 1021–22.

40 *Ibid.*, p. 3, p. 2153. In his Dec. 1891 message to Congress, President Harrison had proposed a federal antilynching law, but it would have applied only to foreign nationals living in the United States. Similar bills were introduced in the Senate in 1893 and 1899 and in the House in 1900, as well as others after the turn of the century (David O. Walter, "Proposals for a Federal Anti-Lynching Law," *American Political Science Review*, 28 [June 1934], 436–38).

in 1895. Louisiana followed in 1898 and North Carolina in 1900.[41] A determined attempt by the Republicans to protect the Negro's vote would have wrecked McKinley's efforts at reconciliation, and the immediate political gains for such a move would not have compensated for the losses. Republicans could not control the South by Negro votes alone, and congressional interference would have destroyed any prospects of building up GOP strength among southern whites.

The suffrage issue was first raised in Congress at this time by the two senators from North Carolina, Marion Butler, a Populist, and Jeter C. Pritchard, a Republican. Both had been sent to Congress as a result of the fusionist victories of 1894 and 1896. In 1898 the Democrats, having regained control of the North Carolina legislature, passed a disfranchising amendment to the state constitution. This provided for a poll tax and literacy test, along with a grandfather clause to protect prospective white registrants. The amendment was submitted to the voters for approval at an election to be held on August 2, 1900. The two senators saw in the Democratic disfranchisement efforts a threat to their base of political power.[42] In early October 1899 Butler condemned the proposed amendment as unconstitutional. Pritchard went even further. On December 12, 1899, he submitted a resolution in the Senate which stated that the North Carolina proposal was a violation of the Fourteenth and Fifteenth Amendments and that any state adopting such provisions as part of its organic law ceased to have a republican form of government as understood and guaranteed by the United States Constitution.[43]

Pritchard's resolution was first brought up for discussion on January 8, 1900. Senator John T. Morgan of Alabama vigorously attacked it, delivering an extended defense of the rights of the states to set qualifications for suffrage.[44] Pritchard answered by asserting that Morgan was espousing "nullification pure and simple." Butler assailed the grandfather clause as "clearly unconstitutional" and denounced the cry about Negro domination as slander.[45] Discussion of the resolution continued intermittently until April, but Pritchard got little support from his northern Republican colleagues. Only Senator Chandler spoke up on its behalf, and he said very little.[46]

[41] C. Vann Woodward, *Origins of the New South, 1877–1913* (Baton Rouge, La., 1951), pp. 321–49.

[42] Edmonds, pp. 178–214; Mabry, *Negro in Politics*, pp. 59–73.

[43] *Cong. Rec.*, 56th Cong., 1st sess., vol. 33, pt. 1, p. 233.

[44] *Ibid.*, pp. 671–77.

[45] *Ibid.*, pt. 2, pp. 1027, 1065, 1544–53.

[46] *Ibid.*, pp. 1033, 1171.

The resolution was referred to the Committee on Privileges and Elections on April 26. Chandler reported on June 1 that a majority of that committee supported a different, weaker suffrage resolution, and on two occasions before adjournment he sought, without success, to obtain unanimous consent for its immediate consideration.[47] Both proposals died in committee.

Republicans at the 1900 national convention also showed little concern about disfranchisement. Former Congressman John R. Lynch, a Negro from Mississippi, raised the issue by proposing a plank favoring the reduction of representation in Congress, in accordance with the Fourteenth Amendment, for states limiting the right to vote. The idea got little support. The convention also ignored an appeal by the National Afro-American Council to take a strong position against disfranchisement and lynching.[48] On Negro rights the platform merely asserted: "It was the plain purpose of the fifteenth amendment to the Constitution to prevent discrimination on account of race or color in regulating the elective franchise. Devices of State governments, whether by statutory or constitutional enactment, to avoid the purpose of this amendment are revolutionary and should be condemned." In this way the Republicans paid homage to their past principles but avoided the fight that would have been necessary to give meaningful protection to Negro suffrage. It was doubtful that any action short of direct supervision of federal elections would have been efficacious. Lynch's suggestion about threatening a reduction in the representation of the disfranchising states clearly had its dangers. Senator Chandler, for example, feared that reducing southern representation under the Fourteenth Amendment would be tantamount to accepting the violation of the Fifteenth. "However imperfectly enforced the 15th amendment may be," he wrote in October 1900, "we should cling to it as the fundamental principle and not sell it or sacrifice it."[49]

Shortly after the 1900 election the disfranchisement issue arose again in the House of Representatives in the course of dealing with the constitutionally required reapportionment of its membership. On December 20, 1900, the Committee on the Census reported out a new apportionment bill based on the twelfth census. To this Con-

47 *Ibid.*, pt. 7, p. 6370, and pt. 8, pp. 6865–66, 6875.

48 New York *Times*, June 17, 18, 1900; *Official Proceedings of the Twelfth Republican National Convention Held in the City of Philadelphia, June 19, 20 and 21, 1900*, p. 100; John Roy Lynch, *Reminiscences of an Active Life: The Autobiography of John Roy Lynch*, ed. John Hope Franklin (Chicago. 1970), p. 423.

49 Chandler to James Lewis, Oct. 4, 1900, William E. Chandler Papers, Manuscript Division, Library of Congress.

gressman Edgar D. Crumpacker, a Republican from Indiana, filed a strongly worded dissent calling attention to the second section of the Fourteenth Amendment. "The language of the Constitution is clear, direct, and mandatory, and it leaves no discretion in Congress whatever." In Louisiana, Mississippi, North Carolina, and South Carolina, he argued, a sufficient number of adult males have been deprived of their vote "by direct and necessary operation of law" to require that each state lose several representatives.[50] "If the negro is not entitled to the protection of political laws," he asked, "under what laws is he entitled to protection?" It had become apparent that "the violation of his rights in one particular suggests it in others. This is seen in the alarmingly frequent exhibitions of mob violence against the negro. He has no rights that the white man is bound to respect, and he may be shot down, hanged, or burned at the stake, without regard to legal procedure or sanction, with absolute impunity." Congress, continued Crumpacker, must act as a "countervailing force" to these tendencies in the South, and in so doing it would help both races. "Legislation can not put brains into the heads nor character into the lives of the people, but it can set in motion forces that will tend to encourage a healthy and honest growth of civil life. . . . The crisis is on, and unless some decisive steps be taken to arrest it, the negro will slowly but surely drift into a condition practically as bad as slavery."[51]

The reapportionment bill came up for consideration on January 8, 1901. Most of the discussion centered on Crumpacker's minority report. Predictably, it was denounced by several southern congressmen. Of greater significance was the fact that only three members spoke on its behalf: White of North Carolina; John F. Fitzgerald, a Massachusetts Democrat; and Charles H. Grosvenor, an Ohio Republican. Crumpacker moved that the reapportionment bill be sent back to committee with instructions to inquire if the right to vote had been unconstitutionally abridged and if so, to report an apportionment bill with appropriate reductions as required by the Fourteenth Amendment. This motion was defeated by a vote of 94 to 136.[52] Within a few years the rest of the South joined Louisiana,

50 *Cong. Rec.*, 56th Cong., 2d sess., vol. 34, pt. 1, p. 486; U.S., Congress, House, Select Committee on the Twelfth Census, *Apportionment among the Several States*, 56th Cong., 2d sess., H. Rept. 2130 (Dec. 20, 1900), pp. 121–22. Crumpacker suggested that Louisiana's representation be reduced from seven to four, Mississippi's from seven to four, North Carolina's from nine to six, and South Carolina's from six to four.

51 *Apportionment among the Several States*, H. Rept. 2130, pp. 132–34.

52 *Cong. Rec.*, 56th Cong., 2d sess., vol. 34, pt. 1, pp. 731–48.

Mississippi, North Carolina, and South Carolina in depriving most of their black citizens of the right to vote. The development was made possible, if not actually encouraged, by the passive attitude of the Republican-controlled federal government.

Despite the spread of disfranchisement in the South, Negroes continued to play a major role in that section's Republican party organizations. They would undoubtedly occupy many of the places in the southern delegations to the 1900 national convention. The Negro delegates were useful to McKinley in 1896, and he still wanted their support in 1900. Thus he was embarrassed when the question of reforming the basis of allotting delegates to the national convention was raised. The subject deserved attention, for the South played an anomalous role in the Republican party. Although it provided a small and declining proportion of the popular vote and no electoral votes in presidential elections, it had great influence in national conventions. The existence of such "rotten boroughs" encouraged shady bargains and corruption. Some Republicans felt that the southern GOP could gain more popular support only if the role of black politicians was reduced or eliminated. One way to do this was to make certain that the number of delegates assigned to a given state bore a closer relationship to the actual strength of the party. Presumably this would provide an incentive for leaders to work for a larger Republican vote, something they had not always done in the one-party states of the South. The immediate effect would be to reduce the bargaining position of southern politicians in the national organization.

According to a rule adopted in 1888, the number of national convention delegates allotted to each state was equal to twice the number of its senators and representatives. In November 1899 Henry Clay Payne, the national committeeman from Wisconsin, made public a resolution he planned to introduce at the December 16 meeting of the national committee. It was similar to a proposal he had tried unsuccessfully to have adopted at the 1896 national convention. Payne hoped to reduce the power of the South by changing the basis for the allotment of district delegates to one for every 10,000 votes, or majority fraction thereof, cast for Republican electors at the last previous presidential election. The number of delegates-at-large would remain unchanged. Black politicians in the North and South were bitterly opposed to such a reform, for it would greatly lessen their influence in the party. Some whites also denounced it as a slap at the South generally. McKinley strongly objected, and on December 15, the day before the national committee was scheduled to meet, he and some of his advisers prevailed upon Payne to drop the idea.[53]

Nevertheless, when the national convention convened at Philadelphia in June 1900 the issue was again brought up, although not by Payne. Strong support for what was widely referred to as the Payne resolution was expressed by several New Englanders and by Senator Matthew S. Quay of Pennsylvania, who had also endorsed a similar proposal in 1896. On June 20 Quay moved the adoption of a rule for the allotment of delegates along the lines of the Payne resolution. If it was accepted, all eleven southern states stood to lose a few delegates, and some a considerable number. The border and most northern states would either hold their own or gain.[54] At this point John R. Lynch introduced his substitute resolution calling for the reduction of representation in Congress, in accordance with the Fourteenth Amendment, of any state that denied the vote to adult males on account of race, color, or previous condition of servitude. If Congress adopted such a change, the South would automatically lose delegates at future Republican conventions according to the old basis for allotment. Lynch's motion was ruled out of order by Chairman Henry Cabot Lodge on the ground that it was a subject not germane to the convention.[55]

Quay's resolution was interpreted as a challenge to the leadership of Hanna and McKinley, who relied upon support from the southern organizations. The alarmed southern delegates let it be known that they would trade their votes on the vice-presidency for the dropping of the proposed reform. On the evening of June 20 Hanna issued a statement explaining that the administration was not against any candidate for the vice-presidency, implying that it had abandoned its opposition to Governor Theodore Roosevelt of New York. The next day Roosevelt won the nomination, and Quay withdrew his resolution. Quay had used the southern issue to score a victory over his enemy Mark Hanna.[56] But southern Republican organizations continued to be a troublesome problem for Hanna, Roosevelt, and their successors. The fight to reform the southern GOP, to make it more acceptable to large numbers of whites, had just begun.

53 William W. Wight, *Henry Clay Payne: A Life* (Milwaukee, 1907), pp. 101–5; Leech, pp. 464–65; Dorothy G. Fowler, *The Cabinet Politician: The Postmasters General 1829–1909* (New York, 1943), pp. 264–65; Horace Samuel Merrill and Marion Galbraith Merrill, *The Republican Command* (Lexington, Ky., 1971), pp. 74–76; John P. Green to George A. Myers, Dec. 20, 1899, Myers Papers.

54 New York *Times*, June 13, 19, 21, 1900; *Proc. 12th Rep. Nat. Conv.*, pp. 93–97.

55 *Proc. 12th Rep. Nat. Conv.*, p. 100.

56 *Ibid.*, p. 114; New York *Times*, June 21, 22, 1900; Leech, pp. 539–40; Arthur W. Dunn, *From Harrison to Harding: A Personal Narrative Covering a Third of a Century, 1888–1921* (New York, 1922), pp. 331–41. Merrill and Merrill. p. 76.

By rejecting their responsibility to protect the rights of Negroes in the South during the McKinley years, Republican leaders had in effect aligned themselves with the forces of racial proscription in the name of national unity. Although dismayed Negroes protested that such a course would lead to defections of black voters in the North, the threatened loss was too small to disturb many politicians.[57] The wooing of the white South paid off by broadening the support for McKinley's foreign ventures. There was little evidence, however, that southern Republicanism had been significantly strengthened. Democrats could always point to the continued role of blacks in the southern GOP and McKinley's acceptance of the support of Negro delegates at the 1900 national convention as evidence of Republican unreliability on the racial issue.

In the 1900 election McKinley's share of the popular vote in the South remained about what it had been four years earlier. The Republican percentage increased in four states—Alabama, Arkansas, Mississippi, and Texas—although the gain was appreciable only in the first two (6.5 and 9.9 percent respectively), neither of which had yet adopted disfranchising devices. However, in Georgia, which had also not revised its election laws, the Republican vote fell off sharply, more than in any other southern state. McKinley's efforts had not been repaid by great gains among white votes in the South as a whole.

After the election McKinley continued to eschew any serious discussion of the divisive racial question, and he reiterated his favorite theme about the virtues of national unity. His second inaugural address concentrated on Cuba and the Philippines and did not mention lynching, disfranchisement, or any of the other pressing problems faced by blacks in America. In late April and early May 1901, McKinley made another journey through the South, stopping in Virginia, Tennessee, Louisiana, and Texas. Southerners greeted him warmly. Ignoring controversial topics, he spoke again and again on the theme of the reconciliation of North and South.[58] His racial policy remained one of calculated neglect.

Many southerners mourned McKinley at the time of his tragic death in September 1901. He had been an attractive president who had honestly preached the message of national unity. A man of

[57] For examples, see Henry A. Rucker to McKinley, June 29, 1900, McKinley Papers; J. Q. Adams to William E. Chandler, July 10, 1900, Chandler Papers; Jere A. Brown to George A. Myers, Dec. 16, 1899, George A. Myers to McKinley, Nov. 15, 1900, Myers Papers. See also Kelly Miller, *Roosevelt and the Negro* (Washington, D.C., 1907), p. 7; Washington *Bee*, Aug. 5, 1899; New York *Times*, June 16, 1900.

[58] For his speeches, see McKinley Papers, microfilm, ser. 4, reel. 84.

goodwill, he apparently believed that such a course was in the best interests of both races. But the sectional peace that McKinley achieved was purchased at a heavy price. It was ironic that the first Republican administration since Reconstruction to have been elected by a clear majority, and one strengthened by Republican control of both houses of Congress, should passively accept the violently anti-Negro actions in the South. Moreover, McKinley's achievement was largely superficial. By 1901 the possibilities of a serious Republican challenge to the Democratic monopoly in the South were less than ever before. And as the determination of southerners to enforce increasingly severe forms of racial proscription grew, so did their sensitivity to any criticism of their section. Had McKinley lived it is possible that he would have had the restraint necessary to preserve the harmonious facade. Such was not always the case with his much more active and outspoken successor. Accordingly, after McKinley's death the question of the Republican party's relationship and responsibility to black Americans became a far more lively and controversial issue in national politics.

CHAPTER II

Roosevelt and "The Door of Hope"

MANY Negroes viewed Theodore Roosevelt's accession to the presidency in September 1901 with considerable misgivings. The colorful former Rough Rider had already been involved in enough controversy to cast serious doubts about his racial attitudes. Any simple generalization in this respect is difficult. In the context of his times, with its hardening of racial stereotypes, many of his public and private utterances suggested a refreshing tolerance. It was also easy to find examples of action and words that support other conclusions. Some Negroes eagerly seized upon Roosevelt's favorable comments or deeds, reading into them far more than they deserved. This helps explain their bitterness and the intensity of their attacks upon him when his words and actions seemed in shocking contrast to their hopes.[1]

During his formative years Roosevelt had little opportunity to gain firsthand knowledge of black Americans. His early training, family associations, and education helped inculcate in him a fierce nationalism and a firm conviction that progress was associated with the rise and dominance of the western or Anglo-Saxon peoples. He was a vigorous Republican partisan, and his early, sympathetic statements on the Negro suggest a stereotyped party position more than a profound conviction.[2] As a member of the Civil Service Commission,

[1] For a summary of Roosevelt's attitude toward Negroes during his presidency, see Seth M. Scheiner, "President Theodore Roosevelt and the Negro, 1901–1908," *Journal of Negro History*, 47 (July 1962), 169–82; Horace Samuel Merrill and Marion Galbraith Merrill, *The Republican Command, 1897–1913* (Lexington, Ky., 1971), chaps. 5–11, passim; Williard B. Gatewood, Jr., *Theodore Roosevelt and the Art of Controversy; Episodes of the White House Years* (Baton Rouge, La., 1970), pp. 32–134. Kelly Miller, *Roosevelt and the Negro* (Washington, D.C., 1907), is an important contemporary assessment written by an influential Negro professor. See also George Sinkler, *The Racial Attitudes of American Presidents: From Abraham Lincoln to Theodore Roosevelt* (Garden City, N.Y., 1971), pp. 308–73; and Edward Wagenknecht, *The Seven Worlds of Theodore Roosevelt* (New York, 1938), pp. 227–36.

[2] For example, see his speech at the 1884 Republican national convention in support of John R. Lynch, a Negro, as temporary chairman, *Official Proceedings of the Republican National Convention Held at Chicago, June 3, 4, 5 and 6, 1884*, p. 10.

however, Roosevelt occasionally had to face the color question, and his stand in defense of "equal and exact justice to all" was praised by Negroes.[3] As governor of New York at the very end of the century he did his best to live by this standard. He appointed a few Negroes to office, and more significantly, he strongly supported the Elsberg bill which ended racial segregation in New York schools.[4] But if Roosevelt's sense of justice led him to believe that individual, deserving Negroes should be given a chance, this did not mean that he regarded blacks as a group as being equal to whites in fact or potentially. Their salvation, he wrote, lay in fitting them "to do ever better industrial work."[5] At other times he readily accepted the charge of rape as a reason for lynching and placed upon Negroes as a group the heavy burden of taking the lead in apprehending one of their number accused of the crime.[6]

While Roosevelt won the applause of some Negroes during his governorship, he also had his detractors. The latter were especially upset by his disparaging comments about the performance of black troops during the Spanish-American War. Such criticism seemed particularly unwarranted because he had praised the Negro soldiers highly at the conclusion of the conflict and had again spoken well of them during his campaign for governor in the fall of 1898. Then in January 1899 Roosevelt's account of *The Rough Riders* began to be published serially in *Scribner's Magazine*. The offending passages appeared in the April installment on "The Cavalry at Santiago." "No troops," he wrote, "could have behaved better than the colored soldiers had behaved so far; but they are, of course, peculiarly dependent upon white officers. Occasionally they produce noncommissioned

3 Roosevelt to Alexander Monroe Dockery, May 24, 1894, in Elting E. Morison, ed., *The Letters of Theodore Roosevelt* (Cambridge, Mass.: Harvard University Press. 1951–54), I, 381.

4 Roosevelt to T. Thomas Fortune, March 27, 1899, Roosevelt to William Henry Lewis, July 26, 1900, *ibid.*, II, 972–73, 1364–65; G. Wallace Chessman, *Governor Theodore Roosevelt: The Albany Apprenticeship, 1898–1900* (Cambridge, Mass., 1965), p. 242; William Henry Harbaugh, *Power and Responsibility: The Life and Times of Theodore Roosevelt* (New York, 1961), p. 129; William Henry Johnson, *Autobiography of Dr. William Henry Johnson* (Albany, 1900). pp. 18, 77; Leslie H. Fishel, Jr., "The Negro in Northern Politics, 1870–1900," *Mississippi Valley Historical Review*, 42 (Dec. 1955), 486.

5 Roosevelt to L. J. Moore, Feb. 5, 1900, in Morison, ed., *Roosevelt Letters*, II, 1169.

6 Roosevelt to John William Fox, Oct. 17, 1899, *ibid.*, 1085. See also Roosevelt's address at the unveiling of the Frederick Douglass monument at Rochester on June 9, 1899 (J. W. Thompson, *An Authentic History of the Douglass Monument* [Rochester, N.Y., 1903], pp. 141–45). As noted below, Roosevelt continued to hold such ideas during his presidency.

officers who can take the initiative and accept responsibility precisely like the best class of whites; but this cannot be expected normally; nor is it fair to expect it." Furthermore, while on the slope under fire "the colored infantrymen (who had none of their officers) began to get a little uneasy and drift to the rear." But he claimed that he had stopped them by threatening to shoot any who retreated.[7] Roosevelt omitted any mention of an explanation for the movement to the rear which allegedly had been presented to him at the time. An account by Sergeant Presley Holliday of the Tenth Cavalry, published in May 1899, stated that the Negroes were moving under orders of Lieutenant Robert J. Fleming in order to remove the wounded and to get rations and tools. Holliday claimed that Fleming had so informed Roosevelt and that Roosevelt had admitted his mistake and apologized for having been so severe with the Negro troops.[8] Somewhat later Roosevelt wrote that he had no memory of such a conversation with Fleming, and he refused to alter his harsh judgment. Roosevelt remained convinced that black troops would do well only when under the supervision of white officers whom they trusted and that while some individuals could be found who performed equally with most whites, the average for the Negro soldiers was not as high.[9]

Soon after Roosevelt became president, some of his Negro detractors ignored their past criticisms and began to hail him as a true friend, a man of courage and sound convictions. Many southern whites, who at first regarded him as an understanding and sympathetic friend of their section, soon became alienated by conduct that they considered deliberately offensive. Roosevelt's attitude and actions with regard to black Americans were of course closely tied to his southern policy. Like all politicians Roosevelt wanted to achieve maximum support for his actions while offending a minimum num-

[7] Theodore Roosevelt, "The Cavalry at Santiago," *Scribner's Magazine,* 25 (April 1899), 435–36.

[8] New York *Age,* May 11, 1899, reprinted in Booker T. Washington, *A New Negro for a New Century* (reprt. ed., New York, 1969), pp. 54–62; and in Willard B. Gatewood. Jr., *"Smoked Yankees" and the Struggle for Empire: Letters from Negro Soldiers, 1898–1902* (Urbana, Ill., 1971), pp. 92–97. The New York *Age,* May 10, 1900, published a letter to the editor written by Holliday, which was accompanied by a letter from Fleming to Holliday, dated July 7, 1899. Fleming told, with only slight variation, an account of the actions of the Negro troops and Roosevelt's response that was in agreement with Holliday's story. Fleming, a professional army officer, strongly upheld the conduct and initiative of the Negro soldiers (clipping in the scrapbooks in the George Foster Peabody Collection, Collis P. Huntington Memorial Library, Hampton Institute, Hampton, Va.).

[9] Roosevelt to Fleming, May 21, 1900, in Morison, ed., *Roosevelt Letters,* II, 1304.

ber of people. Specifically he hoped to maintain the historic ties of the Republican party with the Negro and at the same time to remake his party in the South into an agency of national policy that could win the support of responsible whites as well as blacks. These two objectives were extremely difficult to reconcile. If his actions were supported by one group, they generally alienated the other. His policy followed a tortuous and uncertain course; admirers one week often became detractors the next.

Roosevelt seldom tired of preaching the virtues of national unity. In stressing his ties to all the country, he often expressed pride in his southern ancestors. "I am going to be President of the United States and not of any section," he told three visiting southern congressmen on September 21, 1901. "Half my blood is Southern and I have lived in the West, so that I feel I can represent the whole country."[10] In a speech at Charleston, South Carolina, in April 1902, entitled "The Reunited People," he observed that his mother's people were from Georgia, and before the Revolution from South Carolina. Both North and South, he went on, could glory in the bravery of the men who fought in the Civil War, just as they both could now be proud of their common service in the Spanish-American War.[11] These expressions of pride in the South help account for the enthusiasm of many southerners for him personally. But rhetoric was not in itself a policy. By setting up false expectations, he may have confused southerners and made all the more difficult an understanding of his specific actions.

Once he became president, Roosevelt's first objective in regard to the South was to secure control of the Republican party as a means of assuring his nomination in 1904. The methods varied according to the nature of local conditions; he did not consistently back either the lily-whites or the black-and-tans. If a state organization could be counted upon to support him in 1904, its racial complexion was a secondary matter. With McKinley's death, Senator Hanna was left in apparent control of the party organizations in the South. This was a challenge to Roosevelt. John Morton Blum has noted, "he discriminated not on the basis of color, but on the basis of Hanna."[12] In so

[10] Joseph Bucklin Bishop, *Theodore Roosevelt and His Times* (New York, 1920), I, 154.

[11] *The Works of Theodore Roosevelt* (National Ed., New York, 1927), XVI, 26–27. See also *ibid.*, pp. 343–44.

[12] Blum, *The Republican Roosevelt* (Cambridge, Mass., 1954), p. 46. For other general comments on Roosevelt and the South, see C. Vann Woodward, *Origins of the New South, 1877–1913* (Baton Rouge, La., 1951), pp. 462–67; Vincent P. DeSantis, "Republican Efforts to 'Crack' the Democratic South," *Review of Politics,*

doing he won control of the party. Whether he significantly aided blacks or furthered the cause of national unity in the process is doubtful.

The cause célèbre of the first year of the Roosevelt administration was Booker T. Washington's dinner at the White House.[13] Some weeks before McKinley's assassination, Roosevelt and Washington had been in correspondence concerning a planned visit of the vice-president to the South, including a speech at Tuskegee. The trip was canceled because of McKinley's death, but Roosevelt wrote to Washington asking him to come to the capital to discuss the question of southern appointments. Twice within the next few weeks the two men met. On the second occasion, October 16, Washington stopped at the home of a Negro friend, Whitefield McKinlay, where he received a note from Roosevelt inviting him to dinner that evening. The two dined together and afterwards continued their discussion about southern appointments. Washington departed later in the evening for New York. Neither man indicated at the time that anything extraordinary had occurred. The next day some New York papers carried brief accounts of the meeting and dinner at the White House. Soon a storm of criticism swept across the South.[14]

The vitriolic reaction of some southerners was as shocking as it was revealing of the depth of the fear and hatred of Negroes that had overcome the South. The Memphis *Commercial Appeal* accused the president of committing "the most damnable outrage which has ever been perpetrated by any citizen of the United States . . . when he invited a nigger to dine with him at the White House."[15] Others

---

14 (April 1952), 258–59; Henry F. Pringle, "Theodore Roosevelt and the South," *Virginia Quarterly Review*, 9 (Jan. 1933), 14–25.

13 Dewey W. Grantham, Jr., "Dinner at the White House: Theodore Roosevelt, Booker T. Washington, and the South," *Tennessee Historical Quarterly*, 17 (June 1958), 112–30. See also Bishop, I, 165–67; Gatewood, *Roosevelt and Art of Controversy*, pp. 32–61; Louis R. Harlan, *Booker T. Washington: The Making of a Black Leader, 1856–1901* (New York, 1972), pp. 304–24; Basil Mathews, *Booker T. Washington: Educator and Interracial Interpreter* (Cambridge, Mass., 1948), pp. 233–34; Henry F. Pringle, *Theodore Roosevelt: A Biography* (New York, 1931), pp. 248–50; Samuel R. Spencer, Jr., *Booker T. Washington and the Negro's Place in American Life* (Boston, 1955), pp. 133–35; Mark Sullivan, *Our Times: The United States, 1900–1925* (New York, 1926–35), III, 128–45.

14 Washington to Roosevelt, July 5, 1901, Theodore Roosevelt Papers, Manuscript Division, Library of Congress; Roosevelt to Washington, July 9, Sept. 14, 1901, in Morison, ed., *Roosevelt Letters*, III, 113, 149; Booker T. Washington, *My Larger Education* (Garden City, N.Y., 1911), pp. 175–77.

15 Quoted in the New York *Post*, Oct. 18, 1901. For reports of other southern criticisms, see New York *Times*, Oct. 19, 1901, and *Literary Digest*, 23 (Oct. 26, 1901), 486.

charged that Roosevelt's action was a declaration that the Negro was the "social equal of the white man," or that it was a "studied insult to the South." If such responses seemed hysterical and, as the Boston *Evening Transcript* editorialized, "a teapot tempest,"[16] there is little doubt that the episode damaged Roosevelt in the white South. Certainly he had expected no such outburst when he invited Washington, nor had he intended the dinner to promote the social intermingling of the races or to alienate his southern friends. "The outburst of feeling in the South about it is to me literally inexplicable," wrote Roosevelt a few days after the event. "It does not anger me . . . but I am very melancholy that such feeling should exist in such bitterly aggravated form in any part of our country."[17] In the years that followed, southerners reminded Roosevelt again and again of what they regarded as a great indiscretion.

Many Negroes were elated by the event. Even W. Calvin Chase's Washington *Bee*, which until then had seldom found anything complimentary to say about Roosevelt, ran a front-page story under the headline "The Lie Nailed that he is Opposed to the Negro." It claimed, in contradiction to its earlier articles, that he had been sympathetic to the Negro while governor of New York.[18] The Reverend Francis J. Grimké wrote that at last there was a man in the White House who had both courage and convictions in the right direction.[19] Other words of praise were heard from Negroes north and south. In fact, both Roosevelt's admirers and detractors read too much into the incident. He had not changed his attitude toward Negroes or the South. He met with Washington for the practical reason of discussing southern appointments as part of his efforts to build up the Republican party and his own influence in the South. While he continued to rely heavily on Washington's advice in these matters, he had second thoughts about doing this during dinner at the White House. In later years Roosevelt admitted that perhaps he had made a mistake, not morally, but from the point of view of expediency, for "the effect on the South was injurious and misinterpreted."[20] Sobered by the reaction, Roosevelt did not risk affront-

[16] Oct. 18, 1901.

[17] Roosevelt to Lucius Nathan Littauer, Oct. 24, 1901, in Morison, ed., *Roosevelt Letters*, III, 181.

[18] Oct. 19, 1901.

[19] Francis J. Grimké, *The Roosevelt-Washington Espisode or Race Prejudice* (n.p., n.d.), a sermon delivered Oct. 27, 1901, pamphlet in Roosevelt Memorial Association Collection, Widener Library, Harvard University.

[20] Diary entry of George von Lengerke Meyer concerning cabinet meeting, Feb. 5, 1909, Meyer Paper, Manuscript Division, Library of Congress. See also Roosevelt to Henry S. Pritchett, Dec. 14, 1904, Roosevelt to Owen Wister, April 27, 1906,

ing southern racial sensitivities by repeating the invitation.

With Washington's assistance Roosevelt began to formulate a policy concerning southern Republicanism. It was, as C. Vann Woodward has written, a "quixotic reformism mingled strangely with an old brand of practical politics."[21] The first public indication of Roosevelt's thinking came on October 7, 1901, when he announced that he would appoint Thomas G. Jones judge of the United States District Court in Alabama. Roosevelt had made the decision without consulting Mark Hanna, who up to then had considered it his prerogative to oversee southern appointments. Washington had urged the selection of Jones in his meeting with Roosevelt at the end of September. Southerners praised the appointment. Jones was a former Confederate and a conservative Democrat, but he was a man who believed in fair treatment and protection for the Negro. With his selection Roosevelt was able to bypass the white Republican managers in Alabama who owed allegiance to Hanna and at the same time to select a man who was acceptable to most white southerners and to black leaders.[22]

By mid-October 1901 Roosevelt's southern policy had become a popular subject of speculation. At first the Washington *Bee* praised Roosevelt for attempting to break up the solid South, although it erroneously asserted that Roosevelt and Hanna were working together in this matter. A few months later, the *Bee* blasted Roosevelt for replacing black officeholders with whites and warned him that such actions would cause Negroes to rebel against the Republican party.[23] White southerners also changed their evaluations. For example, in an interview on October 17, 1901, Senator Benjamin R. Tillman of South Carolina praised Roosevelt warmly. "He will make an honest President. I do not believe President Roosevelt will appoint an unworthy man to office."[24] But in a short while Tillman became one of Roosevelt's bitterest critics over, among other things, his appointment policy in South Carolina.

In formulating and carrying out his southern policy, Roosevelt relied heavily on Henry C. Payne and James S. Clarkson during the first few years of his administration. Long active in Wisconsin

---

Roosevelt to Richard Watson Gilder, Nov. 16, 1908, and Roosevelt to Charles Grenfill Washburn, Nov. 20, 1915, in Morison, ed., *Roosevelt Letters*, IV, 1071, V, 227, VI, 1359, VIII, 981.

21 Woodward, p. 463. On Roosevelt's southern appointment policy, see Roosevelt to Carl Schurz, Dec. 24, 1903, in Morison, ed., *Roosevelt Letters*, III, 680–82.

22 Bishop, I, 155; Blum, p. 45; Grantham, pp. 113–114; Woodward, p. 339.

23 Oct. 12, 1901, Jan. 11, Feb. 1, 1902.

24 New York *Times*, Oct. 18, 1901.

politics and vice-chairman of the Republican national committee in 1900, Payne had helped secure Roosevelt's nomination for the vice-presidency. He became Roosevelt's first cabinet appointee in December 1901 when, to the dismay of some reformers, he was named postmaster general, a position he held until his death on October 4, 1904. Payne was selected because of his experience as a party manager, and although he did not purge as many postmasters as some of his predecessors did, he certainly believed in using the spoils system to strengthen the GOP.[25]

Roosevelt's choice of James S. Clarkson on April 17, 1902, as surveyor of customs for the port of New York met with even more adverse criticism. As a longtime leader in Iowa Republican politics before moving to New York in 1891, Clarkson was known as an avowed friend of black Republicans and as a notorious spoilsman. As first assistant postmaster general under Harrison he had removed over 32,000 of the 55,000 fourth-class postmasters.[26] Roosevelt discounted this record by blandly observing that Clarkson had made "new appointments and occasional removals with political considerations, no less than considerations of efficiency of service, in view" and that he was "an honorable and capable man, and a first-class officer."[27] Well versed in the intricacies of southern politics, Clarkson served Roosevelt ably for two years, helping to create and maintain Republican organizations that would stand loyally by the president.

Roosevelt's reliance upon the advice of Booker T. Washington also came under attack. Although the Tuskegee educator alleged that he disliked politics, he became deeply involved in the political machinations of the Roosevelt administration. Roosevelt in turn had the highest respect for Washington and his recommendations. "I do not know a white man of the South who is as good a man as Booker Washington today," he wrote in 1906.[28] No Negro could hope to re-

[25] William Ward Wight, *Henry Clay Payne: A Life* (Milwaukee, 1907), p. 114; Dorothy Ganfield Fowler, *The Cabinet Politician: The Postmasters General, 1829–1909* (New York, 1943), pp. 263–66; Merrill and Merrill, pp. 101–2; New York *Age*, Nov. 14, 1901.

[26] "James S. Clarkson," *National Cyclopaedia of American Biography* (1921), II, 118–19; Blum, p. 44; Harold U. Faulkner, *Politics, Reform and Expansion, 1890–1900* (New York, 1959), p. 96; George H. Mayer, *The Republican Party, 1854–1964* (New York, 1964), pp. 218–19, 222; Merrill and Merrill, p. 103–7; Pringle, *Roosevelt*, p. 344.

[27] Roosevelt to Harriet Sumner Curtis, May 12, 1902, in Morison, ed., *Roosevelt Letters*, III, 263.

[28] Roosevelt to Owen Wister, April 27, 1906, *ibid.*, V, 227. There are numerous

ceive a federal appointment unless approved by Washington, and his influence over the selection of southern whites, as in the case of Judge Jones, was also considerable. Washington was already a highly controversial figure among Negroes. Editor Chase of the Washington *Bee* constantly berated him as a "trimmer and apologist." "If Prof. Washington eats many more dinners with Mr. Roosevelt," wrote Chase in February 1902, "there will not be enough negro office holders in the South left to occupy a space 4 by 6."[29] As Negro opposition to Washington and his accommodationist policies gradually increased, Roosevelt inevitably became involved.

Central to Roosevelt's appointment policy in the South was his so-called referee system, which at times was condemned by both whites and blacks. In each state and district Roosevelt relied upon a few men, usually members of the national or state Republican committees, for advice on federal appointments, but in order to improve the standing of the Republican party with the white community in the South, he was often willing to appoint Democrats rather than some of the old party hacks. Some Negroes saw a strong racial bias in this system.[30] On the other hand, a conservative white Mississippi planter, Alfred Holt Stone, called the system "thoroughly vicious" for it made the referee a "traitor" to his own people like the scalawag of Reconstruction.[31] Incensed by this description, Roosevelt said that Stone had "deliberately, consistently and maliciously falsified the facts." Roosevelt pointed out that the practice had been in existence since Harrison, and that he had consulted many of the same men used by McKinley and Hanna. Moreover, he said that refereees were also used in states outside of the South. Both Democratic and Republican presidents had to rely on someone for advice in those states where they had no senators or congressmen from their own party. Roosevelt concluded that the only difference was that he had made a greater effort than any of his Republican predecessors "to try to

---

laudatory references to Washington in Roosevelt's letters. Shortly after Washington's death, Roosevelt referred to him as "a genius such as does not arise in a generation" (Roosevelt to Julius Rosenwald, Dec. 15, 1915, *ibid.*, VIII, 997). For Roosevelt's final published tribute to Washington, see his preface to Emmett J. Scott and Lyman B. Stowe, *Booker T. Washington, Builder of a Civilization* (Garden City, N.Y., 1918). The preface, written in 1916, is reprinted in Roosevelt, *Works*, XI, 273–77.

29 Washington *Bee*, Feb. 22, 1902; see also Feb. 1, 1902. Later Washington gained Chase's support by means of a subsidy to the *Bee* (August Meier, "Booker T. Washington and the Rise of the N.A.A.C.P.," *Crisis*, 61 [Feb. 1954], 72).

30 Fowler, p. 266; Miller, p. 10.

31 Stone, *Studies in the American Race Problem* (New York, 1908), pp. 340–44.

get the best possible quality of service and the highest possible character of men and women in the offices in the Southern States."[32] That one critic regarded the referee system as evidence of an anti-Negro bias in appointments, while another saw in it aspects of radical Reconstruction, suggests the difficulty that any president was likely to have in carrying out his southern policy.

During the next few years Roosevelt experienced many times the mercurial temper and delicate sensitivity of white southerners, especially when they divined slights to their section. The praise over the Jones appointment was forgotten in the excitement about the Booker T. Washington dinner, an episode that Roosevelt thought illustrated "the continued existence of that combination of Bourbon intellect and intolerant truculence of spirit . . . which brought on the Civil War."[33] In the spring of 1902 Roosevelt once more unintentionally aroused the ire of southerners. Speaking at Arlington National Cemetery on Memorial Day, he made a number of his usual remarks about the reunited country, then went on to discuss the war in the Philippines, with particular reference to the criticism of American troops for brutality to the natives. Deploring any acts of cruelty by American troops that may have occurred under provocation, he asserted that lynchings in the United States had been carried on with far greater "barbarity" and were "infinitely worse," and he denounced those who clamored about what happened in the Philippines without condemning what went on at home.[34] Enraged southern Democrats promptly accused Roosevelt of waving the bloody shirt. Even a few Republicans felt the speech was injudicious, although Roosevelt denied that he had attacked the South and added that what he said about lynching applied "to Kansas & Colorado as much as to Texas & Tennessee."[35] Nevertheless his comments had touched a sensitive spot, and the incident provided still another reminder of the special difficulties of dealing with the South.

In the late summer and fall of 1902 a much more important problem arose as a result of the vigorous movement of lily-whites to capture the Republican party in North Carolina and Alabama. North Carolina then had one Republican senator, Jeter C. Pritchard. Elected to a Senate vacancy in 1895 by the Fusionist, Populist-Republican, legislature, he was supported by whites in the moun-

[32] Roosevelt to John Graham Brooks, Nov. 13, 1908, in Morison, ed., *Roosevelt Letters*, VI, 1343–48.

[33] Roosevelt to Henry Cabot Lodge, Oct. 28, 1901, *ibid.*, III, 184.

[34] New York *Times*, May 31, 1902.

[35] Roosevelt to Silas McBee, June 3, 1902, in Morison, ed., *Roosevelt Letters*, III, 269.

tain and Piedmont regions and Negroes in the eastern sections of the state. As the only Republican senator from the South, he had a large influence on all southern matters. During the McKinley years Pritchard had championed Negro voting and officeholding and denounced the white supremacy campaign in North Carolina which led to the adoption of the disfranchising amendment in 1900. However, after this blow to his electoral base, he reversed himself in favor of the lily-whites.[36]

On August 21, 1902, Pritchard conferred with Roosevelt at his home in Oyster Bay, New York, ostensibly about a vacancy on the United States Court of Claims. Immediately afterwards Pritchard went to Greensboro, North Carolina, where on August 28 he gave the opening speech at the Republican state convention. The meeting, which excluded all Negroes, was a triumph for the lily-whites, and the platform that was adopted failed to condemn the recent disfranchise amendment. In fact, that reform was praised by the convention's permanent chairman as a settlement of the race issue. Pritchard then went on to Alabama, which had passed its own disfranchising amendment in 1901. There he conferred with a number of Democrats, who reportedly were willing, except for the race issue, to bolt their party. Shortly afterwards Alabama Republicans held a convention which carefully excluded Negroes. An effort was clearly being made to attract the leaders of the new South, lawyers, businessmen, and manufacturers, to a new lily-white Republican party.[37]

Pritchard believed that Roosevelt sympathized with that development. On September 15 he wrote to Clarkson that the president's position encouraged "those of us who seek to build up a substantial, vote-getting party in the South. I am sick and tired of the old plan which has obtained in so many of the Southern States."[38] Although Pritchard did not claim as much, his activities, coming as they did after his conference with Roosevelt, gave the impression that he was acting as the president's personal representative.

[36] New York *Times*, Aug. 22, 1902. On Pritchard and North Carolina politics, see *Dictionary of American Biography*; Josephus Daniels, *Editor in Politics* (Chapel Hill, N.C., 1941), pp. 423–24; Helen G. Edmonds, *The Negro and Fusion Politics in North Carolina 1894–1901* (Chapel Hill, N.C., 1951), pp. 91–92; William Alexander Mabry, "Negro Suffrage and Fusion Rule in North Carolina," *North Carolina Historical Review*, 12 (April 1935), 79–102. Also see above p. 16.

[37] *Literary Digest*, 25 (Sept. 6. 1902), 272; *Outlook*, 72 (Sept. 13, 1902), 100; Washington *Bee*, Sept. 6, 1902; New York *Times*, Oct. 21, Nov. 14, 1902; James S. Clarkson to Roosevelt, Sept. 27, 1902, Roosevelt Papers; Clarkson to Booker T. Washington, Oct. 11, 1902, Booker T. Washington Papers, Manuscript Division, Library of Congress.

[38] Pritchard to Clarkson, Sept. 15, 1902, Roosevelt Papers.

Negroes were alarmed. The Washington *Bee* demanded that the national and congressional Republican committees repudiate Pritchard. Veteran Louisiana Negro politician Walter L. Cohen concluded that there was "no doubt that President Roosevelt had turned over the entire patronage of the State to the 'lily white' faction." Booker T. Washington wrote an indignant letter to Clarkson about the movement of the lily-whites against the Negroes. "Unless something is done," he warned, "you will find that when the next election comes, the colored voters at the North, through their ballots, are going to resent what is being done to the colored people in the South." Washington claimed that they held a balance of power in Indiana, New Jersey, and Illinois. Although he did not believe that Roosevelt was in favor of such lily-white schemes, he felt that a word from Clarkson could help bring the "hypocritical Republicans" to their senses.[39]

Clarkson was willing to act. He met twice with Washington and with Charles H. Scott of Montgomery, Alabama, a wealthy white real estate man who had made detailed recommendations concerning appointments and Republican party structure in Alabama. Clarkson felt that the Republican party could not "in any sense indorse or excuse" the ruthless exclusion of Negroes from the Alabama state convention under the direction of William Vaughan, the chairman of the state executive committee, and Julian H. Bingham, a collector of internal revenue. In fact, after the convention Roosevelt dismissed Vaughan from his post as United States district attorney for the Northern District of Alabama on the grounds of "neglect of duty," an action generally seen as a rebuff for his role in excluding Negroes. As Vaughn's successor, Washington favored Thomas Rouhlac of Sheffield, a gold Democrat. In his discussions with Clarkson, Washington emphasized the deep concern of northern Negroes about the lily-white movement. Clarkson was so impressed that he reported to Roosevelt that only the influence of Washington, T. Thomas Fortune, editor of the *Age*, and a few others was what prevented "a stampede of colored men in the North from the Republican Party." Clarkson was surprised to learn that the black leaders held Senator Pritchard responsible for the movement against the Negroes; the senator's recent actions were "untenable" and "unjust" and could only be accepted at a "sacrifice of principle in the South and votes in the North." Clarkson was particularly concerned about the threatened loss of thousands of black votes in close northern states like New York, Ohio, Indiana, Connecticut, and Wisconsin, with the

39 Washington *Bee*, Sept. 6, 1902; Cohen to George A. Myers, Sept. 14, 1902, George A. Myers Papers, Ohio Historical Society; Washington to Clarkson, Sept. 15, 1902, Roosevelt Papers.

possibility that it could cost the Republicans seven or eight congressmen in the 1902 elections. "The question is acute," Clarkson warned Roosevelt, and it had to be met by definite action.[40]

Roosevelt responded promptly. "I agree absolutely with your views as to the Negro question and the Republican party in the South," he wrote to Clarkson on September 29, and he suggested that Roulhac be named immediately to replace Vaughan as the United States district attorney.[41] Black leaders praised this step as a blow to the lily-whites.[42] Significantly, after the appointment had been made, Roosevelt instructed Roulhac to "consult men like Judge Jones, Judge Boyd, and Booker T. Washington."[43] In another effort to reassure Negroes, on October 7 Roosevelt conferred with a delegation from the Afro-American Council, to which he expressed his strong disapproval of any exclusively white party in the South, and as additional evidence of Negro influence on his administration he also made public Booker T. Washington's letter recommending the appointment of Judge Jones.[44] In mid-October, Clarkson released to the press a letter he had just written to Lee Person, a Negro politician in North Carolina, in which he emphasized his and Roosevelt's opposition to efforts to establish Jim Crow parties in Alabama or elsewhere.[45]

After the November elections the administration struck another blow at the lily-whites in Alabama by removing Bingham as collector of internal revenue. His replacement was Joseph O. Thompson, a former gold Democrat and brother of a Democratic congressman. Thompson had opposed the exclusion of Negro delegates from the Alabama Republican convention, and Booker T. Washington had endorsed his appointment. In this instance Payne made the announcement, reiterating the administration's position that the Republican party would not stand for the political exclusion of any group of the population by reason of its race or color.[46] These appointments

40 Clarkson to Roosevelt, Sept. 27, 1902, Roosevelt Papers. See also Washington to Roosevelt, Sept. 27, 1902, *ibid.* On Vaughan, see New York *Times*, Sept. 12, 1902.

41 Roosevelt to Clarkson, Sept. 29, 1902, in Morison, ed., *Roosevelt Letters*, III, 333.

42 Washington to Clarkson, Oct. 7, 1902, Roosevelt Papers; A. D. Wimbs to Washington, Oct. 8, 1902, and Clarkson to Washington, Oct. 11, 1902, Washington Papers.

43 Roosevelt to Thomas Roulhac, Oct. 22, 1902, Roosevelt Papers. See also Clarkson to Roulhac, Nov. 10, 1902, Clarkson Papers, Manuscript Division, Library of Congress.

44 New York *Times*, Oct. 8, Oct. 25, 1902; Woodward, p. 464.

45 New York *Times*, Oct. 20, Oct. 21, 1902; New York *Age*, Oct. 30, 1902.

46 New York *Times*, Nov. 11, 1902.

demonstrated that in Alabama at least Roosevelt was unwilling to give a free hand to the lily-whites.

The situation in North Carolina was less clear. Roosevelt was not prepared to dump Pritchard, although he was obviously unhappy about the turmoil aroused by the senator's tactics. These moves failed to protect the Republicans in North Carolina against the rise of white-supremacist Democrats, and the legislature elected in November refused to return Pritchard to the Senate in 1903, replacing him with a Democrat, Lee S. Overman. Pritchard attempted to square himself with Roosevelt. "My chief object," he wrote on November 21, "has been to build up a strong, respectable and effective Republican organization." He denied that anyone had been excluded from the North Carolina convention on account of race or color. It was only because "they were not elected by duly qualified voters"; moreover, they were troublemakers and Roosevelt's enemies anyway. But he added that if he had to recommend black people for prominent local positions, it would mean a "complete disintegration of the white forces of the state."[47]

In North Carolina, Roosevelt acquiesced to the demands of the lily-whites. One notable instance was the case of Samuel H. Vick, the Negro postmaster of Wilson. After lily-whites got control of the Republican party in Wilson in 1902, they demanded that Vick be replaced by a white. In December, Pritchard pressed the same demand on Roosevelt, claiming that he took his stand not because of Vick's color but on the ground that he had been disloyal to the GOP. Although Vick denied the accusation, in February 1903 Roosevelt replaced him with a white who had been proposed by Pritchard. In addition Roosevelt appointed Pritchard in March 1903 to the Supreme Court of the District of Columbia and a year later elevated him to a judgeship on the Circuit Court of Appeals, Fourth Judicial Circuit.[48]

In Alabama the lily-whites were reported to have been sympathetic to Mark Hanna, so their weakening was to Roosevelt's advantage. But in North Carolina he apparently concluded that his position would have been endangered by continued opposition to the lily-whites, despite Clarkson's and Payne's advice to the contrary. Roosevelt was greatly annoyed by any suggestion that his policies were dictated by such selfish political considerations. In reference to such

47 Pritchard to Roosevelt, Nov. 21, 1902, Roosevelt Papers. See also New York *Times*, Dec. 3, 1902.

48 New York *Times*, Dec. 4, 6, 7, 9, 1902, Feb. 1, Feb. 17, and March 25, 1903; Edmonds, pp. 92–93.

reports he wrote to Clarkson that "the most damaging thing to me . . . is to give the impression that in what I have been trying to do for the Negro I have been actuated by political motives. That is why I have been so insistent that neither you nor Payne nor anyone else shall take any steps to secure Negro or any other delegations from the South. I do not want the nomination unless it comes freely from the people of the Republican States because they believe in me. . . . I want to make it clear as a bell that I have acted in the way I have on the Negro question simply because I hold myself the heir of the policies of Abraham Lincoln and am incapable of abandoning them to serve personal or political ends."[49] It is doubtful, however, that many politicians, black or white, came to such benign conclusions about his southern maneuvers.

While Roosevelt and his lieutenants were struggling with the lily-white problem in North Carolina and Alabama, two other well-publicized controversies arose that damaged the president's standing with white southerners in South Carolina and Mississippi. Roosevelt's objectives in South Carolina were similar to those throughout the South. Wanting to wrest control of the Republican machinery from Hanna and to build up a broader base of support for the party, he sought the backing of respectable whites, but at the same time he did not wish to alienate Negroes. It was a difficult problem. In 1900 McKinley and Hanna had supported the lily-whites, Gold Democrats, and other dissidents in South Carolina in hopes of building a new party dedicated to their brand of Republicanism. They granted control of federal patronage in the state to Senator John L. McLaurin, a protectionist Gold Democrat then at odds with the state's other senator, Benjamin R. Tillman. After McKinley's death McLaurin sought Roosevelt's backing. This the senator was unlikely to receive, given his close association with Hanna. Instead of turning back to the older black-and-tan leaders, however, Roosevelt picked John G. Caspers, an associate of McLaurin in reorganization attempts, as his patronage referee. Although McKinley had appointed him a federal district attorney in South Carolina in 1901 and Hanna had named him to the Republican national committee shortly after the president's death, Caspers switched his loyalty to Roosevelt and publicly declared his support for a Republican party in South Carolina that included both blacks and whites. But evidence of Casper's and Roosevelt's commitment to such a party was slow in materializ-

[49] Roosevelt to Clarkson, March 13, 1903, Roosevelt Papers. See also New York *Times*, Jan. 8, Jan. 29, 1903.

ing—too slow for many Negro Republicans in South Carolina, who before long were openly threatening a break.[50]

Roosevelt faced this troublesome situation in the South Carolina GOP when he visited the Industrial Exposition at Charleston from April 8 to April 10, 1902. Hoping to avoid further difficulties with both whites and Negroes, he discussed appointment possibilities with a number of prominent whites, including James C. Hemphill, editor of the Charleston *News and Courier*, Mayor James Adger Smyth, and banker Robert Goodwyn Rhett. One of the persons considered in this discussion was a Negro, Dr. William D. Crum, although exactly what was said about him later became a matter of considerable dispute.[51] A county chairman for many years and a delegate to every national convention since 1884, Crum had long served the Republican party faithfully. Although most people regarded him as an able man, he had already been involved in one controversy over a federal appointment. His detractors charged that he had improperly voted for Harrison at the 1892 convention, after having been elected as a delegate pledged to Blaine, and as a reward had been appointed postmaster at Charleston. The opposition to him by white residents of Charleston had been so great that Crum requested Harrison to withdraw the nomination. Identified as a Harrison man, Crum's star faded during the McKinley years, especially when Hanna and the president turned to the lily-whites. Roosevelt's interest in Crum in 1902 was another blow at Hanna, as well as a recognition of black Republicans in the state.[52]

During the fall of 1902 reports began to circulate, to the alarm of conservative white Charlestonians, that Roosevelt was planning to appoint Crum to be collector of customs at Charleston to fill a vacancy created by the death of the previous incumbent in September. When the projected nomination was announced in early November, Roosevelt was surprised by the vehement reaction of local whites. This step, wrote Rhett, will "shatter the idol which he [Roosevelt] created in the heads of the people here on his visit last Spring." To be a Republican was to invite social ostracism, Rhett added, and

[50] Gatewood, *Roosevelt and Art of Controversy*, pp. 93–98; Roosevelt to Carl Schurz, Dec. 24, 1903, in Morison, ed., *Roosevelt Letters*, III, 680–81; New York *Age*, Sept. 26, 1901; Washington *Bee*, Oct. 12, 1901.

[51] New York *Times*, April 9–11, 1902; Gatewood, *Roosevelt and Art of Controversy*, pp. 98–99.

[52] On Crum, see Willard B. Gatewood, "William D. Crum: A Negro in Politics," *Journal of Negro History*, 53 (Oct. 1968), 301–8; Vincent P. DeSantis, "The Republican Party and the Southern Negro, 1877–1897," *ibid.*, 45 (April 1960), 84; George B. Tindall, *South Carolina Negroes, 1877–1900* (Columbia, S.C., 1952), pp. 50, 147; New York *Times*, Nov. 28, 1902.

people would support the party only when they realized that the Negro was not in control.[53] Mayor Smyth put the case in stronger words. He objected to Crum on the same grounds as he had in 1892, that is, he regarded the appointment as simply a reward for services rendered. Smyth called Crum absolutely unfit, repeated the familiar story of the degradation suffered during Reconstruction, and concluded that "as Anglo-Saxons, we have sworn never again to submit to the rule of the African."[54] Editor Hemphill was somewhat more charitable to Crum, who he admitted was a "respectable citizen." But he still strongly objected to Crum's appointment on the ground that he was colored, that he was not engaged in commercial pursuits, and that he did not represent the tax-paying, property-holding citizens of the community.[55]

Roosevelt replied carefully to these criticisms. He could not understand how anyone could have gotten the impression during his visit that he "would not appoint reputable and upright colored men to office, when objection was made to them solely on account of their color." He noted that he had appointed Negroes in nearly every state with a considerable black population. There was no question of Negro domination, for nearly all appointments have been of white men; but, Roosevelt concluded, "I cannot consent to take the position that the door of hope—the door of opportunity—is to be shut upon any man, no matter how worthy, purely upon the grounds of race or color."[56] These points were reasonable and restrained. But the South had changed, and Roosevelt misjudged its temper.

Roosevelt's letter to Smyth was dated November 26, 1902. The next day it was released to the press and the Crum case became an open fight. On the last day of December 1902, Roosevelt sent Crum's nomination to the Senate. Thereupon began a nearly interminable struggle for confirmation between an intransigent South and a stubborn president. Bowing to the objections of the South Carolina senators, the Senate adjourned on March 4, 1903, without having taken action. This just whetted Roosevelt's appetite for battle. "The more I have thought it over the more convinced I have been that Crum

53 Rhett to George B. Cortelyou, Nov. 7, 1902, Roosevelt Papers.

54 James Adger Smyth to Cortelyou, Nov. 10, 1902, *ibid.*

55 Hemphill to Roosevelt, Nov. 11, 1902, *ibid.*

56 Roosevelt to James Adger Smyth, Nov. 26, 1902, in Morison, ed., *Roosevelt Letters*, III, 384. See also Roosevelt to Robert G. Rhett, Nov. 10, 1902, *ibid.*, pp. 375–76. Hemphill later wrote that Roosevelt was "distinctly dishonest" about the Crum case in that he had assured some leading whites of Charleston during his visit in April 1902 that he would not disregard the wishes of the whites of Charleston and the South in making appointments (Hemphill to Editor, Dec. 22, 1908, in *Harper's Weekly*, 53 [Jan. 9, 1909], 10, 31).

must be appointed," he wrote to Booker T. Washington. "I shall send in his name again to the Senate tomorrow. If it does not act I shall appoint him as soon as it adjourns."[57] After the special session of the Senate on March 20 also failed to confirm Crum, Roosevelt issued a temporary commission on March 20, 1903. In November 1903 the Senate met again in special session, and Roosevelt submitted the nomination still another time. Once again the Senate adjourned without confirming Crum. On December 1 Roosevelt issued a second temporary commission. The game was repeated for the session that met from December 7, 1903, to April 28, 1904, and Roosevelt issued a third recess appointment at the end of April. In December 1904, Roosevelt submitted Crum's name for the fifth time. On January 6, 1905, the Senate finally yielded and voted for confirmation. More than two years had passed from the time of the original nomination.

Crum's perferment brought him no easy rewards. As a result of a ruling by the Treasury Department he received no pay at all from the federal government during the period of his recess appointments, and he stuck it out only at considerable financial loss.[58] Washington and other Negro leaders did what they could to speed a favorable outcome by urging the senators from northern states to press for confirmation. Indeed, by the spring of 1904 Roosevelt and Republican leaders became concerned about the possibility of the defection of black voters in the North who blamed the Republican Senate for its failure to act.[59] It was still another example of the inherent difficulty of maintaining the Republican party's historic ties with the Negro while trying to attract, rather than alienate, whites in the South. As the clamor over the Crum appointment grew, Roosevelt began to have some doubts about the wisdom of his action. Writing to Carl Schurz at the end of December 1903, he complained that he had "completely lost control of the republican machine" in South Carolina, as well as in Mississippi and in most of the South.[60] Such an assessment was too hastily made, for by early 1904 it became

57 Roosevelt to Washington, March 4, 1903, in Morison, ed., *Roosevelt Letters*, III, 438. For a summary of action on the Crum nomination during the first year of the controversy, see Leslie M. Shaw to Senator Benjamin R. Tillman, Jan. 8, 1904, in *Congressional Record*, 58th Cong., 2d sess., vol. 38, pt. 2, p. 1105.

58 Leslie M. Shaw to William P. Frye, Jan. 27, 1904, in *Cong. Rec.*, 58th Cong., 2d sess., vol. 38, pt. 2, p. 1302; Emmett J. Scott to Mrs. Ellen A. Crum, April 21, 1904, Mrs. Crum to Scott, April 22, 1904, Washington Papers; Gatewood, *Roosevelt and Art of Controversy*, pp. 122–23.

59 Washington to Crum, Feb. 19, 1904, Washington to William H. Lewis, March 3, 1904, and James S. Clarkson to Washington, April 28, 1904, Washington Papers.

60 Roosevelt to Schurz, Dec. 24, 1903, in Morison, ed., *Roosevelt Letters*, III, 682.

obvious that Roosevelt had the firm support of the biracial Republican organization in South Carolina. Nevertheless, his earlier hope of developing a more broadly based party in the state was gone, and on a few occasions thereafter Roosevelt acknowledged that it might have been inexpedient to insist upon Crum's appointment.[61]

Roosevelt did not have any such doubts about his battle with some Mississippians over the Indianola post office. This was an issue, he argued, of "right and wrong in its plainest and simplest form," in which there could be only one proper course of action.[62] The problem arose in the town of Indianola, Mississippi, the county seat of Sunflower County. Blacks made up a large majority of the area's population, and for many years the postmistress of the town had been a Negro, Mrs. Minnie M. Cox. Originally appointed by Harrison, Mrs. Cox was reappointed by McKinley in 1897. In January 1900 her position was raised from a fourth-class to a third-class status and she was reappointed to another four-year term. Mrs. Cox and her husband were intelligent, responsible, property-holding citizens who had the respect of prominent white citizens of the area. Both Mississippi senators had approved of her appointment. Moreover, reports on her work by post office inspectors had been consistently favorable.

Some of the whites in the area coveted Mrs. Cox's position. In June 1901 they first petitioned the postmaster general for the appointment of a new postmaster. Those with designs on the post seem to have been encouraged, although unintentionally, by Roosevelt's efforts to reorganize the Republican party in the South. Convinced that the old GOP leadership in Mississippi was rotten, he selected a gold Democrat, Edgar S. Wilson, as his patronage referee and appointed him marshal of the Southern District of Mississippi in January 1902. After a prominent Negro Republican, James Hill, lost his federal post in the reorganization, some Indianola whites concluded that Roosevelt would agree to the ouster of all black officeholders in the state.[63] One of the hopefuls was A. B. Weeks, the brother-in-law of the mayor, who in April 1902 began the first of numerous requests for the postmastership. In the fall of 1902 Weeks and others took advantage of the intense anti-Negro, white supremacy political campaign being conducted by former governor James K. Vardaman to put

61 Gatewood, *Roosevelt and Art of Controversy*, pp. 124–25; Roosevelt to Henry S. Pritchett, Dec. 14, 1904, and Roosevelt to Owen Wister, April 27, 1906, in Morison, ed., *Roosevelt Letters*, IV, 1071, V, 227. See also Owen Wister, *Roosevelt: The Story of a Friendship* (New York, 1930), p. 18.

62 Roosevelt to Richard Watson Gilder, Nov. 16, 1908, in Morison, ed., *Roosevelt Letters*, VI, 1359.

63 Gatewood, *Roosevelt and Art of Controversy*, pp. 65–68.

pressure on Mrs. Cox to resign. A number of Indianola citizens met and appointed a committee to circulate a petition calling for Mrs. Cox's resignation. At a second meeting they apparently agreed to demand that Mrs. Cox give up her office by January 1, 1903. According to the leader of that meeting, a lawyer named P. C. Chapman, Mrs. Cox's husband, Wayne Cox, came to him before the meeting with a letter of resignation from his wife, to take effect on January 1, 1903. Chapman denied that there had been any intimidation or threats, and he insisted "that the kindest feeling" existed between Mrs. Cox and the white citizens of Indianola.[64]

Apparently Mr. Cox felt differently, for he visited Edgar S. Wilson in Jackson to request his help. While Wilson sought unsuccessfully for a solution, reports of the difficulties in Indianola finally reached the Post Office Department. On November 23, 1902, Charles Fitzgerald, a postal inspector and a friend of Wilson, requested an explanation from the Indianola mayor, J. L. Davis. Davis denied that there had been any intimidation, but he acknowledged that there was much sentiment for Mrs. Cox's resignation, and he stated that he favored the acceptance of her offer to quit. Shortly afterwards Mrs. Cox wrote to Fitzgerald: "If I don't resign there will be trouble and cause the town to lose [its] post-office facilities." On December 4 she sent her resignation to President Roosevelt, to take effect on January 1, 1903, or as soon thereafter as a successor could be appointed.[65]

Inspector Fitzgerald visited Indianola on December 3 and 4. He became convinced that improper pressures had been brought to bear on Mrs. Cox, and he attributed them "to a coterie of Democrats and their friends who are agitating the question of 'nigger domination' and fomenting strife and discord."[66] In his report of December 15 Fitzgerald observed that Mrs. Cox would be in danger if she attempted to remain in office; so he recommended that the Indianola post office be closed. Roosevelt followed this suggestion. Refusing to accept Mrs. Cox's resignation, on January 2, 1903, he directed that until the town accepted her back, its post office would be considered closed and all mail addressed to it would be forwarded to

64 U.S., Congress, House, *Resignation of the Postmaster at Indianola, Miss.*, 57th Cong., 2d sess., H. Doc. 422 (Feb. 26, 1903), pp. 7–11; Chapman to Anselm J. McLaurin, Jan. 6, 1903, in *Cong. Rec.*, 57th Cong., 2d sess., vol. 36, pt. 1, p. 853.

65 Gatewood, *Roosevelt and Art of Controversy*, p. 73; Davis to Fitzgerald, Nov. 29, 1902, Mrs. Cox to Fitzgerald, Dec. (?), 1902, and Mrs. Cox to Roosevelt, Dec. 4, 1902, in *Resignation of the Postmaster at Indianola, Miss.*, H. Doc. 422, pp. 19–20.

66 Fitzgerald to Joe P. Johnston, Dec. 11, 1903, in *Resignation of the Postmaster at Indianola, Miss.*, H. Doc. 422, p. 21.

Greenville. A few days later Mr. and Mrs. Cox left Indianola for Birmingham, where they remained for the next year.[67]

At this point the episode attracted national attention. In defense of the white citizens of Indianola, Senator Anselm J. McLaurin of Mississippi insisted that Mrs. Cox had resigned voluntarily, and he concluded: "In my opinion the main trouble is that you can't make white folks out of negroes."[68] Condemning Roosevelt's action, the New York *Times* held that even if there had been intimidation, it was "an act of gross injustice" to punish a whole community rather than to prosecute the individuals involved.[69] To Roosevelt this was a false issue; it was not he who had closed the post office. The burden lay upon those citizens of Indianola who had forced the resignation and flight of the legally appointed postmistress. He felt no obligation to reward these actions by a new appointment when the office could be opened again at any time she was accepted back. It was a challenge to national supremacy and to presidential authority. For his course Roosevelt had no apologies.[70]

During the early part of 1903 Senator McLaurin and a few other southerners brought the matter up in Congress, strongly attacking Roosevelt's actions and defending Indianola against the charge of wrongdoing. This brought forth a spirited defense of the president by Senator John C. Spooner of Wisconsin, who introduced clear evidence of improper pressures brought to bear on Mrs. Cox.[71] In addition the House of Representatives obtained from Postmaster General Payne copies of correspondence and documents pertaining to the case and printed a report in February 1903 that was very damaging to Indianola. Roosevelt stood by his decision. Only when it was obvious that Mrs. Cox could not be induced to return to her post did he finally make a new appointment and reopen the post office. Moreover, he was careful to appoint, on the recommendation of Edgar S. Wilson, "the one man in the town who had openly and courageously upheld her and done what he could to arouse his fellow citizens to stand by her."[72] Roosevelt's steadfast position in this case

67 *Ibid.*, pp. 25–31; New York *Times*, Jan. 3, 1903; Gatewood, *Roosevelt and Art of Controversy*, pp. 78, 89.

68 New York *Times*, Jan. 5, 1903.

69 Jan. 6, 1903.

70 Roosevelt to Richard Watson Gilder, Feb. 7, 1903, in Morison, ed., *Roosevelt Letters*, III, 420.

71 *Cong. Rec.*, 57th Cong., 2d sess., vol. 36, pt. 1, pp. 853–54, 1175–90, and pt. 3, pp. 2556–68, 2864.

72 Roosevelt to John Graham Brooks, Nov. 13, 1908, in Morison, ed., *Roosevelt Letters*, VI, 1348.

added measurably to the generally favorable impression that he created among Negroes during the first part of his presidency.

Roosevelt's stance in the Crum and Cox cases revealed only one side of his attitude toward black officeholders. When he became president, Roosevelt told Booker T. Washington that although he did not intend to appoint many Negroes to office in the South, all of his nominees, whether white or black, would be men of only the highest character and ability, and that some Negro appointments would be made in the North.[73] After a year and a half in office, he thought that he had upheld this high standard. "The prime tests I have applied have been those of character, fitness and ability," he explained to Clark Howell, editor of the Atlanta *Constitution.* So far as possible, Roosevelt said, he had tried "to consider the feelings of the people of each locality."[74] As he pointed out to Carl Schurz, the great majority of his appointees in the South were Democrats, "and not more than one or two per cent" were Negroes.[75]

Still, Roosevelt managed to make a number of excellent Negro appointments and to take care of at least some of the influential Negroes who sought positions. In the fall of 1901 he named Robert H. Terrell, a successful Washington lawyer, a judge of the Municipal Court of the District of Columbia. The New York *Age* greeted this step as an "innovation of the most dramatic character" which indicated the president's "determination to destroy the color line in politics."[76] The *Age* was oversanguine, but a few other appointments of similar stature followed. Urged by Booker T. Washington to find an important position for another lawyer, John S. Durham of Philadelphia, Roosevelt responded by appointing him an assistant attorney on the Spanish Treaty Claims Commission. He also placed T. Thomas Fortune, the mercurical editor of the New York *Age,* on the special commission to investigate conditions in the United States insular possessions. His selection of William Henry Lewis, a graduate of the Harvard Law School, to be assistant United States attorney for Massachusetts, was of greater significance, and it represented a start toward the fulfillment of his promise to appoint some Negroes to places in the North.[77] In addition Roosevelt saw to it that a num-

73 Washington, *My Larger Education*, pp. 170–71; Mathews, pp. 229–30.

74 Roosevelt to Howell, Feb. 24, 1903, in Morison, ed., *Roosevelt Letters*, III, 431.

75 Roosevelt to Schurz, Dec. 24, 1903, *ibid.*, p. 681.

76 New York *Age*, Nov. 21, 1901. Terrell remained judge until his death in 1925.

77 James S. Clarkson to William Loeb, Jr., Oct. 20, 1902, Philander C. Knox to George C. Cortelyou, Jan. 30, 1903, Roosevelt Papers; New York *Age*, Dec. 11, 1902; New York *Times*, Jan. 13, 1903.

ber of Negro Republican stalwarts retained or acquired some federal governmental position.

At Roosevelt's request his secretary, George B. Cortelyou, made a survey in January 1903 of the number of Negro appointees in all executive departments, as well as of the total number of whites or Negroes appointed during the previous year to positions in Mississippi and South Carolina. The results confirmed Roosevelt's statements about the character of his southern appointments.[78] In a number of instances he had selected whites for offices previously held by Negroes, and Negroes made up a small proportion of the total. In fact by mid-term he had made fewer Negro appointments than either Harrison or McKinley. There was little criticism about the caliber of men selected. "I feel that my course in the south has been absolutely right," insisted Roosevelt in February 1903.[79] Yet because of the general rise of Negrophobia, and the specific furor over the Crum and Indianola affairs, the outcry against Roosevelt by white southerners was far louder than it had ever been against his predecessor.[80]

Roosevelt was surprised and pained by the great outcry against his actions. Somehow he had misjudged the temper of the South. By the end of his first term, however, he had gained a better understanding of that section's growing intransigence on racial matters. He finally came to the conclusion that "as a whole southerners [demanded] . . . the entire exclusion of negroes from office."[81] This he was unwilling to accept. Under such circumstances it was manifestly impossible for him to satisfy both whites and blacks. His few Negro appointments and firm stand in the Crum and Indianola cases antagonized many of the whites; but his many concessions to white prejudices made it impossible to win the full confidence of the blacks.

In one way Roosevelt's southern maneuvers were successful. By gaining control of most of the section's convention delegates, Roosevelt took a major step toward eliminating Mark Hanna as a serious

[78] The responses of the cabinet members in Jan. and Feb. 1903 are in the Roosevelt Papers.

[79] Roosevelt to Silas McBee, Feb. 3, 1903, in Morison, ed., *Roosevelt Letters*, III, 419.

[80] See Roosevelt to Clark Howell, Feb. 24, 1903, *ibid.*, pp. 430–32, for Roosevelt's defense of his appointment policy. For other comments, see Henry Litchfield West, "American Politics," *Forum*, 34 (April 1903), 494–96; *Outlook*, 73 (Jan. 24, 1903), 187–88; *ibid.* (Feb. 7, 1903), p. 273; *World's Work*, 5 (March 1903), 3156–57; New York *Times*, March 3, April 16, 1903.

[81] Roosevelt to Henry S. Pritchett, Dec. 14, 1904, in Morison, ed., *Roosevelt Letters*, IV, 1068. See also Roosevelt to Robert Underwood Johnson, Nov. 12, 1904, *ibid.*, p. 1030.

threat to his renomination in 1904. But this scramble for southern delegates damaged the broader prestige of the party. States that supplied no electoral votes in the presidential election retained skeletal Republican organizations that seemed to exist for no other purpose than obtaining federal offices in return for delegate votes at the national conventions. Although it was not essential for his reelection, Roosevelt would have liked to see the Republican party crack the solid South. In order to do this the regional standing of the GOP had to be raised. Postmaster General Payne argued that a necessary first step was to reform the allotment of convention delegates. Consequently he again proposed, as he had since 1899, changing a state's representation from that based upon the size of the congressional delegation to one based upon actual votes cast for Republican presidential candidates. "When that is changed," Payne wrote to Cortelyou, "and we are able to deal with each locality on its merits as a Republican 'vote getter' instead of a 'delegate getter,' then we may hope for a complete rehabilitation and organization of the Republican party in the South."[82]

But the problem was not easily settled. Many Negroes, in the North and in the South, objected that such a reform would unfairly deprive them of what little political influence they had left in the party. It was not, after all, the fault of southern blacks but of the whites who disfranchised them that the Republican vote in the South was so small. Moreover, such a change was safe only if it could be undertaken without endangering the president's renomination. Roosevelt decided to drop the matter. Like his predecessors, he found that the southern delegates were too immediately useful to sacrifice for the sake of a hoped-for long-range party advantage.

Roosevelt's skill and zest for politics did not prevent him from constantly worrying about his chances. After two years in office he feared that if a convention vote were then taken most of the southern delegates would have been against him. Such apprehension was unnecessary. He had already practically eliminated his chief rival, Hanna, from contention, and with the senator's death on February 15, 1904, Roosevelt's path was clear.[83]

In the pursuit of delegates from the South, Clarkson felt that the best course was to oppose lily-whitism and work within the conventional black-and-tan groups. In practice Roosevelt never hewed

[82] Henry C. Payne to George B. Cortelyou, Dec. 26, 1902, Roosevelt Papers. See also Fowler, pp. 264–66; Wight, pp. 101–5.

[83] Roosevelt to Carl Schurz, Dec. 24, 1903, in Morison, ed., *Roosevelt Letters*, III, 682; Herbert Croly, *Marcus Alonza Hanna: His Life and Work* (New York, 1919), pp. 411–55; Bishop, I, 312.

strictly to any single line. In some states the lily-whites gained in strength, but this was not so everywhere. In February 1904 Booker T. Washington claimed that the lily-white movement had been completely killed in Alabama and that that state would send a mixed black and white delegation to the national convention.[84] A similar situation existed in Georgia. There the leading Negro Republican was Register of the Treasury Judson W. Lyons, initially nominated by McKinley. Roosevelt wooed him away from Hanna in 1901 by a reappointment. At the 1904 convention Georgia sent a black-and-tan group that included Lyons and other prominent Negroes. Lyons was also retained as the national committeeman from Georgia.[85]

The controversy in Louisiana was probably the most acrimonious. On the advice of Booker T. Washington and others in 1902 Roosevelt began making changes in federal officeholders. The state's leading black politician, Walter L. Cohen, who then leaned toward Hanna, was greatly alarmed, fearing that Roosevelt intended to turn over the state's patronage entirely to the lily-whites.[86] Roosevelt denied that he wanted either an all-white party or one dominated by Negroes. "There must certainly be an occasional colored man entitled by character and standing to go to the National Convention," he wrote in February 1904 to Louisiana's new Republican chairman.[87] At the same time even Washington became alarmed over the strength of the Louisiana lily-whites. They controlled the state convention held in May 1904 and selected an all-white slate of delegates-at-large to the national convention. Cohen immediately arranged for a rival delegation, but Washington disapproved, for he felt that if such a contest were to be waged and lost, the Republican party would be hurt in the campaign.[88] Roosevelt was even

84 Washington to Walter L. Cohen, Feb. 23, 1904, Washington Papers.

85 Blum, pp. 44–46; Clarence A. Bacote, "Negro Officeholders in Georgia under President McKinley," *Journal of Negro History*, 44 (July 1959), 222–26; *Official Proceedings of the Thirteenth Republican National Convention Held in the City of Chicago, June 21, 22, 23, 1904*, p. 86; New York *Times*, June 22, 1904.

86 Cohen to George A. Myers, Sept. 14, 1902, Myers Papers. For the comments of one deposed officeholder, see A. T. Wimberly, *A Study in Black and White: An Opinion of the Condition of the Two Races, North and South Combined with an Arraignment of President Roosevelt's Administration* (New Orleans, 1904), copy in Roosevelt Memorial Association Collection, Widener Library, Harvard University. See also Blum, p. 45; and the chart showing changes in federal officeholding in Louisiana between 1901 and 1903 in Morison, ed., *Roosevelt Letters*, III, 281n.

87 Roosevelt to Francis Bennett Williams, Feb. 24, 1904, in Morison, ed., *Roosevelt Letters*, IV, 729.

88 Washington to Cohen, Feb. 23, 1904, Washington Papers; Roosevelt to Washington, May 9, 1904, in Morison, ed., *Roosevelt Letters*, IV, 793; Washington to James S. Clarkson, June 8, 1904, Washington Papers.

unhappier. In a revealing letter to Washington, he pointed out the complexities of the Louisiana situation. The state convention had included some Negroes and thus had not been a purely lily-white affair. Cohen and his crowd simply represented the old office-seekers around whom no successful Republican party could develop. "The safety for the colored man in Louisiana is to have a white man's party which shall be responsible and honest, in which the colored man shall have representation but in which he shall not be the dominant force."[89] Thus in theory Roosevelt did not uphold strict lily-whitism. His position was not substantially different from that taken for other southern states where he had also hoped to develop new, more respectable Republican parties. But at this time, obviously annoyed by Cohen, Roosevelt stated the case without adornment. His frankness alarmed even as sympathetic a person as Booker T. Washington.[90]

On June 16 the Republican national committee voted in a surprise move to seat the Cohen delegation-at-large. But the lily-white delegation, led by former governor Henry C. Warmoth, fought back and denied that it opposed all Negro participation or officeholding. Finally the credentials committee worked out an acceptable compromise. The four delegates-at-large from both factions were seated with each receiving half a vote. Despite Roosevelt's dislike of Cohen, he was kept on as register of the United States Land Office at New Orleans and until 1905 was retained as the state's member of the Republican national committee.[91]

These struggles indicate that it would be misleading to suggest that Roosevelt completely capitulated to the lily-whites in 1904. Rather, he sought delegates and in so doing accepted the situation in each of the various states that would produce them. In many cases, but not all, this policy worked to the disadvantage of black politicians, but it did not result in a great upsurge of a broader-based white Republicanism. The party in the South retained many of the same mixtures and limitations of the past, despite Roosevelt's hope for a change. What he achieved was simply the assurance of his nomination.

Even had Roosevelt desired to follow a pro-Negro policy he was too concerned with immediate political realities to attempt much. He advised Elihu Root that his keynote address to the 1904 Republi-

89 Roosevelt to Washington, June 8, 1904, in Morison, ed., *Roosevelt Letters*, IV, 825.

90 See Washington to T. Thomas Fortune, June 15, 1904, Washington Papers.

91 New York *Times*, June 21, June 22, 1904; New York *Age*, June 23, 1904; *Proc. 13th Rep. Nat. Conv.*, pp. 75–81. In 1905 Pearl Wight, a white man, became the Louisiana national committeeman.

can convention should merely note the high quality of appointments and "that the race question should be treated simply incidentally by an illusion to show that I have set the same standards for black man and for white."[92] At the convention a few efforts were made to attract attention to some of the special problems of black Americans. Henry Lincoln Johnson, a Negro delegate from Georgia, suggested a plank favoring effective congressional legislation against peonage. The National Negro Suffrage League, holding its convention in Chicago at the same time and including among its members many delegates to the Republican convention, appealed for a plank opposed to all forms of disfranchisement based on caste or race prejudice. An interracial civil rights organization, the Constitution League of the United States, also called for an attack on disfranchisement by meaningful enforcement of the Fifteenth Amendment and, if necessary, the reduction of representation according to the Fourteenth Amendment.[93]

The convention ignored these suggestions and adopted instead a weak platform that favored congressional action to "determine whether by special discrimination the elective franchise in any State had been unconstitutionally limited" and, if it had, demanded a proportional reduction of congressional and electoral college representation. In appearance a stand on behalf of disfranchised blacks, in fact this plank meant virtually nothing. As developments soon were to prove, Republican congressmen and the administration had little interest in a vigorous effort to protect the right to vote. The platform ignored all the other evils—peonage, lynching, segregation—that were of vital concern to the daily lives of southern blacks.

As much as possible Roosevelt steered clear of the race issue in the 1904 campaign. He disapproved of the suffrage plank, on which he claimed he had not been consulted, not on moral but on practical grounds. Nothing, he said, would be done. "Where a wrong cannot be remedied," he confided to Lyman Abbott, "it is not worth while to sputter about it." In his judgment he had "nothing to gain and everything to lose by any agitation of the race question. . . . If I can avoid touching upon it and retain my self-respect, I shall do so."[94] His letter of acceptance avoided the word *Negro*, although it included a passage upholding the equality of all men before the

[92] Roosevelt to Root, June 2, 1904, Elihu Root Papers, Manuscript Division, Library of Congress.

[93] New York *Times*, June 22, 1904; Andrew B. Humphrey to Roosevelt, June 2, 1904, Roosevelt Papers; Meier, "Booker T. Washington and the N.A.A.C.P.," p. 73.

[94] Roosevelt to Abbott, July 26, 1904, in Morison, ed., *Roosevelt Letters*, IV, 866–68; Merrill and Merrill, pp. 176–81.

law, whether rich or poor or "whatever their creed, their color, or their birthplace." But he added that in the American system of government, national, as opposed to state, activity was distinctly limited, and "within that sphere all that could be done has been done."[95] Roosevelt said little else about the matter during the campaign. The defense of Negro rights was simply not a useful issue.

Not surprisingly, in 1904 some Negroes were far less than enthusiastic about the Republican party. For example, Chase of the Washington *Bee* continued his long-standing criticism of the Roosevelt administration and asserted that "neither the Democratic nor the Republican party believes in human rights so far as the negro is concerned." But his suggestions as to just what the perplexed black voter should do were vague and amounted to little more than a warning not to be guided simply by sentiment. Later in the campaign Chase softened his criticism and supported Roosevelt, although he still argued that on some local issues it might be best not to follow the Republican party.[96] Another uncertain Negro editor was Fortune of the New York *Age*, who in early 1904 complained that the party was losing its grip on black voters of the North and West because the "leaders do not appear to care a rap for this vote." But Fortune also endorsed Roosevelt in the end. The president, he wrote, "occupies the extraordinary position of having the confidence and respect of ten million people who have been deserted by the Republican party in the last Congress. . . . President Roosevelt stands between these people and utter distrust of the great party which they have loyally supported for thirty-six years."[97] In short, Roosevelt was better than his party. For the most part he was praised by Negroes. He had, after all, invited Booker T. Washington to dinner, and he had stuck by his guns in the Crum and Indianola cases. The very hostility of so many white southerners was evidence of Roosevelt's essential soundness.

Among Negroes, endorsement of Roosevelt was not limited to old-hand politicians, whose jobs and party positions were at stake, or members of the conservative establishment. For example, a new journal, *The Voice of the Negro,* which was not particularly friendly to Booker T. Washington and his followers, strongly advised Negroes to cast their ballots for the Republicans rather than for the party of

95 Roosevelt to Joseph G. Cannon, Sept. 12, 1904, "Letter Accepting the Republican Nomination for President," in Roosevelt, *Works,* XVI, 384.

96 Washington *Bee*, June 25, Sept. 17, Sept. 24, 1904.

97 New York *Age*, Feb. 18, May 19, 1904. For a similar position, see Charles W. Chestnutt, "Peonage, or the New Slavery," *Voice of the Negro,* 1 (Sept. 1904), 396; and the *Colored American Magazine*, Aug. 1904, p. 534, as quoted in Stone, p. 301.

Vardaman, Tillman, and the rest.[98] Howard University professor Kelly Miller, whose later evaluation of Roosevelt was rather hostile, backed the president in 1904 for being "as friendly disposed to the Negro as any of his predecessors since Grant." Miller denied that Roosevelt had been courting the lily-whites. Indeed, he felt that Roosevelt had flown in the face of southern politics and that his attitude was not calculated to advance his political fortunes in that quarter.[99]

The 1904 election was a personal triumph for Roosevelt. Not only did he achieve his primary objective—to become president in his own right—but his 56.40 percent of the popular vote was the highest that any Republican had received. In many states Roosevelt ran ahead of his party, although Republicans also strengthened their control over both houses of Congress. But these gains were in the North and West. Compared to 1900 the GOP just about held its own in the border states, and in every one of the former Confederate states except Arkansas and Florida its vote declined both absolutely and proportionately. In some the fall-off was precipitous, evidence in Alabama, North Carolina, and Virginia of the effectiveness of the recent disfranchisement amendments. Not only were fewer Negroes able to vote, but Roosevelt's vacillating southern policy, especially in regard to the lily-whites, had failed to win over a large number of converts to a new-style Republicanism. Otherwise Roosevelt was heartened by the election, which he saw as a mandate to extend his Square Deal. The needs of no group exceeded those of the blacks, who understandably hoped that with the strengthened Republican position they, too, might be beneficiaries of some of the reforms. Perhaps only the unwary expected much, but few were prepared for some of the disappointments that followed.

98 *Voice of the Negro*, 1 (Sept. 1904), 373.

99 Miller, "Roosevelt and the Negro," *ibid.*, pp. 381–82.

CHAPTER III

Unfulfilled Expectations

DURING his first administration a few well-publicized episodes had created the impression that Roosevelt was a president who would stand fast against southern Negrophobia on behalf of equality of opportunity. This reputation was not really warranted. To be sure, Roosevelt often showed an understanding of the plight of black Americans which surpassed that of most other contemporary Republican leaders. Still, neither he nor his party had taken significant steps to soften the hardening lines of racial proscription. On the contrary, for the most part he tried to placate the white South, although he had found the results disappointing. "The southern question is not one of immediate menace," he wrote after the 1904 election to James Ford Rhodes, the historian of the Civil War and Reconstruction, "but it is one of perpetual discomfort. The southerners show a wrongheadedness and folly the same kind, though not of course in degree, that they showed in the years you write of."[1] Roosevelt claimed that he intended to go on exactly as before in regard to the Negro and the South. But the results of his second term were somewhat different. He made no more dramatic gestures on behalf of Negro rights, and, if anything, he increased his efforts to win the confidence of the white South. Before long the rather inflated reputation he enjoyed among many blacks markedly declined and was replaced by growing feelings of distrust and hostility.

Although many white southerners had strongly criticized Roosevelt during his first term, a few of them appreciated what he had tried to do. One was Edwin Mims, a professor of English at Trinity College in Durham, North Carolina. In January 1905 he published an article which praised Roosevelt for being more in touch with all interests in the country than any previous incumbent. Mims acknowledged that there was great prejudice against Roosevelt in the South but attributed it to lack of understanding of what he was attempting to accomplish, a lack resulting in part from the activities of anti-Negro extremists. Mims believed that Roosevelt was in full

[1] Roosevelt to Rhodes, Nov. 29, 1904, in Elting E. Morison, ed., *The Letters of Theodore Roosevelt* (Cambridge, Mass.: Harvard University Press, 1951–54), IV, 1050. See also Roosevelt to Henry S. Pritchett, Dec. 14, 1904, *ibid.*, 1071.

sympathy with what he called the liberal southerner—the man who condemned extremism, lynching, peonage, and the like; who supported education for Negroes while upholding segregation in school, church, and society and sympathizing with the recent disfranchising amendments.[2] This assessment was close to being an accurate description of Roosevelt's views.

Roosevelt soon outlined the direction that he planned to take in a speech on "The Negro Problem" delivered at a Lincoln Day dinner in February 1905. Intending the speech to be a major statement of his views on the Negro and the South, he prepared it carefully after consulting a number of knowledgeable people, including Booker T. Washington.[3] He began with an appeal for national unity and sectional goodwill, including a sentimental and characteristic comment about how all Americans could now be proud of the glory won by the blue and the gray. As for the Negro problem, Roosevelt pointed out that although it was most acute in the South, the attitude of northerners often fell short of what it should have been. We should "secure to each man, whatever his color, equality of opportunity, equality of treatment before the law." He then observed that the "backward race" must be trained without harming the high civilization of the "forward race." Laziness, shiftlessness, and criminality were particularly likely to bring harm to the Negro. He singled out the black man as having a special responsibility to condemn the crimes of other black men and to bring such criminals to justice. The white neighbor could do much to help the Negro. But at the same time there must be no hint of "social equality." "All reflecting men of both races," concluded Roosevelt, "are united in feeling that race purity must be maintained."[4]

Although this speech was his first extended public statement on the race question, the ideas in it were not new, and Roosevelt may

2 Mims, "President Theodore Roosevelt," *South Atlantic Quarterly*, 4 (Jan. 1905), 48–62. For a similar point of view, see Thomas Nelson Page, "President Theodore Roosevelt from the Standpoint of a Southern Democrat," *Metropolitan Magazine*, 21 (March 1905), 672–74.

3 Roosevelt to Lyman Abbott, Jan. 11, 1905, in Morison, ed., *Roosevelt Letters*, IV, 1099, and note, *ibid.*, pp. 1099–1100; New York *Times*, Jan. 16, 1905; New York *Tribune*, Jan. 16, 1905. See also Baker to his father, Jan. 29, 1905, Ray Stannard Baker Papers, Manuscript Division, Library of Congress. The only part of Roosevelt's speech that particularly worried Washington was a reference to social equality, which he unsuccessfully sought to have deleted (Washington to John S. Durham, Dec. 24, 1904, John S. Durham to Washington, Jan. 8, 1905, Booker T. Washington Papers, Manuscript Division, Library of Congress).

4 "Address at the Lincoln Dinner of the Republican Club of the City of New York, February 13, 1905," in *The Works of Theodore Roosevelt* (National Ed., New York, 1927), XVI, 342–50.

well have felt that they were consistent with his past beliefs and actions. Yet the tone of the message—the choice of words, the emphasis on problems that seemed to confirm southern racial stereotypes—created the impression that there had been a change of policy. Many white southerners who praised the speech saw in it an indication that Roosevelt was going to adopt a more favorable attitude toward their section. Some even interpreted it as an acceptance of their method of handling racial problems with the implication that the North would thereafter keep its hands off.[5]

The speech helped to improve Roosevelt's popularity in the South. This was a development that he continued to encourage. Two southern trips in 1905 showed that southerners would respond warmly to him as an individual, regardless of their opinion of his party. Shortly after his inauguration Roosevelt went hunting in Oklahoma. The excursion gave him a chance to stop for a few days in Texas, where he was greeted by large and enthusiastic crowds. He made no notable speeches, but he pleased his listeners with sentimental references to his southern ancestry.[6] In the fall of 1905 he made an extensive southern tour. His first speech, entitled the "North and South," was delivered at Richmond on October 18. Praising the glory and daring of the troops on both sides in the Civil War and the healing of the wounds thereafter, he struck just the right note to win the cheers and sympathies of his southern white listeners. It was a theme that he used throughout the tour. After Richmond Roosevelt spoke at Atlanta, Jacksonville, Birmingham, Montgomery, Little Rock, New Orleans, and other smaller places. Everywhere he was warmly welcomed. His principal address to a black audience was delivered at Tuskegee Institute on October 24. Devoted to the topic "The Education of the Negro," his speech had been carefully reviewed beforehand by Booker T. Washington. Predictably, Roosevelt praised the work of Tuskegee and pointed out that there was a demand for skilled labor in the South. The Negro, like members of all races, needed training in more than agriculture, mechanics, and household duties, but these were the fields in which he "can at present

[5] See Henry Edwin Tremain, *Sectionalism Unmasked* (New York, 1907), p. 76. For other reactions, see the New York *Times*, Feb. 14, 1905, and the newspaper clippings in the George Foster Peabody Collection, Collis P. Huntington Memorial Library, Hampton Institute. James S. Clarkson, no appeaser of the South in the past, referred to it as "in every respect great and satisfactory" (Clarkson to Washington, Feb. 21, 1905, Washington Papers; see also Washington to T. Thomas Fortune, Feb. 24, 1905, *ibid.*; Roosevelt to James Ford Rhodes, Feb. 20, 1905, in Morison, ed., *Roosevelt Letters,* IV, 1125).

[6] New York *Times*, April 6–9, 1905.

do most for himself and be most helpful to his white neighbors." Roosevelt repeated familiar themes about the virtues of self-help, sobriety, and industriousness, as well as his particular notion that Negroes had a duty to make war against all crime, especially that committed by members of their own race. The address was fully in accord with conservative, if well-intended, sentiment on the race issue. Few white southerners would have found the ideas disturbing.[7]

The only discordant note on this trip occurred at Little Rock, Arkansas. In his welcoming remarks Governor Jeff Davis mentioned the race problem in a manner that implied a defense of lynching. In reply Roosevelt added to his conventional speech in praise of national unity a condemnation of the "hideous crime" of lynching, with a pointed reminder that all persons in authority had a responsibility to wipe it out. Even then, however, he was careful to balance this comment with a reference to "the negro criminal, and above all the criminal of the hideous type so often hideously avenged," and an admonition that the Negro had a "duty to himself and to his race to hunt down that criminal."[8]

The tour increased speculation about Roosevelt's objectives regarding the South. One prominent southern writer, William Garrott Brown, observed that although the president had expressed no new policy, what he said and did not say suggested a new attitude. Brown was impressed by the extent of southern interest in Roosevelt's comments on economic matters, particularly about railroads, the Isthmian Canal, and industrial development. He felt that it was inconceivable that Roosevelt would agree to any attempt by his party to restore the ballot to the mass of Negroes or to carry out the party plank regarding the reduction in southern representation. Brown saw the tour as helping to conclude a *modus vivendi* between the South and the Republican party.[9]

As the anti-Washington *Voice of the Negro* immediately pointed out, if this sort of analysis was correct, the arrangement was concluded at the expense of black Americans. Roosevelt "was lacking in the elements of bravery that used to be characteristic of him." The *Voice* also attacked his educational doctrine for Negroes as preposterous and said that the great need was for doctors, teachers, preach-

[7] Roosevelt, *Works*, XVI, 32–35, 351–55; Roosevelt to Washington, Oct. 12, 1905, Washington to Roosevelt, Oct. 16, 1905, Washington Papers.

[8] New York *Times*, Oct. 26, 1905; Joseph Bucklin Bishop, *Theodore Roosevelt and His Times* (New York, 1920), I, 441–42.

[9] Brown, "President Roosevelt and the South," *Independent*, 59 (Nov. 9, 1905), 1086–89.

ers, and lawyers. It warned Roosevelt that the South's admiration for him was only skin deep and could not be counted upon.[10]

Such criticism was not isolated. The *Voice of the Negro* surveyed the Negro press and found that over half had commented adversely upon Roosevelt's southern trip. Even Booker T. Washington was worried that it meant a change in policy that would be detrimental to the Negro. Roosevelt denied that he "intended to inaugurate a new white party" or to undertake any other changes.[11] Indeed his opinions about blacks and the South probably had not greatly changed. Certainly he had expressed many ideas earlier that were wholly consistent with those of his 1905 speeches. But in apparent deference to the sensitivities of southern whites the emphasis had shifted, and this was enough to arouse the suspicions of many Negroes. Having exaggerated the significance of some favorable events earlier in his presidency, they regarded Roosevelt's remarks and actions in 1905 as indicative of a major shift in attitude.

These considerations were minor in comparison to the event that really shook their faith in Roosevelt's goodwill, the Brownsville affair. During the summer of 1906 three companies of the Negro Twenty-fifth Regiment were sent to Fort Brown in Brownsville, Texas. Many local citizens resented their presence, and a few minor scuffles occurred between the whites and the black troops. On August 13 one of the soldiers allegedly assaulted a white woman. Around midnight that evening about a dozen armed men raided the town. Many shots were fired; one citizen was killed and a couple of others were wounded. The mayor blamed the affair on the Negro troops, although an immediate check by Major Charles W. Penrose uncovered no evidence of their involvement. In the morning the mayor produced a number of shells, apparently from army rifles, which were found near the scene of the shooting, and this evidence convinced Major Penrose, for the time being at least, that the guilty must be some of his men. Racial tension ran high in the town. Mobs of whites posted themselves along the road and threatened to shoot any soldier attempting to leave the fort. A few days later Roosevelt responded to the request of a committee of Brownsville citizens and ordered the soldiers to another post.[12]

10 *Voice of the Negro*, 2 (Dec. 1905), 823–27.

11 *Ibid.*, p. 827; Roosevelt to Jeter C. Pritchard, Jan. 9, 1906, in Morison, ed., *Roosevelt Letters*, V, 130; Washington to Whitefield McKinlay, Jan. 24, 1906, William Loeb, Jr., to Theodore Roosevelt, n.d. (Jan. 1906?), Carter G. Woodson Collection, Manuscript Division, Library of Congress.

12 Two books have recently been published on this subject. John D. Weaver, *The Brownsville Raid* (New York, 1970), contends that the evidence pointed to the

Shortly after the shooting an investigation was made by Major Augustus P. Blocksom, an assistant inspector general. Blocksom's report blamed the raid on an unidentified number of Negro soldiers and accused the others of a "conspiracy of silence" to protect the guilty. Accepting Blocksom's conclusions, Roosevelt ordered Inspector General Ernest A. Garlington to warn the soldiers that all might be punished if the guilty were not uncovered. When this threat brought no result, Garlington recommended the discharge of all three companies without honor. Completely convinced of the soldiers' guilt, on November 5 Roosevelt signed the order that ended the military career of over 160 men. Included in the dismissed were six winners of the Medal of Honor. A number of others were near retirement. None had been convicted of any offense; indeed, none had even been formally charged or tried. For those who were innocent, the loss of their profession and financial benefits, and the impugning of their honor, was a personal disaster. For all Negroes who were proud of the service of their fellows in the armed forces of the United States the dismissal was a cruel affront.

Never were Negroes so united in their bitter denunciations of the President. "He has adopted the methods of the Georgia Mob," cried the Washington *Bee*. The dismissal was "vicious and contrary to the spirit of our Constitution," declared the New York *Age*. William Monroe Trotter's Boston *Guardian* said that Roosevelt had been guilty of an act of "meanness, injustice, and unwarranted cruelty." One of the most harmful aspects of the order "is its accord with the altogether too general accepted notion among white Americans that while white men are not held responsible for the detection of white criminals, yet colored men can rightly be so held. This notion . . . endangers the personal safety of innocent colored persons." In the

---

innocence of the black troops. Ann J. Lane, *The Brownsville Affair: National Crisis and Black Reaction* (Port Washington, N.Y., 1971), more cautiously concludes that the case against the soldiers was not proved. An older, short summary, critical of Roosevelt, is in Henry F. Pringle, *Theodore Roosevelt: A Biography* (New York, 1931), pp. 458–64. William Henry Harbaugh, *Power and Responsibility: The Life and Times of Theodore Roosevelt* (New York, 1961), pp. 303–8, also condemns Roosevelt's actions, although Harbaugh is less sympathetic than Pringle to Senator Foraker's defense of the accused soldiers. George E. Mowry, *The Era of Theodore Roosevelt, 1900–1912* (New York, 1958), pp. 212–13, is a very brief account that assumes the guilt of some of the Negroes and that has no criticism of Roosevelt's actions *per se*. James A. Tinsley, "Roosevelt, Foraker, and the Brownsville Affray," *Journal of Negro History*, 41 (Jan. 1956), 43–65, concludes that there is doubt about the soldiers' guilt, and he is critical of Roosevelt's methods. See also Emma Lou Thornbrough, "The Brownsville Episode and the Negro Vote," *Mississippi Valley Historical Review*, 44 (Dec. 1957), 469–93.

Negro press and pulpit, protests came forth with unprecedented unanimity. Moreover, there was much criticism from whites. The New York *Times* called Roosevelt's action "improper" and "in flat contravention . . . of the Constitution." It was an "executive lynching," said the New York *World.* According to the *Literary Digest,* the northern white press was almost united in denouncing the punishment of the innocent with the guilty.[13]

Roosevelt was unbending in his decision. Criticism, in fact, only heightened his obstinacy. Certain though he was of his rectitude, however, his political sense did not completely leave him, for the dismissal order was not made public until after the November 6 mid-term elections. Even Booker T. Washington was disturbed by Roosevelt's action, although he remained publicly silent. Informed of the impending dismissal, he did his utmost to stay the president's hand and failing that, to have him postpone action until after his trip to Panama.[14] But it was to no avail. On November 8 Roosevelt departed, leaving Secretary of War William H. Taft to carry out the discharges. It was an unpleasant duty. Pressure to delay action continued, and reports of much agitation on the subject, among white Republicans as well as Negroes, convinced Taft that it might be well to hold off and have a rehearing. The dismissals began on November 16, but on the next day Taft instructed Roosevelt's private secretary, William Loeb, to wire to the president about the appeals and to suggest a suspension. Roosevelt's answer was unequivocal. "Under no circumstances is that order to be suspended and it will only be revoked if a totally different state of facts can be shown. . . . I am absolutely clear as to the course I took and mere agitation no matter how extended will receive no attention whatsoever from me."[15] The fate of the soldiers was sealed.

But the controversy over the Brownsville affair had just begun. Throughout the remainder of his presidency the issue continued to plague Roosevelt. Although the bitterness eventually lessened, the damage to his reputation among blacks was never fully repaired. Most Republicans did not wish to confront the president directly,

[13] Washington *Bee,* Nov. 10, 1906; *Literary Digest,* 33 (Nov. 17, 1906), 710; *ibid.,* 33 (Dec. 8, 1906), 832–34; New York *Times,* Nov. 8, 1906. See also Kelly Miller, *Roosevelt and the Negro* (Washington, D.C., 1907), p. 16; Thornbrough, pp. 471–73; Lane, pp. 70–75.

[14] Roosevelt to Washington, Nov. 5, 1906, Washington to Whitefield McKinlay, Nov. 7, 1906, Woodson Collection.

[15] Taft to Loeb, Nov. 17, 1906, Taft Papers, Manuscript Division, Library of Congress; Mary Church Terrell, "Secretary Taft and the Negro Soldiers," *Independent,* 65 (July 23, 1908), 189–90; Roosevelt to Taft (telegram), Nov. 21, 1906, Taft Papers.

although some believed that he had acted unjustly and unwisely. Senator Joseph B. Foraker of Ohio, however, made the cause of the Brownsville soldiers his own. After the dismissals he carefully read the reports on which Roosevelt had acted and came to the conclusion that a grave wrong had been committed. In taking up the defense of the soldiers, Foraker began a long and unpleasant struggle with the president.

When the second session of the 59th Congress met on December 3, 1906, Senator Boies Penrose of Pennsylvania presented a resolution asking the president to give to the Senate all relevant information on the case. Foraker then proposed a similar resolution directing the secretary of War to answer specific questions about the soldiers and their rights. Both were passed. In the meantime Foraker received additional support from John E. Milholland's Constitution League of New York, which on December 10 issued a preliminary report of its own findings and appealed for an investigation by Congress. The league report, which Foraker presented to the Senate, described the hostility of the local citizens and the prejudice of General Garlington and concluded that the evidence did not support the assumption of guilt.[16] Roosevelt sent the documents on the case to the Senate on December 19, along with a letter upholding executive authority in the matter. At the end of the letter Roosevelt took cognizance of the implications that his actions implied prejudice against the Negroes, and he restated his position that each man must be dealt with "on his merits as a man, and not . . . merely as a member of a given race." In defense of his record he added that "so far as was in my power, I have sought to secure for the colored people all their rights under the law."[17] Unfortunately Roosevelt did not grasp the point that the Brownsville soldiers had not been treated on their merits as individuals, and that without benefit of trial, all had been discharged as a group.

Foraker responded to the president's message by requesting that the Committee on Military Affairs, of which he was a member, undertake an investigation of the case. A spirited debate followed. Roosevelt intervened again on January 14, 1907, when he submitted additional documents, including a report of an investigation by Ma-

16 *Congressional Record*, 59th Cong., 2d sess., vol. 41, pt. 1, pp. 2, 55, 97–106; U.S., Congress, Senate, *Preliminary Report of the Commission of the Constitution League of the United States on the Affray at Brownsville, Tex.*, 59th Cong., 2d sess., Senate Doc. 107 (Dec. 10, 1906), pp. 1–18.

17 U.S., Congress, Senate, *Message from the President of the United States Transmitting a Report from the Secretary of War . . .*, 59th Cong., 2d sess., Senate Doc. 155 (Dec. 19, 1906), p. 9.

jor Blocksom and Assistant Attorney General Purdy. He explained that since the Senate had questioned the sufficiency of his evidence, he had sent these men out to make another report. Although Roosevelt insisted that the dismissals had been justified, this additional inquiry suggested some inner doubt. Also, his January 14 message revoked his original order barring the soldiers from civil employment by the United States and added that "if any one of the men discharged hereafter shows to my satisfaction that he is clear of guilt, or of shielding the guilty, I will take what action is warranted." The Senate finally approved, in amended form, Foraker's request for an investigation, wording the resolution that it did not question the "legality or justice of any act of the President."[18]

The investigation dragged on intermittently for over a year. On March 11, 1908, the Senate Committee on Military Affairs reported its findings. A majority, composed of four Republicans and four Democrats, concluded that the shooting was done by members of the Twenty-fifth Infantry, but that the individual soldiers could not be identified. Appended to the report was a bill that provided for the reenlistment of any man who could prove his innocence to the satisfaction of the president within a year after the passage of the act. Roosevelt had requested this bill because the time limit for similar proceedings authorized by the secretary of War in December 1906 had expired. Foraker and three other Republicans filed a minority report stating that the evidence had failed to identify the guilty or to prove a conspiracy of silence. Senators Foraker and Morgan G. Bulkeley of Connecticut added a separate statement to the effect that the weight of the testimony clearly suggested the innocence of the men. The minority also prepared a bill to allow the reenlistment of a member of the regiment upon simply taking an oath that he was not involved in and knew nothing about the shooting.[19]

On April 14, 1908, Foraker delivered a long speech in the Senate in support of his reenlistment bill. Before galleries packed with applauding Negroes, he reviewed the whole case and dramatically argued that the evidence suggested the innocence of the men. It was, said the New York *Times*, "a cogent statement of the facts in a matter of national importance, in which the powers of the Executive

[18] *Cong. Rec.*, 59th Cong., 2d sess., vol. 41, pt. 2, pp. 1066, 1434, 1502–12.

[19] *Ibid.*, 60th Cong., 1st sess., vol. 42, pt. 4, pp. 3122–48; U.S., Congress, Senate, *The Brownsville Affray: Report of the Committee on Military Affairs*, 60th Cong., 1st sess., Senate Rept. 355 (March 11, 1908); Joseph B. Foraker, *Notes of a Busy Life* (Cincinnati, 1916), II, 260–61. See also Roosevelt to Francis Emroy Warren, March 9, 1908, and Roosevelt to Ernest Hamlin Abbott, March 12, 1908, in Morison, ed., *Roosevelt Letters*, VI, 966–67, 968.

have been strained desperately and outrageously to wrong a number of brave and loyal soldiers of the United States Army. To this wrong, as the proof of it has unfolded, the Executive has shown a mind singularly impermeable to all sense of right."[20] But Foraker could do little to help the discharged soldiers. His reenlistment bill got nowhere.

During the summer of 1908 Roosevelt authorized Taft to hire Herbert J. Browne, a journalist, and William G. Baldwin, a Negro detective, to make a secret investigation. They attempted to uncover evidence of guilt from the former soldiers. Instead they only succeeded in embarrassing the administration when it was shown that they had lied in claiming to have uncovered the names of some of the guilty. In December, Foraker introduced a resolution calling for Taft to submit the details on this investigation and proposed another reenlistment measure. The latter failed, but Taft was required to send in the information concerning the private detectives. These revelations gave Foraker another opportunity to blast Roosevelt and Taft, but little else.[21] In February 1909, a revised reenlistment bill, which Roosevelt found acceptable, was finally enacted. This authorized a court of high officers to take testimony and pass on the eligibility for reenlistment of any of the soldiers. Such a court ultimately heard the statements of a number of them, but its report in April 1910 authorized the reenlistment of only fourteen. Of these, eleven finally reenlisted.[22]

Roosevelt refused to concede that he had erred in his handling of the Brownsville case. But that some doubt emerged is suggested by his reinvestigations and by his acceptance of the reenlistment bill. Race, he reiterated, had nothing to do with it, and he insisted that he would have acted the same had white troops been involved. It was a matter of maintaining the "discipline and honor of the American Army," and in such a situation no extraneous considerations, political or otherwise, would be permitted to stand in the way.[23] Possibly Roosevelt would have taken the same stand had the soldiers been white. On the other hand, as one student of the affair has suggested, he may have been compensating unconsciously for the

20 *Cong. Rec.*, 60th Cong., 1st sess., vol. 42, pt. 5, pp. 4709–23; Foraker, II, 261–98; New York *Times*, April 15 and April 18, 1908.

21 Tinsley, pp. 59–60; Henry F. Pringle, *The Life and Times of William Howard Taft* (New York, 1939), p. 328; Weaver, pp. 192–99; *Cong. Rec.*, 60th Cong., 2d sess., vol. 43, pt. 1, pp. 183–95, 304–11, 792–809. Foraker delivered his speech on Jan. 12, 1909.

22 *Ibid.*, pt. 3, pp. 2947–48, 3386–3400; Tinsley, pp. 59–61; Lane, p. 165.

23 Roosevelt to Curtis Guild, Jr., Nov. 7, 1906, in Morison, ed., *Roosevelt Letters*, V, 489–90.

earlier hostile criticisms about his favoritism toward Negroes.[24]

As the case dragged on Roosevelt became concerned about political damage to him and his party. Thus he decided to mend some political fences in the black community, beginning in Foraker's home state. In February 1907 he let it be known that he planned to appoint a Negro, Ralph W. Tyler of Columbus, to the post of surveyor of customs for the port of Cincinnati. Booker T. Washington had recommended Tyler, and at an earlier date Foraker had endorsed him for a consular post. But Roosevelt's move, taken without Foraker's recommendation, was obviously designed to embarrass the senator. It also was discomforting to Roosevelt's son-in-law, Representative Nicholas Longworth from Cincinnati, who faced a difficult reelection battle. So Tyler's appointment was put off, and instead about a year later he was made auditor of the Navy. Some blacks regarded Roosevelt's action as a crude and inadequate effort to recoup some of his lost prestige among them. In the opinion of Chase of the Washington *Bee*, it was all a waste of time. After Brownsville, he said, Negroes could no longer support the president.[25]

Not all blacks felt so strongly. Booker T. Washington was very unhappy over Roosevelt's actions, but he worked hard to allay Negro hostility to the president. Because of his own close ties with the administration, attacks upon it were also damaging to him. In January 1907 Washington blamed Milholland's Constitution League, with which he was already on bad terms, as largely responsible for keeping agitation alive, a fact he pointedly made known to Postmaster General Cortelyou, from whose department Milholland obtained much of his income through the sale of pneumatic tube equipment. Later in the year Washington reported that most Negroes still felt kindly toward the administration and that few had been lost to the party because of Brownsville.[26] By May 1908 he claimed that "the bulk of our people are coming around to the point where they understand the President and Secretary Taft and are ceasing to be misled by a few paid agitators."[27] Washington painted too rosy a picture, for reports of serious Negro disaffection were also common, and as Roosevelt himself acknowledged, many congressmen

[24] Tinsley, p. 63.

[25] *Literary Digest*, 34 (Feb. 16, 1907), 241–42; Washington *Bee*, April 20, 1907; Thornbrough, p. 479; Everett Walters, *Joseph Benson Foraker, an Uncompromising Republican* (Columbus, Ohio, 1948), pp. 240–41.

[26] Washington to George B. Cortelyou, Jan. 28, 1907, Washington to Roosevelt, Sept. 19, 1907, and Dec. 16, 1907, Washington Papers; August Meier, "Booker T. Washington and the Rise of the N.A.A.C.P.," *Crisis*, 61 (Feb. 1954), 74–75.

[27] Washington to William Loeb, May 20, 1908, Taft Papers.

feared the alienation of black voters.[28] But the long-range impact had yet to be shown.

Roosevelt's handling of the Brownsville case did not mean that he had radically altered his opinion about Negroes. The timing of the event was accidental, and he might well have acted in the same way had it occurred during his first administration. Nevertheless, the position he took tended to support the more favorable image he had been developing in the white South. He also found support for the claim of southern whites that even decent Negroes shielded wrongdoers in the fact that so many blacks stood by the soldiers.[29] But he still insisted that he was sympathetic to the Negro people. "I not only hope, but believe, that I have stood as valiantly for the rights of the negro as any President since Lincoln," wrote Roosevelt to Lyman Abbott, "and I should be a traitor to the negro as well as to the white man and to the country if I now sanctioned a crime in order to placate the negro vote."[30]

The Brownsville affair was the most important, but not the only reason for Roosevelt's declining reputation among black Americans. His response to the problem of lynching was particularly upsetting to them. Although the lynching rate had declined since the mid-1890's, the total number of deaths each year remained high. In 1901, 135 people were killed, of whom 108 were Negroes. During the years of the Roosevelt presidency, from 1901 through 1908, the annual death toll averaged slightly over 89. Nearly 89 percent of the victims were Negroes.[31] Republican politicians, like most people in the country, showed little concern. The Republican platform made no comment on lynching in 1900 and in 1904. After Congressman White of North Carolina departed from the House in 1901 Congress showed virtually no interest in the matter. Only once during the Roosevelt years was an antilynching measure introduced, by Congressman William H. Moody of Massachusetts in December 1901. It was abandoned in committee.[32] A few years later another Massachusetts congressman, Frederick H. Gillett, condemned a speech by Congressman Thomas Spight of Mississippi in which he had avowed that the men

28 New York *Times*, March 12, 1908, editorial; Roosevelt to Lyman Abbott, May 10, 1908, in Morison, ed., *Roosevelt Letters*, VI, 1026; Miller, pp. 19–20.

29 Roosevelt to Ray S. Baker, March 30, 1907, in Morison, ed., *Roosevelt Letters*, V, 634–35.

30 Roosevelt to Abbott, May 10, 1908, *ibid.*, VI, 1026.

31 National Association for the Advancement of Colored People, *Thirty Years of Lynching in the United States, 1889–1918* (New York, 1919), p. 29. Arthur Raper, *The Tragedy of Lynching* (Chapel Hill, N.C., 1933), pp. 480–81, has similar but slightly higher figures.

32 *Cong. Rec.*, 57th Cong., 1st sess., vol. 35, pt. 1, p. 51.

of the South would do anything to protect the honor of their women even "if it requires the extermination of the negro."[33] But congressional references to the problem of lynching and mob violence were infrequent.

In so far as people thought about it, the notion was widely held that lynching was likely to be a response to rape or to the delays and uncertainties in the administration of justice. In 1905 the first detailed book on lynching was published by James E. Cutler, an instructure in economics as Wellesley College. His figures showed that between 1882 and 1903 rape was the alleged cause of the lynching of Negroes in only about a third of the cases.[34] Later studies demonstrated that rape was charged, let alone proved, even less frequently. Nonetheless, the belief persisted that Negroes were prone to rape and that lynching was primarily a response to this crime.

Before 1906 Roosevelt had made an occasional public reference to lynching, but he had never treated it as a matter of major concern.[35] After the race riot at Atlanta in September 1906, however, he decided to devote a portion of his next message to Congress to the problem of mob violence. Roosevelt called upon Booker T. Washington, Clark Howell, and others for advice. Howell suggested that a commission be created to study the race issue. He believed that the situation was "more menacing now than it has been since the days of reconstruction" and that something had to be done. Howell and the other white advisers approved of Roosevelt's proposed message.[36] But Washington was less happy. After a session with the president, he reported to Whitefield McKinlay that Roosevelt "did not take all the medicine which we prescribed for him, but he did take a portion of it. He agreed to modify most of the objectionable expressions except those in the first paragraph; when I tackled him on that, he gritted his teeth and absolutely refused to budge a single inch."[37] Roosevelt's obstinacy concerned the in-

[33] *Ibid.*, 58th Cong., 2d sess., vol. 38, pt. 4, pp. 3342, 3826–29. Spight delivered his speech on March 16, 1904.

[34] Cutler, *Lynch Law: An Investigation into the History of Lynching in the United States* (New York, 1905), p. 173.

[35] Note his Memorial Day address, May 30, 1902, his Lincoln Dinner Speech, Feb. 13, 1905, and his comments at Little Rock on Oct. 25, 1905.

[36] Howell to Roosevelt, Oct. 24, Oct. 31, 1906, Theodore Roosevelt Papers, Manuscript Division, Library of Congress; Roosevelt to Howell, Oct. 26, 1906, in Morison, ed., *Roosevelt Letters*, V, 472; William H. Fleming to Roosevelt, Nov. 2, 1906, Silas McBee to Roosevelt, Nov. 3, 1906, Roosevelt Papers. See also Horace Samuel Merrill and Marion Galbraith Merrill, *The Republican Command, 1897–1913* (Lexington, Ky., 1971), pp. 240–42.

[37] Washington to McKinlay, Nov. 9, 1906, Woodson Collection. Washington,

clusion of comments about the Negro's responsibility for crime. His position was influenced by the Brownsville case, especially the outcry among Negroes against the dismissal of the soldiers. "I have been amazed and indignant at the attitude of the negroes and of shortsighted white sentimentalists as to my action," he wrote to Silas McBee, one of his consultants on his 1906 message. He saw the protests as further support for his notion that "negroes too often band together to shelter their own criminals."[38]

Roosevelt's December 3, 1906, annual message to Congress aggravated his already strained relations with the black community. To be sure, he asserted that "each man, whatever his color, his creed, or his social position" should be treated "with even-handed justice on his real worth as a man," and he upheld the need for improved Negro education. But most of what he said was far from complimentary. Protesting against lynching as a bestial crime which represents a "loosening of the bands of civilization," he went on to a lengthy criticism of the role that blacks played in such lawlessness. Despite the evidence to the contrary, he referred to rape as the greatest cause of the lynching of Negroes. Their worst enemy, he said, was "the negro criminal, and above all the negro criminal who commits the dreadful crime of rape." Even in the paragraphs on Negro education, Roosevelt observed that rapists were usually those who had little or no education. In condemning the inflammatory speeches of demagogues, he pointed out that their attention to the "hideous deed" tended to incite in those with "brutal and depraved natures thoughts of committing it." Equally disurbing was Roosevelt's notion that Negroes "must learn not to harbor their criminals, but to assist the officers in bringing them to justice. This is the larger crime and it provokes such atrocious offenses as the one at Atlanta." Negroes were thus charged with a special responsibility for tracking down those of their own race who were accused of crime.[39] If Roosevelt intended his message to be

---

however, was not enthusiastic about federal intervention to protect Negroes from violence, and he defended Roosevelt for not sending troops to Atlanta at the time of the riot. Such action, he said, would not only have been politically difficult but practically unwise. Although local authorities in Atlanta had been slow in taking action, Washington felt that Negroes were more secure, once local officials had assumed responsibility and controlled the mob, than they would have been had federal authorities taken over (Washington to C. J. Perry, Oct. 5, 1906, Roosevelt Papers).

38 Roosevelt to McBee, Nov. 22, 1906, in Morison, ed., *Roosevelt Letters*, V, 509.

39 Roosevelt, *Works*, XV, 351–55. Although the Brownsville episode was probably on Roosevelt's mind when he emphasized the Negro's special responsibility to bring Negro criminals to justice, he had expressed this idea before on a number of occasions. For example, see Roosevelt to John W. Fox, Oct. 19, 1899, in Morison,

an attack upon lynching, it was a curious one that seemed to place far more blame upon the victims—and other members of their race—than upon the lynchers.

It was not surprising that the drafts of the message had disturbed Booker T. Washington and that other blacks strongly criticized the address. The New York *Age* condemned his comments as an "adoption of the Southern white man's viewpoint."[40] Kelly Miller was bitter. "However holy and righteous may have been the president's intentions, this message is calculated to do the Negro more harm than any other state paper issued from the White House."[41] Coming on top of the Brownsville dismissals and the apparent shifts in the administration's southern policy, Roosevelt's message, instead of reassuring Negroes, had increased their apprehensions.

In a number of other areas black Americans found the record of Roosevelt's second term to be a mixture of the good, the bad, and the doubtful. On the whole they were pleased by the fact that he continued to carry out his announced intention of appointing Negroes to significant positions in the North, even though he was reluctant to risk another battle on behalf of a nominee in the South. For example, in March 1905 Roosevelt nominated Charles W. Anderson, an influential New York politician, to be collector of internal revenue at New York, possibly the most important federal office then awarded to a Negro. Anderson was an admirer and skillful defender of Booker T. Washington, and for several years Roosevelt had sought a satisfactory federal post for him. The collectorship was ideal. Negroes, at least those in the Washington camp, were delighted. It was a radical departure from established precedent, proclaimed T. Thomas Fortune. "No other President has given an appointment of that high character in the domestic service in the North to an Afro-American."[42]

In the fall of 1907 Roosevelt made another well-received appointment, by naming James A. Cobb, an able Washington lawyer, to be a special assistant United States attorney for the District of Columbia.[43] A further example was his selection in early 1908, on Booker T.

ed., *Roosevelt Letters*, II, 1085; his Lincoln Dinner Speech, Feb. 13, 1905; and his comments at Little Rock, Arkansas, Oct. 25, 1905.

40 Quoted in *Literary Digest*, 33 (Dec. 15, 1906), 891.

41 Miller, p. 17.

42 New York *Age*, March 9, 1905; New York *Times*, March 5, March 8, 1905; James S. Clarkson to William Loeb, Jr., Oct. 20, 1902, Roosevelt Papers. On Anderson, see Gilbert Osofsky, *Harlem, the Making of a Ghetto: Negro New York, 1890–1930* (New York, 1966), pp. 161–67.

43 Washington *Bee*, Nov. 23, 1907. See also William Loeb, Jr., to Charles J. Bonaparte, March 26, 1907, Charles J. Bonaparte Papers, Manuscript Division, Library of Congress.

Washington's recommendation, of S. Laing Williams of Chicago as a special attorney for naturalization. In thanking Roosevelt, Washington observed with some satisfaction that "the Williams appointment takes care of every colored man whom we discussed for office when you first went into the Presidency. Besides you have appointed more men than was decided upon."[44]

Besides these appointments in the North, Roosevelt continued the traditional practice of selecting blacks for consular and ministerial posts in such countries as Haiti, Liberia, and Sierra Leone. As he explained to Secretary of State Elihu Root, "We find the utmost difficulty in getting places where colored men can be put without causing such friction as to offset any possible benefit." These posts, where "there can be no such objection," served a useful purpose.[45] That purpose, presumably, was to placate the masses of Negroes by rewarding a favored few.

In addition to the few who received presidential appointments were the many Negroes who held a variety of other federal government jobs, mostly ones of a routine or unskilled nature. Here the government's, if not the president's, attitude began to arouse suspicions, as Negroes noted a decrease in the number of promotions and new appointments. Many attributed this fact to the discriminatory application of the Civil Service Commission rule that allowed a department chief to select any one of the three top candidates who were qualified by examination for a given position.[46]

Even more disturbing were the questions raised about the attitude of federal government officials toward racial segregation. During the Roosevelt years Republicans made no serious effort to prevent the

44 Washington to Roosevelt, March 30, 1908, Washington Papers. On Williams, see J. W. Gibson and W. H. Crogman, *Progress of a Race, or the Remarkable Advancement of the American Negro* (Atlanta, 1902), p. 573, and Allan H. Spear, *Black Chicago: The Making of a Negro Ghetto, 1890–1920* (Chicago, 1967), pp. 66–69. Like Anderson in New York, Williams was a friend of Washington, and he kept a check on the activities of Washington opponents such as Du Bois and others associated with the Niagara Movement.

45 Roosevelt to Root, Nov. 30, 1905, in Morison, ed., *Roosevelt Letters*, V, 101–2. Under Roosevelt there were eleven such consular and diplomatic appointments, one less than during McKinley's presidency.

46 According to the *Republican Campaign Text-Book: 1908*, p. 302, there were 13,978 Negroes then in federal government service. As of 1899, the Republicans claimed 15,868 (*Republican Campaign Text-Book: 1900*, p. 149). Both sets of figures may well have been exaggerated, although it seems clear that the number had declined. Constance McLaughlin Green, *The Secret City: A History of Race Relations in the Nation's Capital* (Princeton, N.J., 1966), pp. 158–59, says that the number of Negro federal employees in the District of Columbia dropped from 1,537 in 1892 to 1,450 in 1908.

extensive southern movement to enact Jim Crow into law. Indeed, after 1900 a number of instances of racial segregation in the federal government departments at Washington began to appear. Chase's Washington *Bee*, which had never shown much sympathy for Roosevelt, was chiefly responsible for bringing these conditions to light. In 1904 it found evidence of racial discrimination, particularly the practice of putting Negro clerks together in separate rooms or divisions, in nearly every one of the executive departments, especially Treasury, War, and Interior. The *Bee* condemned the conditions in the Jim Crow corner of the Bureau of Engraving and Printing as being particularly bad. By 1905 it also reported that a number of government restaurants refused service to Negroes. The *Bee* charitably placed the blame for these conditions on the subordinate officials, and it appealed to the department heads to take corrective action. There is no evidence that Roosevelt or high administration officials made any effort to put a stop to such segregation. The problem was limited; but its appearance was an ominous sign.[47]

At the same time the federal government did show some concern about the problems Negroes faced as a result of segregation on the interstate railroads. During the Roosevelt years the Interstate Commission received a number of complaints about inequitable treatment. A case in 1907 arose as a result of the ejection of a black woman from a railroad coach set aside for whites. In this instance the Nashville, Chattanooga and St. Louis Railway Company had provided no smoking compartment for Negroes, no towels and washbowls, and no separate toilets for men and women, although the white sections had all of these amenities. The commission did not challenge the constitutionality of racial segregation, but it upheld the principle that there must be no discrimination in the nature of the accommodations furnished to each race and ordered railroads to provide such equal facilities.[48] These were not easily obtained. Booker T. Washington wrote to the president and to the commission in March 1908 asking that something be done. He pointed out that Negroes on the whole opposed the principle of segregation and that it would be un-

[47] Washington *Bee*, March 19, Sept. 3, Oct. 8, 1904, July 22, Aug. 26, 1905, Aug. 4, Aug. 18, 1906; Constance McLaughlin Green, *Washington: Capital City, 1879–1950* (Princeton, N.J., 1963), pp. 216–17; Green, *Secret City*, pp. 165–66; August Meier and Elliott Rudwick, "The Rise of Segregation in the Federal Bureaucracy, 1900–1930," *Phylon*, 28 (Summer 1967), 178–84.

[48] *Georgia Edwards* v. *Nashville, Chattanooga and St. Louis Railway Company, Operating the Western and Atlantic Railroad*, 12 I.C.R. 247 (1907). See also United States, Interstate Commerce Commission, *Twenty-First Annual Report of the Interstate Commerce Commission* (Washington, D.C., 1907), pp. 65–67.

fortunate if Roosevelt said anything that seemed to endorse it. At the least, he insisted, the separate facilities should be equal, whereas they were often too small, filthy, and generally inadequate.[49] As a result of this prodding, Roosevelt wrote a letter to the attorney general stating that where there was separation, the facilities must be equal. He suggested that a court injunction be sought if necessary to force the Nashville, Chattanooga, and St. Louis Railway to comply with the commission's order. In this instance relief was obtained. But other complaints continued to come about the conditions on southern railroads, and the commission did not always act upon them. Moreover, neither the administration nor the commission challenged the principle of segregation itself, despite the increasingly cumbersome burdens it was placing on interstate commerce.[50]

The administration's record was considerably better in regard to another and more serious threat to black Americans, the problem of peonage.[51] Compulsory service for debt was not a new problem. During Reconstruction an act of March 2, 1867, had declared null and void any state statute which attempted to establish enforced service in liquidation of a debt and made it a crime to "hold, arrest, or return" a person to peonage. But in various forms the evil continued, particularly in the South, and Negroes were the chief victims. Some states fostered the practice by passing laws that made the failure to perform services contracted for and for which money had been advanced *prima facie* evidence of an intent to defraud and punishable as theft. Alabama passed three such statutes in the first two decades of the twentieth century, all of which were invalidated by the courts.

In the spring of 1903 federal grand juries in Georgia and Alabama reported uncovering shocking conditions of peonage and brought in a number of indictments. The United States district judge in Alabama was Thomas G. Jones, a Roosevelt appointee. In response to questions by the grand jury, he held that the Alabama statute of 1901, which made the breaking of a labor contract a penal offense,

49 Washington to Roosevelt, March 23, 1908, Washington Papers.

50 Roosevelt to the Department of Justice, April 2, 1908, Roosevelt to Washington, April 2, 1908, in Morison, ed., *Roosevelt Letters*, VI, 987–88; Washington to Roosevelt, March 28, 1908, Washington Papers; *Winfield F. Cozart* v. *Southern Railway Company*, 16 I.C.R. 226 (1909) and *Wesley J. Gaines et al.* v. *Seaboard Airline Railway et al.*, 16 I.C.R. 471 (1909).

51 Peonage was defined by the United States Supreme Court "as a status or condition of compulsory service, based upon the indebtedness of the peon to the master. The basal fact is indebtedness" (*Clyatt* v. *United States*, 197 U.S. 207 [1905]).

was unconstitutional.[52] In December 1904 the United States Supreme Court heard a case from Florida involving the federal antipeonage statutes. The defendants had been convicted of holding two men in peonage. Although their conviction was reversed on a technicality, the validity of the federal law was affirmed.[53]

These actions were merely small skirmishes in the struggle against peonage. The practice was far more widespread and deeply seated than was apparent from the few cases that were publicized in the courts. Roosevelt made an effort to arouse his complacent associates. "I wish I could agree with you that no one in the South wishes to reestablish slavery," he wrote to James Ford Rhodes. "In my judgment this is so far from the fact that in reality there are at this very moment not only active but partially successful movements for the reintroduction of slavery under the form of peonage in at least three Southern States."[54] He explained that these efforts had been broken up temporarily, but he realized that it was not possible to leave a matter of that sort in the hands of the states.

Even Roosevelt was too sanguine about the extent to which federal investigation and prosecutions had cut down peonage. Many unsuspecting workers were entrapped into long periods of servitude by the contract labor laws. In some areas planters, with the collusion of local authorities, rounded up field hands as needed by having them arrested on various petty or trumped-up charges. The planters then paid the fines, in return for which the victims were obliged to labor on the plantations. In other instances the state leased—in effect sold to the highest bidder—their convicts to work in mines, lumber mills, and turpentine farms. Most of the victims were blacks, although some whites were also snared. The revelation of these practices by Judge Jones and others may have helped, but the traffic in human labor could not be stopped as long as state officials themselves were partners to the evil.[55]

At the end of 1907 over eighty complaints of peonage were pending

[52] 123 Federal Reporter 673 (June 16, 1903); New York *Times*, May 30, July 12, and July 27, 1903.

[53] *Clyatt* v. *United States*, 197 U.S. 207 (March 13, 1905).

[54] Roosevelt to Rhodes, Nov. 29, 1904, in Morison, ed., *Roosevelt Letters*, IV, 1050–51. See also Roosevelt to Henry S. Pritchett, Dec. 14, 1904, *ibid.*, p. 1067.

[55] For some contemporary exposures of peonage, see Mary Church Terrell, "Peonage in the United States: The Convict Lease System and the Chain Gang," *Nineteenth Century*, 62 (Aug. 1907), 306–22; Hamilton Holt, *The Life Stories of Undistinguished Americans as Told by Themselves* (New York, 1906), pp. 183–99, reprinted in Herbert Aptheker, ed., *A Documentary History of the Negro People in the United States* (New York, 1951), pp. 832–38; Ray Stannard Baker, *Following the Colour Line* (New York, 1908), pp. 96–97.

at the Department of Justice. Many of the complainants were immigrants; a few were children. The helpless condition of the peons made it impossible for many others to file charges. Moreover, as Attorney General Bonaparte acknowledged, convictions were very difficult to obtain because "of local sympathy with the defendants in such cases and the poverty and ignorance of the sufferers, who are also the principal witnesses." Bonaparte said it was his policy to prosecute even if likelihood of conviction was not strong, for the revelations brought in a trial helped to stimulate public condemnation and to warn possible victims.[56] The Department of Justice placed Assistant Attorney General Charles W. Russell in charge of peonage investigations, and at the end of 1906 and in early 1907 he spent four months in the South. His recommendations called for an incessant fight against peonage, for the federal supervision of interstate labor-supplying businesses, and for the broadening and strengthening of the federal statutes relating to involuntary servitude. In addition he called for the abolition or amendment of state laws on vagrancy, contract labor, absconding debtors, and so on, which were used to uphold peonage.[57] Subsequently the government argued successfully against a 1907 Alabama law, although the Supreme Court did not make its final ruling against its validity until 1911.[58] The tenacity with which several southern states sought to preserve this form of involuntary servitude made the fight difficult. But the Roosevelt administration at least recognized the evil and took some steps against it.

Even more intractable than peonage was the problem of disfranchisement. The movement to deprive Negroes of their votes continued unabated during the Roosevelt years until most southern states had successfully accomplished their objectives. Northern Republicans made little protest. After the United States, under GOP leadership, set up colonial governments in the Philippines, Hawaii and Puerto Rico with educational tests that prevented most of the native population from voting, it became difficult for many Republicans to oppose similar exclusions of the black population in the South. In addition, an increasing number of northerners openly accepted southern notions about the Negro's inherent racial inferi-

[56] *Annual Report of the Attorney-General of the United States* (Washington, D.C., 1907), I, 11.

[57] *Ibid.*, pp. 207–15.

[58] *Bailey* v. *Alabama*, 219 U.S. 219 (1911). Both Roosevelt and Booker T. Washington took a special interest in this case. See Pete Daniel, "Up from Slavery and Down to Peonage: The Alonzo Bailey Case," *Journal of American History*, 57 (Dec. 1970), 558–61, and below, pp. 98–99.

ority as a valid reason for depriving him of the vote. Many Republicans now conceded that it had been unwise to grant the vote to the freedmen during Reconstruction and that the Fourteenth and Fifteenth Amendments had failed.

Numerous examples of this changed northern position could be cited. In a speech to the Union League Club of New York on February 6, 1903, Secretary of War Elihu Root frankly admitted, and tacitly accepted, the South's exclusion of the Negro from politics. Despite the setting, Root's comments apparently met with no objections. Democrats had long held that it was an error to grant the Negro the ballot, commented *Harper's Weekly*, "but now for the first time we learn that the conviction is held also by many candid and thoughtful Republicans."[59] The Boston *Herald* joined in with an attack upon the suffrage policies of Reconstruction, while the New York *Sun* called the Fifteenth Amendment not only the "most deplorable mistake in our history" but one that the nation would have to rectify by its repeal.[60] In 1906 Charles Francis Adams decided, after a brief visit to Africa, that the Negro simply was inferior. Therefore, he said, Reconstruction was not only wrong but was "work done in utter ignorance of ethnological law and total disregard of unalterable fact."[61] During these same years the studies of Reconstruction published by John W. Burgess, James Ford Rhodes, and William A. Dunning took similar anti-Negro positions and added greatly to the respectability in the North of the trend to denounce the work of the Radicals.[62]

Others accepted at face value the South's claims of progress in the handling of the race issue. Clergyman and publisher Lyman Abbott of the *Outlook* magazine held that political injustice in the

59 Root, *Miscellaneous Addresses* (Cambridge, Mass., 1917), pp. 123–27; New York *Times*, Feb. 7, 1903; "Elihu Root on the Negro Problem," *Harper's Weekly*, 47 (Feb. 21, 1903), pp. 306–7. See also Merrill and Merrill, pp. 110–12.

60 On the Boston *Herald* story, see Richard P. Hallowell, *Why The Negro Was Enfranchised: Negro Suffrage Justified* (Boston, 1903), p. 4, and Moorfield Storey, *Negro Suffrage Is Not a Failure* (Boston, 1903), p. 6; New York *Sun*, April 30, 1903.

61 Adams, "Reflex Light from Africa," *Century*, 72 (May 1906), 107.

62 See Burgess, *Reconstruction and the Constitution, 1866–1876* (New York, 1902); Rhodes, *History of the United States from the Compromise of 1850 to the Final Restoration of Home Rule at the South* (New York, 1906), V, VI; Dunning, *Reconstruction, Political and Economic, 1865–1877* (New York, 1907). See also Thomas F. Gossett, *Race: The History of an Idea in America* (Dallas, 1964), pp. 284–85; George M. Fredrickson, *The Black Image in the White Mind: The Debate on Afro-American Character and Destiny, 1817–1914* (New York, 1971), pp. 297–304; I. A. Newby, *Jim Crow's Defense: Anti-Negro Thought in America, 1900–1930* (Baton Rouge, La., 1965), pp. 64–68.

South was lessening and that if that section were let alone there would be little difficulty in solving the race question. Accepting the property and literacy tests as desirable, Abbott denied that they were simply enacted to disfranchise Negroes.[63] Another publisher, Albert Shaw, held that "the legal disfranchisement of negro illiterates paved the way for a more stable political condition in the South. . . . When, after another decade or two, the political life of the white voters of the South has reasserted itself in a wholesome way, the negroes who possess fitness will undoubtedly be admitted to . . . their political rights."[64] Secretary of War Taft also had kind things to say about the disfranchising laws. In a speech at Greensboro, North Carolina, on July 9, 1906, he asserted that they would end the specter of Negro domination, reduce the demoralizing effects that resulted from the open flouting of the law as a means of depriving the Negro of his vote, provide a legal means to achieve the same purpose, and in the long run establish a basis for the extension of the suffrage impartially to those who meet the legal requirements.[65]

Some northerners still upheld the older Republican position. Moorfield Storey, a distinguished lawyer and former secretary to Charles Sumner, emphatically rejected the view that it had been wrong to grant the vote to the freedmen. On the contrary, he argued, it had been essential to do so in order to preserve their freedom. Moreover, the experiment had not been a failure, for since 1876 it had not been fairly tried. Storey warned of the dangers of disfranchisement. "Let it once be agreed that the negro is inferior and that on this account he may be deprived of political rights, and it will not be long before other men are discovered who are also unfit to hold them. . . . The moment the doctrine of equal rights is abandoned, who shall draw the line?"[66] Another Republican from the past, Carl Schurz, raised a somewhat similar protest. Suffrage had prevented enslavement, he argued. If it was dangerous because Negroes were ignorant, it was equally so in the case of whites, a large portion of whom had similar shortcomings. Schurz rejected the notion that it was no business of the North to discuss the Negro ques-

[63] Abbott to Katherine Coman, May 2, 1903, Washington Papers; Abbott to Ray S. Baker, March 28, 1907, Baker Papers; Boston *Transcript*, Feb. 23, 1904. The *Transcript*, a conservative, Republican journal, reported on a speech delivered by Abbott in Boston, which it criticized as being "worth to the Negrophobists a dozen Vardamans." On Abbott's views, see Ira V. Brown, *Lyman Abbott, Christian Evolutionist* (Cambridge, Mass., 1953), pp. 205–7.

[64] Shaw, *Political Problems of American Development* (New York, 1907), p. 125. Shaw was editor of the *Review of Reviews*.

[65] New York *Times*, July 10, 1906.

[66] Storey, p. 18.

tion. The violation of the Thirteenth, Fourteenth, and Fifteenth Amendments was not to be indefinitely tolerated. Either recognize the Negro as a true citizen, Schurz declared, or he will be reduced to permanent serfdom.[67]

Such forthright defenses of the Negro's right to vote were becoming rare. The prevailing opinion was closer to that of the Supreme Court, which continued its abandonment of the Negro. In the case of *Giles* v. *Harris* in 1903, a Negro who had been refused registration as a voter argued not only that the administration of the suffrage provisions of the new Alabama Constitution of 1901 worked to exclude Negroes but that the record of the constitutional convention clearly showed this to be the intent of the new requirements. Nevertheless, Justice Holmes rendered the opinion of the majority that Giles could get no relief from the courts. Giles then sued the registrars for damages and applied for a writ of mandamus to compel them to register him. This second effort also failed.[68] In effect, the United States Supreme Court had sanctioned the South's disfranchisement of blacks by holding that suffrage provisions, no matter how unfairly administered, were beyond reach of the federal courts.

As James S. Clarkson lamented, these were decisions of a Republican Supreme Court, and they profoundly discouraged those who still looked for a means to stem the anti-Negro current.[69] One reaction was to press for congressional action. Could we not, asked the *Nation,* look beyond the face of the credentials of southern Congressmen and inquire into the registration of voters? Negroes were "entitled to the full and equal protection of the laws." The Republican party must set about "the work of completing its mission in behalf of the negro." Another demand came from the Union League Club of New York City, which in December 1903 voted a resolution in favor of reducing the congressional representation of the disfranchising states.[70]

Congress only occasionally discussed the suffrage question. At times the issue was brought up by southerners who opposed the Negro's right to vote. For example, Congressmen William W. Kitchin of North Carolina, Oscar W. Underwood of Alabama, and Thomas W. Hardwick of Georgia regularly introduced resolutions to repeal

67 Schurz, "Can the South Solve the Negro Problem?" *McClure's Magazine,* 22 (Jan. 1904), 259–65.

68 *Giles* v. *Harris,* 189 U.S. 475 (1903); *Giles* v. *Teasley,* 193 U.S. 146 (1904).

69 Clarkson to Booker T. Washington, Feb. 26, 1904, Washington Papers.

70 *Nation,* 76 (April 30, 1903), 346; New York *Times,* Dec. 11, 1903; *Independent,* 55 (Dec. 17, 1903), 3008–10.

the Fifteenth Amendment and that part of the Fourteenth Amendment providing for the reduction of representation of states that abridge the right to vote. On one occasion a northerner, William O. Smith, a Republican from Pennsylvania, also proposed repeal of the relevant part of the Fourteenth Amendment.[71] Some Republican congressmen had other objectives. Four resolutions calling for investigations of suffrage restrictions were introduced between December 1901 and November 1902 by Congressmen Charles Dick of Ohio and Edgar D. Crumpacker of Indiana.[72] In April 1904 Congressman Edward de V. Morrell of Philadelphia responded to a long diatribe against Negro suffrage by Congressman Hardwick with a forthright defense of the Fourteenth and Fifteenth Amendments. Condemning the excesses of Negrophobes like Governor James K. Vardaman of Mississippi, Morrell said that the time had come for a general discussion of the Negro question. But such talk on behalf of the Negro's voting right was then rarely heard in Congress.[73]

Only one member of the administration, Postmaster General Payne, expressed interest in enforcing the Fourteenth Amendment's suffrage provision by reducing the South's congressional representation. Roosevelt was not enthusiastic. Although he agreed that representation in Congress and the electoral college should be reduced, he did not think that it would be "wise to attempt to act and fail." In order to get anything passed, he explained in July 1903, it would first be necessary to change the Senate's rules on unlimited debate, a move that would be "bitterly opposed even by many Republicans."[74] Roosevelt wrote to Carl Schurz in December 1903 that he agreed with him "about the nullification of the 14th, 15th and even 13th Amendments in the South," but he added that "as it has not yet seemed absolutely necessary that I should notice this, I have refrained from doing so."[75] In short, Roosevelt was in no mood to fight.

Even if a reduction in the congressional representation of the disfranchising states could have been achieved, defenders of the Negro were divided over the advisability of such a step. Booker T. Washington and his friends opposed it. In late November 1904 he dis-

71 *Cong. Rec.*, 59th Cong., 1st sess., vol. 40, pt. 4, p. 3248 (March 1, 1906).

72 *Ibid.*, 57th Cong., 1st sess., vol. 35, pt. 1, p. 58, and pt. 3, p. 2764; 58th Cong., 1st sess., vol. 37, pt. 1, pp. 165, 236.

73 *Ibid.*, 58th Cong., 2d sess., vol. 38, pt. 2, pp. 1270–78 (Jan. 27, 1904), and pt. 5, pp. 4258–63 (April 4, 1904).

74 Roosevelt to Rollo Ogden, July 9, 1903, in Morison, ed., *Roosevelt Letters*, III, 514.

75 Roosevelt to Schurz, Dec. 25, 1903, *ibid.*, p. 680.

cussed the matter at some length with Roosevelt, arguing that it would be of no help. Indeed, the more Washington thought about it, the more dangerous the proposition appeared. It would legalize a wrong in the South and thus possibly establish the right to disfranchise Negroes elsewhere.[76] Others, notably John E. Milholland of the Constitution League, W. E. B. Du Bois, and some of the founders of the Niagara Movement in 1905 supported the idea as a necessary step to force the South to respect the Negro's right to vote.[77] The Republican Club of New York City prepared a measure which was introduced on December 7, 1904, by Senator Thomas C. Platt of New York. Under it representation in the House would be reduced for those states where the right to vote in federal elections was denied to males age twenty-one or over for causes not permitted in the Constitution. The eleven southern states would loose a total of nineteen seats.[78]

The introduction of the Platt bill created a brief stir. But congressional support was very limited, and the bill never emerged from the Committee on the Census. Roosevelt opposed the measure on the grounds of political realism. "As conditions are now," he observed in mid-December 1904, in regard to the Fourteenth Amendment, "it is unwise and would do damage rather than good to press for its active enforcement by any means that Congress has at its command."[79] As one reporter noted after Roosevelt's return from his southern trip in the fall of 1905, "It is hardly conceivable that the President will countenance any attempt of his party, either to restore the ballot to the mass of them [the Negroes] at once, or to carry out the plank of the party platform which demands a reduction in the South's representation in Congress."[80] Roosevelt not only feared damage to his own and his party's standing in the South; beyond these considerations was the fact that he had doubts about the wisdom of the original enfranchisement of Negroes during Reconstruction. He believed that the passage of the Fifteenth Amend-

76 Washington to T. Thomas Fortune, Nov. 22, 1904, Emmett Scott to Washington, Nov. 23, 1904, Washington to John S. Durham, Dec. 24, 1904, Washington Papers. Fortune's New York *Age*, Jan. 5, 1905, also opposed the proposal to reduce representation.

77 Meier, "Washington and Rise of N.A.A.C.P.," p. 74; Elliott M. Rudwick, "The Niagara Movement," *Journal of Negro History*, 42 (July 1957), 183.

78 *Cong. Rec.*, 58th Cong., 3d sess., vol. 39, pt. 1, p. 47; New York *Times*, Dec. 8, 1904.

79 Roosevelt to Henry S. Pritchett, Dec. 14, 1904, in Morison, ed., *Roosevelt Letters*, IV, 1067.

80 W. G. Brown, p. 1089.

ment had been a mistake, and he referred to the "folly of the Congressional scheme of reconstruction based on universal negro suffrage."[81] Apparently Roosevelt did not appreciate the importance of the ballot in protecting other basic rights of the freedmen. These doubts reinforced his decision not to make an issue of Negro disfranchisement during his presidency.

During his second term Roosevelt had disillusioned and angered many black Americans. As the 1908 election approached, they sought an effective means of expressing their discontent with the Republican leadership. A few supported Senator Foraker for the presidency. Others rejected the Republican party altogether. The most outspoken of the disaffected were the opponents of Booker T. Washington and his philosophy of accommodation. Their principal spokesman was W. E. B. Du Bois, a professor at Atlanta University, whose critical essay on Washington had been published in *Souls of Black Folk* in 1903. With Du Bois's participation in the creation of the Niagara Movement in 1905 a militant protest movement had emerged. Dedicated to a forthright equalitarianism, this small group of blacks and their white allies became a threat to the dominance of Washington.[82] The close identification of Washington with Roosevelt meant that the Niagara Movement would inevitably clash with the president also. At its third conference, held at Boston in August 1907, the Niagara Movement published a pamphlet addressed to the black voters in the North, calling upon them to "defeat Theodore Roosevelt, William Taft, or any man named by the present political dictatorship."[83] In March 1908 Du Bois announced his intention to support the Democrat William J. Bryan. "An avowed enemy" he declared, is "better than [a] false friend."[84]

In the months before the 1908 Republican national convention there were many other signs of Negro discontent throughout the North. Meetings of Negroes in Boston and in Brooklyn condemned Taft for his role in the Brownsville affair and for alleged anti-Negro remarks. In Washington a conference of Negro Methodist bishops passed a resolution warning the Republicans not to nominate either

81 Roosevelt to James Ford Rhodes, Feb. 20, 1905, in Morison, ed., *Roosevelt Letters,* IV, 1125. See also Roosevelt to Henry S. Pritchett, Dec. 14, 1904, and Roosevelt to Owen Wister, April 27, 1906, *ibid.,* IV, 1066, V, 225–26.

82 Rudwick, "Niagara Movement," pp. 177–95; Meier, "Washington and Rise of N.A.A.C.P.," pp. 72–74; August Meier, *Negro Thought in America, 1880–1915: Racial Ideologies in the Age of Booker T. Washington* (Ann Arbor, Mich., 1963), pp. 190–206. See also Aptheker, pp. 897–915.

83 Quoted in *Outlook,* 87 (Sept. 14, 1907), 48.

84 Rudwick, "Niagara Movement," p. 194.

Roosevelt or Taft and condemning the party's flirtations with the lily-whites.[85] An astute political observer in Cleveland, the Negro barber George A. Myers, complained "that never before was there so much unrest among the colored voters of Ohio."[86] Such feelings were widespread enough to worry Booker T. Washington. "The colored people are making a mistake, from which it is going to take years for them to recover, in opposing Secretary Taft and abusing the President of the United States in the way that they are now doing," he wrote in late February 1908. "The Democratic party does not want the Negro, and if he puts himself in a position of enmity to the Republican party he will soon find himself without any political influence in the country."[87]

This unrest, although troublesome, did not seriously endanger Roosevelt's control of the party. Long before the national convention, he worked carefully to ensure that most state delegations would be loyal to Taft. Postmaster General George von L. Meyer and Assistant Postmaster General Frank H. Hitchcock were the president's chief lieutenants in this task. In February 1908 Hitchcock resigned his post to devote full time to the canvass for Taft delegates, especially in the South. The administration had matters well in hand. In March, Hitchcock claimed that Taft could then count on 552 of the 980 delegates, including a large majority of those from the South. This was more than enough for the nomination.[88]

As usual Roosevelt worried, fearing that the opposition would stoop to bribery and corruption in challenging the seats of the regular delegates. Contests did arise over the delegations from nearly every southern state, but they proved to be no great cause for alarm. On June 5 the national committee met at Chicago to begin hearings on the challenges and to draw up the temporary roll. By June 12 it had completed its labors. Of the 219 cases it decided, 216 seats went to Taft and only 3 to Foraker.[89] By the time the convention opened on June 16 the opposition had largely collapsed. Two days later Taft was nominated on the first ballot with over 200 votes to spare.

85 "Negroes and Secretary Taft," *Independent*, 64 (Feb. 13, 1908), 374; John Daniels, *In Freedom's Birthplace: A Study of the Boston Negroes* (Boston, 1914), p. 294; Washington *Bee*, Feb. 22, 1908.

86 Myers to T. E. Burton, March 20, 1908, James R. Garfield Papers, Manuscript Division, Library of Congress.

87 Washington to C. B. Purvis, Feb. 26, 1908, Washington Papers.

88 Dorothy G. Fowler, *The Cabinet Politician: The Postmasters General, 1829–1909* (New York, 1943), p. 243; George H. Mayer, *The Republican Party, 1854–1964* (New York, 1964), p. 301; Pringle, *Taft*, p. 347.

89 Roosevelt to Thomas Jefferson Coolidge, Feb. 8, 1908, in Morison, ed., *Roosevelt Letters*, VI, 933–34; New York *Times*, June 13, 1908.

Included among the southern delegates were several dozen Negroes, few of whom were willing to risk their political fortunes by openly opposing the president. During the proceedings at Chicago their loyalty was bolstered by the activity of Negro federal officeholders like Auditor of the Navy Ralph W. Tyler and Register of the Treasury William T. Vernon.[90] Despite the increase in white influence in the southern parties, the delegate contests seem to have been decided primarily on political (i.e., loyalty to Taft) rather than racial lines. Taft told Hitchcock that he was "very anxious that he should not take a position in favor of Lily White delegations like that one in Louisiana"; and a contest between the lily-white and black-and-tan delegations from that state, both of whom favored Taft, was resolved by seating both and giving half a vote to each delegate.[91]

The perennial scramble for delegates from the South's rotten boroughs offended Taft. Several months earlier he had expressed the wish that votes in the national convention should be made proportional to a state's Republican vote in a general election. A proposal along these lines, which would reduce the size of the southern delegations, was introduced at the convention by anti-Taft forces. It was defeated by a narrow margin. At that time Roosevelt wanted no part of such a change, even though Taft could have been nominated on the first ballot without southern support. Roosevelt was not prepared to see his successor deprived of so useful a political device. Ironically, had the reform passed, Roosevelt might have won the nomination from Taft four years later.[92]

Possibly in response to the recent indications of Negro dissatisfaction with the Republican party, the convention adopted a plank on the "Rights of the Negro." "The Republican Party," it proclaimed, "has been for more than fifty years the consistent friend of the American Negro. It gave him freedom and citizenship. It wrote into the organic law the declarations that proclaim his civil and political rights." The plank then demanded "equal justice for all men," and "the enforcement in letter and spirit of the Thirteenth, Fourteenth and Fifteenth Amendments," while it condemned

[90] Tyler to William Loeb, Jr., June 6, 1908, Taft Papers; New York *Times*, June 16, 1908.

[91] Taft to Washington, June 6, 1908, Washington Papers. On Louisiana, see Francis B. Williams to Taft, Taft Papers; Roosevelt to Pearl Wight, April 18, 1908, Roosevelt to Frank H. Hitchcock, June 9, 1908, in Morison, ed., *Roosevelt Letters*, VI, 1012, 1070–71; New York *Times*, June 10, 1908.

[92] Pringle, *Taft*, 347; New York *Times*, June 11–18, 1908; James E. Watson, *As I Knew Them* (Indianapolis, 1932), pp. 128–29; Roosevelt to Richard Watson Gilder, Nov. 16, 1908, in Morison, ed., *Roosevelt Letters*, VI, 1363.

all devices aimed at "disfranchisement for reasons of color alone." These sentiments were not, however, backed by any promises of action in regard to specific grievances. As in 1904 Roosevelt strongly opposed the inclusion of any proposal about cutting down southern representation as "insincere" and "an empty threat." Booker T. Washington similarly objected, preferring more general statements.[93] The Republicans also included a ten-page section on the Negro in their *Campaign Text-Book* in which they associated Jim Crow laws and disfranchisement with Democratic state governments and reminded readers about the number of Negroes who had positions in the United States government. These proclamations, which Taft reiterated in his July 28 acceptance speech, avoided any serious confrontation with America's racial problems. Nevertheless, 1908 was the last time that the Republican platform called for the enforcement of the Civil War amendments, even in general terms, and the last time until 1932 that it felt compelled to have a section devoted specifically to Negroes.

The Republican professions of goodwill may have helped to keep most black voters in line, but they failed to satisfy all. Aggressive and independent men like Bishop Alexander Walters, the Reverend J. Milton Waldron, William Monroe Trotter, and a number of others associated with the Niagara Movement continued to oppose Roosevelt and Taft. In June they formed the National Negro-American Political League and threw their support to Bryan. Du Bois also stuck by his decision to back the Democratic candidate.[94] Reports of Negro discontent continued throughout the campaign. In October, Roosevelt admitted that "the defection in the Negro vote" was real, but he predicted that it would be important only in a very close election.[95]

Taft showed more concern about the South than the Negro. Urged on by Roosevelt, he became the first Republican presidential candidate to campaign below the Mason and Dixon line, giving speeches in Louisville, Chattanooga, Greensboro, and Richmond. Although he had no serious hopes of winning electoral votes in the South, he did wish to encourage Republicans there.[96] These efforts paid off.

93 Roosevelt to Herbert Parsons, April 10, 1908, in Morison, ed., *Roosevelt Letters*, VI, 999; Washington to Taft, June 4, 1908, Taft Papers.

94 Aptheker, pp. 857–58; Meier, *Negro Thought*, pp. 186–87; August Meier, "The Negro and the Democratic Party, 1875–1915," *Phylon*, 17 (1956), 185–88; Thornbrough, pp. 487–92; Washington *Bee*, July 11, 1908. After the election the organization was renamed the National Independent Political League.

95 Roosevelt to Kermit Roosevelt, Oct. 20, 1908, in Morison, ed., *Roosevelt Letters*, VI, 1304.

96 Roosevelt to Taft, Sept. 1, 1908, Taft to Roosevelt, Oct. 9, 1908, Taft Papers;

Taft won a larger popular vote in every southern state than Roosevelt had in 1904, and in all of these states but Arkansas his percentage of the total vote was also greater. In view of the disfranchisement of most of the Negroes, these gains meant that a substantial number of white southerners had turned to the Republican party. The solid South had not yet been cracked, but it seemed to be weakening. Many Republicans found this prospect of considerably more interest than their traditional ties to black Americans.

Roosevelt's presidency coincided with a drastic worsening of the Negro's position in America. This was the case especially in regard to the extension of segregation laws and practices and to disfranchisement. But it was also apparent in the spread of racist ideas, as much of the North accepted the moderate South's rationale for its handling of race relations. It was Roosevelt's misfortune to have been in office during this triumph of racism. Effective challenges to the Negrophobic practices were extremely difficult to make. The mildest gestures of goodwill toward the black man aroused passionate denunciations from southerners. Few of his fellow Republicans cared enough about the Negro's plight to support the president in any serious challenge to the prevailing racial practices. Added to this was Roosevelt's romantic attachment to the South and his strong desire to be liked, both for personal and political reasons. It was little wonder that he preferred Booker T. Washington's counsels of accommodation and moderation to forthright assaults upon the innumerable injustices.

Roosevelt, too, had been influenced by racism. His own views of the Negro contained many contrasting elements. He remained skeptical of any dogmatic approach to the subject of race and impatient with the absurdities of some of the extremists. He praised individual achievement, like that of Booker T. Washington, generously.[97] At the same time, he rendered unflattering judgments about blacks as a group. "As a race and in the mass," he said, "they are altogether inferior to the whites."[98] Whether he felt that this inferiority was due

---

C. Vann Woodward, *Origins of the New South, 1877–1913* (Baton Rouge, La., 1951), pp. 467–68.

97 Note Roosevelt's review of Houston Stewart Chamberlain, *Foundations of the Nineteenth Century*, in *Outlook*, 98 (July 29, 1911), 718–31. See also Gossett, pp. 318–19.

98 Roosevelt to Owen Wister, April 27, 1906, in Morison, ed., *Roosevelt Letters*, V, 226. See also Roosevelt to Ray S. Baker, June 3, 1908, *ibid.*, VI, 1048, where he calls misconduct by Negroes a question of race, noting Haiti in particular; and Roosevelt to Harry H. Johnston, July 11, 1908, *ibid.*, p. 1126, in which Roosevelt refers to Negroes as members of "the most utterly underdeveloped races of mankind."

to genetic disability or present discrimination was not always clear. But as his biographer William H. Harbaugh suggests, "a mild undercut of racism seems to have lingered in his unconsciousness."[99]

Under Roosevelt's leadership the Republicans and the nation failed to find a formula for the working out of America's racial problems that was consistent with democratic and equalitarian principles. Certainly none emerged which thoughtful Negroes could wholeheartedly endorse or regard as true to the best heritage of the Party of Lincoln. It was unlikely that Taft would be much more successful.

99 P. 220.

CHAPTER IV

In Troubled Waters
The Taft Administration

FROM the very outset of his presidency Taft sought to convince all America of his benevolent intentions. Undoubtedly a man of goodwill, Taft, like Roosevelt, condemned those who fomented racial hatreds and warmly praised the achievements of individual Negroes. "Personally, I have not the slightest race prejudice or feeling," the new president insisted in his inaugural address. In such an intensely race-conscious society his words were an unintended mockery; prejudice simply did not have the same meaning for Taft, or other white Americans, no matter how kindly disposed, that it had for their black countrymen. The fact that he could deny having a sense of racial feeling was indicative of the gulf that separated the two Americas. Predictably, some Negroes were skeptical about Taft's intentions. Pointing to his close association with Roosevelt's ill-regarded administration, they concluded long before his inauguration that his understanding of the race problem was limited. Listening to Taft's professed concern for black Americans, these skeptics doubted that he was the man who could revive the Republican party's ideals and lead a serious assault upon the prevailing discriminatory racial practices.

The key to Taft's Negro policy lay in his attitude toward the South. Like his predecessor, he was fascinated by that region. He greatly desired to be liked and respected by its leaders, and he sympathized with them in respect to their economic and social problems. Beyond that, of course, Taft very much hoped to strengthen southern Republicanism and so develop a meaningful two-party system. His problem then was to reconcile a conciliatory approach toward the white South with a positive program for the Negro. It was highly improbable that he could be successful at both; priorities had to be established.

Taft began his overtures to the South several years before he became president. For example, on July 9, 1906, on the eve of the Republican state convention at Greensboro, North Carolina, he delivered a speech in which he argued that nothing could be of greater advantage to the country as a whole and to that region in particular than a dissolution of the solid South. The condition, he said, that had been mainly responsible for the one-party supremacy, fear of Negro domination, had now been eliminated by the new property and educational qualifications for suffrage. Believing that the tests would ultimately be applied impartially, he accepted this "legal" exclusion of Negroes—in contrast to the older techniques of violence and intimidation—as being consistent with the Fifteenth Amendment.[1]

At Kansas City, Missouri, on February 10, 1908, Taft again praised the South for moving away from violent methods of excluding Negroes from voting and referred to the recent suffrage laws as an indication of a "turn for the better."[2] On several other occasions during the two or three years before he became president, Taft publicly expressed similar ideas. To heighten the attractiveness of his party, he frequently added that the South stood to gain by various Republican programs, particularly economic ones like the tariff.[3] His precedent-breaking southern campaign tour in 1908 was another indication of his interest in Dixie.

Taft's approval of suffrage limitations based on educational and property requirements was consistent with his conservative views about popular democracy. However, he overestimated the South's goodwill and underestimated its determination to keep Negroes in a servile status. In effect he was reassuring the South that it would have a free hand in its handling of racial matters and that it need fear no intervention by the federal government.

After the election the southern-born journalist Walter Hines Page invited Taft to speak at a dinner of the North Carolina Society in New York City on December 7. This provided him an opportunity

[1] New York *Times*, July 10, 1906. See also Josephus Daniels, *Editor in Politics* (Chapel Hill, N.C., 1941), pp. 488–89. On Taft and the South, see E. Merton Coulter, "The Attempt of William Howard Taft to Break the Solid South," *Georgia Historical Quarterly*, 19 (June 1935), 1–11; and C. Vann Woodward, *Origins of the New South, 1877–1913* (Baton Rouge, La., 1951), pp. 467–69.

[2] William H. Taft, *Present Day Problems* (New York, 1908), p. 277. Taft drew the line at grandfather clauses, however, which he condemned as inconsistent with the Fourteenth and Fifteenth Amendments (see Jane L. Phelps, "Charles J. Bonaparte and Negro Suffrage in Maryland," *Maryland Historical Magazine*, 54 [Dec. 1959], 348–49).

[3] For examples, see Taft's speeches at Greensboro, N.C., July 9, 1906, and Kansas City, Mo., Feb. 10, 1908, cited above; at Lexington, Ky., Aug. 22, 1907, in *Present Day Problems*, pp. 221–40; at Plymouth Church, Brooklyn, March 16, 1908, and at the North Carolina Society dinner in New York, Dec. 7, 1908, in New York *Times*, March 17, Dec. 8, 1908; and at New Orleans, Feb. 12, 1909, in William H. Taft, *Political Issues and Outlooks* (New York, 1909), pp. 268–74.

to make a major presentation of his projected southern policy. Booker T. Washington assisted Taft by preparing a memorandum stressing the need for Negro education and for the equal application of the franchise laws to whites and blacks alike. Although Washington recognized that there were many in the South who would support the Republican party if Taft gave assurances that he would reject the Negro's educational and political rights, he argued that a strong Republican party could be gradually built up while doing justice to the Negro.[4] To a degree Taft followed Washington's suggestions. Emphasizing the value of education, he also said that he did not sympathize with efforts to exclude qualified Negroes from the Republican party. They "should be given an equal opportunity with whites."[5] However, on the whole the speech was consistent with his previous statements about the South, and it was far more calculated to reassure white southerners than had been the ideas in Washington's memorandum. In stressing the importance of dissolving the solid South, Taft again pointed out that there no longer ought to be fear of domination by "an ignorant electorate, white or black," for this could now be prevented by the new election laws without violating the Fifteenth Amendment. He also assured his audience that the federal government would have nothing to do with the promotion of social equality. This speech once again revealed the dilemma Republicans faced in attempting to square their supposed commitment to the Negro with their desire to woo the white South. On balance, his words contained little comfort for black Americans.

In January 1909 Taft visited Georgia, supposedly to rest, but also to do a little missionary work for his party. The Georgia Republicans had been heartened in 1908 by a substantial increase in the size of their vote, an improvement attributed in part to the work done by the newly organized Taft clubs throughout the state. These were lily-white groups opposed to the lethargic older organization headed by a Negro, Judson W. Lyons, the former national committeeman.[6]

[4] The memorandum is quoted in Basil Mathews, *Booker T. Washington: Educator and Interracial Interpreter* (Cambridge, Mass., 1948), pp. 236–38. See also Washington to Taft, Nov. 9 and 19, 1908, Booker T. Washington Papers, Manuscript Division, Library of Congress.

[5] New York *Times*, Dec. 8, 1908.

[6] In 1908 the presidential vote in Georgia for the Republicans was nearly double what it had been in 1904, and it amounted to 31.40 percent of the total. The Democratic percentage was 54.53, the smallest received by that party until it lost the state to Goldwater in 1964. Lyons, who had become identified with the critics of Booker T. Washington, lost his place on the national committee in 1908.

After the election Roosevelt advised Frank Hitchcock "that it would be a mistake to disturb the Taft organizations there." Instead they should be encouraged and built up.[7] During his Georgia visit Taft did nothing to discourage these whites, and the warm reception he received further strengthened his belief in a Republican renaissance in the South. Of his speeches to white and to black audiences, his remarks to the Atlanta Chamber of Commerce on January 15 attracted the most attention. "I realize," he said, "that expressions of sympathy for the South . . . will have comparatively little weight unless . . . accompanied by such appointments as shall prove this sympathy to be real and substantial. . . . I expect . . . to select those whose character and reputation and standing in the community commend them to their fellow citizens as persons qualified and able to discharge their duties well, and whose presence in important positions will remove, if any such thing exists, the sense of alienism in the Government which they represent."[8] The meaning was clear: Taft did not intend to appoint Negroes to federal government positions in the South unless the individual was fully acceptable to the community. Since any black candidate was likely to arouse some white objections, the implication seemed to be that Negroes would be virtually excluded. Many Negroes were understandably alarmed. The principle was all wrong, wrote Francis J. Grimké to Taft, for it tended "to make the prejudices or the animosities of one class the measure of the rights of another class." Moreover, it would greatly discourage all black people and strengthen whites in their opposition to the civil and political rights of Negroes.[9]

Another illustration of Taft's willingness to achieve harmony by making concessions to the white South was shown before his inauguration when, with Booker T. Washington's help, he persuaded Dr. Crum to resign his post as collector of customs at Charleston, South Carolina. Crum's resignation, effective March 4, 1909, ended a long-standing grievance and relieved Taft of an embarrassing situation.

[7] Roosevelt to Hitchcock, Dec. 3, 1908, in Elting E. Morison, ed., *The Letters of Theodore Roosevelt* (Cambridge, Mass.: Harvard University Press, 1951–54), VI, 1408–9. See also the Washington *Bee*, Nov. 14, 1908. Hitchcock was generally inclined to favor more traditional Republicans rather than the lily-whites with whom Taft flirted (see Guy B. Hathorn, "The Political Career of C. Bascom Slemp" [Ph.D. diss., Duke University, 1950], p. 78).

[8] "Trying to Melt the Solid South," *Literary Digest*, 38 (Jan. 23, 1909), 121; New York *Times*, Jan. 16, 1909.

[9] Grimké to Taft, Feb. 19, 1909, in *The Works of Francis J. Grimké*, ed. Carter G. Woodson (Washington, D.C., 1942), IV, 116–17. See also Archibald H. Grimké, "The Shame of America, or The Negro's Case against the Republic," in American Negro Academy, *Occasional Papers*, no. 21 (Washington, D.C., 1924), p. 15.

But it also gave substance to his announcement that appointments would not be made against the wishes of the local community.[10]

Taft, like Roosevelt, sought the advice of Booker T. Washington in developing his overall Negro and southern policies. "I certainly shall expect to call on you at all times to assist me in matters with reference to the colored people in my administration," wrote Taft to Washington on December 3, 1908.[11] Roosevelt also encouraged this relationship. "There is not a better or truer friend of his race than Booker Washington," Roosevelt advised Taft, "and yet he is so sane and reasonable that following his advice never gives cause for just criticism by the white people."[12]

Taft's views on Negro education were close to those of Washington.[13] He believed that most blacks needed manual and industrial training. They, like the great majority of whites, had to look forward to hard manual labor as a means of earning a living. By 1908 Taft acknowledged that in order to train doctors, clergymen, lawyers, and teachers, higher education among Negroes should also be encouraged, although he admitted that he had not always believed this was desirable. He regarded formal education as particularly valuable in developing the traits of self-help so praised by the philosophers of the gospel of success. The Negro "must make himself worthy of respect. He must cultivate those virtues of providence, of industry, of thrift, which will make him respected . . . as a man contributing to the wealth of the community in which he lives."[14] Moreover, Taft believed that as the Negro developed his talents and made himself

[10] Taft to Theodore Roosevelt, Feb. 25, 1909, Roosevelt to Taft, Feb. 26, 1909, William H. Taft Papers, Manuscript Division, Library of Congress; New York *Times*, March 2, 1909; Henry F. Pringle, *The Life and Times of William Howard Taft* (New York, 1939), 390; Willard B. Gatewood, Jr., *Theodore Roosevelt and the Art of Controversy: Episodes of the White House Years* (Baton Rouge, La., 1970), pp. 132–33. In June 1910 Crum was compensated by being appointed Minister to Liberia.

[11] Taft to Washington, Dec. 3, 1908, Washington Papers. See also Washington to Taft, Nov. 30, 1908, quoted in Mathews, pp. 234–35.

[12] Roosevelt to Taft, Jan. 20, 1909, Taft Papers. See also Washington to Roosevelt, Jan. 18, 1909, *ibid.*

[13] In addition to some of Taft's speeches already noted above in n.3, see his speech at Fisk University, May 22, 1908, copy in Washington Papers, and his speeches at Allen Temple in Cincinnati, Sept. 15, 1908, and at Haines Normal and Industrial School, Augusta, Ga., Jan. 19, 1909, in Taft, *Political Issues*, pp. 66–70, 261–67; "The Future of the Negro," Sept. 15, 1908, *ibid.*, p. 70.

[14] Speech to Colored YMCA, Augusta, Ga., Jan. 17, 1909, New York *Times*, Jan. 18, 1909; see also Taft's speech at Fisk University, May 22, 1908, Washington Papers; at Plymouth Church, Brooklyn, March 16, 1908, New York *Times*, March 17, 1908; and at Carnegie Hall, New York City, Feb. 23, 1909, *Political Issues*, pp. 291–99.

indispensable to the industrial interests, as he improved his economic standing, political barriers and racial prejudice would fade away. No pessimist on the race question, Taft felt that time was on the side of progress and that justice was bound to triumph. This belief reinforced his own proclivity to leave matters alone, to avoid interference by the federal government, and to let things work out by themselves. It was also compatible with his desire to placate the South and avoid unpleasant controversy, and probably reflected the view of many other white Americans.

Taft's inaugural address on March 4, 1909, confirmed the fears of some black Americans and the hopes of many southerners. Asserting his desire to promote good feeling between the sections, he reminded the South that the danger of Negro domination had passed and promised that as long as its laws establishing electoral qualifications met the test of the Fifteenth Amendment "and are not otherwise in conflict with the Constitution and laws of the United States, it is not the disposition or within the province of the Federal Government to interfere with the regulation by Southern States of their domestic affairs." Again Taft assured the South that he would not appoint a Negro "to a local office in a community in which the race feeling is so widespread and acute as to interfere with the ease of facility with which the local business can be done." He also praised the progress made by Negroes since emancipation and added a few cautious words against racial prejudice. But the message remained clear. Taft intended to accept the white South's handling of the Negro question.[15]

Responding to this attitude, many political observers predicted the impending breakup of the solid South. With Negro domination no longer a threat, they said, the reason for such solidity had ended. "Hardly a sincere and respectable protest against the disfranchisement of the negro has yet been made by the Republican party," wrote Professor James W. Garner of the University of Illinois, "and recent events would seem to justify the conclusion that it has virtually abandoned him so far as his political rights are concerned."[16] The fact that Taft and others had accepted the necessity of the "social segregation of the races" and the "elimination of illiterate voters" meant that the South no longer had to fear federal interference or

[15] William Howard Taft, *Presidential Addresses and State Papers* (New York, 1910), pp. 63–66. Roosevelt read and approved Taft's inaugural address before it was delivered (Taft to Roosevelt, Feb. 25, 1909, Roosevelt to Taft, Feb. 26, March 1, 1909, Taft Papers).

[16] Garner, "New Politics for the South," *Annals of the American Academy of Political and Social Science*, 35 (Jan. 1910), 174.

Negro rule, insisted another writer. "In this agreement may be found the basis for a more complete understanding between the two sections than has existed for half a century."[17] Because the South was released from the social necessity of one-party control, it was now possible for those southerners who favored Republican tariff and monetary policies to abandon their Democratic ties.[18] Alabama-born author and historian William Garrott Brown was impressed at the progress being made in ending the Democratic monopoly. The 1908 election showed notable Republican increases among white voters, he said, and if the present tendencies continued, he felt that it would be "only a question of time when in more than one Southern State those who in their hearts favor the Republican Party will be . . . the majority."[19]

Similar predictions were often expressed throughout 1909 and well into 1910, as Taft's wooing of the South appeared to be leading to success. His views on the Negro seemed perfectly suited for this end. "As to the race question, the administration's course invites no criticism," wrote Brown to Taft's secretary in October 1910.[20] The optimism ended with the November elections. In the South, as elsewhere, the rise of reform spirit hurt the conservative Republicans. Farmers in particular had been alienated by Taft's defense of the Payne-Aldrich tariff. Extensive Democratic gains demonstrated that once again the predictions about the demise of the solid South had been premature. The elections, which resulted in loss of the Republican control of the House of Representatives as well as a number of governorships, were a rebuke to Taft and his party. As for the South, remarked the Washington *Bee*, they proved that nothing had been gained by the surrenders to the Democrats and the lily-whites.[21] After

17 William P. Few, "President Eliot and the South," *South Atlantic Quarterly*, 8 (April 1909), 185. Professor Few was dean of Trinity College in North Carolina.

18 Enoch M. Banks. "The Passing of the Solid South," *ibid.*, 101–6. Banks was a professor at the University of Florida.

19 Brown, "President Taft's Opportunity," *Century*, (June 1909), 256. See also Brown, "The South in National Politics," *South Atlantic Quarterly*, 9 (April 1910), 103–15, and Bruce L. Clayton, "An Intellectual on Politics: William Garrott Brown and the Ideal of a Two-Party South," *North Carolina Historical Review*, 42 (Summer 1965), 319–34. For a similar viewpoint, see Henry L. West, "President Taft and the South," *Forum*, 41 (April 1909), 289–96.

20 Brown to Charles D. Norton, Oct. 13, 1910, Taft Papers. See also W. W. Russell to Taft, Aug. 16, 1910, Thomas G. Caffey to Norton, Aug. 18, 1910, Taft Papers.

21 New York *Times*, Nov. 9, Nov. 10, 1910; *Literary Digest*, 41 (Nov. 19, 1910), 915–18; Thomas D. Clark and Albert D. Kirwan, *The South since Appomatox: A Century of Regional Change* (New York, 1967), p. 131; Dewey W. Grantham, Jr.,

1910 far less was heard about Republican prospects in the South. Taft became more and more involved with the progressive opposition within his own party, and as the time approached for rounding up all possible delegates to the 1912 national convention, his enthusiasm for reforming the older Republican organizations in the South waned.

Negroes were understandably less than enthusiastic about Taft's actions. His policy on appointments was particularly disappointing. In a memorandum to the president in June 1909, Booker T. Washington pointed out that he had tried to explain to black people that Taft would in his own way and in his own time "see that the best thing is done." But he warned that they were "becoming not a little stirred up." Taft's answer was rather feeble. "The matter of appointments and filling places is a most difficult one to carry out, for the reason that the places are so few and the vacancies come so rarely that it is difficult to shape a plan of action."[22]

Within the administration Ralph W. Tyler, the auditor of the Navy, handled much of the correspondence and statements on Negro political problems. The president's friendship for Negroes was real, Tyler explained in an interview in the Washington *Bee*, and should not be judged simply by the number he appointed to office. They should note Taft's interest in education and in Liberia, and his expressions of sympathy toward the race.[23] Tyler's explanations failed to quell the alarm of even moderate and sympathetic Negroes. In August 1910 Judge Robert H. Terrell wrote to Washington about the "startling" situation he had found among black voters in several cities in Ohio and in Detroit. They were "bitter in their expressions and their attitude against the national administration" and seemed likely to desert the Republican party in large numbers.[24] United States Attorney William H. Lewis reported that similar feelings prevailed at a meeting of members of the National Negro Business League. "To put it mildly," he wrote toTaft's secretary Charles D. Norton, "most of them are very much discouraged and disappointed" with the administration.[25] At the same time Fred R. Moore, editor of the influential New York *Age*, published a strong editorial

The Democratic South (Athens, Ga., 1963), pp. 54–55; Woodward, p. 469; Washington *Bee*, Dec. 3, 1910.

22 Washington to Taft, June 18, 1909, Taft to Washington, June 24, 1909, Washington Papers.

23 Washington *Bee*, March 26, 1910. For Tyler's correspondence on Negro problems, see File 190, Presidential Ser. no. 2, Taft Papers.

24 Terrell to Washington, Aug 10, 1910, Robert H. Terrell Papers, Manuscript Division, Library of Congress.

25 Lewis to Norton, Aug. 24, 1910, Taft Papers.

about the bad effect on Negroes of Taft's appointment policy, which he blamed on Postmaster General Frank H. Hitchcock.[26] Chase of the Washington *Bee* was equally critical of the administration's surrender of "the political rights of colored Americans" in its effort to bring the white South into the Republican party. He predicted that the effort would fail and that "the South will forever remain Democratic no matter what is surrendered."[27] Even a white congressman, John W. Langley, a Republican from Pikeville, Kentucky, became alarmed about the extent of Negro dissatisfaction. He claimed that the 60,000 black voters in his state held the balance of power and that the Republicans would lose a large number of them unless something was done.[28]

These complaints failed to convince Taft that he should alter his appointment policy. An incident recorded in September 1910 by Archie Butt, Taft's military aid, revealed just how intractable the president had become. Norton brought in a stack of letters and telegrams urging certain appointments that would be for the benefit of the Republican party. Included were a number of recommendations for the South by Hitchcock. According to Butt, Taft "slammed his fist on the desk and said almost angrily: 'I will not be swerved one iota from my policy to the South, and I want Hitchcock to understand it now, once and for all. I shall not appoint Negroes to office in the South, and I shall not appoint Republicans unless they be good men. I shall not relinguish [*sic*] my hope to build up a decent white man's party there, politics or no politics.' "[29]

Taft's aids did not fully share his unconcern about Negro discontent. Norton sought advice from William H. Lewis on what the president might say about Negro education that would have a good effect. Lewis submitted a lengthy memorandum devoted mostly to an attempted clarification of Taft's appointment policy.[30] Norton also asked publisher and philanthropist Oswald Garrison Villard to suggest the names of three or four Negro editors or public men whose opinion might carry weight and whom presumably he hoped

26 New York *Age*, Aug. 25, 1910. See also Moore to Norton, Sept. 30, 1910, Taft Papers. Moore replaced Fortune as editor of the *Age* in October 1907.

27 Washington *Bee*, Aug. 27, 1910. Otherwise Chase had been sympathetic to Taft and blamed the trouble on bad advisers (*ibid.*, Sept. 3, 1910). See also Kelly Miller, "The American Negro as a Political Factor," *Nineteenth Century*, 68 (Aug. 1910), 285–302; John Lynch, *Reminiscences of an Active Life: The Autobiography of John Lynch*, ed. John Hope Franklin (Chicago, 1970), pp. 503–5.

28 Langley to Norton, June 29, 1910, Taft Papers.

29 Butt, *Taft and Roosevelt: The Intimate Letters of Archie Butt, Military Aid* (Garden City, N.Y., 1930), II, 511.

30 Lewis to Norton, Sept. 27, 1910, Taft Papers.

to influence to support the administration. Villard warned against too great a reliance upon Booker T. Washington, against whom opposition was steadily increasing. "The great majority of the men who have risen above the ranks consider him a traitor to his race." In particular he criticized Washington for allowing himself to become an "office-broker" for Negroes under Roosevelt and Taft.[31] Villard listed eight Negroes opposed to Washington and five supposed "Washington Men." Of these five, Kelly Miller and Bishop Alexander Walters had already publicly criticized Taft because of his attitude on disfranchisement, Negro appointments, and other matters.[32] Later, Villard also forwarded to Taft a blistering two-page critique of these same points prepared by W. E. B. Du Bois.[33] In fact, it had become difficult to find any well-known Negro who was not at least a little discouraged by Taft's concessions to the white South. Even Ralph W. Tyler became worried about the reaction to Taft's removal of "practically all Negro officeholders in the south." He warned that petty officials had so interpreted the president's policy as to "exclude or keep down all colored men holding clerical or inconsequential positions," and he pointed out that Negroes working for Democrats or insurgent Republicans had made the policy an issue in states where there was a large black vote. Tyler suggested that if Taft could not make appointments in the South, he should at least make an additional number in the North, so that the total number of Negroes holding office was as large as before.[34]

Taft apparently agreed, for outside the South he did make some effort to assuage Negro discontent with a number of showcase appointments. Most of the appointees were followers of Washington. In two cases he selected Negroes for positions not previously held by members of their race. One was the collectorship of customs for Georgetown, D.C., to which in the summer of 1910 Taft named Whitefield McKinlay.[35] The most important was the promotion of

[31] Villard to Norton, Sept. 20, 1910, *ibid.* Until that time Villard had maintained good relations with Washington (August Meier, "Booker T. Washington and the Rise of the N.A.A.C.P." *Crisis*, 61 [Feb. 1954], 75–76, 117–21).

[32] Miller, p. 301. Villard's inclusion of Walters was surprising in view of his role in the National Negro-American Political League, which had opposed Taft in 1908. That organization (renamed the National Independent Political League) also strongly attacked Taft in its call, dated June 22, 1910, for its third annual meeting (Washington *Bee*, July 2, 1910; Herbert Aptheker, ed., *A Documentary History of the Negro People in the United States* [New York, 1951], pp. 859–60).

[33] Du Bois to Villard, Sept. 26, 1910, Taft Papers.

[34] Tyler to Charles D. Hilles, Aug. 17, 1911, *ibid.*

[35] Taft to Washington, July 1, 1910, Washington to Taft, July 9, 1910, *ibid.*; New York *Tribune*, July 20, 1910; Washington *Bee*, July 23, 1910.

William H. Lewis, in March 1911, to be assistant United States attorney general, the highest federal office held by a Negro up to that time. Lewis was understandably elated. "While it means much to me personally," he explained to Norton, "yet it is hard to estimate how much more it means to millions of my countrymen, (in accordance with the President's policy) as an encouragement and inspiration to good citizenship."[36] In an exception to his usual practice of naming friends or nominees of Washington, in the spring of 1910 Taft selected Henry Lincoln Johnson to be recorder of deeds for the District of Columbia, replacing a Washington appointee, John C. Dancy. Johnson, a Georgia lawyer and an old-style Republican politician, was rewarded for his service to Taft in helping to oust Judson W. Lyons as Georgia national committeeman in 1908.[37] For another traditional Negro post, register of the Treasury, Taft named an associate of Washington, James C. Napier of Nashville, Tennessee.[38]

In addition to a few other domestic appointments, Taft maintained the usual number of Negro diplomatic and consular positions. In 1909 he also sent a special commission to Liberia to study its boundary and financial problems. One of the three commissioners was Booker T. Washington's secretary, Emmett J. Scott of Tuskegee.[39] Furthermore, Taft retained or reappointed a number of Negro officials who were in office at the time he became president. A few of these held positions in the South, like Nathan Alexander, register of the Land Office at Montgomery, Alabama; Robert Smalls, collector of customs at Beaufort, South Carolina; and Joseph E. Lee, internal revenue collector, Jacksonville, Florida. They also included such defenders of Booker T. Washington as Charles W. Anderson,

[36] Lewis to Norton, March 3, 1911, Taft Papers. On Lewis, see Stephen R. Fox, *The Guardian of Boston: William Monroe Trotter* (New York, 1970), pp. 158–60; August Meier, *Negro Thought in America, 1880–1915: Racial Ideologies in the Age of Booker T. Washington* (Ann Arbor, Mich., 1963), p. 241.

[37] Washington *Bee*, March 5, 1910; Meier, *Negro Thought*, p. 252. See also John C. Dancy, *Sand against the Wind: The Memoirs of John C. Dancy* (Detroit, 1966), pp. 60–63 (written by the son of Roosevelt's recorder of deeds for the District of Columbia).

[38] Washington *Bee*, Sept. 3, 1910; Ralph W. Tyler to George A. Green, Jan. 9, 1912, Taft Papers. On Napier, see Meier, *Negro Thought*, pp. 253–54; J. W. Gibson and W. H. Crogman, *Progress of A Race, or the Remarkable Advancement of the American Negro* (Atlanta, 1902), pp. 567–69.

[39] On the diplomatic and consular appointments, see *Republican Campaign Text-Book: 1912*, pp. 239–40. On the Liberian issue, see Louis R. Harlan, "Booker T. Washington and the White Man's Burden," *American Historical Review*, 71 (Jan. 1966), 441–67; Mathews, pp. 241–54; J. H. Mower, "The Republic of Liberia," *Journal of Negro History*, 32 (July 1947), 265–306; U.S., Congress, Senate, *Affairs in Liberia*, 61st Cong., 2d sess., Senate Doc. 457 (March 25, 1910).

collector of internal revenue in New York; Robert H. Terrell, judge of the Municipal Court of the District of Columbia; and Ralph W. Tyler, auditor of the Navy.[40]

But Taft remained true to his original promise of not forcing Negroes on the South. During the 1912 campaign he told his campaign chairman Charles D. Hilles that he did "not intend to appoint any except . . . to places in the central government where the appointments will not prejudice the race by bringing the Southern whites into hostility with them."[41] Negroes close to the administration worked hard to present Taft's record on appointments in a favorable light. For example, in 1912 Tyler prepared a number of detailed lists of presidential appointees to be used by Negro politicians in defending the president. Booker T. Washington staunchly defended the president's appointment policy in public. "The present administration has always been alive to the interest of the Negro," he wrote in July 1912 in a statement for campaign use. It "has sought from time to time to place colored men of distinguished ability and character in important positions, not only in recognition of the worth of those individuals but that they might be held up as an object lesson to other members of their race. Without undue self-praise, I think I can safely say that this administration has gone further in placing colored men in distinguished and high positions than is true of any administration in the past."[42]

Actually, even by the highest administration estimates, the number of blacks who held important federal government positions anywhere in the country had increased little since McKinley. In August 1912 Tyler was able to find only forty-four with presidential appointments, including those retained from the Roosevelt administration and the twelve with diplomatic or consular posts. This list included several performing essentially routine jobs, like Mingo Sanders, a Medal of Honor winner who had been dismissed from the army in 1906 as a result of the Brownsville affray and who was made a special messenger by Taft in August 1912.[43]

In a number of other areas Negroes learned that the assistance

40 Tyler to George A. Green, Jan. 9, 1912, Tyler to Taft, Feb. 9, 1912, and "Colored Federal Officials Appointed by President Taft," a list prepared by Tyler and dated Aug. 5, 1912, Taft Papers.

41 Taft to Hilles, Aug. 3, 1912, *ibid.*

42 Washington memorandum, dated July 20, 1912, quoted in Mathews, pp. 238–39. See also Booker T. Washington, *My Larger Education* (Garden City, N.Y., 1911), pp. 172–73.

43 "Colored Federal Officials Appointed by President Taft," Aug. 5, 1912, Taft Papers.

they were likely to receive from the federal government was decidedly limited. The Washington *Bee* continued its investigations into discrimination and segregation in federal government employment and reported that the problem was increasing. For example, in the Department of the Interior, Negro laborers were denied regular hours and forced to do night work, even though Secretary Richard A. Ballinger had not ordered any done. Many complained that they were treated worse than convicts.[44] In an "Open Letter to President Taft" on January 7, 1911, editor Chase asked Taft what he intended to do about discrimination in the executive departments. He particularly attacked Attorney General George W. Wickersham. There is no evidence of any presidential response. At other times the *Bee* called attention to discrimination in the War, Navy, and Post Office Departments. Negroes complained that they could not receive promotions, although their fellow white employees were regularly advanced. Moreover, the practice of department heads choosing appointees from among the top three candidates certified as eligible by the Civil Service Commission continued to be used in a racially discriminatory manner. In early 1912 Whitefield McKinlay presented Taft with a number of grievances of this nature, but the administration took no action.[45]

Prospects for Republican action on disfranchisement were even less favorable. Taft's assurances to the South made a mockery of the 1908 Republican platform pledge to enforce the Thirteenth, Fourteenth, and Fifteenth Amendments. Congressional action was no more likely than executive. A bill for the reapportionment of the House of Representatives according to the 1910 census was passed in 1911 without any reference to the Fourteenth Amendment and the reduction of southern representation.[46] The most persistent interest in the Fourteenth and Fifteenth Amendments was shown by a few southern congressmen, notably Hardwick of Georgia and Under-

44 Washington *Bee*, Nov. 6, 1911.

45 Constance McLaughlin Green, *Washington: Capital City, 1879–1950* (Princeton, N.J., 1963), p. 210; Thomas A. Johnson to McKinlay, March 2, 1912, Taft Papers; August Meier and Elliott Rudwick, "The Rise of Segregation in the Federal Bureaucracy, 1900–1930," *Phylon*, 28 (Summer 1967), 180–81. See also *Crisis*, 3 (Feb. 1912), 141, and J. Milton Waldron to Taft, June 10, 1911, Taft Papers, for related complaints about the failure of the army to promote Negro soldiers and the lack of Negro officers.

46 U.S., Congress, House, *Apportionment of Representatives*, 61st Cong., 3d sess., H. Rept. 1911 (Jan. 13, 1911); *ibid.*, 62d Cong., 1st sess., H. Rept. 12 (April 25, 1911); U.S. Congress, Senate, *Apportionment of Representatives*, 62d Cong., 1st sess., Senate Rept. 94 (July 6, 1911), and pt. 2 (July 31, 1911).

wood of Alabama, who introduced several resolutions for their repeal.[47]

Test of northern sentiment about the Negro's disfranchisement in the South arose over the proposed constitutional amendment for the popular election of United States senators. On January 11, 1911, Senator William E. Borah of Idaho presented a report of the Senate Judiciary Committee favoring such a reform. However, the committee's proposal included an amendment, sponsored by southern Democrats, taking away Congress's power, as stated in Article I, section 4 of the Constitution, to alter state regulations pertaining to the times, places, and manner of holding elections for senators. This change was intended, of course, to prevent any possible basis for federal interference with the South's franchise laws. Determined to win passage of the popular election amendment, the Senate insurgents, with the exception of Albert J. Beveridge of Indiana, were willing to agree to the provision in order to win southern support.[48]

Senate conservatives immediately seized upon the southern provision as raising the wholly new issue of placing limits upon congressional authority over the regulation of federal elections. Senator George Sutherland, a Republican from Utah, countered the committee version by offering an amendment to restore the resolution to its original form.[49] A few weeks of heated debate followed, during which the question of Negro suffrage played a central role. Senator Thomas H. Carter, a Republican from Montana, asserted that the adoption of the southern amendment "would give substantial though limited national sanction to the disfranchisement of the Negroes in the Southern States."[50] Senators Chauncey M. Depew of New York, Henry Cabot Lodge of Massachusetts, and other conservatives agreed. Seldom in recent years had so many Old Guard Republicans indicated such concern for the political rights of Negroes.

But their interest failed to impress the insurgents. Senator Borah in particular took up this point. In a long speech on February 16 he denounced the North for playing "the hypocrite or the moral coward on this Negro question." It had no business telling the South how to handle a problem not found in its own section. Moreover, Borah

47 *Congressional Record*, 61st Cong., 1st sess., vol. 44, pt. 2, pp. 1364, 1689, and pt. 4, p. 4387; *ibid.*, 62d Cong., 1st sess., vol. 47, pt. 1, pp. 184, 270.

48 *Ibid.*, 61st Cong., 3d sess., vol. 46, pt. 1, pp. 766, 847; U.S., Cong., Senate, *Report to Accompany S. J. Res. 134*, 61st Cong., 3d sess., Senate Rept. 961 (Jan. 11, 1911). On the fight for the Seventeenth Amendment, see George H. Haynes, *The Senate of the United States* (Boston, 1938), I, 106–16; Claudius O. Johnson, *Borah of Idaho* (New York, 1936), pp. 124–28.

49 *Cong. Rec.*, 61st Cong., 3d sess., vol. 46, pt. 1, p. 847.

50 *Ibid.*, pt. 2, p. 1222.

added, if Congress already did have such authority under Article I, section 4, why had it not exercised it to protect the Negro? A narrow constructionist on this matter, Borah denied that the section in question gave Congress any such power, and he insisted that it ought to cease handing Negroes "soporific applications of rhetoric" and "give him the substantial food of hard facts and simple truths." For Borah this meant letting Negroes know that "no law will be proposed, no statute passed, no voice will be raised in this Chamber again for years. The silence of the last decade will be followed by the silence of the next."[51]

The insurgents did not succeed. On February 24 the Sutherland amendment was adopted, over the opposition of southerners and several insurgents, by a vote of 50 to 37. The resolution for a constitutional amendment, which had thus been restored to its original form, required a two-thirds majority for passage. Lacking full southern support, it was narrowly defeated four days later by a vote of 54 to 33.[52] The controversy delayed congressional passage of the Seventeenth Amendment by only a little over a year. But the episode demonstrated that Republican senators, whether progressives or conservatives, had little concern for the political rights of black Americans.

Another test of the administration's and Congress's attitude was presented by the continued occurrences of lynching, mob violence, and other forms of physical assault against Negroes. The annual toll of lynching deaths dropped only slightly during the Taft presidency.[53] Nevertheless, Taft could find no basis for federal action, and he was reluctant to make any public reference to the problem. On May 31, 1911, a delegation from the newly organized National Association for the Advancement of Colored People, the National Independent Political League, and the Constitution League met with Taft in the White House and asked him to request congressional action. "Repeated appeals have been made to Governors, state legislatures and sheriffs to prevent lynchings, but to no avail," they declared. "The spirit of murder and lawlessness has spread to

[51] *Ibid.*, pt. 3, pp. 2656–57.

[52] *Ibid.*, pt. 4, pp. 3307, 3639; New York *Times*, Feb. 25, March 1, 1911.

[53] According to the National Association for the Advancement of Colored People, *Thirty Years of Lynching in the United States, 1889–1918* (New York, 1919), p. 29, the following number of lynchings occurred during the Taft years:

Year	*Negro*	*Total*
1909	75	89
1910	80	90
1911	63	71
1912	61	64

such an alarming extent in this country until human life—if it be that of a colored person—is not safe any where in America." Taft replied that he could not "ask Congress to do what it has no power to do. . . . The remedy must be sought through the State governments."[54] In the light of the persistent failure of the states to act, this was useless advice. Taft's belief that congressional action would not be constitutional was widely shared, but his reluctance to use the prestige of his office to help create a climate of opinion against lynching was difficult to defend. Tyler pleaded with him "to take some step to generate a popular and effective sentiment against the crime of lynching." As a start Tyler suggested calling a meeting of governors.[55] In November the NAACP expressed great regret that in the face of lawlessness and even burnings at the stake, "President Taft has not as yet seen fit to voice a single public protest or recommend any course of action."[56] Not until the spring of 1912, during the hotly contested presidential primary campaign, did Taft publicly condemn lynching, in an address before a black audience in Washington, D.C.[57] The Republican national convention that summer adopted a brief plank which merely called upon "the people . . . to condemn and punish lynchings and other forms of lawlessness."

Taft's administration, like Roosevelt's, showed considerably more initiative in dealing with peonage. Action initiated during the Roosevelt years led to the most important decision by the United States Supreme Court involving a contract labor law, *Bailey* v. *Alabama*, which was decided on January 3, 1911. Alonzo Bailey, a Negro, had accepted a $15.00 advance payment from a company in return for signing a contract to work for one year at the rate of $12.00 a month. Of this sum $1.25 was to be applied to his debt. After about a month he left his employment without having paid back his obligation. He was then arrested and convicted under an Alabama law which held that his failure to perform the contracted services was *prima facie* evidence of intent to defraud. Bailey was sentenced to pay a fine of $30.00 and costs, or in default thereof to work 20 days to pay off the fine and 116 for the costs. On appeal the Alabama Supreme Court upheld the conviction and the statute in question. But the United States Supreme Court ruled that the *prima facie* sec-

[54] NAACP to Taft, May 31, 1911, and Taft's statement to delegation, May 31, 1911, Taft Papers.

[55] Tyler to Taft, Aug. 22, 1911, *ibid.* There is no reply from Taft in the Taft Papers.

[56] NAACP resolution, Nov 15, 1911, File 158260, Record Group 60, National Archives.

[57] Washington *Bee*, April 13, 1912.

tion of the Alabama law was unconstitutional under the Thirteenth Amendment.[58]

This ruling did not halt the practice of peonage. Alabama and other southern states continued to pass and apply laws that promoted involuntary servitude, while convictions under federal antipeonage statutes were extremely difficult to obtain. Nevertheless, Attorney General Wickersham attempted to enforce the federal laws relating to peonage. On October 31, 1910, he requested all the United States attorneys in states where peonage seemed to be a problem to prepare a special report about cases in their districts, prosecutions, and state laws that could be used to produce involuntary servitude.[59] The reports from some states, notably Alabama, Florida, Georgia, and Mississippi, were very revealing. The United States attorney for the Southern District of Georgia, Alexander Akerman, reported that since January 1, 1909, there had been six indictments by grand juries under the antipeonage laws but that subsequent convictions were extremely difficult to obtain regardless of the evidence. Moreover, grand juries refused to return indictments in over half the cases that Akerman considered worthy of "vigorous prosecution," "We are almost daily called upon by negroes in a state of abject fear," reported Akerman. Georgia's contract labor law accounted for the majority of the instances of peonage in that state, but the problem went beyond that. He felt that if Congress would enact a short and simple statute keeping close to the language of the Thirteenth Amendment and with milder penalties it would be far easier to obtain convictions than under the existing federal antipeonage statutes.[60] The United States attorney in Oxford, Mississippi, William D. Frazee, reported that after a wealthy planter was convicted and sentenced in 1908 on a peonage charge, the crime, in a technical sense, had declined in his area. However, his investigations occasionally showed the existence

[58] *Bailey* v. *Alabama*, 219 U.S. 219 (1911). See also Pete Daniel, "Up from Slavery and Down to Peonage: The Alonzo Bailey Case," *Journal of American History*, 57 (Dec. 1970), 654–70. Deeply concerned about the case, Washington secretly organized support for Bailey's suit.

[59] See File 50–0, Record Group 60, National Archives. The extensive files on peonage for these years in the records of the Department of Justice, National Archives, give some suggestion of the great scope of the problem. Although Wickersham pressed the federal attorneys to act vigorously, I could find no correspondence on the subject by President Taft in the National Archives or in the Taft Papers. Wickersham not only wanted federal action under the act of March 2, 1867, but also recommended use of other statutes relating to the deprivation of federal civil rights of citizens or aliens on account of race, color, or alienage.

[60] Akerman to Attorney General Wickersham, Nov. 9, 1910, File 50–0, Record Group 60, National Archives.

of "involuntary servitude, or slavery pure and simple" without a condition of indebtedness. "This is a violation of the 13th amendment to the Constitution of the United States: but no statute has ever been enacted by Congress imposing a penalty that exactly covers the case."[61]

In his annual report for 1911 Wickersham requested amendments to the federal statutes, including a revision along the lines suggested by Akerman.[62] But neither Taft nor Congress responded. Wickersham also insisted that the Justice Department continue its work in the field. Investigations and prosecutions in Alabama led to the Supreme Court case in 1914 of *United States* v. *Reynolds,* which held that another Alabama law designed to promote peonage was an unconstitutional violation of the Thirteenth Amendment.[63]

In 1912 the Republican party boasted that Taft's administration had "done much toward stamping out peonage in the South."[64] The claim was exaggerated. The Department of Justice deserved credit for its work, but neither Congress nor the country generally recognized the magnitude of the problem. The ignorance and helplessness of many southern Negroes made them easy prey for those who could profit by their labor. Involuntary servitude was still very much a fact of life in America fifty years after emancipation.

Black Americans had ample cause for dissatisfaction with Repub-

[61] Frazee to Attorney General Wickersham, Jan. 5, 1911, *ibid.*

[62] *Annual Report of the Attorney-General of the United States* (Washington, D.C., 1911), p. 27. The report of the Immigration Commission (Dillingham Commission), presented on Dec. 5, 1910, included a brief section on peonage which noted the many complaints that had arisen concerning immigrant laborers. But it had nothing on the far more serious problem of Negro peonage (U.S., Congress, Senate, *Reports of the Immigration Commission,* 61st Cong., 3d sess., Senate Doc. 747 [Dec. 5, 1910], II, 443).

[63] *United States* v. *Reynolds,* 235 U.S. 133 (1914). This case involved the nature of the labor contracts used extensively in certain counties of Alabama. After a Negro had been convicted of some petty offense (among the offenses listed on contracts in the files of the Department of Justice were "abusive language," "vagrancy," "false pretenses," "horse racing," and "changing name"), his fine and costs would be paid by a planter. In return the Negro was induced to sign a contract binding him to labor for the planter to pay off that debt. Even a small fine could lead to a term of forced labor for several months. Many such contracts may be found in U.S. Attorney: Alabama Southern, Peonage Cases, 1907–1912, Box 12, Record Group 118, National Archives. See also George W. Wickersham to William H. Armbrecht, Aug. 22, 1912, File 50–106, Record Group 60, *ibid.,* for material on Wickersham's role in prosecuting such cases.

[64] *Republican Campaign Text-Book: 1912,* p. 241. See also Cyrus Field Adams, *The Republican Party and the Afro-American: A Book of Facts and Figures* (New York, 1912), p. 21.

lican leadership, a dissatisfaction that would have been troublesome in 1912 even had the party remained united. But when Roosevelt broke with Taft and began his own campaign for the presidential nomination, the Negro question took on a new significance. In catering to southern white prejudices, Taft had long-range hopes of building a meaningful GOP in the South. In 1912, however, his immediate objective was to control the national convention, and for this purpose the regular southern organizations, which still included some Negroes, were very useful. Moreover, once he was nominated, it would be desirable to keep border and northern state black voters loyal, especially if the election were close. On January 24, 1912, Taft conferred at some length in the White House with five Negro officeholders about the best tactics to take to present his policies in a favorable light. Among other things they recommended that Taft should insist that the Civil War amendments be upheld and that he make it clear that he would oppose any effort to nullify them. They also wanted him to explain that his inaugural statement had not been meant to imply that he would appoint no Negroes in the South but only that he intended to act with discretion. In addition they asked him to express sympathy for the injustices suffered by Negroes.[65] The long memorandum was actually a summary of Taft's numerous sins of commission and omission. There was obvious need to present the president in a better light if he were to win and maintain the support of Negro leaders.

On March 12 a group of eighteen bishops, fifty-seven ministers, and several black educators from thirteen northern and five southern states issued a statement declaring that "at no time, since the Negro has been a citizen, has he been so thoroughly ignored as a part and parcel of this great government, as he has been since William Howard Taft has been President of the United States." Negroes should support Roosevelt, they said, despite Brownsville. Give him "a chance to right a hasty act," for he is "the only man . . . in the Republican Party who will revive the principles of Lincoln, Grant and Stevens from their shattered and disorganized state."[66]

Taft made some effort to counter such sentiment. On April 9 he

65 Present were Henry Lincoln Johnson, William H. Lewis, Whitefield McKinlay, James C. Napier, and Ralph W. Tyler (Washington *Bee*, Jan. 27, 1912; memorandum dated Jan. 12, 1912, Ralph W. Tyler to Taft, Feb. 9, 1912, and "Memorandum for the President," Feb. 9, 1912, Taft Papers).

66 *Negroes against Taft* (n.p., n.d), pamphlet in scrapbook of "Campaign Literature: 1912," Roosevelt Memorial Association Collection, Widener Library, Harvard University (hereafter cited as RMA Collection).

spoke to a Negro audience at the Metropolitan Methodist Church in Washington, D.C., and publicly condemned lynching for the first time since he became president.[67] This was his principal preconvention effort. W. E. B. Du Bois requested that he prepare a fuller statement of his views on black people for publication in the NAACP's journal, the *Crisis*, but Tyler advised Taft not to publish such a piece, possibly fearing the divisive effects of any involvement with known enemies of Booker T. Washington. Instead the White House staff settled for sending Du Bois a copy of Taft's April 9 speech.[68]

During the bitter preconvention struggle between Roosevelt and Taft, Washington declined to take sides publicly. Nevertheless he was very concerned about the lily-whites in the South. In March he warned Taft that they were completely eliminating Negroes from party councils in Virginia, North Carolina, and Texas, and he expressed fear that such actions would alienate "hundreds and thousands of Negro votes in the North and West, where the Negroes' votes are counted," without gaining a single electoral vote. Washington claimed that in most of the other southern states the Republican party still included Negroes; yet it was just as effective as in states where the lily-whites were strong.[69]

For the moment, the complexion of the state organizations was less important to Taft than their loyalty. To win renomination he needed delegates, whether black or white. Fortunately for Taft the 1908 convention had not reduced the representation of the southern states; in 1912 he, like so many of his predecessors, was able to take advantage of the southern rotten boroughs that provided many delegates but no electoral votes. The South was allotted 252 seats, or nearly half the number needed for a convention majority. To begin with such a base of delegates was therefore very important. Roosevelt had to fight for as many of these seats as possible to keep his chances alive; for this reason, of the 254 contests, most came from the South. Had Roosevelt been able to win 40 or 50 of them he could have at least prevented Taft's renomination. With a few more he would have won. But the national committee, which began its hearings at Chicago on June 7, was loyal to the incumbent president. All but 19 of the contested seats were awarded to Taft.[70]

After that the only thing that could stop Taft was to entice as

[67] Washington *Bee*, April 13, 1912.

[68] Du Bois to Charles D. Hilles, April 13, 1912, Taft Papers.

[69] Washington to Hilles, March 29, 1912, *ibid.*

[70] George E. Mowry, *Theodore Roosevelt and the Progressive Movement* (Madison, Wis., 1946), p. 239.

many delegates as possible to support Roosevelt. Tremendous pressure was brought to bear upon the 60 or more Negro delegates pledged to Taft. An agent from the Roosevelt camp, Ormsby McHarg, was sent to work on them, and soon charges and countercharges of corruption flew. "Negroes Tell of Bribes to Beat Taft" headlined a typical story in the New York *Times*.[71] Some of the alleged bribes were in the form of payments that the Negro delegates received to cover their expenses at the national convention, a practice that had prevailed for some time. The extent to which votes were actually influenced by the exchange of money cannot, of course, be determined. Tyler circulated among the Negro delegates, doing his best to keep them loyal, and promised Taft that they could be counted upon.[72] On June 22, Taft was renominated on the first ballot with most of the Negroes standing firm to their pledges.

The role played by the Negro delegates became the subject of considerable discussion. Taft naturally praised their conduct. "You stood like a solid rock" he said to a group of them who called at the White House on July 18.[73] Victor Rosewater, the Republican national chairman, minimized their alleged misconduct. Some changed their minds, he admitted, but he found them no less dependable than white delegates. William Jennings Bryan viewed the matter quite differently. Corruption and uncertain loyalties, he asserted, were characteristic of the Negro delegates.[74] After the convention the Roosevelt forces placed great emphasis upon the alleged scandal of the southern delegations, although they did not, of course, mention the pressure they had put upon the Negro delegates to change sides.[75] The *Nation* referred to the part played by the Negro delegates as "altogether deplorable," but it blamed the white Republican politicians who had used money to corrupt black politicians for years. Negroes saw the matter in a different perspective. Chase, a Taft supporter, argued that the events at Chicago proved that the

71 June 18, 1912. See also *Crisis*, 4 (Sept. 1912), 235–36.

72 Tyler to Charles D. Hilles, June 8, 1912, Tyler to Taft, June 21, 1912, Taft Papers.

73 *Republican Campaign Text-Book: 1912*, p. 246.

74 Victor Rosewater, *Backstage in 1912: The Inside Story of the Split Republican Convention* (Philadelphia, 1932), pp. 99–101; Bryan, *A Tale of Two Conventions* (New York, 1912), pp. 7–9.

75 For example, see the "official account" of the formation of the Progressive party, George H. Payne, *The Birth of the New Party or Progressive Democracy* (n.p., 1912), pp. 128–52, and the following editorials by Theodore Roosevelt: "Mr. Taft's Majority: An Analysis," *Outlook*, 101 (July 6, 1912), 520–21; "Thou Shalt Not Steal," *ibid.*, 101 (July 13, 1912), 571–76; "Two Phases of the Chicago Convention," *ibid.*, 101 (July 20, 1912), 620–30.

Negro could not be bought. Du Bois, who was disgusted with both Taft and Roosevelt, read the matter in still another light. The effort by Roosevelt's cohorts to purchase the votes of the Negro delegates proved their lack of respect for the black man.[76]

The administration's laissez-faire conservatism on the race question was reflected in the 1912 Republican platform. Failing to mention the Negro by name, it merely called upon the people to show greater interest in public affairs and to condemn lynching and other forms of lawlessness. At least the Republicans could not be accused of arousing false hopes by making wild promises. A few campaign documents, such as the *Republican Campaign Text-Book* and a sixty-four-page pamphlet prepared by Assistant Register of the Treasury Cyrus Field Adams on *The Republican Party and the Afro-American: A Book of Facts and Figures,* said considerably more. But even in these the emphasis was on the defense of past policies and a condemnation of the Democrats, rather than on an explication of programs to meet present and future needs.[77]

Adams was but one of the Negroes holding presidential appointments who labored diligently for Taft in 1912. Ralph W. Tyler, William H. Lewis, Henry L. Johnson, among others, all gave their services to the same cause. Although the split between Taft and Roosevelt was painful and embarrassing to Booker T. Washington, after Taft's renomination he too endorsed the Republican ticket.[78] So did most Negro politicians, who apparently concluded that their interests would be best served by maintaining a record of party regularity.

One of the few Negro delegates to support Roosevelt at the Republican convention was Perry Howard of Mississippi, a man who had the distinction of having been selected by both of his state's competing conventions. When Roosevelt walked out of the national convention, Howard followed him over to the rump meeting at Orchestra Hall. Later he appeared in Chicago as a delegate to the

76 *Nation,* 94 (June 20, 1912), 606; Washington *Bee,* June 29, 1912; *Crisis,* 4 (Sept. 1912), 235–36.

77 Adams first prepared such a book as a campaign document in 1908. On his role in 1912, see Franklin MacVeagh to Taft, Aug. 17, 1912; Cyrus F. Adams to Taft, Aug. 22, Sept. 11, and Oct. 21, 1912; Taft to Adams, Oct. 22, 1912, Taft Papers. For a rebuttal to Adams by the Progressives, see "The Bull Moose Party and the Negro," *Progressive Bulletin,* 1 (Oct. 7, 1912), 10.

78 Mathews, pp. 238–39. Washington sent a memorandum to Taft praising his administration. See also Lewis's attack on the Progressive party and defense of the Taft administration in the Boston *Evening Transcript,* Sept. 12, 1912, reprinted in Leslie H. Fishel, Jr., and Benjamin Quarles, eds., *The Negro American: A Documentary History* (Glenview, Ill., 1967), pp. 388–89.

Progressive convention, and there too he found that the race question was a matter of considerable contention.[79] Roosevelt's decision to form a third party presented black voters with a new, non-Democratic alternative to the Republicans. Although many harbored bitter memories of the Brownsville affair and remained disillusioned by the later years of Roosevelt's presidency, the idea of backing the Progressives had some attraction. For one thing Roosevelt's supporters included many social reformers, some of whom, like Jane Addams, were committed to racial justice. At first there seemed at least a possibility that the Progressive party might be induced into taking a strong stand on Negro rights.

It was a false promise. Attempts by Addams and others from the NAACP to have a strong plank in favor of the repeal of discriminatory laws and on behalf of equal voting rights written into the Progressive platform failed.[80] Their hopes were further dashed by Roosevelt's decision to create a lily-white party in the South. Roosevelt had wished to say as little as possible on the question of Negro participation in the party. But when several southern states sent black delegates to the national convention and their places were contested by whites, it became necessary to come to a decision about the composition of the southern parties. Understandably, Roosevelt resented the role of the southern delegates had played at the recent Republican convention. Representing states that would give the party no electoral votes, they had, by remaining loyal to Taft, deprived Roosevelt of the presidential nomination. Nearly one-fourth of these delegates were black despite the fact that Negroes no longer voted in significant numbers in most of the South. Indeed, Roosevelt believed that the Republican party had failed to win broad popular support in the South precisely because of its racial identification. Accepting the advice of his chief southern supporter, John M. Parker of New Orleans, Roosevelt decided that the Progressives must not make this same mistake. Theirs would be a lily-white party. On August 1, just before the Bull Moosers assembled for their national convention, he stated these views in a letter to Julian Harris of At-

79 Rosewater, p. 98. Roosevelt had considered having Howard second his nomination at the Republican convention (Roosevelt to Sidney D. Redmond, June 11, 1912, in Morison, ed., *Roosevelt Letters*, VII, 561). Ironically, Howard subsequently was unseated at the Progressive convention by a lily-white.

80 Charles Flint Kellogg, *NAACP: A History of the National Association for the Advancement of Colored People*, Vol. I: 1909–1920 (Baltimore, 1967), p. 155; Allen F. Davis, "The Social Workers and the Progressive Party, 1912–1916," *American Historical Review*, 69 (April 1964), 676–77; Allen F. Davis, *Spearheads for Reform: The Social Settlements and the Progressive Movement, 1890–1914* (New York, 1967), pp. 198–201.

lanta that was immediately made public. Trying to soften the blow to Negroes, he reiterated his belief in "treating each man on his worth as a man," and he welcomed them into the party organization in the northern and border states where they were accepted as voters. As for the South, however, the Progressives had to face reality. They must not imitate the Republican rotten-borough system and have a party alienated from the majority of the community. There it had to be a white man's party, at least for the time being. Only in this manner could justice ultimately be done to all.[81]

When the provisional national committee of the Progressive party met to draw up the preliminary roll of delegates, it either had to ratify Roosevelt's decision or repudiate its leader. The long discussions about the nature of the party revealed the lily-white or even racist inclinations of many Progressives. For example, on August 3, after a long debate about the voting rights of the territories at the convention, Medill McCormick of Illinois had this to say concerning Hawaii: "Now, as I understand it, gentlemen, this is to be a white man's party. Are we going to go back upon this proposition and confer upon 70,000 Asiatics or other foreigners who are out there, the right to vote in this convention?"[82] John M. Parker agreed. It had to be a white man's party, at least in the South. But this identification worried some northern members. William Flinn of Pennsylvania declared: "I am not going to join any white man's party. I live in a particularly intelligent state, and the negro in our state is no trouble to us, none whatever. . . . I could not sit in a convention that would be designated a white man's party." Flinn felt the policy would kill the party in Pennsylvania, although he admitted that if he lived in the South he might well feel like Parker.[83]

Roosevelt's letter to Julian Harris provided a way out of this difficulty. In the South the party would be lily-white; in the North it could be otherwise. No overall labels were necessary. Matthew Hale of Massachusetts felt that all members of the committee could agree

[81] Roosevelt to Julian La Rose Harris, Aug. 1, 1912, in Morison, ed., *Roosevelt Letters*, VII, 584–90. See also Arthur S. Link, ed., "Correspondence Relating to the Progressive Party's 'Lily White' Policy in 1912," *Journal of Southern History*, 10 (Nov. 1944), 480–90; Link, "The Negro as a Factor in the Campaign of 1912," *Journal of Negro History*, 32 (Jan. 1947), 81–99; Link, "Theodore Roosevelt and the South in 1912," *North Carolina Historical Review*, 23 (July 1946), 313–24; George E. Mowry, "The South and the Progressive Lily White Party of 1912," *Journal of Southern History*, 6 (May 1940), 237–47.

[82] "Official Report of the Proceedings of the Provisional National Progressive Committee . . ." (Aug. 3–5, 1912), p. 47, typed MS, RMA Collection. Quoted by permission of the Harvard College Library.

[83] *Ibid.*, pp. 51–52.

to this, and he proposed a resolution endorsing Roosevelt's positions. Hale's comments about the Negro members of the contesting delegations made his order of priorities clear. "I don't care whether their fathers are apes," he said. "It is not the question, the question is whether our action here is going to hurt Colonel Roosevelt's candidacy, or whether it is going to help it."[84] By August 5 the provisional national committee had completed its work. It failed to reach a decision in the Georgia contest, and the state went unrepresented at the convention. But it seated the white delegations from Alabama, Florida, and Mississippi. It also went on record as unanimously endorsing the views expressed in Roosevelt's letter, and it passed a resolution recognizing the inherent right of each state to determine the qualifications and manner of election of its own delegates to national conventions.[85]

Roosevelt arrived at Chicago on August 5. The alarm of northern Negroes over the party's lily-white stand was pointed out to him, but he was not deterred. After an all-night session the credentials committee accepted the decisions of the provisional national committee, and on August 6 its report was adopted by the convention. All contesting black delegates from the South were purged from the roll.[86] On the same day Roosevelt delivered his speech, "A Confession of Faith." Near the end he was interrupted by a number of questions from the audience. One concerned the problem of Negro representation. "No man can ask me a question that I am afraid of," retorted Roosevelt. He then reiterated the stand he took in his letter to Julian Harris. Also, he pointed out that the Progressives, unlike the Republicans, had Negro delegates from states outside of the South. Thus, "from Maryland and West Virginia there have come to this convention colored delegates sent because they represent an element of colored men who have won the esteem and respect of their white neighbors, so that all the honest and decent men can join in sending delegates of both colors. And they send them here honestly. They send them here of their own free will. . . . I propose to take toward the southern states the exact attitude that we take to West Virginia and Maryland. And I believe that adopting that action we shall naturally and spontaneously see from those

[84] *Ibid.*, p. 212.

[85] *Ibid.*, pp. 265–66; Link, "Theodore Roosevelt and the South in 1912," p. 318. On Aug. 6 the convention approved the provisional national committee's resolution about selection of delegates.

[86] New York *Times*, Aug. 6, 7, 1912; "First National Convention of the Progressive Party Held at Chicago, August 5, 6 & 7, 1912," pp. 138–40, typed MS, RMA Collection.

southern states a repetition of the conditions in West Virginia and Maryland."[87]

Despite this bold stand at the convention, Roosevelt felt defensive about the policy he had laid down for the Bull Moosers. In the August 24 issue of the *Outlook* he attempted a further clarification of "The Progressives and the Colored Man." Again he contrasted Republican hypocrisy with Progressive honesty, noting that black delegates were present from several northern and border states. He included in the latter Tennessee and Arkansas, which had sent uncontested mixed delegations to the Progressive convention. "Unlike the Democratic party, the Progressive party stands for justice and fair dealing toward the colored man; and, unlike the Republican party, it proposes to secure him justice and fair dealing in the only practicable way. . . . Therefore it is merely the part of wisdom to try our plan, which is to try for the gradual re-enfranchisement of the worthy colored man of the South by frankly giving the leadership of our movement to the wisest and justest white men of the South."[88] The Negro delegates to the Progressive convention published a similar defense in an effort to refute the lily-white label. They were proud to be charter members of a new party "which knows no north, no south, no east, no west, no race, no creed, no sex—but only American citizenship as a party requisite."[89]

For at least a few Progressives, like Jane Addams, the decision was hard to accept. Nevertheless, she decided to stay with the new party, believing that its positive and forward-looking aspects outweighed the bad.[90] During the campaign the Progressives made serious efforts to attract black voters in the North and the West, and they established special bureaus for that purpose in New York and Chicago. In Illinois a Negro was selected as one of the party's presidential electors. In Ohio and New York many Negroes were delegates to the state Progressive conventions, and in New York four Negroes

87 "First National Convention of the Progressive Party . . . ," pp. 127–24, *ibid.* Quoted by permission of the Harvard College Library. Roosevelt's speech, "A Confession of Faith," appears in *The Works of Theodore Roosevelt*, (National Ed., New York, 1927), XVII, 254–99, but without the exchange with members of the audience.

88 Roosevelt, "The Progressives and the Colored Man," *Outlook*, 101 (Aug. 24, 1912), 109–12. See also Roosevelt, *Works*, XVII, 300–305.

89 *The Negro Question: Attitude of the Progressive Party toward the Colored Race* (n.p., 1912), p. 14, pamphlet, RMA Collection.

90 *Crisis*, 4 (Sept. 1912), 216; Addams, "The Progressive Party and the Negro," *ibid.*, 5 (Nov. 1912), 30–31; Roosevelt to Amos Pinchot, Dec. 15, 1912, in Morison, ed., *Roosevelt Letters*, VII, 665–66.

were elected to the state committee.[91] Although the national platform had no specific plank on racial issues, some of the northern state organizations adopted their own. For example, Progressives in New York called for the "enforcement in letter and spirit of the Empire State's laws forbidding discrimination on account of race, creed or color."[92] The disparity between the party's position in the North and South emphasized the continuing dilemma American politicians faced in attempting to reconcile different sectional objectives within one national party.

For years dissatisfied Negroes had threatened to abandon the Republican party, but in the absence of a meaningful alternative the defections were never great. In 1912 the possibility existed that a sizable number might actually go over to the new Progressive party or even to the Democrats. A few disgruntled Negro leaders had been flirting with the latter for several years, and some like J. Milton Waldron, Alexander Walters, and William M. Trotter had even cast their lot with the Democrats in 1908. The political vehicle of these radicals was the National Independent Political League. For some time Tyler and other loyal Taft men refused to take that group seriously. In June 1911 he dismissed it contemptuously as a "paper army" of Negro Democrats, mostly from Washington, D.C., who were merely "voteless residents in a voteless community."[93] A year later, however, the threat of a substantial bolt could not be passed off so easily.

After Wilson's nomination in 1912 the Democratic party took the unprecedented step of seeking black votes outside of the South. It approved the establishment of a National Negro Wilson League in Richmond, Virginia, to provide campaign speakers for the North, and it spent money for speakers and literature. Wilson personally acknowledged the National Independent Political League for its work on his behalf.[94] To persuade Negroes to back the Democrats, it was essential to reassure them about Wilson's position. On July 16 he conferred with Waldron and Trotter. Somewhile after this meeting Waldron prepared a summary, from memory, of his understanding of Wilson's views. Oswald G. Villard, a member of the

91 *Negro Year Book: 1913*, p. 15; "The Bull Moose Party and the Negro," *Progressive Bulletin*, 1 (Oct. 7, 1912), 10; James H. Hayes, "Why a Negro Should Be a Progressive," *Progress*, 1 (Nov. 1912), 58–59.

92 "Campaign Literature: 1912," and "Campaign Literature: Progressive: 1913–15, Campaign: 1916," scrapbooks in RMA Collection.

93 Tyler to Charles D. Hilles, June 24, 1911, Taft Papers.

94 Link, "Negro as Factor in Campaign of 1912," p. 85; Meier, *Negro Thought*, p. 187.

NAACP board of directors, sent Wilson a copy of this unauthorized statement on August 14. The day before, Villard had met with Wilson and had come away delighted. Wilson had said he would be president of all the people, would appoint Negroes on their merits, and would speak out against lynching. But he was unwilling to accept the statement attributed to him by Waldron, which claimed that he had promised to veto legislation hostile to Negroes. Wilson wrote to Villard on August 23 denying that he had promised such a veto or that he said he needed Negro votes, and he asked Villard to prepare a revised statement. Villard replied by sending a moderate document written by W. E. B. Du Bois which merely welcomed the support of all citizens and opposed voting laws that discriminated on grounds of race. Even this was too strong for the Democratic candidate. The furthest Wilson was willing to go was a promise contained in a letter to Alexander Walters, then head of the National Colored Democratic League, on October 16. He assured Negroes of his "earnest wish to see justice done them in every matter. . . . Should I become President of the United States they may count upon me for absolute fair dealing and for everything by which I could assist in advancing the interests of their race in the United States."[95]

This statement pointedly omitted reference to specific grievances. Still, it was a dramatic contrast to what any previous Democratic presidential candidate had been willing to promise. Together with their disgust with both Taft and Roosevelt, it was enough to convince a number of black leaders that they should support Wilson. The most notable of them was Du Bois, who, although wary, felt that the experiment was worth the try. He could find little good in any of the major parties, Republican, Progressive, or Democratic. Only the Socialists stood for human rights, but they were out of the running. Therefore, Du Bois concluded that it would be "better to elect Woodrow Wilson President of the United States and prove once [and] for all if the Democratic party dares to be Democratic when it comes to black men. It has proven that it can be in many Northern States and cities. Can it be in the nation? We are willing to risk a trial."[96]

Negro opinion was probably more divided in 1912 than in any

[95] Ray S. Baker, *Woodrow Wilson: Life and Letters* (Garden City, N.Y., 1927–39), III, 387–88; Henry Blumenthal, "Woodrow Wilson and the Race Question," *Journal of Negro History*, 48 (Jan. 1963), 4–5; *Crisis*, 4 (Sept. 1912), 216–17; Fox, p. 167; Kellogg, pp. 157–59; Link, "Negro as Factor in Campaign of 1912," pp. 88–93; Arthur S. Link, *Wilson: The Road to the White House* (Princeton, N.J., 1947), 502–5.

[96] *Crisis*, 5 (Nov. 1912), 29.

previous presidential election. Most of the militant leaders had little use for Roosevelt, a view stemming to a considerable degree from the Brownsville affair and reinforced by his lily-white strategy as a Progressive. Many of this group were willing to take a chance on Wilson. Conservatives, and the officeholders, both of whom were associated with Booker T. Washington, remained loyal to Taft and the Republican party. As for the rank-and-file Negro voters, the estimates are not particularly reliable. In October 1912 the *Crisis* reported that a New York *Times* survey had been able to discover very little support for Roosevelt among blacks. Writing in 1913, however, Kelly Miller estimated that possibly 60 percent of the Negro vote went to the Progressives, with the rest divided approximately evenly between the Republicans and the Democrats. A recent scholar, August Meier, follows Miller, but Arthur S. Link feels that probably the majority of northern Negroes were loyal to the GOP, although he suggests that possibly as many as 100,000 voted for Wilson. All agree that never before had so many Negroes turned against the Republican party.[97]

Taft's southern strategy, which had been the principal reason for Negro disaffection from the GOP, had failed. The prospects for splitting the solid South had largely faded after the 1910 setback, and in 1912 the Republican vote in the South sank to all-time lows. Much, but not all, of this decline can be explained by the loss of votes to the Progressive party, which polled a larger presidential vote than the Republican in most of the South. Nevertheless, the combined totals for Roosevelt and Taft amounted to a smaller percentage of the popular vote than the Republicans alone had received in 1908 in every southern state except Alabama and Louisiana. The Progressives too had failed to cut seriously into the Democratic strength, despite Roosevelt's acceptance of lily-whitism. As Roosevelt lamented several years later, not only had the Progressives found less support in the South than in any other region, but much of the vote they received came "not from among former members of the Democratic Party, but from the best men in the minute Republican Party organizations."[98] A two-party South seemed as far away as ever before.

In the North and border regions the support that Negroes gave the Democrats and Progressives in 1912 did not mean more than a

[97] *Ibid.*, 4 (Oct. 1912), 283; Miller, "The Political Plight of the Negro," *Kelly Miller's Monographic Magazine*, 1 (May 1913), 3; Meier, *Negro Thought*, p. 188; Link, "Negro as Factor in Campaign of 1912," p. 99; *Negro Year Book: 1913*, p. 14.

[98] Roosevelt to T. H. Wannamaker, June 24, 1916, in Morison, ed., *Roosevelt Letters*, VIII, 1079. See also Roosevelt to Whitmell Pugh Martin, June 23, 1916, *ibid.*, pp. 1077–78.

temporary shift away from their historic association with the Republican party. Within a few years the Progressive organization was dead, and the actions of Wilson and the Democrats proved to be bitterly disappointing. Before long most Negroes could see no alternative, however unsatisfactory, than to return to or stay with the GOP. The Democratic interlude provided the Republicans an opportunity, if they cared to take advantage of it, to reconfirm their commitment to the Negro.

CHAPTER V

"All Else Is the Sea" Democratic Interlude–Republican Opportunity

NEGROES who supported Wilson in 1912 gambled that the action of enlightened Democrats would be at least as acceptable as the broken promises and neglect they had received at the hands of the Republicans. But they expected too much. After the inauguration, matters rapidly went from bad to worse. Before the end of 1913 it was obvious that their experimental association with the Democrats had failed. Wilson was far too tied to the anti-Negro southerners within his party to challenge the pressures for racially discriminatory policies. Unsatisfactory though the Republican party had become, the Democrats were not yet an acceptable alternative.

The first grievance was the rapid extension of racial segregation in several of the government departments at Washington, notably the Bureau of Engraving and Printing, the Treasury, and the Post Office.[1] The segregation introduced during the Roosevelt and Taft administration had been limited and apparently without the sanction of highest authority. It was otherwise in 1913. Although Wilson did not specifically order racial segregation in the departments, he knew and approved of it. Yet less than a year had passed since he had promised that Negroes would receive "absolute fair dealing." Responding to many appeals, the NAACP assumed the lead in attempting to reverse the development of this segregation. In answer to a

[1] For general discussions of government racial policies during the Wilson years, see Henry Blumenthal. "Woodrow Wilson and the Race Question," *Journal of Negro History*, 48 (Jan. 1963), 1–21; Charles F. Kellogg, *NAACP: A History of the National Association for the Advancement of Colored People*, vol. I: 1909–1920 (Baltimore, 1967), pp. 155–82; Arthur S. Link, *Wilson: The New Freedom* (Princeton, N.J., 1956), pp. 243–54; George C. Osborn, "The Problem of the Negro in Government, 1913," *Historian*, 23 (May 1961), 330–47; Morton Sosna, "The South in the Saddle: Racial Politics during the Wilson Years," *Wisconsin Magazine of History*, 54 (Autumn 1970), 30–49; Nancy J. Weiss, "The Negro and the New Freedom: Fighting Wilsonian Segregation," *Political Science Quarterly*, 84 (March 1969), 67–79; Kathleen L. Wolgemuth, "Woodrow Wilson and Federal Segregation," *Journal of Negro History*, 44 (April 1959), 158–73.

strong letter of protest from Oswald Garrison Villard in July 1913, Wilson offered the explanation that segregation was not a movement against Negroes, but something done in their own best interests.[2] An official protest from the NAACP board of directors, made public in mid-August, stimulated more adverse comment from blacks.[3] From conservatives aligned with Booker T. Washington to radicals like William Monroe Trotter they decried the administration's policy. In the face of the many protests Wilson's suggestion that a number of influential Negroes approved of such segregation carried little weight. His argument that it protected Negroes and lessened racial prejudice was equally unconvincing. As NAACP secretary Mary C. Nerney observed in a report she prepared in the fall of 1913, "Those segregated are regarded as a people set apart, almost as lepers. Instead of allaying race prejudice, as some of the advocates of segregation would have us believe, recognition has emphasized it. In fact, government approval in some cases has aroused it where it did not exist."[4]

By promoting segregation, the Wilson administration sorely embarrassed those who had advised Negroes to support the Democrats. Villard, who had taken such a position, now warned Wilson that his actions would put an end to that promising development. Segregation was not only wrong, it was also a political blunder, for it gave the Republicans an issue "if they have the sense to use it."[5] As a matter of fact, it was not easy to arouse the interest of Republican leaders. "The safeguarding of the Negro has always been the prime duty of the Republican Party," Villard reminded Senator Elihu Root, and he noted that two progressive senators, Robert M. La-Follette of Wisconsin and Moses E. Clapp of Minnesota, had protested. "Will you not likewise lift up your voice and thus prove the Republican Party true to its ideals on this subject?"[6] Root did not

[2] Wilson to Villard, July 23, 1913, quoted in Ray S. Baker, *Woodrow Wilson: Life and Letters* (Garden City, N.Y., 1927–39), IV, 221. See also Wilson to H. A. Bridgman, Sept. 8, 1913, *ibid.*, p. 223; Kellogg, pp. 161–65. For notes on the cabinet meeting of April 11, 1913, when Postmaster General Albert S. Burleson first brought up the racial question, see *The Cabinet Diaries of Josephus Daniels, 1913–1921*, ed. E. David Cronon (Lincoln, Nebr., 1963), pp. 32–33.

[3] NAACP to Wilson, Aug. 15, 1913, Arthur B. Spingarn Papers, Manuscript Division, Library of Congress; New York *Times*, Aug. 18, 1913.

[4] "Segregation in Government Departments," report of an investigation, New York, Nov. 1, 1913, by Mary Childs Nerney, Spingarn Papers.

[5] Villard, "The President and the Segregation at Washington," *North American Review*, 198 (Dec. 1913), 800–807.

[6] Villard to Root, Aug. 20, 1913, NAACP Papers, Manuscript Division, Library of Congress. Senator Clapp was an active supporter of the NAACP. "With one possible exception," wrote Du Bois, "Senator Clapp is the only member of the Senate who can be absolutely relied on to support every measure in the interests

respond. Nor did congressional Republicans generally show much interest. Clapp was discouraged. "One great political party is arrayed against us and the other evinces very little sympathy with the fight," he wrote to Miss Nerney.[7] Even Clapp was cautious about taking action against segregation, and he warned that an NAACP confrontation with Wilson might just precipitate action on anti-Negro bills then in the Democratic-controlled Congress.[8]

The protests by blacks and liberal whites did have some beneficial effect. In August 1913 the Treasury Department took down its "For Colored" signs in the rest rooms, although in practice segregated facilities were still insisted upon.[9] By 1914 there was some mitigation of the practice in other government departments; at least its advocates were less blatant. Nevertheless, when Wilson conferred with a delegation headed by Trotter on November 12, 1914, he defended segregation as being in the best interest of both races and stated that it would continue.[10] It did, and from time to time instances of newly established separate facilities occurred during the remaining years of the Wilson administration, including such places as the galleries of the Senate, the Senate lunchroom in the Capitol building, and the lunchroom of the Library of Congress.[11]

A second grievance concerned Wilson's attitude toward presidential appointments. Bowing to strong pressure from his southern supporters, Wilson was reluctant to appoint any Negroes to office, especially where they would have supervision over whites. Negroes assumed that members of their race would at least continue to hold their traditional posts. Instead by the spring and summer of 1913 many incumbents had been dismissed and pressure was put on others to resign. Among the more important black officeholders dropped were Assistant Attorney General William H. Lewis, Auditor of the Navy Ralph W. Tyler, and Register of the Treasury James C. Napier.[12] More than a dozen lost their positions in 1913, and others

of colored people, and to fight prejudice and injustices without cessation" (*Crisis*, 11 [April 1916], 306).

[7] Clapp to Mary C. Nerney, Sept. 30, 1913, NAACP Papers.

[8] Clapp to Nerney, Dec. 4, 1913, *ibid.*

[9] Washington *Bee*, Aug. 30, 1913; Kellogg, p. 167; Wolgemuth, p. 171.

[10] New York *Times*, Nov. 13 and 14, 1914; "Race Segregation at Washington," *Independent*, 80 (Nov. 23, 1914), 275; *Crisis*, 9 (Jan. 1915), 119–20; Weiss, p. 71; Stephen R. Fox, *The Guardian of Boston: William Monroe Trotter* (New York, 1970), pp. 179–82.

[11] August Meier and Elliott Rudwick, "The Rise of Segregation in the Federal Bureaucracy, 1900–1930," *Phylon*, 28 (Summer 1967), 181; Kellogg, pp. 181–82.

[12] Kathleen L. Wolgemuth, "Woodrow Wilson's Appointment Policy and the Negro," *Journal of Southern History*, 24 (Nov. 1958), 457–71; Washington *Bee*, May 3, 1913; *Negro Year Book: 1914/15*, p. 27.

soon followed. During that year Wilson nominated only one Negro, Adam E. Patterson, an Oklahoma Democrat, to be register of the Treasury. Senate opposition was great, and Wilson failed to support his nominee; Patterson agreed to withdraw. This post, and others traditionally held by Negroes, went to deserving Democrats. Only in the case of Robert H. Terrell, who was reappointed judge of the District of Columbia Municipal Court in February 1914, did Wilson defy vigorous southern opposition. After a delay of two months the nomination was confirmed.[13] In 1915 the Senate accepted with little protest another Negro, James L. Curtis, to be minister to Liberia. But that was all. Wilson appointed only two Negroes during his first term, retained only eight or nine others, and dropped nearly two dozen.[14]

Another complaint was about increased racial discrimination within the civil service. On May 27, 1914, the Civil Service Commission ordered that photographs accompany all applications.[15] Previously they had been required for positions in the territories, but never for those within the continental United States. The ostensible reason was to prevent fraud by assuring that the person who was appointed was the one who had been examined. Negroes immediately suspected that the order was really directed against them, although when questioned by the NAACP the commission denied the charge. The pictures were for identification only, claimed the acting president of the Civil Service Commission, Charles M. Galloway. Another commissioner, John A. McIlhenny, asserted that the step was taken "without any view to discriminating against any class of applicants."[16] These answers were unconvincing. "There is no doubt in my mind that the order was determined upon as a new means of discouraging the colored applicant for examination," observed one

13 New York *Times*, Feb. 19, March 24, April 25, 1914; Baker, IV, 224; Kellogg, p. 173. On Terrell, see George C. Osborn, "Woodrow Wilson Appoints a Negro Judge," *Journal of Southern History*, 24 (Nov. 1958), 480–93.

14 Wolgemuth, "Wilson's Appointment Policy," pp. 467–68; George B. Tindall, *The Emergence of the New South, 1913–1945* (Baton Rouge, La., 1967), p. 144. The *Republican Campaign Text-Book: 1916*, pp. 379–80, names twenty-five Negroes who were replaced by whites. The *Negro Year Book: 1916/17*, pp. 165–66, lists nine Negroes holding presidential appointments.

15 *Thirty-First Annual Report of the United States Civil Service Commission* (Washington, D.C., 1915), pp. 26–27. See also Lawrence J. W. Hayes, *The Negro Federal Government Worker: A Study of His Classification Status in the District of Columbia, 1883–1938* (Washington, D.C., 1941), pp. 54–55; Paul R. Van Riper, *History of the United States Civil Service* (Evanston, Ill., 1958), pp. 241–42.

16 McIlhenny to James C. Walters, Aug. 3, 1914, NAACP Papers. See also Chapin Brinsmade to McIlhenny, July 23, 1914, Galloway to Brinsmade, July 28, 1914, McIlhenny to Brinsmade, Aug. 29, 1914, *ibid.*

NAACP official after talking with McIlhenny.[17] Joel E Spingarn of the NAACP wrote directly to Wilson requesting that the photograph order be repealed.[18] Wilson did not reply to this letter, and no reversal was forthcoming. The order may not have been directed solely against Negroes, but the effect was still adverse. In 1910 Negroes had comprised a total of 6 percent of the civil service; by 1918 the figure had dropped to 4.9 percent.[19]

The news from Capitol Hill was not much better. Never before had so many discriminatory measures been introduced as in the Democratic 63rd and 64th Congresses. Some were intended to enforce by statute the segregation in the government departments that was then being promoted by less formal methods.[20] Among the others were bills to require segregation in the public transportation of the District of Columbia; to acquire Mexican territory for the purpose of colonizing American Negroes; to forbid the appointment of Negroes as commissioned or noncommissioned officers in the army or navy; to prohibit the enlistment of any Negroes in the armed forces; to prohibit intermarriage in the District of Columbia; to exclude all colored immigrants; and to repeal the Fourteenth and Fifteenth Amendments. Most of these proposals died in committee, and none was passed. But on a few occasions they provided an opportunity for some of the strongest expressions of anti-Negro racism ever heard in Congress.[21]

One of the few congressmen to speak out against such measures was Martin B. Madden, a Republican from a Chicago district with a large black constituency. On June 8, 1914, he delivered a lengthy praise of the service and bravery of Negro troops in America since the Revolution. Noting the recent flood of anti-Negro measures, he

17 Laurence Todd to Chapin Brinsmade, Aug. 27, 1914, *ibid.*

18 Spingarn to Wilson, March 23, 1915, *ibid.*

19 Van Riper, pp. 241–42.

20 See the bills introduced by Congressman B. Aswell of Louisiana, June 10, 1913, and by Congressman Charles G. Edwards of Georgia, Feb. 23, 1914, in *Congressional Record*, 63d Cong., 1st sess., vol. 50, pt. 2, p. 1985, and *ibid.*, 2d sess., vol. 51, pt. 4, p. 3814. Three similar bills were also introduced in the next Congress in Dec. 1915 by Congressman Aswell and Edwards and Carl Vinson of Georgia (*ibid.*, 64th Cong., 1st sess., vol. 53, pt. 1, pp. 14, 24, 295). Aswell's bill included a section providing that no "white clerk or employee [shall] be placed under the orders, direction, or supervision of any person of African blood or descent" (U.S., Congress, House, *Segregation of Clerks and Employees in the Civil Service: Hearings before the Committee on Reform in the Civil Service*, 63d Cong., 2d sess [March 6, 1914], pp. 9–10).

21 See the speech by Senator James K. Vardaman of Mississippi delivered on Feb. 6, 1914, during discussion of the Smith-Lever bill (*Cong. Rec.*, 63d Cong., 2d sess., vol. 51, pt. 3, pp. 3036–40).

appealed to Congress to "call a halt in this matter of color discrimination."[22] Few such defenses of the Negro and equality were heard in Congress at that time.

The Smith-Lever bill for federal aid for agricultural education presented another opportunity for the Negro's friends to be counted. As passed by the House in January 1914, the measure left the state legislatures free to decide which agricultural colleges would receive federal assistance; a southern state could allot all its funds to white and none to black institutions. Some senators openly acknowledged to representatives of the NAACP that such discrimination was intended.[23] In response, an NAACP attorney, J. Chapin Brinsmade, prepared an amendment which was introduced by Senator Wesley L. Jones, a Republican from Washington, on February 5, 1914. It provided that none of the money was to be used by any college that made distinctions on the basis of race or color in its admissions, except that in those states with separate white and black institutions the money could be "equitably divided" between them, subject to the approval of the secretary of Agriculture.[24] On February 7 this amendment was defeated by a vote of 23 to 32. Sixteen of the negative votes were cast by senators from the North or the West.[25] Southern Democrats introduced these anti-Negro measures; but as this vote indicated, Negroes found few defenders among northern Republicans.

The problems that black Americans encountered from the Democratic administration and Congresses were reflections of the maltreatment accorded them throughout the land. North or South, racism was never more respectable. Few Republicans were then inclined to fight for an aggrieved minority, especially one that lacked effective political power. Disfranchised throughout most of the South, Negroes could no longer be considered the base for a Republican revival there. With some local exceptions, their vote was also not regarded as decisive in the border of northern states, certainly not in a presidential contest.

With the Democrats in power, national Republican leaders became more willing than ever before to encourage reform of the party organization in the South. The efforts of the preceding years had

22 *Ibid.*, pt. 10, pp. 10021–25. See also *Segregation of Clerks and Employees in the Civil Service: Hearings* (March 6, 1914), pp. 7–8.

23 Mary C. Nerney to Members of the NAACP, Jan. 27, 1914, Spingarn Papers. On the Smith-Lever Act, see Dewey W. Grantham, Jr., *Hoke Smith and the Politics of the New South* (Baton Rouge, La., 1958), pp. 256–64; Austin F. MacDonald, *Federal Aid: A Study of the American Subsidy System* (New York, 1928), pp. 54–84, Sosna, pp. 42–45.

24 *Cong. Rec.*, 63d Cong., 2d sess., vol. 51, pt. 3, p. 2925; Kellogg, p. 191.

25 *Cong. Rec.*, 63d Cong., 2d sess., vol. 51, pt. 3, p. 3124.

made it clear that most southern whites regarded the GOP as too tainted by Negroes to be an acceptable alternative to the Democrats. Even with disfranchisement, black politicians still played a major role in many of the state parties. The reformers' next move was to work for their elimination so as to make the Republican party in the South truly lily-white and "respectable." For the national organization two related problems were involved. One was the disproportionate influence of the South at national conventions, despite the fact that it had not cast an electoral vote for a Republican presidential candidate since 1876. The other was the important, and allegedly scandalous, role played by southern Negro delegates. The efforts made since the 1890's to reduce the South's representation at national conventions had always been blocked, chiefly because the existing arrangement was useful to the men who controlled the national organization. McKinley, Roosevelt, and Taft all had benefited from the relatively easy manipulation of the southern rotten boroughs. With the Republicans out of the White House it at last became possible to attempt to reduce the size of the southern delegations without arousing the opposition of an incumbent president. Some, but not all, white southerners agreed that this reduction would be a useful first step in making the party more respectable in the South. It would strike at the basis of the Negro politician's influence, lessen corruption, and provide an incentive for state leaders to seek more popular support instead of patronage.

A group of progressive Republican senators and other leaders who met at Chicago from May 10 to 12, 1913, took a tentative step in this direction. As a means of reforming and reuniting their party, they wanted to change the basis of a state's representation at national conventions, to provide that contests would be settled at the state level, and to have delegates to state and national conventions selected by primary elections. All agreed that the South's representation at conventions had to be cut. To effect these reforms the progressives suggested the calling of a special national convention. Conservatives sneered at this idea and the Republican executive committee rejected it when it met in Washington on May 24. But it did appoint a legal committee to study the problem of delegate allotment and to determine if the national committee could by itself change the basis of a state's representation.[26] In November 1913 the legal committee reported that the national committee had no such authority. Shortly afterwards the Republican congressional committee proposed the

[26] New York *Times*, May 8, 11–14, 24, 25, 1913; Howard Scott Greelee, "The Republican Part in Division and Reunion, 1913–1920" (Ph.D. diss., University of Chicago, 1950), pp. 58–63.

summoning of a special national convention. This was turned down by the national committee at its meeting on December 16. Instead it agreed upon a change in the basis of representation that would go into effect when ratified by conventions in enough states to constitute a majority of electoral votes. Under this plan each state would be allotted four delegates-at-large, one delegate for each congressman, and an additional delegate for each congressional district in which the Republican vote for president in 1908 or for congressman in 1914 was at least 7,500. Thus the state organizations would be rewarded for successful efforts to get out the vote and penalized for failures.[27]

By October 1914 twenty-two states, including several in the South, had ratified the plan, and chairman Charles D. Hilles announced that it would be in effect in 1916.[28] Under it there would be 93 fewer delegates than in 1912. Of these losses 78 were sustained by the eleven southern states. It was a damaging blow to one of the last remaining areas of influence of southern Negro politicians, and it alarmed Negroes in other sections as well. Although the reform was not put forth merely as a means of getting rid of Negro delegates, everyone recognized that this had been a major consideration. And such indeed was the result. In 1912 there had been some 62 Negro delegates from the South. Four years later their number was reduced to about 32.[29] With a Democratic administration in power that was clearly hostile to the interests of Negroes, any such diminution of their political influence made their position all the more precarious.

This fact became obvious in 1916 when Republicans showed that they were far more interested in the issues of war and preparedness, and in the reuniting of Bull Moosers with their party, than in the politically unprofitable matter of Negro rights. The platform adopted at the 1916 Republican national convention omitted any specific mention or reference to the Negro and civil rights. The party of Lincoln thus failed to make any official challenge to the anti-Negro actions of the first southern administration since the Civil War.[30]

27 New York *Times*, Nov. 9, Dec. 5, 13, 16–18, 1913; Greelee, pp. 64–66.

28 New York *Times*, Oct. 26, 1914. Of states holding conventions only Texas rejected the new plan.

29 The figures are from the *Negro Year Book: 1921/22*, p. 38. The number of Negro delegates is difficult to determine from available evidence, and the estimates vary somewhat. See also *Crisis*, 10 (May 1915), 28; *Negro Year Book: 1916/17*, p. 37; and S. Herbert Giesy to Robert H. Terrell, Sept. 16, 1914, Robert H. Terrell Papers, Manuscript Division, Library of Congress.

30 The *Republican Campaign Text-Book: 1916*, pp. 376–81, included a section, written by Henry Lincoln Johnson, on "The Negro under Wilson." Although this

Not admiration for the Republicans but disgust with the Democrats accounted for the decision of many Negroes to stay with or return to their traditional party affiliation in 1916. "My distrust and dislike of the attitude of the Administration centered upon Woodrow Wilson," wrote the usually mild-mannered author and diplomat James Weldon Johnson, "and came nearer to constituting keen hatred for an individual than anything I have ever felt." He supported Republican nominee Charles Evans Hughes in order to overthrow the southern oligarchy and maintain the national citizenship rights of Negroes.[31] Many others acted similarly. As for Hughes, said W. E. B. Du Bois, "under ordinary circumstances the Negro must expect from him, as chief executive, the neglect, indifference and misunderstanding that he has had from recent Republican presidents. Nevertheless, he is practically the only candidate for whom we can vote."[32]

There was not much in Hughes's background to suggest any particular interest in or knowledge of the Negro. His record as governor of New York from 1906 to 1910 was admirable, but the experience had done little to enlarge his understanding of the problems of race relations.[33] As a justice of the United States Supreme Court he had no reason to question the wisdom of the separate-but-equal principle of *Plessy* v. *Ferguson* when he wrote an opinion in 1914 that in effect upheld an Oklahoma law requiring separate railroad coaches.[34] Hughes had not been hostile to Negroes; he had been indifferent. During the 1916 campaign he showed no inclination to change.[35]

---

attacked Wilson's treatment of the Negro, it did not state what actions the Republicans would take.

31 *Along This Way: The Autobiography of James Weldon Johnson* (New York: The Viking Press, Inc., 1933), p. 306.

32 *Crisis*, 12 (Oct. 1916), 268. Cf. George A. Myers to James Ford Rhodes, Oct. 26, 1916, in John A. Garraty, ed., *The Barber and the Historian: The Correspondence of George A. Myers and James Ford Rhodes, 1910–1923* (Columbus, Ohio, 1956), p. 58.

33 In Hughes's collected addresses there is only one speech dealing with the Negro question prior to the 1916 campaign, an address delivered at Carnegie Hall in New York on Jan. 17, 1908, at a meeting held in the interest of Tuskegee Institute. In it he upheld the right of Negroes to their chance in life and concluded that "we cannot maintain our democratic ideals as to one set of our people, and ignore them as to others." But he did not accompany this generality with any specific recommendations on how to deal with contemporary problems (*Addresses and Papers of Charles Evans Hughes, Governor of New York, 1906–1908* [New York, 1908], p. 286). Merlo J. Pusey, *Charles Evans Hughes* (New York, 1952), has virtually no references to Negroes or the race issue.

34 *McCabe* v. *Atchison, Topeka & Santa Fe Railway Company*, 235 U.S. 151.

35 In the files on the 1916 compaign in the Hughes Papers, Library of Congress, there is no material bearing on Negroes and their problems.

In September of that year the NAACP sent Hughes a letter asking him to state his views on lynching, disfranchisement, and segregation, all matters on which he had been silent.[36] Hughes declined to answer. Late in the campaign he made one comment on the race issue, telling a group of Negroes in Nashville, Tennessee, that he believed in "equal and exact justice to all" and "the maintenance of the rights of all American citizens, regardless of race or color."[37] Searching for something else to report to black voters, the Republicans' Colored Advisory Committee reprinted a speech Hughes had delivered on November 6, 1906, in which he had condemned lynching, upheld equality before the law, and promised to be governor of all the people.[38] But not much else could be done to demonstrate his interest in racial problems.

Understandably, Negroes developed little enthusiasm for Hughes. Near the end of the campaign Du Bois began to doubt that it was even worthwhile to vote for him at all. Of course, he argued, no intelligent Negro could back Wilson, but one could register a protest by voting for the Socialist Allan I. Benson or by simply staying home on election day. Nevertheless, the evidence suggests that, though they may have been disappointed in the Republican candidate, most blacks who did vote supported Hughes. Few believed that they had any alternative.[39]

By 1916 Negroes had few illusions left about the author of the New Freedom. Still, during Wilson's second term new and serious problems arose, many as a result of the World War. Constant vigilance was needed to protect the rights of Negroes in the armed forces. For example, provision for the training of Negro army officers was made only after a strenuous fight. In the navy Negroes were allowed to serve only as mess corpsmen, and the marines excluded them entirely. Negroes in the army complained, among other things, about abuse from officers, inadequate recreational facilities, and discriminatory treatment by supporting agencies like the YMCA. Wilson tried to deal with some of these problems by appointing Emmett J. Scott, the former secretary to Booker T. Washington, as a special assistant to the secretary of War to advise on Negro matters. But neither

36 *Crisis*, 13 (Nov. 1916), 17.

37 Quoted, *ibid.*, pp. 33–34.

38 *Ibid.*, pp. 7–8.

39 *Ibid.*, p. 12; Arthur S. Link, *Woodrow Wilson and the Progressive Era, 1910–1917* (New York, 1954), p. 251, n. 70. See also Weiss, pp. 75–76; Harold F. Gosnell, *Negro Politicians: The Rise of Negro Politics in Chicago* (Chicago, 1935), pp. 27–28; David Burner, *The Politics of Provincialism: The Democratic Party in Transition, 1918–1932* (New York, 1968), pp. 237, 241.

Scott nor anyone else could find easy answers to problems that were rooted so deeply in the racist attitudes of the country.[40]

Friction between black servicemen and white civilians was common, and at times it led to serious clashes. The worst incident occurred at Houston, Texas, on August 23, 1917, when members of the Negro Twenty-fourth Infantry Regiment rioted after abusive treatment by local police. More than a dozen townspeople were killed and many others were wounded. Punishment of the Negroes was prompt and severe. After a quick court-martial thirteen soldiers were hanged in December 1917, forty-one were sentenced to life imprisonment, and four to shorter terms. As a result of this and another trial, sixteen others were also condemned to death. Appeals to Wilson led to the reprieve of ten, but six were subsequently hanged. No white policemen were brought to trial.[41]

During the war years, outbreaks of mob violence against Negroes increased greatly. At least eighteen major interracial disturbances occurred between 1915 and 1919. The worst was at East St. Louis, Illinois, in early July 1917, where at least nine whites and thirty-nine blacks were killed. The violence culminated during the summer of 1919 with bloody outbreaks in Washington, Chicago, Omaha, and other cities. Alarmed Negroes protested to the White House and requested federal protection of their rights. Thousands marched in a great silent protest parade in New York on July 28, 1917. Wilson's response was discouraging; he could find no basis for federal action.[42] "The black man asks for justice and is given a theory of government," cried Kelly Miller. "He asks for protection and is confronted with a scheme of governmental checks and balances."[43]

Congress conducted an investigation of the East St. Louis riot during the fall of 1917. It took nearly 5,000 pages of testimony but never authorized publication of its hearings.[44] Despite the continued outrages, Wilson remained silent until July 26, 1918, when he finally

40 *Cong. Rec.*, 64th Cong., 1st sess., vol. 53, pt. 1, p. 138, pt. 4, p. 3721, and pt. 12, p. 11,717; Kellogg, pp. 247–75; Fox, pp. 217–21. See also Scott, *The American Negro in the World War* (Washington, D.C., 1919), and John Hope Franklin, *From Slavery to Freedom* (3d ed., New York, 1967), chap. 24, pp. 452–76.

41 Edgar A. Schuler, "The Houston Race Riot, 1917," *Journal of Negro History,* (July 1944), 300–338; Martha Gruening, "Houston: An N.A.A.C.P. Investigation," *Crisis,* 15 (Nov. 1917), 14–19; Kellogg, 260–62.

42 See, for example, Wilson to Leonidas C. Dyer, July 28, 1917, in Baker, VII, 198. On the East St. Louis riot, see Elliott M. Rudwick, *Race Riot at East St. Louis, July 2, 1917* (Carbondale, Ill., 1964).

43 Miller to Wilson, Aug. 4, 1917, an open letter, printed in Kelly Miller, *The Everlasting Stain* (Washington, D.C., 1924), pp. 136–60.

44 Rudwick, pp. 139, 283 n. 44.

issued a statement denouncing lynchings, mob spirit and violence.[45] Negroes welcomed this belated message, inadequate as it was for quelling the outbreaks.

Despite these problems Negroes gave substantial support to the war effort. Even the irascible critic W. E. B. Du Bois counseled Negroes to "forget our special grievances and close ranks shoulder to shoulder with our white fellow citizens and the allied nations that are fighting for democracy."[46] In turn, the war taught some valuable lessons. It dramatized the contrast between America's professed democratic objectives abroad and its racism at home. It also revealed a new world to thousands of Negro soldiers. After fighting in the great crusade and sampling life in France, the Negro veteran was far less likely to acquiesce in his status in the United States. The war helped to bring forth a new militancy, an aggressive spirit that characterized the "New Negro." "We return fighting," wrote Du Bois in May 1919. "Make way for Democracy! We saved it in France, and by the Great Jehovah, we will save it in the United States of America, or know the reason why."[47]

This new mood, coupled with the emergence of a considerably enlarged black electorate in the North, suggested the need for Republicans to begin a serious reexamination of their relationship with American Negroes. In 1918 the GOP regained control of Congress, and it looked forward with confidence to recapturing the White House in 1920. It was a time for Republicans to consolidate and strengthen their traditional sources of support. Already there was evidence that the Negroes' intense dislike of Wilson might not be enough to keep them loyal to the GOP. To continue to take the votes of Negroes for granted, while ignoring their grievances and acquiescing in southern racism, could be risky, at least in the long run. Thus the circumstances called for a new Republican political strategy that would take into account the emergence of new and aggressive Negro leaders and organizations and the steadily increasing number of Negro voters in the North.

The northern migration of Negroes was not a new phenomenon.

[45] New York *Times*, July 27, 1918; Ray S. Baker and William E. Dodd, eds., *The Public Papers of Woodrow Wilson: War and Peace, Presidential Messages, Addresses, and Public Papers (1917–1924)* (New York, 1927), I, 238–40; Kellogg, pp. 227–28; Baker, VIII, 218, 289, 314; Robert L. Zangrando, "The Efforts of the National Association for the Advancement of Colored People to Secure Passage of a Federal Anti-Lynching Law, 1920–1940" (Ph.D. diss., University of Pennsylvania, 1963), p. 62.

[46] *Crisis*, 16 (July 1918), 111. Some Negroes strongly criticized Du Bois for his editorial, however.

[47] *Ibid.*, 18 (May 1919), 14.

Since the Civil War the number living outside the South had been slowly increasing, both absolutely and as a proportion of the total black population. Lured by promises of higher wages and by hopes of a freer life, most of the migrants sought their opportunity in the rapidly growing cities of the North. During the decade of the 1890's the Negro population roughly doubled in such cities as New York, Chicago, Cleveland, Philadelphia, and Pittsburgh. Still, until well into the twentieth century this movement was relatively small. The overwhelming majority of Negroes lived below the Mason-Dixon line. In 1902 Kelly Miller raised the question of why there was not a greater exodus from the South, considering the harsh treatment the Negro received there. His answer was simply that the North did not welcome Negroes. It was not the cold climate, but the "frigidity of the social atmosphere. . . . Between industrial exclusion in the North and political suppression in the South there is not much to choose."[48]

With World War I this picture altered dramatically. In 1915 a massive migration to the North began. The first phase continued until 1918, and it was followed by another wave in the early 1920's. Possibly 450,000 moved to the North during the first wave, but because some returned to the South, the net migration was certainly less. The totals for the years 1922 and 1924 were equally large. The United States Department of Labor reported that for the year ending September 1, 1923, a total of 478,700 left from thirteen southern states. Between 1915 and 1928 possibly as many as 1,200,000 Negroes migrated from the South to the North and West, although the net total was smaller because of returnees. Still, the migration was very significant. The 1920 census showed that the geographical center of Negro population, which from 1790 to 1910 had followed the westward movement, had moved eastward and northward. Between 1910 and 1930 the number of Negroes living in the North and West increased from 1,078,336 to 2,529,566, a change from some 11 percent to 21.3 percent of the total Negro population in the United States.[49]

48 Miller, "The Expansion of the Negro Population," *Forum*, 32 (Feb. 1902), 674.

49 "Negro Migration in 1923," *Monthly Labor Review*, 18 (April 1924), 762; Charles S. Johnson, "The Changing Economic Status of the Negro," *Annals of the American Academy of Political and Social Science*, 140 (Nov. 1928), 131. See also Henderson H. Donald, "The Urbanization of the American Negro," in *Studies in the Science of Society*, ed. G. P. Murdock (New Haven, 1937), pp. 181–99; Reynolds Farley, "The Urbanization of Negroes in the United States," *Journal of Social History*, 1 (Spring 1968), 241–58; T. Lynn Smith, "The Redistribution of the Negro Population of the United States, 1910–1960," *Journal of Negro History*, 51 (July 1966), 155–73; U.S., Department of Commerce, Bureau of the Census, *Negroes in the United States, 1920–32* (Washington, D.C., 1935); U.S., Department of Com-

The causes of this great migration were primarily economic. Depressed wages in the South, floods, and damage to cotton crops by the boll weevil all played a role. Even more important were the increased labor needs of the North created by the defense and war production. Northern employers actively recruited Negro labor. After the war the demand slackened, but in the early 1920's it was renewed for a while as a result of the restriction of foreign immigration. However, the migration cannot be explained wholly in economic terms. The continued oppression and violence in the South certainly were also significant factors. With some encouragement many Negroes were only too glad to leave the land of Jim Crow for the promise of a new life.[50] As Du Bois wrote in 1920: "The migration of Negroes from the South to North continues and ought to continue. The North is no paradise—as East St. Louis, Washington, Chicago, and Omaha prove; but the South is at best a system of caste and insult and at worst a Hell. . . . We can vote in the North. We can hold office in the North. As workers in northern establishments, we are getting good wages, decent treatment, healthful homes and schools for our children. Can we hesitate? COME NORTH!"[51]

Tens of thousands followed Du Bois's advice. Nevertheless, by the end of the 1920's Negroes still comprised only a small proportion of the population of the North and the West—2.5 percent in 1910 and 4.3 percent in 1930. As the overwhelming majority of the migrants settled in a few urban areas, the full impact of the change was greater than these figures might suggest. Traditionally most Negroes in the North—76.9 percent in 1910—had been city dwellers. By 1930 the percentage of those living in cities had risen to 88.3. During the same two decades the black population increased from 91,709 to 327,706 in New York City; from 44,103 to 233,903 in Chicago; and

merce, Bureau of the Census, *Negro Population, 1790–1915* (Washington, D.C., 1918); U.S., Department of Labor, Division of Negro Economics, *Negro Migration in 1916–17* (Washington, D.C., 1919).

50 In addition to the works previously cited, see Henderson H. Donald, "The Negro Migration of 1916–1918," *Journal of Negro History,* 6 (Oct. 1921), 383–498; W. E. B. Du Bois, "The Migration of Negroes," *Crisis,* 14 (June 1917), 63–66; Rollin L. Hartt, "When The Negro Comes North: I, An Exodus and Its Cause," *World's Work,* 48 (May 1924), 83–89; "Letters of Negro Migrants of 1916–1918," *Journal of Negro History,* 4 (July 1919), 290–340; "Additional Letters of Negro Migrants of 1916–1918," *ibid.,* 4 (Oct. 1919), pp. 412–65; William Pickens, "Migrating to Fuller Life," *Forum,* 72 (Nov. 1924), 600–607; Emmett J. Scott, *Negro Migration during the War* (New York, 1920), esp. pp. 13–25; Carter G. Woodson, *A Century of Negro Migration* (Washington, D.C., 1918).

51 *Crisis,* 19 (Jan. 1920), 105.

from 5,741 to 120,066 in Detroit.[52] The potential political power of these Negroes, concentrated in a limited number of urban areas, and in turn within rather restricted residential districts, was far greater than it would have been had they been evenly distributed throughout the population. A politician at the local, state, or even congressional level could not ignore such a change in his constituency.

At the same time new and more aggressive Negro leaders and organizations were emerging. With the death of Booker T. Washington in November 1915 an era ended. No man before or since had such influence over American blacks and over whites interested in the race problem. "His career," eulogized the New York *Times*, "is one of the most remarkable that our history affords. It is doubtful if any American, within the forty years of his active life, has rendered to the nation service of greater or more lasting value than his."[53] Du Bois dissented. "Of the good that he accomplished there can be no doubt," but "we must lay on the soul of this man a heavy responsibility for the consummation of Negro disfranchisement, the decline of the Negro college and public school and the firmer establishment of color caste in the land."[54] With the publication of his *Souls of Black Folk* in 1903, Du Bois became the outstanding Negro critic of Washington's philosophy of conciliation. In the short-lived Niagara Movement (1905–9), Du Bois had attempted to give organized form to this opposition. Most members of the Niagara Movement in turn joined the National Association for the Advancement of Colored People, the organization that emerged after Washington's death as the most effective agency working for the rights of the American Negro. The NAACP developed out of a National Negro Conference held in New York City on May 31 and June 1, 1909, called by a number of whites led by the southern writer William English Walling, the social workers Mary White Ovington and Henry Moskovitz, and the publisher Oswald Garrison Villard, who wrote the call for the first conference. The next year a permanent organization was established which adopted the name by which it has since been known. Interracial from the start, the NAACP included many educated and outspoken Negroes, although with the exception of Du Bois, who had been enticed away from his position as professor at Atlanta University to become director of publications and research, its principal national officers were white. In the fall of 1910 publication of the NAACP's official monthly journal, the *Crisis*, began, and in a few

52 *Negroes in U.S., 1920–32*, pp. 13, 53, 55.

53 New York *Times*, Nov. 16, 1915.

54 *Crisis*, 11 (Dec. 1915), 82.

years, under the able but often controversial editorship of Du Bois, it became the most influential magazine of Negro protest thought in America.[55]

The resolutions adopted at the preliminary conference on June 1, 1909, strongly denounced "the ever-growing oppression of our 10,000,000 colored fellow citizens as the greatest menace that threatens the country" and called for strict enforcement of the civil rights guaranteed by the Fourteenth Amendment, equal educational opportunities for Negro and white children, and the right of Negroes to vote on the same terms as other citizens. Although this was a fairly mild statement, Mary White Ovington reported that it "was denounced by nearly every white man who gave to Negro institutions."[56]

Booker T. Washington and his friends were also far from happy about the new organization. Villard had invited Washington to attend the first conference in 1909, but he had tactfully declined. Thereafter relations between the two men became strained. The NAACP was a challenge to Washington's leadership, and he was never reconciled to it. "I happen to know the individuals who compose this conference," he wrote to Ray Stannard Baker, a speaker at the May 1910 meeting. "Nothing that has any real sense in it would be received with any degree of enthusiasm. What they want is nonsense. I would have some sympathy with this organization if I did not know that a majority, not all, of the white men who are leading in the matter are not sincere, and that a majority of the colored people in it are not sincere. . . . It is sinful in the highest degree for any set of white men to lend their influence of deceiving the colored people into the idea that they can get what they ought to have in the way of treatment merely by making demands, passing resolutions and cursing somebody."[57]

Washington underrated the sincerity of the NAACP leaders and

[55] On the founding of the NAACP, see Kellogg, pp. 9–65; August Meier, "Booker T. Washington and the Rise of the N.A.A.C.P.," *Crisis*, 61 (Feb. 1954), 69–76, 117–23; Meier, *Negro Thought in America, 1880–1915: Racial Ideologies in the Age of Booker T. Washington* (Ann Arbor, Mich., 1963), passim, esp. chap. 10; Mary White Ovington, *The Walls Came Tumbling Down* (New York, 1947), pp. 100–111; Wilson Record, "Negro Intellectual Leadership in the National Association for the Advancement of Colored People, 1910–1940," *Phylon*, 17 (1956), 375–89.

[56] Mary White Ovington, "The National Association for the Advancement of Colored People," *Journal of Negro History*, 9 (April 1924), 111. The resolution is reprinted in Kellogg, pp. 302–3.

[57] Washington to Baker, May 24, 1910, Ray S. Baker Papers, Library of Congress. On Booker T. Washington's relationship to the NAACP during its early years, see Kellogg, pp. 27–29, 67–88.

their skill in developing a variety of means to pursue their goals. One was the traditional device of publicity, which the NAACP employed to arouse the conscience of the country to the plight of the Negro. Another was political pressure. The NAACP kept a careful watch over developments in Congress, opposed undesirable measures, advised the Negro community about sympathetic and hostile legislators, and lobbied for desired legislation. The NAACP also made extensive use of legal action. Among its white leaders were a number of able lawyers, including the association's first president, Moorfield Storey of Boston, who was an acknowledged leader of the American bar, and a vice-president, Arthur B. Spingarn of New York, who headed the legal committee. The NAACP won its first big victory in 1915 in the case of *Guinn* v. *United States* when the Supreme Court accepted Storey's argument that the grandfather clause of the Oklahoma constitution was an unconstitutional violation of the Fifteenth Amendment. After the death of Washington no single individual or group spoke from a position of acknowledged leadership such as he had enjoyed, but the NAACP clearly became the outstanding organization concerned with the rights of Negroes.

An enlarged and more militant press also helped to awaken a new spirit among Negroes and to defend their rights. An early example was the Boston *Guardian,* founded in 1901 by the erratic firebrand William Monroe Trotter, who to a large extent went his own way independent of both Booker T. Washington and the NAACP. Robert S. Abbott's Chicago *Defender,* founded in 1905, had a greater impact. Highly sensational, this paper did much to encourage Negroes to migrate from the South and to seek fulfillment of their rights. By 1915 the *Crisis* had become, under Du Bois's skillful leadership, a significant example of the militant new press. The First World War had an important effect on the Negro newspapers. Frequently they pointed out the inconsistency between the government's propaganda about the war to save democracy and the abuse of Negroes in America. As many new papers were established, the number of Negroes reached by the printed word increased considerably. Moreover, these newspapers wrote about the problems and achievements of black Americans that usually went unnoticed by the general press.[58]

[58] G. James Fleming, "The Negro Press" (research memorandum prepared for the Carnegie-Myrdal study of the Negro in America, 1940), chap. 3, pp. 1–2 (copy in Schomburg Collection of the New York Public Library); Frederick G. Detweiler, *The Negro Press in the United States* (Chicago, 1922), pp. 61–100, 130–202; Gunnar Myrdal, *An American Dilemma: The Negro Problem and Modern Democracy* (New York, 1944), pp. 913–14. On Trotter and the Boston *Guardian,* see Fox. On the Chicago *Defender,* see Roi Ottley, *The Lonely Warrior: The Life and Times of Robert S. Abbott* (Chicago, 1955). For a collection of articles from various Negro

Far more conservative in manner and objectives than the sensational Negro press or the NAACP, but significant for its attention to the problems created by life in the city, was the National Urban League. Founded in New York City in 1911, the league was a union of three older organizations involved in social work among Negroes. It was supported largely by white philanthropy, but its first director was a Negro, George E. Haynes, a graduate of Columbia University with a Ph.D. in sociology who was then teaching at Fisk University. Many other Negroes were active in the organization, including supporters of both Washington and Du Bois. The league was mainly concerned with improving housing conditions, neighborhoods, and playgrounds and with finding jobs for Negroes, rather than with civil rights. Its importance grew considerably with the great migration to the North, and in 1916 it sponsored a national conference on migration in New York City. During the war Haynes was brought into the government as head of a division of Negro economics under the Department of Labor. Unlike the NAACP, the Urban League had the blessing of many conservative Negro leaders. Yet its approach was not simply one of accommodation and conciliation, for it helped stimulate an awareness of some of the problems and needs of the expanding Negro population in a changing, urban America.[59]

On quite a different side of the political spectrum were a few Negro radicals, men who crossed swords not only with white racists and Negro conservatives but also with militants like Du Bois. The most important of the new radicals were Chandler Owen and A. Philip Randolph. Professed socialists, they were for a while instructors of Marxism at the Rand School of Social Science in New York. They sought the unionization of black and white workers on an equal basis. In order to present their ideas to a larger audience in 1917, they founded the *Messenger*, a "journal of scientific radicalism." The next year they rejected Du Bois's appeal to "close ranks" behind the war effort. During the postwar red scare, the Lusk committee of the New York state legislature singled out the *Messenger* as a dangerous publication, "distinctly revolutionary in tone."[60] Owen

newspapers at this time, see Robert T. Kerlin, *The Voice of the Negro* (New York, 1920).

59 Guichard Parris and Lester Brooks, *Blacks in the City; A History of the National Urban League* (Boston, 1971), pp. 32–40; L. Hollingsworth Wood, "The Urban League Movement," *Journal of Negro History*, 9 (April 1924), 117–26; Seth M. Scheiner, *Negro Mecca: A History of the Negro in New York City, 1865–1920* (New York, 1965), pp. 155–58.

60 New York, Legislature, *Revolutionary Radicalism: Report of the Joint Legislative Committee Investigating Seditious Activities, Filed April 24, 1920, in the Senate of the State of New York* (Albany, 1920), II, 1477. See also Abram L. Harris,

and Randolph did not have the widespread influence the committee feared, but their efforts to organize Negroes into a radical labor movement and their trenchant criticism of many conventional verities did help to shatter the illusion that Negroes were passive and contented citizens.

An organization that, more than any other, appealed to the imagination of the black masses was Marcus Garvey's Universal Negro Improvement Association. Founded in Jamaica in 1914, Garvey brought it to America in 1916, and it soon attracted a considerable following, especially among the less educated urban masses in New York and some other big cities. The movement reached its peak in the early 1920's but rapidly declined with Garvey's indictment in 1922 and imprisonment the next year for fraudulent use of the mails. Du Bois and many other Negro leaders strongly attacked Garvey's back-to-Africa movement. However, his emphasis upon pride in things black was a psychologically important corrective to the prevailing assumptions. Garvey's ideas did little to advance white acceptance of Negroes on equal terms as citizens of America, but his arousal of the poor was an important aspect of the new spirit beginning to develop among American blacks.[61]

At another level was the outburst of activity among Negro writers, musicians, and artists. Although few of them had kind words for Garvey, they too exhibited a new pride in their race. Centered in New York City the important creative achievement of the postwar period has been styled the "Harlem Renaissance." Many of the works were ones of a racial protest, and to that extent writers like James Weldon Johnson, Claude McKay, and Langston Hughes helped to keep before the American public the record of Negro grievances and aspirations.[62] As these and other examples indicate, by the middle of the second decade of the twentieth century a new

"The Negro Problem as Viewed by Negro Leaders," *Current History*, 18 (June 1923), 414; Elbert L. Tatum, *The Changed Political Thought of the Negro, 1915–1940* (New York, 1951), pp. 41–42; and James Weldon Johnson, *Black Manhattan* (New York, 1930), pp. 246–51.

[61] Edmund D. Cronon, *Black Moses: The Story of Marcus Garvey and the Universal Negro Improvement Association* (Madison, Wis., 1955), and Elton C. Fax, *Garvey: The Story of a Pioneer Black Nationalist* (New York, 1972), are the fullest accounts. See also E. Franklin Frazier, "Garvey: A Mass Leader," *Nation*, 123 (Aug. 18, 1926), 147–48; *Philosophy and Opinions of Marcus Garvey*, ed. Amy Jacques-Garvey (New York, 1925).

[62] On the Harlem Renaissance and the New Negro, see Robert A. Bone, *The Negro Novel in America* (New Haven, 1958), pp. 51–107; Meier, *Negro Thought*, pp. 256–78; Franklin, pp. 498–522; Nathan Irvin Huggins, *Harlem Renaissance* (New York, 1971). For works by participants, see Alain Locke, ed., *The New Negro* (New York, 1925); Langston Hughes, *The Big Sea* (New York, 1940).

spirit was emerging among American Negroes that found expression in a variety of organizations, journals, and literary and artistic endeavors. Representatives of the "New Negro" were no longer content with the accommodations of the age of Washington, and they exhibited greater racial pride and championed their rights more aggressively than had many of the Negro spokesmen of the past.

What most of them wanted—that they be truly accorded equal rights as citizens of a democracy—was far from revolutionary. As one Negro wrote in 1922, "They are asking for the protection of life, for the security of property, for the liberation of their peons, for the freedom to sell their labor on the open market, for a human being's chance in the courts, for a better system of public education, and for the boon of the ballot. They ask, in short, for public equality under the protection of the Federal Government."[63] These were precisely the things that white America had so obdurately refused to grant. But now some Negroes felt that the changing conditions—the rapidly growing Negro population in the North and the new Negro leadership and spirit—might prod Republican politicians into promoting these egalitarian principles.

Some encouraging signs appeared during the two years before the presidential election of 1920. In Congress, for example, a few Republicans from urban areas sponsored measures designed to protect Negro rights. In April 1918 Congressmen Leonidas C. Dyer of St. Louis, Missouri, and Merrill Moores of Indianapolis, Indiana, introduced antilynching bills. Neither saw the light of day after being referred to committee, but they marked the opening round of a long struggle for federal legislation.[64] In January 1919 Congressman Martin B. Madden, who represented a predominantly black district in Chicago, submitted a bill to ensure equal accommodations and prohibit discrimination on account of race or color in interstate transportation.[65] In 1919 and 1920 Congressman William E. Mason of Chicago and Senator Selden P. Spencer of St. Louis introduced separate proposals to investigate racial problems in the United States. In defense of his bill Spencer delivered on May 22, 1920, an unusually forthright speech on behalf of Negro rights. "The colored man of the United States is a citizen precisely as the white man of the United States is a citizen," said Spencer. "Each is an American. . . . Each is entitled to the equal protection of the law in his life, in his property, and in his liberty." He condemned the gross in-

[63] Mordecai W. Johnson, "The Faith of the American Negro," *Nation*, 115 (July 19, 1922), 65.

[64] *Cong. Rec.*, 65th Cong., 2d sess., vol. 56, pt. 5, p. 4821, and pt. 6, p. 5362.

[65] *Ibid.*, 3d sess., vol. 57, pt. 3, p. 2335.

equalities between the educational expenditures for whites and those for Negroes in the southern states. But he also insisted that the race issue had become a national problem demanding national attention.[66]

The Republican-controlled 66th Congress passed none of these measures. Many Negroes in turn were skeptical about the intentions of the Republican leaders. To make it clear to the GOP that no party had an automatic claim to their votes, they counseled independence: reward friends and punish enemies regardless of party. Du Bois expressed these sentiments in an article published in the *Nation* just before the 1920 Republican national convention. "Negroes as a mass," he warned, "have done more thinking in the last four years than ever before. . . . They have long-standing grievances against the Republican Party, and it cannot therefore count on the absolute necessity of a black man voting Republican." Du Bois pointed out that in many local and state districts, New York City for example, the Democrats gave the Negro much more consideration than the Republicans. Hoping to influence Republicans by claiming that Negroes held or could hold the balance of power in a close national election, he noted particularly the states of Illinois, Indiana, Kentucky, and Maryland, as well as many congressional districts, where Negro votes could be decisive.[67] The balance-of-power argument had been used occasionally in the past with little effect. After 1920 it was heard more and more frequently, and with the increased Negro population in the North it became more plausible. But Du Bois's figures for the size of the Negro vote were inflated, for they were based on estimates of the number eligible to vote rather than those who were registered or were likely to cast a ballot. His argument also assumed an unwarranted degree of independence among black voters. Nevertheless, a big increase in Negro population living outside of the South had occurred, and some local politicians were already sensitive to this fact.

In 1920, however, most presidential aspirants, Republican or Democratic, were unwilling to make public statements about matters of direct concern to Negroes. In February 1920 the NAACP sent out a questionnaire to seventeen men who had been mentioned as presidential possibilities. Each was asked his opinion about a federal antilynching law, Negro disfranchisement, enforcement of the Fourteenth Amendment's provision for reduction of representation for

66 *Ibid.*, p. 2259; *ibid.*, 66th Cong., 1st sess., vol. 58, pt. 5, 4883; *ibid.*, 2d sess., vol. 59, pt. 5, p. 5927, and pt. 7, pp. 7481–82.

67 Du Bois, "The Republicans and the Black Voter," *Nation*, 110 (June 5, 1920), 757. For other calls for Negro political independence, see Woodson, pp. 181–83, and *Messenger*, 2 (Jan. 1918), 12.

disfranchising states, the appointment of a United States commission to enforce the Fifteenth Amendment, abolition of Jim Crow cars in interstate traffic, withdrawal of American forces from Haiti, federal aid to elementary education without discrimination against Negroes, enlistment of Negroes in the armed forces in proportion to their numbers in the total population, and abolition of racial segregation in the United States Civil Service.[68]

The responses were disappointing. No one answered the questions directly, and only three replied at all. Senator Miles Poindexter of Washington said that he was "in favor of maintaining the legal rights and opportunities of all our citizens, regardless of color or condition." General Leonard Wood replied cryptically that reports of his attitude toward colored officers were not true and were "enemy propaganda." Senator Warren G. Harding gave the longest answer. After assuring the NAACP of his cordial interest in its work, he stated that it was "not consistent with my views to take up the categorical questions which you address to me, because I am a very firm believer in the doctrine that conventions are called upon to enunciate platforms and policies for our Party, and the candidate selected must be expected to stand on the platform thus made. I believe in judgment which comes from the counsels of many; that is the theory of representative government."[69] As for the fourteen who did not answer at all, Du Bois observed sardonically, "we will forget these gentlemen neither in our prayers nor in our votes."[70] Walter White, the assistant secretary of the NAACP, was equally disturbed by this negative response. "The patience and faith of all of the colored people of America have been sorely tried by the dishonesty of the Republican party," he wrote in March 1920. "Negative goodness will not suffice. Positive action in correcting the evils of American life is the only thing that can appease colored voters and enlist their support at the polls next November."[71]

During the preconvention campaign the Republican presidential aspirants followed many of the old ways, including both inadequate attention to Negro grievances and active pursuit of southern delegates. The most diligent wooer of the South was former Postmaster General Hitchcock, who began his efforts in 1919 and in early 1920 threw his support to General Wood. Testimony presented to a Sen-

[68] Letters dated Feb. 18, 1920, NAACP Papers. See also NAACP, *Annual Report: 1920*, p. 24.

[69] Harding to John R. Shillady, Feb. 20, 1920, NAACP Papers; *Crisis*, 20 (June 1920), 69; NAACP, *Annual Report: 1920*, p. 24.

[70] *Crisis*, 20 (June 1920), 69.

[71] White to C. P. Dam, March 2, 1920, NAACP Papers.

ate committee investigating campaign expenses showed that the Wood-Hitchcock forces outdid all others in their expenditure of money in the South. Their tactics stimulated the demand for more sweeping reform of the southern GOP. Harding, too, was interested in the South. In March, for example, he became the first prospective Republican presidential nominee to campaign in person in Texas.[72]

These efforts in the South led to many contested seats, often between lily-white and black-and-tan factions. At the end of May the national committee, led by Will H. Hays, began hearings on the contests. Selected as national chairman in 1918 because of his effectiveness as a conciliator, Hays was mainly concerned about keeping the party united. In 1920 he did not have to protect the interests of an incumbent president, and the race for the presidential nomination was wide open. Hays held the hearings in public session, but most black-and-tan delegates did not fare well. The first decision concerned the Arkansas delegation and favored the lily-whites, despite the fact that they had excluded blacks from their state convention. No Negroes were seated from Alabama, Arkansas, North Carolina, Texas, and Virginia. Even one of the most important Negro politicians of the 1920's, Robert R. Church, Jr., from Memphis, Tennessee, was unseated by the credentials committee after having been put on the temporary roll by the national committee.[73]

Negroes were not entirely excluded from the southern delegations. Several disputed seats from Georgia were awarded to a group headed by Henry Lincoln Johnson, who was also named the state's national committeeman. This action incensed many Georgia whites, who complained that it would only perpetuate the Democratic control of the state.[74] A few other decisions also favored the black-and-tans, and the convention even adopted a resolution presented by Charles B. Warren, the Michigan national committeeman, that was directed

[72] U.S., Congress, Senate, *Presidential Campaign Expenses: Hearings before a Subcommittee of the Committee on Privileges and Elections,* 66th Cong., 2d sess. (May 24—Oct. 18, 1920), esp. pp. 454–78, 542–58, 945–66. See also Greelee, pp. 364–65; Andrew Sinclair, *The Available Man: The Life behind the Masks of Warren Gamaliel Harding* (New York, 1965), p. 130; New York *Times,* March 2, March 4, 1920; *Crisis,* 19 (April 1920), 297.

[73] George H. Mayer, *The Republican Party, 1854–1964* (New York, 1964), p. 351; New York *Times,* April 29, May 26, June 1–6, 1920; *Official Report of the Proceedings of the Seventeenth Republican National Convention Held in Chicago, Illinois, June 8, 9, 10, 11, and 12, 1920,* p. 44; *Crisis,* 19 (April 1920), 297; *Negro Year Book: 1921/22,* p. 38.

[74] New York *Times,* June 2, 6, 9, 1920; Walter Akerman to Harding, June 23, 1920; B. F. Brimberry to Harding, June 24, 1920; C. Bascom Slemp to D. C. Cole, Sept. 7, 1920, Warren G. Harding Papers, Ohio Historical Society. Henry Lincoln Johnson was the first Negro Republican national committeeman since 1912.

against the lily-whites. Apparently inspired by events in Arkansas, Texas, and Virginia, it provided that in the future no delegations should be seated if they were elected at conventions held in places where Negroes were barred. This resolution came too late to do any good in 1920, and was not a serious restraint on the lily-whites in any case.[75]

Many Republicans were embarrassed by the perpetual squabbles between warring factions in the southern parties and by the temptation to corruption that always seemed present in the pursuit of southern delegates. If a major break in the solid South was seriously contemplated, they felt that far more sweeping changes would have to be made. Accordingly, on June 5 the national committee appointed a special committee to "study the whole political situation in the South" and to make recommendations "how the Republican Party in the States of the South may be . . . [made] a more effective agent." Shortly before adjournment the convention passed a resolution directing the national committee to prepare within twelve months a new "just and equitable basis of representation in future national conventions." The national committee carefully asserted that it was not attacking the right of Negroes to representation at national conventions. But, as Walter L. Cohen of Louisiana said in opposing the resolution, reform in the southern parties or a change in the basis of representation really meant further reduction in the role played by Negroes in the Republican party in the South.[76]

This was a future danger. Of more immediate concern to Negroes in the North and South was the amount of recognition that Republicans would give to the host of other racial problems. Despite the efforts of the NAACP and others to create an awareness of these issues, the platform was disappointing. Five Negroes, including James Weldon Johnson, were included among 171 members of a special advisory committee on the platform. As Johnson later noted, the appointment was "quite an empty honor."[77] Only one plank, that on lynching, was specifically directed to Negroes. It urged Congress "to consider the most effective means to end lynching in this country

[75] New York *Times*, June 4, 1920. Warren's resolution referred to hotels or similar facilities that excluded Negroes. It did not specifically attack other devices that whites might use to bar Negroes from state Republican conventions. If enforced it would have been an inconvenience to lily-whites, but not a serious blow. By 1920 the role of the southern Negro politician in the GOP had obviously declined over what it had been earlier in the century. According to one report only 27 of the 169 delegates from the South in 1920 were Negroes, 5 less than in 1916 and 35 less than in 1912 (*Negro Year Book 1921/22*, p. 38).

[76] New York *Times*, June 6, 14, 1920; *Proc. 17th Rep. Nat. Conv.*, p. 233.

[77] J. W. Johnson, *Along This Way*, p. 357; *Crisis*, 19 (April 1920), 340.

which continues to be a terrible blot on our American civilization." This promised little, although it was a more specific recommendation on an issue concerning Negro rights than had appeared in a Republican platform in many years.

Although Republicans were fascinated by the prospects of a southern breakthrough based on lily-white parties, they still were unwilling to make an unqualified commitment in this direction. They were listening to two voices. One argued that if the Negro were thrown out, a strong Republican party could rise in the southern states. The other was heard less distinctly, but it was present. It said, in the words of James Weldon Johnson, "The Republican party would increase its chances of national success more by standing by the Negro, and thus making sure of the pivotal states in the North where the Negro holds the balance of power."[78] The 1920 convention seemed to listen more to those who would sacrifice the Negro. But it equivocated enough to satisfy neither side entirely.

After the convention Johnson and other black leaders continued their efforts to get the Republicans to support Negro rights. In mid-July Robert R. Moton, the president of Tuskegee Institute, wrote to Hays and to Harding urging the Republican nominee to make a strong statement in favor of justice for Negroes in his acceptance speech. Hays advised Harding to consider this suggestion.[79] On July 22 Harding took a position that went beyond that of the Republican platform. Not only did he declare that "the Federal government should stamp out lynching and remove that stain from the fair name of America," but he also affirmed his belief that "Negro citizens of America should be guaranteed the enjoyment of all their rights, that they have earned their full measure of citizenship bestowed, that their sacrifices in blood on the battlefields of the republic have entitled them to all of freedom and opportunity, all of smypathy and aid that the American spirit of fairness and justice demands."[80] These florid phrases inspired the editor of a Negro newspaper in Birmingham, Alabama, to praise the address as a "masterpiece" that gave Negroes of this country more incentive than any speech that has been made since the demise of the immortal Lincoln."[81] Radicals like Chandler Owen and A. Philip Randolph were not so favorably im-

[78] New York *Age*, June 19, 1920.

[79] Moton to Will H. Hays, July 14, 1920; Moton to Harding, July 14, 1920, Hays to George B. Christian, Jr., July 14, 1920, Harding Papers.

[80] *Republican Campaign Text-Book: 1920*, p. 50. Vice-Presidential candidate Calvin Coolidge took a similar, if vaguer, stand in favor of the "constitutional rights" of Negroes a few days later in his own acceptance speech (New York *Times*, July 28, 1920).

[81] Henry F. Arnold to Harding, Aug. 26, 1920, Harding Papers.

pressed. Harding had done nothing for the Negro, they reminded their readers, and his "cynical interest" was "amusing at this late date."[82]

Harding made a greater effort to attrack black voters in the northern and border states than other Republican candidates had in recent elections. His organization included Negro advisors for each section of the country, and they in turn sponsored the formation of local and state Negro Republican clubs. Henry Lincoln Johnson assisted these clubs with pamphlets and other campaign literature. Under the direction of Robert R. Church, Jr., and James C. Napier, special attention was given to Tennessee. According to its Republican chairman, it was the one southern state that the GOP had a good chance of winning if it rejected lily-whitism and organized all elements of the electorate including Negroes. As this was the first presidential election after ratification of the Nineteenth Amendment, considerable effort was also made to get black women registered, especially in Harding's home state of Ohio. A Colored Women's Bureau was set up under the chairmanship of Mrs. Lethia C. Fleming of Cleveland. Mary Church Terrell, wife of the District of Columbia municipal judge, ably directed the eastern division of this bureau. To ensure the broadest possible support, a Negro ministerial campaign committee was also established to sponsor prayers for the success of Harding and Coolidge.[83]

In keeping with Harding's front-porch campaign, Henry Lincoln Johnson promoted the idea of a "Colored Voters Day," which was held at Marion, Ohio, on September 10. Most of those attending this carefully arranged affair were conservative representatives of two branches of the Baptist church and of the African Methodist Episcopal church. To the chagrin of Johnson, William Monroe Trotter and a few members of the National Equal Rights League were also present. In his comments to the gathering Harding made no specific promises. Instead he praised the progress Negroes had made in America, counseled hard work, and cautioned against all unlawful violence. After his speech Harding conferred privately with several of the Negro leaders, including Trotter, and according to newspa-

[82] *Messenger*, 2 (Sept. 1920), 82.

[83] New York *Times*, July 3, Oct. 2, 22, 27, 1920; Wesley M. Bagby, *The Road to Normalcy: The Presidential Campaign and Election of 1920* (Baltimore, 1962), p. 152; Randolph C. Downes, "Negro Rights and White Backlash in the Campaign of 1920," *Ohio History*, 75 (Spring and Summer, 1966), 88–90; William F. Nowlin, *The Negro in American National Politics* (Boston, 1931), p. 85; John C. Houk to Harry M. Daugherty, June 23, 1920, J. C. Napier to Robert J. Harlan, July 23, 1920, Henry A. Wallace to Will H. Hays, Aug. 23, 1920, Harding Papers; Mary Church Terrell Papers, Box 3, Manuscript Division, Library of Congress.

per reports of the meeting he promised to make a careful study of such grievances as lynching and the segregation of federal government employees.[84]

Meanwhile representatives of the NAACP did their best to inform Harding of specific steps needed to be taken in order to improve the position of Negroes. At James Weldon Johnson's request an interview was arranged with Harding for August 9 at Marion. Accompanying Johnson was Harry E. Davis, a member of the NAACP's board of directors from Cleveland. Johnson and Davis tried to acquaint Harding with the work of the NAACP and urged him to make statements on a number of points: action to protect the right of Negroes to vote, abolition of segregation in the government departments in Washington, federal antilynching legislation, an investigation of conditions in Haiti, federal aid to education on a racially nondiscriminatory basis, fair apportionment of Negroes in the armed forces, and abolition of Jim Crow in interstate travel. Harding answered that he agreed in principle with all of those points, but that he was unwilling to make a campaign issue of any of them, except possibly Haiti. According to Johnson's report of the meeting, Harding not only said that he was "in favor of the Negro having the full right to the ballot" but that he was "in favor of securing him that right by a force bill if necessary." As for segregation, Harding "virtually promised he would abolish it in government departments by executive order if elected." Harding frankly admitted that he felt "practical politics" prevented his making a campaign issue of most of these points. Johnson and Davis considered their visit "not an entirely lost effort," for they had acquainted him with many aspects of the race question with which he was unfamiliar. Moreover, Johnson reported, "the personal impression made by Mr. Harding on Mr. Davis and myself was a favorable one. He is a finer type of man than Governor Cox and although a hard-headed and practical politician, he does not give the impression of being shifty and 'smooth.' "[85]

After this meeting Johnson continued his efforts to get Harding to take a public stand on the issues he had presented. Writing to Harding's secretary on August 28, he argued that it would only be good practical politics to pay attention to the greatly increased Negro vote. Johnson did not believe that many Negroes would vote

[84] New York *Times,* Sept. 11, 1920; Downes, pp. 90–94.

[85] "Report of the Field Secretary in Interview with Senator Warren G. Harding, Marion, Ohio, August 9, 1920," NAACP Papers; "Report of the Committee Waiting upon Senator Harding," in NAACP "Minutes of Meeting of Board of Directors, September 13, 1920," Spingarn Papers.

Democratic, but he warned that many were so disgusted that they might not vote at all or only for one of the radical parties, especially in some of the northern and border states where the election might be close. "I am not unaware of the effect that such statements would have on the South, but . . . I believe that a solid Negro vote in the North in the hand is worth more than a solid white vote in the South in the bush."[86]

Apparently Harding saw it otherwise. On one of the few occasions during the campaign when he commented on Negro rights, in a speech at Oklahoma City on October 9, he did so in a manner that was more acceptable to southern whites than to blacks. On the day of Harding's arrival the *Daily Oklahoman* prominently published on its front page three questions. The first concerned his attitude toward Irish independence, but the other two involved Negroes. Did he favor racial segregation, and did he favor a force bill to guarantee the right to vote? Harding responded to all three. As for segregation, he said, "I can't come here and answer that for you. It is too serious a problem for some of us who don't know it as you do in your daily lives. But I wouldn't be fit to be president of the United States if I didn't tell you the same things here in the south that I tell in the north. I believe in race equality before the law. You can't give one right to a white man and deny it to a black man. But I want you to know that I do not mean that white people and black people should be forced to associate together in accepting their equal rights at the hands of the nation." His answer to the last question was more forthright. "The Force bill has been dead for a quarter of century. I'm only a normal American citizen, and a normal man couldn't resurrect the dead if he wanted to." His reply was of little comfort to Negroes, nevertheless, it caused his managers to fear that it would lose him votes in segregationist areas. Silence was a safer tactic.[87]

The only point raised by Johnson which Harding was willing to take up as a campaign issue was the American presence in the Negro republic of Haiti, an intervention that had begun under the Wilson administration in 1915.[88] On August 28, in reply to an indiscreet

[86] Johnson to George B. Christian, Jr., Aug. 28, 1920, NAACP Papers.

[87] *Daily Oklahoman*, Oct. 9–11, 1920; Downes, p. 95.

[88] For the United States relations with Haiti, see Rayford W. Logan, *Haiti and the Dominican Republic* (New York, 1968); Arthur C. Millspaugh, *Haiti under American Control, 1915–1930* (Boston, 1931); Ludwell L. Montague, *Haiti and the United States, 1714–1938* (Durham, N.C., 1940); Hans Schmidt, *The United States Occupation of Haiti, 1915–1934* (New Brunswick, N.J., 1971). See also J. W. Johnson, *Along This Way*, pp. 344–60, and Johnson's reports on his 1920 investigation,

boast by Democratic vice-presidential candidate Franklin D. Roosevelt that "I wrote Haiti's Constitution," Harding promised that if he became president he would "not empower an Assistant Secretary of the Navy to draft a constitution for helpless neighbors in the West Indies and jam it down their throats at the point of bayonets borne by United States marines."[89] Harding renewed the attack on September 17, asserting that thousands of natives had been killed by United States Marines and that Roosevelt's statement was the first official admission of the American "rape of Haiti."[90] Secretary of the Navy Josephus Daniels responded to such criticism on October 15 by ordering an official hearing by a naval board of inquiry. NAACP leaders discounted this step as merely an attempt to whitewash American offenses and continued to press for withdrawal.[91] Despite the NAACP's concern, however, the Haitian issue was not of major political significance in 1920. It may have slightly embarrassed the Democrats, but it probably lost them few votes. It was also remote from the daily problems of most Negroes.

During the 1920 campaign Harding failed to comment publicly on any of the other points brought up by Johnson in their August 9 meeting. The race issue was raised in other ways, however, particularly in Ohio, the home state of both major party candidates. There the Democrats denounced the Republicans for courting the Negro and accused them of favoring social equality. In October the Ohio Democratic organization issued pamphlets entitled *A Timely warning to the White Men and Women of Ohio* and *The Threat of Negro Domination*, which told of the dangers created by the immigration of Negroes from the South.[92] Even Democratic candidate James M. Cox took up the theme. In a speech at Columbus, Ohio, on October 14 he denounced Harding for soliciting the backing of seventeen selfish groups and especially for catering to Negroes in states where they

---

"Self-Determining Haiti," *Nation*, 111 (Aug. 28, Sept. 4, Sept. 11, Sept. 25, 1920), 236–38, 265–67, 295–97, 345–47.

89 New York *Times*, Aug. 29, 1920. Roosevelt's remarks delivered at Helena and Butte, Montana, are quoted in Frank Freidel, *Franklin D. Roosevelt: The Ordeal* (Boston, 1954), p. 81.

90 New York *Times*, Sept. 18, 1920.

91 For the proceedings of the Naval Court of Inquiry, see U.S., Congress, Senate, Select Committee on Haiti and Dominican Republic, *Inquiry into Occupation and Administration of Haiti and Santo Domingo: Hearing Pursuant to Senate Res. 112*, 67th Cong., 1st sess. (1921), pt. 7. See also James W. Johnson to Harding, Oct. 27, Dec. 21, 1920, Harding Papers; Johnson to Daniels, Dec. 2, 1920, in *Press Service of the NAACP*, Dec. 2, Dec. 20, 1920, NAACP Papers.

92 New York *Times*, Oct. 22, 1920; *Crisis*, 19 (Dec. 1920), 55; NAACP, *Annual Report: 1920*, pp. 25–26; Bagby, p. 152; Downes, pp. 98–100.

supposedly had the balance of power. "There is behind Senator Harding the Afro-American party, whose hyphenated activity has attempted to stir up troubles among the negroes upon false claims that it can bring about social equality."[93]

The race issue also appeared by the revival of the charge, especially during the final days of the campaign, that Harding had Negro ancestry. The stories prompted Ohio Republicans to reply with a considerable volume of material defending the purity of their candidate's forebears. With such accusations and rebuttals both sides succeeded in lowering the tone of American politics, but in little else. Possibly the matter raised the hopes of some Negroes that Harding would be more sympathetic to them. But it seems doubtful that it seriously affected the Republican vote.[94]

In 1920 many black leaders strongly recommended independence from commitments to either major political party, especially in local and congressional elections. As Du Bois put it, "vote for friends *of our race and defeat our enemies.*"[95] Unlike the election of 1912, however, no important Negroes wanted to gamble with another Democratic president. Most black voters supported Harding, if not with enthusiasm, then at least with the expectation that a Republican administration would be an improvement over Wilson's.[96]

Republican leaders were less impressed by the Negro vote in the 1920 election than by the results in the southern and border states. Every one of the latter went Republican except Kentucky, which was lost by a mere fraction of 1 percent of the total vote. In every southern state the Republicans registered distinct gains. Most important, they carried Tennessee, the first presidential victory in the South since Reconstruction. Moreover, seven Republican congressmen were

93 New York *Times*, Oct. 15, 1920. See also Cox's letter to Frank L. Stanton, published in the New York *Times*, Oct. 27, 1920, in which Cox again denounced Republicans for allegedly raising the prospect of social equality.

94 Downes, pp. 100–106. On Harding's alleged Negro ancestry, see also Francis Russell, "The Four Mysteries of Warren Harding," *American Heritage*, 14 (April 1963), 7–9; Francis Russell, *The Shadow of Blooming Grove: Warren G. Harding in His Times* (New York, 1968), pp. 372, 403–5, 412–16.

95 *Crisis*, 20 (Sept. 1920), 24. For other recommendations for political independence, see Ernest R. McKinney, "The Election Comes," *Crisis*, 20 (Oct. 1920), 274–76; *Negro Year Book, 1921/22*, pp. 39–40.

96 On the black vote in Chicago and New York, see John M. Allswang, *A House for All Peoples: Ethnic Politics in Chicago, 1890–1936* (Lexington, Ky., 1971), pp. 42, 52–53, 187; Allswang, "The Chicago Voter and the Democratic Consensus: A Case Study, 1918–1936," *Journal of the Illinois State Historical Society*, 60 (Summer 1967), 150–52; Gosnell, p. 28; Burner, pp. 237, 241; Gilbert Osofsky, *Harlem, the Making of a Ghetto: Negro New York, 1890–1930* (New York, 1966), pp. 242–43, nn. 36 and 37.

elected in Tennessee, Texas, and Virginia, an increase of four over the previous Congress.[97] The solid South had been marred by a distinct crack. Never before in the twentieth century had the outlook for the emergence of a two-party South appeared more promising.

What sort of a party the Republicans wanted and could get in the South was another matter. For years there had been much talk about a "New Republicanism" there, a Republicanism that was based, not on the Negro or on the few old white anti-Bourbon counties, but rather on the northerners who had migrated to the South and especially on new converts among southerners who accepted Republican economic doctrines and saw the evils of the one-party system. This "New Republicanism" required that the party purge itself of its close association with the Negro, and despite the results of the 1920 election in Tennessee, where many Negroes could still vote, its proponents continued to believe that the prospects for a two-party South depended upon strengthening the lily-whites. By further reducing the role of Negroes, who supplied few votes in most of the South anyway, the gains of 1920 might be turned into future victories.[98]

The desire to break into the South was not prompted by political necessity as it had been in the latter nineteenth century. In 1920 Harding received over 60 percent of the popular vote, and Republicans won control of both houses of Congress. The GOP was the majority party. The South could merely provide additional insurance that it would retain this status. At a less partisan level, the existence of a two-party South would finally end the Republican party's narrow regional identification and lessen the divisive effects of sectionalism.

Ironically, this renewed interest in the South occurred at a time

97 In Tennessee five Republicans and five Democrats were elected to the House of Representatives, a gain of three for the Republicans. In Texas one Republican was elected, replacing a Democrat. In Virginia one Republican was reelected. Another successfully contested the election apparently won by a Democrat, and he was finally seated in Dec. 1922. Thus as a result of the 1920 elections there were eventually eight Republican congressmen from the eleven southern states in the 67th Congress compared to three in the 66th. On Tennessee, see Gary W. Reichard, "The Aberration of 1920: An Analysis of Harding's Victory in Tennessee, "*Journal of Southern History*," 36 (Feb. 1970), 33–49.

98 On the New Republicanism, see C. Vann Woodward, *Origins of the New South, 1877–1913* (Baton Rouge, La., 1951), pp. 461–69; V. O. Key, Jr., *Southern Politics in State and Nation* (New York, 1949), passim, esp. pp. 277–97; Paul Lewinson, *Race, Class, and Party. A History of Negro Suffrage and White Politics in the South* (New York, 1932), pp. 110–11, 166–70; Tindall, pp. 167–70; Ralph J. Bunche, "The Political Status of the Negro" (research memorandum prepared for the Carnegie-Myrdal study of the Negro in America, 1940), pp. 1175–1226 (copy in Schomburg Collection of the New York Public Library).

when black constituencies were rapidly growing in northern urban districts and when black organizations and leaders were becoming more and more outspoken and willing to question the patterns of the past. To woo the white South while retaining the allegiance of Negroes in the North required considerable political dexterity. To some extent Harding had shown this ability in his 1920 campaign, and he had enjoyed a measure of success. But he also had had the advantage of the Negroes' reaction against the Wilson administration. In the future, with a Republican record to defend, it might not be as easy to hold their allegiance. The Republicans might be able to write off the northern Negro vote as not important enough to matter in presidential elections, but such a step was impossible for an increasing number of congressmen and other officials with large black constituencies. Moreover, to take such a course meant a more explicit rejection of the Republican party's ideals than many were willing to make. However much the GOP had failed to live up to its rhetoric in favor of equality, it was another matter to turn away entirely from its traditional association with the Negro. Negroes in turn hoped to convince Republicans that such action was neither necessary nor desirable. On the contrary, they argued that promotion of the party's democratic ideals would be good practical politics rewarded by black voters in key areas holding a balance of power. Once again, to reconcile the demands of both the white South and the Negro was difficult proposition, and its resolution would reflect on the Republicans' ability to come to grips with the changing conditions of the mid-twentieth century.

CHAPTER VI

The Limits of Normalcy

If Harding had thought deeply or clearly about America's racial problems, it was not readily apparent during his 1920 presidential campaign. On this, as with other major issues, he was reluctant to take an unequivocal position, and his remarks often obscured as much as they clarified. He had, however, listened with apparent sympathy as black spokesmen pleaded their case. Such cordiality did not mean that Harding really understood or sympathized with the Negroes' difficulties and aspirations. Nor did it mean that he was prepared to give meaningful support to programs designed to protect their rights. But his manner did arouse the hope that some changes would be forthcoming.

After the election James Weldon Johnson renewed his efforts to educate Harding in matters of special interest to Negroes. On January 15, 1921, the two men conferred at Marion, Ohio. Johnson brought up the problems of Negro disfranchisement, the Ku Klux Klan, lynching, and Haiti. He also asked Harding to appoint an interracial commission and Negro assistant secretaries in some of the government departments and to pardon the members of the Twenty-fourth Infantry who were still imprisoned because of their involvement in the Houston riot. Johnson found the president-elect to be a friendly and willing listener but reluctant to make public statements or commitments. Harding agreed to review the case of the Twenty-fourth Infantry, and he gave Johnson the impression that he would take some action on behalf of an interracial commission. Privately Harding condemned the Klan. As for Negro suffrage in the South, he would do no more than say that the problem would be resolved in time. In his report to the NAACP, Johnson associated this response with Harding's desire "to break the solid South, or, at any rate, to set up a functioning Republican Party in the Southern states. . . . The gist of his solution was that colored people in the South should willingly accept white leadership until such time as prejudice was worn down." Johnson felt that the discussion had gone as well as could be expected. "He is an average, decent American citizen," he concluded, "but also a hard, practical and perhaps timid politician. More serious still, from our point of view, is the fact that he knows absolutely nothing about the race question. . . . Also, he has undoubtedly been influenced by southern men during his trip South, and he is going South again next week." Nevertheless, he felt that "Harding intends to be just and fair. . . . Harding will need to be educated on the race question. Perhaps he can be. The Secretary regards it as hopeful, at any rate."[1] One good sign was that Harding invited Johnson to come to Washington after the inauguration to discuss racial matters.

Before he took office Harding met with delegations of Negroes at St. Augustine, Florida, on two occasions to discuss the race situation in the South. One interview was arranged by Johnson and took place on February 22, 1921, with a group that included Bishop John Hurst of the AME church, Captain James W. Floyd of Jacksonville, and several other business and professional men. The other meeting was held at the instigation of Dr. Robert R. Moton of Tuskegee Institute. On February 14 Moton sent Harding a number of suggestions about the racial situation. Among these were pleas that Negroes be included in any plans for the reorganization of the Republican party in the South, that Harding refer to lynching in his inaugural address, and that he appoint a commission of white and black Americans to study the situation in Haiti and the Dominican Republic and to make recommendations for its improvement.[2] Moton, with no desire for public office for himself, wanted to be introduced to Harding and hoped to establish contacts with the White House similar to those he had developed under Wilson. He finally secured an appointment along with Dr. Will Alexander of the Commission on Interracial Cooperation, John J. Eagan, president of the American Cast Iron Pipe Company and chairman of the C.I.C., and the Reverend M. Ashby Jones. After some confusion the group was ushered into Harding's suite in the Ponce de Leon Hotel. Harding's ignorance of the southern racial situation soon became apparent. Not only had he never heard of Dr. Moton, but he did not even know about Booker T. Washington and the Tuskegee Institute. Harding, who apparently thought that the members of the delegation were job-seeking politicians, embarrassed the group by his rambling discussion of politics and by his swearing. Upon leaving, Dr. Moton commented to his associates, "I'm afraid we'll have to see the President-elect

[1] "Report of the Secretary's Visit to Senator Harding, January 15, 1921," NAACP Papers, Manuscript Division, Library of Congress; NAACP, *Annual Report: 1921*, p. 8.

[2] Johnson to Harding, Feb. 11, 1921, and Harding to Johnson, Feb. 14, 1921, NAACP Papers; NAACP, *Annual Report: 1921*, pp. 8–9; William H. Hughes and Frederick D. Patterson, eds., *Robert Russa Moton of Hampton and Tuskegee* (Chapel Hill: University of North Carolina Press, 1956), pp. 192–94.

again sometime. We have completely failed." Dr. Woofter then added, "If you'd eliminate damn from that fellow's vocabulary he couldn't do anything but stutter."[3]

Through the efforts of Johnson, Moton, and others, many items of concern to black Americans were presented to Harding.[4] Of these men Johnson was the most successful in impressing the new president. Meeting with him on April 4, 1921, Johnson spoke "frankly of the great unrest among colored people and their dissatisfaction with conditions which allowed lynching, disfranchisement, peonage and other forms of racial injustice." He gave Harding an NAACP memorandum which asked that the president recommend action to end lynching, that the Department of Justice investigate peonage, that the government investigate Negro disfranchisement, that a national interracial commission be appointed to study race relations, that Congress investigate the American occupation of Haiti, that the administration appoint colored assistant secretaries in the Departments of Labor and Agriculture, and that the president abolish by executive order racial segregation in the government departments in Washington and in the Civil Service.[5] Harding now had a list of specific objectives desired by many black Americans.

On April 12 Harding sent a special message to Congress that aroused hope in even some usually skeptical observers. In it he called upon Congress to "wipe the stain of barbaric lynching from the banners of a free and orderly representative democracy," and he cautiously noted, without explicitly recommending, the proposal for an interracial commission to study race relations.[6] The message was actually very vague. It failed to mention most of the issues brought up by Johnson and others, and it did not specifically endorse the Dyer antilynching bill then before Congress. But its tone seemed

3 Will Winton Alexander, "Reminiscences," pp. 303–7, MS in Oral History Research Office, Butler Library, Columbia University. See also Wilma Dykeman and James Stokely, *Seeds of Southern Change: The Life of Will Alexander* (Chicago, 1962), pp. 122–23; Hughes and Patterson, pp. 218–32.

4 For some examples, in addition to those mentioned, see Ralph W. Tyler to George Christian, Jr., Feb. 15, 1921, Harding to Tyler, Feb. 20, 1921, Emmett J. Scott to Harding, Feb. 18, 1921, Harding to Scott, Feb. 22, 1921, George B. Kelly *et al.* to Harding, March 6, 1921, James W. Johnson to Harding, March 12, 1921, George E. Cannon to Christian, March 21, 1921, Harding Papers, Ohio Historical Society.

5 "Memorandum to the Honorable Warren G. Harding, April 4, 1921," NAACP Papers; "Report of the Secretary, April 6, 1921," Arthur B. Spingarn Papers, Manuscript Division, Library of Congress, NAACP, *Annual Report: 1921*, pp. 9–10. Johnson wrote that he had had a "very satisfactory interview with the President" (Johnson to Walter F. White, April 4, 1921, NAACP Papers).

6 New York *Times*, April 13, 1921.

warmly sympathetic, and Negroes generally received the message enthusiastically. "They have been stirred as seldom before by your straightforward words," Johnson wrote to Harding.[7] Even W. E. B. Du Bois was elated. "This is the strongest pronouncement on the race problem ever made by a President in a message to Congress," he wrote in the *Crisis*. "It offers hope that the eleven years of effort during which the NAACP has been stinging the conscience of America by bringing to light the conditions affecting the Negro, are about to bear fruit."[8]

Du Bois's unusual optimism was short-lived. By the early summer of 1921 he noted bitterly that nothing had been done about the interracial commission and that work on the antilynching bill was going on at a languid pace. He regarded Harding's consideration of William Howard Taft for the Supreme Court as "almost disastrous" and his nomination of a lily-white leader, Frank A. Linney, to be a United States attorney for the Western District of North Carolina as even worse.[9] Eventually, many other Negroes felt a similar disappointment. Harding had aroused expectations that he did not fulfill. After his message of April 12, 1921, he never again pressed Congress for legislation desired by Negroes. He was silent on the race question in both of his annual messages in December 1921 and 1922. Congress, firmly controlled by the Republicans, also showed little concern for such matters, with the exception of the antilynching bill. Harding was not hostile. His public remarks were usually friendly, if general, and on the occasions when he met with Negro delegations his manner was cordial. But his understanding of racial problems remained superficial, and he seemed to feel neither a moral urgency nor a strong political necessity to deal with them.

Harding made his most extensive public statement about the race question in the United States on October 26, 1921, in a speech to several thousand Negroes and whites assembled at Woodrow Wilson Park in Birmingham, Alabama. Amidst his wordy and repetitious rhetoric were some positive statements that attracted considerable attention. As for the two races, he observed that

> Politically and economically there need be no occasion for great and permanent differentiation, for limitations of the individual's opportunity, provided

[7] Johnson to Harding, April 20, 1921, NAACP Papers. See also Johnson to Harding, April 13, 1921, *ibid.*; Eugene Kinckle Jones to Harding, April 19, 1921, Harding Papers.

[8] *Crisis*, 22 (June 1921), 68.

[9] *Ibid.* (July 1921), p. 101. For two similar opinions, see Robert R. Church, Jr. to James W. Johnson, May 21, 1921, and Johnson to Church, June 1, 1921, NAACP Papers.

that on both sides there shall be recognition of the absolute divergence in things social and racial. When I suggest the possibility of economic equality between the races, I mean it precisely the same way and to the same extent that I would mean if I spoke of equality of economic opportunity as between members of the same race. In each case I would mean equality proportional to the honest capacities and deserts of the individual.

Men of both races may well stand uncompromsingly against every suggestion of social equality. Indeed, it would be helpful to have the word "equality" eliminated from this consideration; to have it accepted on both sides that this is not a question of social equality, but a question of recognizing a fundamental, eternal and inescapable difference. . . .

Take the political aspect. I would say let the black man vote when he is fit to vote; prohibit the white man voting when he is unfit to vote. Especially would I appeal to the self-respect of the colored race. I would inculcate in it the wish to improve itself as a distinct race, with a heredity, a set of traditions, an array of aspirations all its own. Out of such racial ambitions and pride will come natural segregations . . . such as are proceeding in both urban and rural communities now in Southern States, satisfying natural inclinations and adding notably to happiness and contentment.

On the other hand I would insist upon equal educational opportunity for both. . . . There must be such education among the colored people as will enable them to develop their own leaders, capable of understanding and sympathizing with such a differentiation between the races as I have suggested. . . . Racial amalgamation there cannot be. Partnership of the races in developing the highest aims of all humanity there must be if humanity, not only here but everywhere, is to achieve the ends which we have set for it.[10]

Reaction to the speech was mixed, both in the North and in the South.[11] Some observers felt that Harding's comments about political and economic equality were bold, particularly since they were de-

[10] New York *Times,* Oct. 27, 1921.

[11] *Ibid.,* Oct. 28, 1921; "The Negro's Status Declared by the President," *Literary Digest,* 71 (Nov. 19, 1921), 7–9; "President Harding Discourses on the Color Line," *Current Opinion,* 71 (Dec. 1921), 708. For a sampling of the extensive newspaper comment on the address, see the two scrapbook volumes of clippings in the George Foster Peabody Collection, Huntington Library, Hampton Institute. A sizable collection of letters referring to the speech is in the Harding Papers, Box 359. Recent Harding biographers still present a varied assessment of the speech. Andrew Sinclair, *The Available Man: The Life behind the Masks of Warren Gamaliel Harding* (New York, 1965), p. 233, asserts that it revealed Harding as a "racist and segregationist." Francis Russell, *The Shadow of Blooming Grove: Warren G. Harding in His Times* (New York, 1968), pp. 470–72, calls it a "Negro rights speech" that was advanced for its time. Robert K. Murray, *The Harding Era: Warren G. Harding and His Administration* (Minneapolis, 1969), pp. 399–400, praises Harding for his sincerity and courage and says that he merely wanted to encourage the growth of a situation in the South in which blacks belonged to both parties and were dominated by neither.

livered in the deep-South city of Birmingham. A number of southern newspapers responded favorably. But others, along with many southern congressmen, denounced the speech vigorously. Senator Pat Harrison of Mississippi, assailed the encouragement to political equality as "a blow to the white civilization of this country that will take years to combat."[12] Among Negroes one of the most favorable reactions was that of Dr. Moton, who called the speech "the most important utterance on this question by a President since Lincoln," and one containing a platform that could be supported by both whites and Negroes.[13] For quite different reasons Marcus Garvey also praised it in a statement denouncing social equality and social amalgamation which showed the common ground that existed between the black nationalist and the white segregationist. Not surprisingly, politicians like Henry Lincoln Johnson of Georgia and Perry Howard of Mississippi wrote letters of congratulations. But many Negroes were far from pleased. Du Bois tried hard to be fair. He commended the president for calling for political, educational, and economic equality, but he strongly regretted the remarks about social equality that devaluated the effect of the message.[14] Others were less reserved, "The President's speech supports the worst Negro-phobist element of the South," cried the New York *Crusade*.[15] Professor Kelly Miller found the emphasis upon racial differences "calculated in the long run to do the Negro as great harm as the Taney Dictum."[16]

These varied reactions stemmed largely from the speech's own contradictions. There is evidence to suggest that Harding decided to speak directly on the race question in hopes of allaying the growing Negro criticism of his administration.[17] But he also wished to reassure the white South. He could not reconcile these two objectives with complete success. Most Negroes considered his reference to "social equality" very unfortunate. Yet his remarks about political, educational, and economic rights for Negroes were so extensive as to

12 New York *Times*, Oct. 28, 1921.

13 Moton to Harding, Nov. 4, 1921, Harding Papers. See also "The South and the President," *Outlook*, 129 (Nov. 9, 1921), 383–85.

14 New York *Times*, Oct. 27, 1921; New York *Sun*, Oct. 27, 1921; Johnson to Harding, Oct. 28, 1921, Howard to Harding, Oct. 28, 1921, Harding Papers; *Crisis*, 23 (Dec. 1921), 53–56.

15 Quoted in Elbert L. Tatum, *The Changed Political Thought of the Negro, 1915–1940* (New York, 1951), p. 96.

16 An open letter to Harding, quoted in *Negro Year Book: 1921/22*, p. 50.

17 See, for example, John T. Adams (chairman of the Republican national committee) to Harding, Sept. 28, 1921; W. H. Hunt to Harding, Oct. 5, 1921, Melvin J. Chisum to George W. Perkins, Jr., Oct. 15, 1921, Harding Papers.

arouse the ire of the Negrophobes to a degree that could not be assuaged by assurances about eternal differences.[18] He should have known that "social equality" was an imprecise and threatening phrase cast about by those who opposed virtually any amelioration of the Negro's condition. As James Weldon Johnson observed, "It is never defined; it is shifted to block any path that may be open; it is stretched over whole areas of contacts and activities; it is used to cover and justify every form of restriction, injustice, and brutality practised against the Negro. The mere term makes cowards of white people and puts Negroes in a dilemma."[19] Whatever Harding's intent may have been in proscribing social equality, his rambling address indicated a good deal of confusion in his thinking about racial matters and clearly demonstrated the problems he faced in attempting to appeal to both white segregationists and black Americans.

By the end of his first year in office Harding's popularity with Negroes had markedly declined, due in considerable measure to his continued attempts to woo white southerners. Many Negroes concluded that Harding was more interested in supporting the lily-white New Republicanism in the South than in backing programs that they wanted. One indication of this was Harding's reliance upon Congressman C. Bascom Slemp of Virginia for advice on southern matters. Slemp represented an area in the extreme southwest portion of the Old Dominion that had long shown Republican strength. His father had been elected Republican congressman from the ninth Virginia district in 1902, and upon his death in 1907, C. Bascom was elected to the seat, which he held for the next fifteen years. From 1905 to 1918 he was also chairman of the Republican state committee and from 1918 to 1932 the national committeeman from Virginia. No more favorably disposed toward the Negro in politics than the Democrats in his state, Slemp concentrated upon the development of a white man's Republican party in Virginia. After his rise to power no more black-and-tan delegations from Virginia were seated by the national convention. During the 1920 presidential campaign Slemp was put in charge of the southern headquarters of the Republican party, and after the election he became Harding's chief adviser

[18] For example, Senator Thomas E. Watson of Georgia insisted that the South would not admit Negroes to political equality because that was "inseparately connected with social equality" ("The Negro's Status Declared by the President," *Literary Digest*, 71 [Nov. 1921], 8).

[19] *Along This Way: The Autobiography of James Weldon Johnson* (New York: The Viking Press, Inc., 1933), p. 311. For an analysis of the issue of social equality, see Gunnar Myrdal, *An American Dilemma: The Negro Problem and Modern Democracy* (New York, 1944), chaps. 28–30, esp. pp. 586–592.

on southern patronage. His position seemed clear evidence of the intention of Republican leaders to build up a lily-white party in the South.[20]

Early in 1921 an article by former President Taft stimulated further talk on the subject. Noting the favorable prospect for the growth of the Republican party in the South, Taft cautioned against arousing white resentment by appointing Negroes there; "they should not be forced into public duty which they must exercise counter to strong local feeling." Rather, he said, they should be placed in the North or in the District of Columbia. Although Harding claimed that he was unaware of Taft's article until Emmett J. Scott called it to his attention, its publication caused considerable concern among Negroes who feared a revival of the much criticized appointment policy followed during Taft's presidency.[21]

Shortly after his inauguration Harding gave considerable attention to the reorganization of the Republican party in the South.[22] In Georgia, a Negro, Henry Lincoln Johnson, had been selected as the state's Republican national committeeman in June 1920. During the campaign whites complained that this would impede the party's growth. The appointment surely pleased the Democrats, wrote one Atlantan to Harding, for "Georgia will be solid Democratic for 100 years with a negro leadership."[23] Slemp, too, feared that this difficulty might hurt the Georgia Republicans, and just at the time when they had a good prospect of receiving a large vote. After the election he discussed possible changes with some white leaders. They warned that despite the strong showing in the 1920 election all their efforts

20 On Slemp, see Guy B. Hathorn, "The Political Career of C. Bascom Slemp" (Ph.D. diss., Duke University, 1950); Hathorn, "Congressional Campaign in the Fighting Ninth: The Contest between C. Bascom Slemp and Henry C. Stuart," *Virginia Magazine of History and Biography*, 66 (July 1958), 337–44; *Selected Addresses of C. Bascom Slemp,* comp. and ed. J. Frederick Essary (Washington, D.C., 1938).

21 Taft, "The Negro Problem in America," *Southern Workman,* 50 (Jan. 1921), 16; Scott to Harding, Feb. 18, 1921, Harding to Scott, Feb. 22, 1921, Harding Papers.

22 For material on the Republican party in various southern states, see *ibid.*, boxes 213–221. Harding received conflicting advice, but innumerable letters came from southern whites warning him that if the GOP were to get anywhere in the South it had to purge itself of Negroes and become a white man's party.

23 B. F. Brimberry to Harding, June 24, 1920, *ibid.* See also Walter Akerman to Harding, June 23, 1920, and T. T. Flagler to Harding, June 25, 1920, *ibid.* On the Georgia party and Henry Lincoln Johnson's selection as national committeeman, see U.S., Congress, Senate, *Presidential Campaign Expenses: Hearings before a Subcommittee on Privileges and Elections,* 66th Cong., 2d sess. (May 24, 1920–Oct. 18, 1920), pp. 945–66.

would be lost unless they could get rid of Johnson.[24] On June 8, 1921, the national committee responded by approving a plan for the reorganization of the Republican party in Georgia that was intended to be a model for the rest of the South. The committee called for a sharply reduced role by Negroes in party affairs. Included in the reform was another change in the allotment of delegates at national conventions that would further reduce the number from the South.[25] Harding then sent a group of advisers to Georgia to assist in the reorganization. A new state chairman was named, and a new state committee was put together. Negroes had been in the majority of the old committee; they had only two members on the new one. Harding attempted to get rid of Johnson by nominating him to be recorder of deeds for the District of Columbia, a plan that was thwarted in November 1921 when the Senate blocked confirmation because of the personal objection of Senator Thomas E. Watson.[26]

These changes aroused a considerable amount of Negro protest. Former Register of the Treasury Judson W. Lyons warned that the reorganization might backfire politically by alienating black voters. In close elections, he asserted, Republicans could be defeated in eight states—New Jersey, New York, Connecticut, Maryland, West Virginia, Ohio, Indiana, and Illinois—in 1922 if they lost the Negro vote.[27] These warnings did not inhibit the administration from encouraging other changes in the southern GOP.

The situation in Louisiana remained as it had been for many years, a battle between the regular black-and-tan forces and the lily-whites who had the backing of many of the business and sugar-planting interests. Negroes composed a majority of the state organization, which was led by a Negro, Walter L. Cohen, and a white,

24 Slemp to D. C. Cole, Sept. 7, 1920, Harding Papers; Hathorn, "Slemp," p. 175; New York *Times*, Jan. 22, 1921.

25 New York *Times*, May 19, June 8–9, 1921; Clarence B. Miller to Harding, May 2, 1921, Harding Papers. At this meeting John T. Adams of Iowa was elected to succeed Will H. Hays as national chairman. Adams was regarded as more sympathetic than Hays to the southern reforms pushed by Slemp.

26 C. W. McClure to Harding, July 28, 1921, O. M. Duke to Harding, July 28, 1921, Harding Papers; Benjamin J. Davis to James W. Johnson, Jan. 8, 1924, NAACP Papers; *Negro Year Book: 1921/22*, p. 39; New York *Times*, June 29, 1921; *Congressional Record*, 67th Cong., 1st sess., vol. 61, pt. 8, p. 8124. Taft had originally appointed Johnson recorder of deeds for the District of Columbia in 1910, and he served until 1914. Although his influence lessened, Johnson remained on the national committee from 1920 until his death in 1925.

27 Lyons to Harding, May 24, 1921, Harding Papers. See also Lyons to Harding, Sept. 10, 1921, *ibid.*

Emile Kuntz, the state's national committeeman. Despite the changes that Harding had approved in Georgia, he told the opponents of the Cohen-Kuntz faction that he was reluctant to cast aside all the old leaders of the GOP who had stuck with the party through thick and thin. Nevertheless, he sent assistant Secretary of Commerce Claudius H. Huston to New Orleans to arrange a meeting between the regular group and the lily-white Republican Club of Louisiana. After some preliminary difficulty because the members of the Republican Club were unwilling to attend any conference at which Negroes were present, a reorganization plan was worked out. The number of black members on the state committee would be cut from 58 to 20 percent, with some places on the new committee going to Republican Club members. Negro representation on the executive committee would be cut from thirteen to five, and the ways and means committee and the advisory committee would become all white. Cohen, whose "fine spirit" was praised by Huston, was willing to accept the plan, even though it weakened the Negro's position in the state organization.[28] "The whole program sounds very pleasing to me," wrote Harding to the president of the Republican Club "and I shall be more delighted than I can tell you if we are able to carry it out effectively and happily."[29] On November 28, 1921, representatives of the old state committee accepted the plan with only slight modification, and in December new officers were nominated. As a result, wrote the optimistic chairman of the state central committee, "all party factions have been wiped out in Louisiana."[30] The reforms in Louisiana, like those in Georgia, did not mean a complete victory for lily-whitism, for Negroes continued to play a role in party affairs. But the direction of the change was clear.

A controversial appointment in North Carolina provided other evidence of Harding's support of the lily-whites. This was his nomination of Frank A. Linney, the chairman of the Republican state committee, to be the United States attorney for the Western District of North Carolina. Linney was a lily-white who had taken a strong segregationist stand as the Republican candidate for governor in 1916 and who had declared himself in favor of Negro disfranchisement during the 1920 campaign. The NAACP, which attempted to block his confirmation, reported that Linney had said, "The Re-

28 Henry C. Warmoth to Harding, May 6, 1921, Harding to Bishop C. Perkins, May 16, 1921, Huston to Harding, Aug. 25, 1921, Kuntz to Harding, Aug. 29, 1921, Warren Kearny to John T. Adams, Sept. 28, 1921, Kearny to Harding, Oct. 7, 1921, *ibid.*

29 Harding to Warren Kearny, Oct. 11, 1921, *ibid.*

30 D. A. Lines to George B. Christian, Jr., Dec. 18, 1921, *ibid.* See also D. A. Lines to John T. Adams, Dec. 18, 1921, Emile Kuntz to Harding, Dec. 3, 1921, *ibid.*

publican Party has not made any effort to organize the Negroes in this campaign, men or women, nor will it openly, secretly or otherwise connive at any such political strategy. . . . I pledge to the women of North Carolina that if we carry the state in this election, you will have a strictly white government, honorable and efficient; and I further assure the good women of the state that in the future the Republican Party's policy will be to let the Negro stay out of politics."[31] Despite the opposition of the NAACP, and reportedly, of a few senators, the Senate, meeting in executive session, confirmed Linney's nomination on August 10, 1921.[32]

It was a different story in the neighboring state of South Carolina. There Negroes controlled much of the party machinery, although the dominant figure was a white, Joseph W. Tolbert. For years the regular black-and-tan organization had the dubious distinction of polling the smallest percentage of Republican presidential votes of any state, and it was under attack by lily-whites, who, in the words of one, hoped to "open the door for a decent Republican doctrine."[33] The lily-whites wanted to reorganize the state party under the leadership of former Senator John L. McLaurin. After he conferred with Slemp at the White House on May 26, 1921, rumors spread that the administration would throw its support to him. On the same day Harding accepted Slemp's recommendation to hold up all of South Carolina's appointments "until some satisfactory solution" was worked out.[34] In this case none was forthcoming. The anti-Tolbert forces claimed that many of the best men of the state would flock to the Republican party if it would get rid of the Negroes. The evidence suggested, however, that the dissidents were more interested in federal appointments for themselves than in the broader welfare of the party. Thus the administration was not convinced that there was such potentially broad support for a reorganization. The regular

31 "Report of the Secretary, June 9, 1921," Spingarn Papers. See also James W. Johnson to W. T. Wills, Jr., May 17, 1921 (and many similar letters from Johnson to other branch officers of the NAACP), and Johnson to William E. Borah, June 7, 1921, NAACP Papers; *Crisis*, 22 (July 1921), 101–2.

32 *Cong. Rec.*, 67th Cong., 1st sess., vol. 61, pt. 5, p. 4828; New York *Times*, Aug. 11, 1921; New York *Tribune*, Aug. 11, 1921.

33 B. F. Bruce to Harding, June 4, 1921, Harding Papers. See also Bruce to Harding, May 30, 1921, A. W. Litschgi to Harding, May 20, 1921, *ibid.* On Tolbert and South Carolina Republicanism, see V. O. Key, Jr., *Southern Politics in State and Nation* (New York, 1949), p. 288; Ralph J. Bunche, "The Political Status of the Negro" (research memorandum prepared for the Carnegie-Myrdal study of the Negro in America, 1940), p. 1185 (copy in Schomburg Collection of the New York Public Library).

34 Slemp to Harding, May 20, 1921, Harding to Slemp, May 26, 1921, B. M. Edwards to Harding, May 30, 1921, Harding Papers.

black-and-tans retained control, and the state remained at the bottom of the Republican vote column. In August 1922 John T. Adams, the Republican national chairman, wrote the state off as incorrigible. "Every suggestion to improve conditions in South Carolina that has come to my notice" he told Harding's secretary, George B. Christian, Jr., "has been made by someone who either wants a federal appointment, or who wishes to control patronage in the place of our present referee. If the South is ever redeemed, South Carolina will be at the tail end of the procession."[35]

Lily-whites were much more successful in Virginia. Under Slemp's leadership white Republicans had already greatly reduced the influence of Negroes in party affairs. In 1920, for example, they had been excluded from the state convention at Roanoke. On July 14, 1921, another state Republican convention was held at Norfolk from which all except two Negro delegates were barred. Henry W. Anderson of Richmond, the leader of the eastern section of the Virginia Republicans, got control of the lily-whites and was nominated for governor. The Republicans took a stronger stand than ever before in claiming to be a white man's party. Negro Republicans then held their own convention and nominated a full slate of candidates for state office. The white Republicans had had hopes of carrying the state, but Anderson polled somewhat less than half of the vote received by his Democratic opponent E. Lee Trinkle, while John Mitchell, the Negro Republican, came in a poor third. Some people attributed this result to the reaction to Harding's Birmingham address, which had allegedly aroused fears of Negro domination, fears that the Democrats exploited. Nevertheless, Anderson's vote was substantial, the largest received by a Republican since Reconstruction. In Virginia, at least, the lily-white Republicans were considerably more than an insignificant faction.[36] If Harding played no direct part in the development of the lily-whites in Virginia, his association with Slemp added to the Negroes' suspicions that he favored a reorganization of the southern Republicans at their expense.

The continued effort to change the formula for representation at national conventions was another indication of the interest of the

[35] Adams to Christian, Aug. 15, 1922, *ibid.* Adams also mentioned the "colored situation in the North" as a reason for not pressing forth with southern reorganization at that time, suggesting that he feared the political reaction in the North among Negro voters.

[36] Andrew Buni, *The Negro in Virginia Politics, 1902–1965* (Charlottesville, Va., 1967), pp. 81–89; Hathorn, "Slemp," pp. 159–64; New York *Times*, July 15, Sept. 11, 1921, Nov. 9, Nov. 10, 1921; Paul Lewinson, *Race, Class and Party: A History of Negro Suffrage and White Politics in the South* (New York, 1932), pp. 159–60, 176–78, 275 n. 35.

party leaders in promoting the New Republicanism in the South. The 1920 Republican national convention had approved a proposal to create a special committee to study and make recommendations on how the Republican party could be made more effective in the South. At the end of January 1921 national chairman Will H. Hays announced the appointment of the "committee on reconstruction." Its chairman was C. Bascom Slemp.[37] By May the special committee had prepared its recommendations. The national committee considered them at its meeting on June 8, 1921, and over the protest of Henry Lincoln Johnson and a few other members, voted to alter the basis for convention representation. Under the 1916 revision a Republican vote of 7,500 in a congressional district in the last election was required in order to have more than one delegate from that district; this had restricted most districts in the South to one delegate. Under the new plan a minimum vote of 2,500 for the Republican candidate in the last presidential or congressional election was necessary for the district to be entitled to any delegate, and a vote of 10,000 or the election of the Republican nominee to Congress was required in order to be allotted a second delegate.[38] Unless there was a marked increase in Republican votes in the 1922 congressional elections, most southern states stood to lose several seats at the next national convention.

Most Negroes, of course, opposed the change, having no illusions about the effect of the reform on their participation in party affairs. Henry Lincoln Johnson chided his fellow national committeemen for jamming the reduction through while the Republican Congress did not "have the guts" to enforce the Fourteenth and Fifteenth Amendments.[39] Even national chairman Adams became worried by the Negroes' reaction. In September he warned Harding that the Democrats had taken advantage of the situation to spread propaganda designed to alienate further "our colored friends" and that the Negro press had become "distinctly hostile." "It is a serious situation and worthy of our most careful consideration."[40]

The 1921 revision was discarded before the next convention took place; on December 12, 1923, the Republican national committee restored the basis for apportioning delegates. Indeed, it agreed to increase the total number of actual delegates at the 1924 convention. The reasons for this reversal were complex. The votes in the 1922

37 New York *Times*, Jan. 31, 1921.

38 Clarence B. Miller to Harding, May 2, 6, 1911, Harding Papers; New York *Times*, June 9, 1921.

39 New York *Times*, June 9, 1921.

40 Adams to Harding, Sept. 28, 1921, Harding Papers.

congressional election were one consideration. On the basis of these returns some northern, as well as most southern states, would have had their delegates cut back, although Virginia and Florida would have gained. The vigorous and continuing Negro opposition to the plan also played a part. Some Republicans did fear a loss of Negro votes. Quite probably the most important reason was a consequence of Harding's death in August 1923 and the elevation of Coolidge to the presidency. As an accidental president, Coolidge was concerned about ensuring his own nomination in 1924, and one of the traditional means was to begin with control of as large a block of southern delegates as possible. This was not the moment to reduce their number. Significantly, the anti-Coolidge hopefuls, like Senator Hiram Johnson of California, denounced the reversal, which they attributed to dictation by the administration.[41]

The problem of reconciling the conflicting demands of Negroes and southern whites was by no means restricted to intraparty conflicts. A particularly troublesome example arose in regard to the Negro veterans' hospital that had been constructed at Tuskegee, Alabama. To some Negroes the idea of building a segregated hospital, and locating it in the South, was unfortunate. In 1921 the NAACP's board of directors voted to oppose the proposal on both counts. But Tuskegee Institute welcomed the hospital and donated a site of 300 acres.[42] The new 600-bed institution, built at a cost of $2,500,000, was dedicated on February 12, 1923. Long before this Dr. Moton had urged the Veterans Bureau to plan on appointing Negroes to responsible positions at it, including the headship, and he had understood that he would be consulted about the personnel. Nevertheless, in January 1923 Colonel Robert H. Stanley, a white man from Alabama, was put in command of the hospital, two days before Moton was even notified. On February 3, Moton talked with Brigadier General Frank T. Hines, the new director of the Veterans Bureau, and discovered that "matters there seemed somewhat confused." Moton explained to Harding that he had gone to see Hines because he "had been informed that this hospital . . . is to be manned entirely by a white staff, no colored persons holding positions above the rank of laborers." Moton was temperate in his comments about Stanley's

41 New York *Times*, Dec. 11–14, 1923; *Nation*, 117 (Dec. 26, 1923), 725; "The Southern Delegate Scandal," *Literary Digest*, 80 (Jan. 5, 1924), 14–15; Stuart A. Rice, "What Do the Different Party Labels Mean?" *Current History*, 20 (Sept. 1924), 908.

42 NAACP, *Annual Report: 1923*, p. 6; Hughes and Patterson, p. 128; Walter White, *A Man Called White* (New York, 1948), p. 69. For an account of the struggle over the hospital, see Pete Daniel, "Black Power in the 1920s: The Case of Tuskegee Veterans Hospital," *Journal of Southern History*, 36 (Aug. 1970), 368–88.

appointment. "I think it entirely proper that the Commanding Officer of the Hospital should be someone already experienced in Government service of this kind, and that his expert assistants should also be people of experience." But he warned Harding that

> if Negro physicians and nurses are debarred from service in this Hospital without at least being given the chance to qualify under the civil service, where that requirement is necessary, it will bring down on my head, and on Tuskegee Institute, an avalanche of criticism. . . . What is more, it will bring down upon your administration throughout the country a storm of protest on the part of the Negro press and from Negroes, North and South, which would be most unfortunate.[43]

On February 23 Harding discussed the issue with Moton and assured him that Negro applicants would be examined for positions at the hospital. On the same day Christian instructed Hines that the president wanted an effort made to secure eligible Negroes. Hines endeavored to do so. But little progress was made, partly because Stanley took the position that he would hire Negroes only as menials, at least initially. Moton turned to the NAACP for help. As a result James Weldon Johnson also warned Harding about the reaction if such discrimination became known, and he asked that at least some Negro physicians and nurses be appointed.[44] On April 28 Christian replied to another NAACP letter and stated flatly that it was "the plan of the Director of the Veterans Bureau, with the approval of the President, to man this institution completely with a colored personnel."[45]

Meanwhile the administration faced growing pressures from southerners to prevent Negro appointments. A number of Alabama political leaders, including the governor of the state, regarded any black officials at the hospital as a threat to white supremacy and, apparently attracted by the federal salaries, demanded an entirely white staff.[46] In answer to a telegram from Governor William W. Brandon, Harding stated that although the decision was not final, the government was planning to organize the hospital with Negroes and that a survey

43 Moton to Harding, Feb. 14, 1923, quoted in Hughes and Patterson, pp. 196–97. See also "The Tuskegee Hospital," *Crisis*, 26 (July 1923), 106. Walter White referred to Stanley as "bitterly anti-Negro" (p. 69).

44 Hughes and Patterson, pp. 130–31; "Tuskegee Hospital," *Crisis*, 26 (July 1923), 107; Daniel, p. 371; Johnson to Harding, March 31, 1923, NAACP Papers; NAACP, *Annual Report: 1923*, p. 26.

45 Herbert J. Seligmann to Christian, April 19, 1923, Christian to Seligmann, April 28, 1923, NAACP Papers.

46 Hughes and Patterson, p. 131; "Tuskegee Hospital," *Crisis*, 26 (July 1923), 106; *Nation*, 116 (July 27, 1923), 750; New York *World*, Aug. 26, 1923.

was being made to find qualified people.[47] A little later Christian wrote in reply to another NAACP query that there was "no change in the attitude of the President" in the matter of Negro appointments.[48] On June 18 Hines reported to Harding "that through the efforts of the professional colored medical associations and the Civil Service Commission, we have been able to obtain practically sufficient colored personnel to man Tuskegee. . . . I hope in the very near future to be able to advise you that the hospital has been completely manned by colored personnel."[49]

By late June, the opposition of Alabama whites to the hiring of Negro personnel became even more intense, and threats of possible riot and bloodshed were heard. On June 26 Hines announced a temporary halt in his recruitment, although he reiterated that the policy of staffing the hospital completely with blacks remained. Under heavy pressure from Tuskegee whites, including two Institute trustees, Moton feared for the safety of the Institute, and on July 1 backed down to the extent of asking Hines to let the hospital continue under white control for the time being. White resistance climaxed on the evening of July 3, when several hundred white-robed Ku Klux Klansmen paraded through the streets of Tuskegee in protest against the placing of Negroes on the hospital staff.[50] Accounts differ as to just how far the Klansmen were willing to go in pressuring local Negroes and Tuskegee Institute. A Negro reporter, Nahum D. Brascher, told the NAACP that the parade had been all "stage-set" and that the officials at the Institute had been notified that the marchers would not actually pass through any of the school thoroughfares; no one there needed to fear being hurt. People at the Institute, he said, looked at the parade not with "awe and silence" as a Montgomery newspaper reported, but with curiosity. They were "depressed but not afraid."[51]

The NAACP thought the Klan threat was extremely serious. On July 5 James Weldon Johnson asked Harding to send federal troops

47 Harding to Brandon, May 1, 1923, quoted in Hughes and Patterson, p. 197; Daniel, p. 373.

48 Herbert J. Seligmann to Christian, May 12, 1923, Christian to Seligmann, May 16, 1923, NAACP Papers. By this time the NAACP took the position that the hospital personnel should be entirely Negro (James W. Johnson to Harding, May 16, 1923, NAACP Papers).

49 Hines to Harding, June 18, 1923, Harding Papers.

50 Daniel, pp. 376–77; Hughes and Patterson, p. 132; White, p. 70; New York *Times*, July 4, 1923; New York *World*, July 5, 1923.

51 Report of Brascher to NAACP, July 4, 1923, NAACP Papers. Albion L. Holsey, who was Moton's secretary, later wrote in a similar vein about the demonstration (Hughes and Patterson, pp. 133–38).

to protect the Institute, the hospital, and Dr. Moton. That same day Hines arrived at Tuskegee and told an assembly of local white citizens that he would not be a party to any movement that would bring disorder upon the community. Hines asked them to appoint a committee of three to discuss the problem of the hospital staff with him. This committee apparently informed Hines that the whites, who had not wanted the hospital there in the first place, intended to run it as they wished.[52] Some of the early reports of this meeting suggested that Hines capitulated. "Whites Win First Round in Tuskegee Hospital Battle" headlined a story in the New York *World*. The Baltimore *Sun* claimed Hines said that he had a moral obligation to appoint white personnel to the hospital. Officials at the Veterans Bureau denied such stories and affirmed that there had been no change in the plan to have an all-Negro staff.[53]

Several days later Hines attempted to reassure the NAACP about the government's intentions. He explained to Johnson that the whole affair was being "unduly agitated" and it would be best for all if the press would stop writing about it. Have "patience and faith in the right thing being done and there will be no question as to the final outcome."[54] The NAACP was not satisfied. It wanted some concrete steps taken to ensure the Negroes' positions at Tuskegee Hospital. On July 24 it asked Hines to remove Stanley as head of the hospital for failing to protect Negro subordinates and for possibly conniving with the Klan. An NAACP report claimed that during the demonstration on the evening of July 3 ten hospital sheets had been used by Klansmen and that all but a few guards left the hospital. It said that Klansmen were allowed to search the premises for John H. Calhoun, a young Negro graduate of Hampton who had been sent by the Civil Service Commission to assume the position of disbursing officer, and that a white woman, the chief dietitian, had prepared a table of hospital food for the Klan marchers. At the same time Johnson wrote an open letter to Harding asking for Stanley's removal and for the fulfillment of his pledge to appoint a black staff.[55]

Not all white southerners endorsed the Klan activity at Tuskegee.

[52] Johnson to Harding, July 5, 1923, Hines to Johnson, July 23, 1923, NAACP Papers; New York *Times*, July 6, 1923; New York *Tribune*, July 6, 1923; Hughes and Patterson, pp. 134–35; White, p. 71.

[53] New York *World*, July 6, 1923; Baltimore *Sun*, July 6, 1923; New York *Herald*, July 10, 1923, copies in NAACP Papers.

[54] Hines to Johnson, July 23, 1923, NAACP Papers.

[55] Johnson to Hines, July 24, 1923, *ibid.*; *Press Service of the NAACP*, undated, July 1923, *ibid.* See also the Report of Nahum D. Brascher to NAACP, July 4, 1923, *ibid.*

Some major newspapers pointed out the inconsistency of segregationist whites opposing Negro personnel in a Negro hospital. Will Alexander of the Commission on Interracial Cooperation even persuaded the Alabama Power Company to object to the presence of the Klan after the Klan demonstration frightened away some blacks working on a nearby company dam. Alexander also obtained signatures, including that of Bishop James Cannon of the Methodist Church, on a resolution condemning the Klan actions, and he pointed out to Senator Oscar Underwood's managers that the affair was hurting the senator's chances for a presidential nomination.[56]

In August, after several conferences with Tuskegee whites, Hines announced what was described in the press as a "compromise arrangement." Temporarily the directorship and two other positions would remain in white hands. All other vacancies were to be filled by blacks. At the same time Hines insisted that the original policy of installing a completely Negro personnel had not been changed.[57]

The Tuskegee whites had not won, but neither had the government quite lived up to its earlier pledge. After Harding's death on August 2, the responsibility passed to his successor. "Unless Calvin Coolidge thus fulfills the promise of President Harding," wrote Du Bois in an editorial denouncing the compromise, "he cannot hope for the votes of intelligent black folk."[58] Moton and the officials at Tuskegee Institute were more willing to accept the compromise than were some of the others involved in the struggle. Albion L. Holsey, Moton's secretary, objected strongly to a statement in the NAACP's annual report for 1924 that "the final victory . . . was lost when the authorities at Washington became convinced that the heads of Tuskegee Institute would be content with a mixed staff." Holsey claimed that Tuskegee was "helpless in the matter" and pointed out that there was a definite promise that the few remaining whites would be gradually replaced.[59] Holsey's faith was justified, for with the appointment of a Negro, Joseph H. Ward, as director in July 1924, the hospital finally became all black. In many ways it was a remarkable triumph of the Negro interests against white opposition, one for which both Harding and Hines deserve credit. But the dispute left scars. Some Negroes regarded the government's position during

56 Hughes and Patterson, pp. 137–38; Alexander, pp. 314–16.

57 New York *Tribune*, Aug. 7, 1923; New York *Times*, Aug. 16, 1923; Daniel, p. 382. Stanley resigned as director on Aug. 22, but he was replaced by another white, Charles M. Griffith.

58 *Crisis*, 27 (Nov. 1923), 8.

59 Holsey to James A. Cobb, May 10, 1924, James W. Johnson to Cobb, May 14, 1924, NAACP Papers. On the disagreement between the NAACP and Tuskegee, see also Shelby J. Davidson to Walter White, Jan. 5, 1924, *ibid.*

most of 1923 as weak and vacillating. Doubts were raised about the administration's intentions or its ability to act. At the same time Harding's position antagonized many white southerners. Once again Republican leaders found that reconciliation of the demands of both black Americans and white southerners was very difficult.

The struggle at Tuskegee provided one example of the threat that the Ku Klux Klan presented to Negroes during the early years of the 1920's. The rapid growth of this organization led to demands by the NAACP, the Commission on Interracial Cooperation, and other groups for an investigation by the executive department or by Congress. The NAACP also tried, with little success, to obtain statements on the Klan from all members of Congress.[60] No investigation by the Justice Department or any other agency of the executive was forthcoming, but a number of Democratic and Republican congressmen did introduce resolutions for an inquiry. The House Rules Committee held a brief public hearing from October 11 to 17, 1921.[61] Several witnesses testified in favor of a full congressional investigation, but most of the time was spent listening to Imperial Wizard William Joseph Simmons. Having provided the Klan leader with a national forum from which he could air his convictions, the committee ended the hearings and reported adversely on the proposals for an investigation.

The press reported that Harding looked favorably upon the proposal for a Justice Department investigation, but he made no public statement on the Klan during the abortive House hearings. In the spring of 1922 he was plagued by stories, spread in part by a Klan lecturer, Joe G. Camp of Atlanta, that Harding, Attorney General Harry M. Daugherty, and some other members of the administration were either Klan members or in strong sympathy with the organization. Christian attempted to squelch such rumors. "Any statement of the President's interest in or approval of the Ku Klux Klan is a complete and egregious misrepresentation of the President's attitude," he wrote in a letter released to the press. "In some quarters it has been represented that the President is a member of this organization. Not only is this untrue, but the fact is that the President

[60] James W. Johnson to Harding, Sept. 19, 1921, *ibid.*; *Press Service of the NAACP,* Sept. 16, 1921, Spingarn Papers; Alexander, p. 195; New York *Times,* Sept. 21, 1921; Johnson to George W. Norris, Oct. 4, 1921, George W. Norris Papers, Manuscript Division, Library of Congress. Similar letters were sent to other members of Congress.

[61] U.S., Congress, House, *Ku-Klux Klan: Hearings before the Committee on Rules,* 67th Cong., 1st sess. (Oct. 11–17, 1921); New York *Times,* Oct. 18, 1921. Technically the hearings were only on the resolution calling for a congressional investigation, although they dealt with substantive matters.

heartily disapproves of the organization and has repeatedly expressed himself to this effect."[62]

A forthright public condemnation of the Klan by Harding himself would have been more effective. But the president was at a loss as to what action he ought to take. "I do not know the most practical method of dealing with the Ku Klux Klan," he wrote on November 12, 1922, to the Texas member of the Republican national committee, "but I think every organization of that sort is a menace to American freedom and American institutions."[63] Harding was reluctant to use the power of the federal government. To Governor John M. Parker of Louisiana, who had written about the inability of his state's government to deal with Klan offenses, he expressed not only his surprise but also his disapproval of Parker's suggestion that federal assistance was needed. Such interference with the police powers of a state, answered Harding, would be deeply resented throughout many parts of the country. Attorney General Daugherty took a similar view. In answer to a request by Senator David I. Walsh of Massachusetts that the Department of Justice take action against the Klan, Daugherty asserted that it could find no cases within the jurisdiction of the federal government.[64] In 1923, during the difficulties at the Tuskegee Veterans Hospital, Walter White talked with members of the Justice Department about Klan activity. Assistant Attorney General John W. Crim was sympathetic with the Negro's position, but otherwise he was not reassuring. Indeed, Crim told White that he believed "that the administration at Washington was playing politics with the Klan."[65] A number of other people agreed. The cautious manner in which Congress and the executive branch handled the Klan during the Harding presidency added to the doubts that many Negroes had about the basic goodwill of the Republican leaders.

Harding's response to a number of the problems inherited from the Wilson administration reinforced these doubts. The return of the Republicans to power did not result in the changes that many Negroes had hoped for. For example, in 1920 Harding had made a minor campaign issue of the American occupation of Haiti, and his

62 Christian to Mrs. Frank L. Applegate, April 12, 1922, Harding Papers. In the Harding Papers, box 317, are several letters inquiring about Harding's association with the Klan and similar answers from Christian; see especially Charleston A. Kleinman to Christian, April 14, 1922, Christian to Kleinman, April 18, 1922, Will W. Alexander to Christian, May 3, 1922.

63 Harding to H. F. MacGregor, Nov. 13, 1922, *ibid.*

64 Harding to Parker, Nov. 8, 1922, *ibid.*; New York *Times*, Nov. 28, Dec. 5, 1922.

65 "Minutes of the Meeting of the Board of Directors, July 9, 1923," NAACP Papers.

statements provided a reasonable basis for believing that the Republicans would institute some significant changes. A special committee headed by Republican Senator Medill McCormick of Illinois began a Senate investigation in 1921, but it disappointed the NAACP by failing to make a full report on the alleged American atrocities and by not recommending the immediate withdrawal of the United States Marines. By the summer of 1921 Harding had concluded, in line with the views of Secretary of State Charles Evans Hughes, that American forces would have to remain as long as the stability of the islands, including the protection of American investments, required it. Instead of ending the occupation the Republicans provided a reorganization and rationalization of it.[66]

Another legacy of the Wilson presidency was the problem of increased racial segregation in the federal government. At his meeting with Johnson on August 9, 1920, Harding had "virtually promised he would abolish it in government departments by executive order if elected."[67] Republicans on Capitol Hill, however, had already shown their reluctance to challenge such segregation. After they regained control of Congress in 1919 they took no steps to end segregation in areas under congressional jurisdiction such as the lunchroom of the Library of Congress and the Senate restaurant.[68] The NAACP included the abolition of segregation in its list of demands which Johnson presented to Harding on April 4, 1921, and subsequently numerous other individuals and groups appealed for this reform. The results were disappointing. Harding did not issue any order abolishing segregation. In fact the government appeared to be remarkably insensitive to the feelings of Negroes in regard to the practice.

The ceremony dedicating the Lincoln Memorial on May 30, 1922, was an example. The guests were all carefully segregated, apparently at the behest of Colonel C. O. Sherrill, the superintendent of public buildings and grounds. Some Negroes were indignant. The District of Columbia branch of the NAACP protested to Harding and other

66 Hans Schmidt, *The United States Occupation of Haiti, 1915–1934* (New Brunswick, N.J., 1971), pp. 121–34; U.S., Congress, Senate, Select Committee on Haiti and Dominican Republic, *Inquiry into Occupation and Administration of Haiti and Santo Domingo*, 67th Cong., 2d sess., Senate Rept. 794 (June 26, 1922); James W. Johnson to McCormick, July 26, 1922, NAACP Papers; Johnson, p. 360; *Crisis*, 24 (June 1922), 60; Hughes to Harding, July 19, Aug. 15, Aug. 20, 1921, Harding to Hughes, Aug. 20, 1921, Harding Papers.

67 "Minutes of the Meeting of the Board of Directors, September 13, 1920" (NAACP), Spingarn Papers.

68 *What Has the Branch Done: A Record of the Efforts and Achievements of the D.C. Branch of the NAACP during the Year 1919*, pamphlet, NAACP Papers.

government leaders. "It would be a rude awakening and a painful disillusionment to us to realize that this party was approving and following a practice which was an incident of chattel slavery. Such a realization, in the case of a self-respecting people, could only result in the severing of ties which until now have bound us to that party."[69]

Within the departments segregation even increased to some extent during the Harding period. Its introduction into the office of the register of the Treasury was particularly upsetting. Wilson had given this post, traditionally held by a black, to a white. Harding failed to restore it to Negro hands and named another white, Harley V. Speelman. In July 1923 Speelman began the segregation of black and white clerks by erecting partitions. He also required the separate use of the elevators and segregated rest rooms for the women. Vigorous protests resulted in some mitigation of these orders, but it was a disillusioning experience. Harding had failed to live up to his promise to Johnson, and, at the time of his death, governmental segregation was still widespread.[70]

Harding's record was also disappointing in the related issue of Negro appointments. Among the NAACP's proposals presented by Johnson was one for the naming of black assistant secretaries in the Departments of Labor and Agriculture. Not only did Harding ignore this request; he was slow to fill posts that had been traditionally held by Negroes, at least before Wilson. At the end of March 1921 Emmett J. Scott informed the administration that Negroes were becoming impatient over the delay, and he hinted that more should be done.[71] Harding responded on April 7 with a memorandum to members of the cabinet asking them to find "a couple of suitable places for colored appointees," so that he could put "a few representative colored Republicans into administrative activity."[72] Not until June 28, 1921, did Harding attempt his first significant Negro appointment by nominating Henry Lincoln Johnson to be recorder of deeds for

[69] Copy of the resolution in NAACP Papers. It was signed by Archibald H. Grimké and Shelby J. Davidson. The resolution also claimed that segregation placards had recently been placed in Rock Creek Park, which was also under the jurisdiction of the superintendent of public buildings and grounds.

[70] August Meier and Elliott Rudwick, "The Rise of Segregation in the Federal Bureaucracy, 1900–1930," *Phylon*, 28 (Summer 1967), 182; James W. Johnson to L. M. Hershaw, May 14, 1923, NAACP Papers; Pittsburgh *Courier*, July 16, 1927.

[71] Scott to Christian, March 30, 1921, Harding Papers. See also Eugene McIntosh to Harding, June 3, 1921, *ibid.*

[72] Harding to James J. Davis, April 7, 1921, quoted in Sinclair, p. 230. See also Harding to Harry S. New, June 20, 1921, Harding to Davis Elkins, June 20, 1921, Harding Papers.

the District of Columbia. As already noted, this move seems to have been motivated mainly by a desire to get Johnson out of the way in order to facilitate the reorganization of the Republican organization in Georgia, and it was upset by the Senate's refusal to confirm Johnson in November 1921. The post later went to another Negro, Arthur G. Froe of West Virginia, whose appointment had been recommended by Senator Davis Elkins as a means of recognizing the substantial number of black voters in his state.[73]

Harding's reluctance to appoint Negroes seems to have been largely a consequence of his interest in reorganizing the Republican party in the South along lily-white lines. The nomination of Negroes to positions anywhere, even outside of the South, was likely to detract from his image among most white southerners. At the same time, however, the reaction of Negroes to this policy of calculated neglect alarmed Republican politicians in states with a sizable number of black voters. Thus during the final months of 1921 several Republican politicians, including Senator Joseph S. Frelinghuysen of New Jersey, Senator Elkins of West Virginia, Congressman Charles L. Knight of Ohio, and a number of party leaders in Maryland, urged Harding to make some appointments as a means of holding the significant Negro vote in their states.[74]

Eventually some Negroes did receive office, although the number was small, especially of those in higher positions.[75] Two influential southern political figures were included. The first was Perry Howard of Mississippi, a state in which the administration accepted black-and-tan control of a Republican party that had only minuscule popular support anyway. In May 1921 Howard was named a special assistant to the attorney general. The other was Walter L. Cohen of Louisiana, who in November 1922 was nominated comptroller of customs at New Orleans, one of the most lucrative federal jobs in the South. A veteran of some thirty years of Louisiana politics, Cohen

[73] New York *Times*, June 29, 1921, Feb. 3, 1922; *Cong. Rec.*, 67th Cong., 1st sess., vol. 61, pt. 3, p. 3161, and pt. 8, p. 8124; Elkins to Harding, Dec. 5, 1921, Harding Papers.

[74] Frelinghuysen to Harding, Sept. 24, 1921, Knight to Christian, Oct. 18, 1921, Elkins to Harding, Dec. 5, 1921, W. P. Jackson *et al.* to Harding, Dec. 13, 1921, Harding Papers.

[75] See *ibid.*, box 140, for reports prepared in April and May 1922 at the request of Senator Coleman du Pont of Delaware listing Negroes holding positions paying over $3,000. The Department of State listed five; Interior listed four (including Emmett J. Scott, secretary treasurer of Howard University, only part of whose salary came from the federal government); Treasury listed three; and Agriculture, Labor, and Justice listed one each. The Commerce, Navy, and Post Office Departments listed none.

had many enemies, and he was rejected by the Senate in March 1923. He later received a recess appointment from Harding, was renominated by Coolidge, and after a second rejection was finally confirmed in March 1924.[76] Harding also recognized one important northern Negro politician, Charles W. Anderson of New York, with an appointment in March 1923 as collector of internal revenue for the Third District of New York.[77] On the other hand two previously Negro-held posts, the register of the Treasury and the auditor of the Navy, remained in white hands, as did several other lesser positions in Washington. Of the twelve diplomatic and consular positions traditionally held by Negroes a number had been lost under Wilson; another two went to whites under Harding. Only the posts of minister to Liberia, three consuls, and the first secretary of the legation at Monrovia, Liberia, continued to be occupied by Negroes.[78]

Black leaders generally, and not merely the officeseekers, were keenly disappointed by Harding's record on appointments. Conservatives and radicals alike complained. In July 1921 Du Bois angrily pointed out that with the exception of Henry Lincoln Johnson, Harding had made no Negro appointments of consequence.[79] When Harding reappointed Judge Robert H. Terrell to the municipal court of the District of Columbia in the spring of 1922, Emmett J. Scott observed that he had done "about the only decent thing of his administration, so far as we are concerned."[80] In July 1923 a group of Negro leaders from several states met at Atlantic City and drew up a highly critical statement denouncing the administration for its continued neglect of black Americans. The leader of this gathering,

[76] Harry M. Daugherty to Christian, April 22, 1922, Harding Papers; Key, p. 286; New York *Times*, Nov. 5, Nov. 23, 1922, March 2, Dec. 11, 1923, Feb. 19, Feb. 26, March 18, 1924; *Nation*, 115 (Dec. 6, 1922), 594; memorandum on Cohen in "Foreign Affairs-Liberia," Presidential Papers, Herbert C. Hoover Papers, Hoover Presidential Library, West Branch, Iowa.

[77] New York *Times*, March 6, 1923; Gilbert Osofsky, *Harlem, the Making of Ghetto: Negro New York, 1890–1930* (New York, 1966), p. 167.

[78] The minister to Liberia was Solomon Porter Hood of New Jersey, who was nominated and confirmed without difficulty in Oct. 1921 (*Cong. Rec.*, 67th Cong., 1st sess., vol. 61, pt. 7, pp. 6654, 6809). For Negro officeholders under Harding, see the memoranda to Christian prepared by various department heads in April 1922, Harding Papers; *Negro Year Book: 1921/22*, p. 183; *Republican Campaign Text-Book: 1924*, p. 321.

[79] *Crisis*, 22 (July 1921), 102.

[80] Scott to Terrell, June 26, 1922, Robert H. Terrell Papers, Manuscript Division, Library of Congress. See George A. Myers to James Ford Rhodes, May 22, 1922, in John A. Garraty, ed., *The Barbor and the Historian: The Correspondence of George A. Myers and James Ford Rhodes, 1910–1923* (Columbus, Ohio, 1956), p. 144, for a similar comment.

Dr. George E. Cannon of Jersey City, complained bitterly that Harding had given them less recognition than any previous Republican president. Although Cannon and many others at the Atlantic City conference had long been active supporters of the GOP they publicly threatened to bolt the party if Republican policies were not changed.[81]

The Republican response to the continuing problem of disfranchisement was no more satisfactory. By 1920 most of the various "legal" devices to deprive Negroes of their vote had been in operation for several years. No serious effort had been made in Congress to enact legislation to protect the right to vote since the Lodge bill of 1890–91, and no Republican platform since 1908 had explicitly condemned disfranchisement. The southern practices had been accepted without protest by most northerners and, except for the grandfather clauses, sanctioned by the Supreme Court. There seemed little likelihood that Republicans would attempt any remedial action.

Nevertheless, Harding told Johnson during their conference on August 9, 1920, "I am not only in favor of the Negro having the full right to the ballot, but personally, I am in favor of securing him that right by a force bill if necessary."[82] Johnson brought the subject up again in his meeting with Harding shortly after the inauguration and requested an investigation as a start toward ensuring equal voting rights. But no more was heard on the subject.

In the meantime the NAACP had decided that a serious effort should be made to apply the Fourteenth Amendment to the problem of disfranchisement, despite the possibility that a reduction of representation might be interpreted as a sort of constitutional sanction for the continued denial of the suffrage to Negroes. "It may be that the best way of inducing the South to respect the rights of the colored people is to make them feel that their voice in the nation depended upon it," explained Moorfield Storey to Johnson. "Rather than give up rights they might be willing to concede votes. If we can once put them in that position and any dissension arises between the whites, the party that needs votes will probably agitate in favor of giving them to the colored people."[83]

After the 1920 election the NAACP sent a telegram to Congress-

[81] New York *Times*, May 11, July 21, July 22, 1923; Pittsburgh *Courier*, July 28, 1923. See also Cannon to Christian, March 21, 1921, Cannon to Harding, May 24, 1922, Harding Papers.

[82] "Minutes of the Meeting of the Board of Directors, September 13, 1920" (NAACP), Spingarn Papers.

[83] Storey to Johnson, Dec. 18, 1919, NAACP Papers.

man Isaac Siegel of New York, chairman of the House Committee on the Census, urging a reapportionment of representation in accordance with the terms of the Fourteenth Amendment. It claimed that there had been "open and flagrant disfranchisement of colored voters in a number of states" in the presidential election, and offered to furnish evidence.[84] On December 3, 1920, Johnson and Herbert Seligmann discussed the matter with Siegel, who said he was going to introduce a bill that would raise the question of southern representation.[85] But the only congressman who showed a strong interest in the question of Negro suffrage was George H. Tinkham of Massachusetts. Somewhat of a maverick, Tinkham was not known for his liberal sentiments, but like his abolitionist predecessors from the Bay State, he showed a determined interest in Negro rights. In early December 1920 Tinkham presented a resolution calling for a House investigation of Negro disfranchisement and for a reapportionment of representation according to the actual voting population. The NAACP immediately telegraphed Tinkman, endorsing the proposal and offering to provide documentary proof of disfranchisement.[86] On December 29 and 30, 1920, several NAACP representatives appeared before the Committee on the Census at hearings on the decennial reapportionment bill. The sessions were stormy; a number of southern congressmen heckled and harassed the NAACP spokesmen, apparently trying to prevent testimony unfavorable to the white South from getting on the record. Nevertheless, the NAACP managed to present evidence of disfranchisement in the 1920 election and asked for a congressional investigation. Wherever disfranchisement was found, they wanted remedial action to secure the vote or an appropriate reduction in representation in Congress.[87]

On May 6, 1921, Tinkham introduced a resolution calling for an investigation by the Committee on the Census into the denial of the vote to citizens and for the committee to report its findings as the basis for a reapportionment of representatives. Tinkham claimed that his resolution was constitutionally privileged and therefore entitled to immediate consideration. His criticism of southern suffrage re-

[84] "Minutes of the Meeting of the Board of Directors, November 8, 1920" (NAACP), Spingarn Papers.

[85] "Report of the Secretary, December 8, 1920," *ibid.*

[86] New York *Times*, Dec. 6, 7, 8, 1920; "Report of the Secretary, December 8, 1920," Spingarn Papers.

[87] Report by Walter White on the Dec. 29–30 hearings, NAACP Papers; *Crisis*, 21 (Feb. 1921), 165; NAACP, *Annual Report: 1920*, pp. 27–28; New York *Times*, Dec. 30–31, 1920; Walter White to George H. Tinkham, Jan. 20, 1921, NAACP Papers. See also the pamphlet prepared by the NAACP, *Disfranchisement of Colored Americans in the Presidential Election of 1920*, Spingarn Papers.

strictions and of GOP inaction was severe. The issue, he said, concerns "the most colossal electoral fraud the world has ever known. On this question moral cowardice and political expediency dominate the Republican leadership of this House."[88] Tinkham found scant support for his resolution. Majority floor leader Frank W. Mondell of Wyoming even denounced Tinkham's comments as those of a "stump speech." Finally Speaker Frederick H. Gillett of Massachusetts ruled unfavorably on the matter of constitutional privilege, and the House upheld the decision by a vote of 286 to 47.[89] Thus the Republican-controlled House killed any chance for action at that time.

Tinkham did not readily admit defeat. During debate on the apportionment bill in October, he proposed an amendment for the reduction of representation of those states which denied the vote to citizens. The Fourteenth Amendment, he argued, uses the verb "shall" in this connection, and therefore such a reduction was mandatory.[90] Tinkham was no more successful this time than earlier. His Republican colleagues in Congress were no more interested in fighting for Negro voting rights than was the president.

Republican leaders did little better on several other lesser issues. Another of the items of the NAACP's agenda was the creation of a national interracial commission to study race relations in America. The NAACP had discussed the idea as early as 1912, and Oswald Garrison Villard had presented such a proposal to President Wilson in May 1913.[91] But it had been lost in the turmoil that shortly after erupted over segregation in the government. Harding apparently supported the idea in his message of April 12, 1921.[92] Two related bills were then introduced into Congress, one by Senator Selden P. Spencer of Missouri and another by Congressman Caleb R. Layton of Delaware. Spencer's measure proposed a broad study of race relations; Layton's called for a Negro Industrial Commission that would be primarily concerned with economic conditions. Johnson wrote to Harding that he considered the Spencer bill the better of the two, although he suggested changes in the proposed membership of the commission. But his hopes faded rapidly. After a visit to Washington in June 1921 Johnson concluded that there was little chance that

88 *Cong. Rec.*, 67th Cong., 1st sess., vol. 61, pt. 2, p. 1126.

89 *Ibid.*, p. 1130.

90 *Ibid.*, pt. 6, pp. 6311–12. Another effort by Tinkham in May 1922 to force the Census Bureau to collect data on disfranchisement was simply ignored (see New York *Times*, May 15, 1922; *Cong. Rec.*, 67th Cong., 2d sess., vol. 62, pt. 7, p. 7009).

91 Charles F. Kellogg, *NAACP: A History of the National Association for the Advancement of Colored People*, vol. I: 1909–1920 (Baltimore, 1967), pp. 159–61.

92 New York *Times*, April 13, 1921. Harding's language was equivocal, but he acknowledged that "the proposal has real merit."

Congress would seriously consider either measure.[93] Although Harding urged members of the Judiciary Committee to report out the Spencer bill, they failed to act.[94] Once again the proposal was abandoned.

Serious questions about the rights of Negroes were occasionally raised in other measures before Congress not directly concerned with race relations. The Sheppard-Towner Act, passed in November 1921, was one example. This measure granted money to the states on a dollar-matching basis to be used to promote the welfare of mothers and children.[95] As the states were given nearly a free hand in administering the act, however, there was no guarantee that the funds would be distributed on a racially nondiscriminatory basis. The social worker Florence Kelley had long been a strong supporter of such federal aid, but during the debates over the bill she was torn by her knowledge that the measure would be of little help to Negroes in the South. For a while Johnson hoped that a provision for the equitable distribution of funds could be written into the bill. But, as Mrs. Kelly pointed out, such a provision would only ensure the defeat of whole measure. Despite her misgivings, Mrs. Kelley supported passage of the bill, for even if it were unjustly administered in the South she believed that it would surely aid Negro mothers and children in other sections.[96] In this, as in other instances, most congressmen showed little sensitivity to the racial implications of the bill.

Another example was afforded by the proposals to create a Department of Education and to authorize under it the expenditure of federal funds for the support of education in the states. Sponsored by the National Education Association, the idea had the backing of a number of reformers. To allay fear of federal control, the N.E.A. carefully pointed out that the measures provided that the money granted to the states would "be spent under the exclusive direction of State and local educational authorities." [97] Local control, how-

93 *Cong. Rec.*, 67th Cong., 1st sess., vol. 61, pt. 1, pp. 144, 218; Johnson to Harding, June 1, 1921, NAACP Papers; "Report of the Secretary, June 9, 1921," Spingarn Papers.

94 Medill McCormick to Harding, Oct. 17, 1921, Christian to McCormick, Oct. 24, 1921, Harding to C. Bascom Slemp, May 22, 1922, Harding Papers.

95 New York *Times*, Nov. 8, 20, 22, 1921; Austin F. MacDonald, *Federal Aid: A Study of the American Subsidy System* (New York, 1928), pp. 210–34; J. Stanley Lemons, "The Sheppard-Towner Act: Progressivism in the 1920's," *Journal of American History*, 55 (March 1969), 776–86.

96 Kelley to James W. Johnson, April 4, April 8, 1921, Johnson to Kelley, April 7, 1921, NAACP Papers.

97 *Journal of the National Education Association*, 12 (Dec. 1923), 412. See also MacDonald, pp. 268–69; George D. Strayer, "The Towner-Sterling Bill," *Journal of the National Education Association*, 11 (Oct. 1922), 311.

ever, was precisely what Negroes feared. At a meeting of the NAACP directors in February 1923, Florence Kelley warned that the education bill (then known as the Sterling-Towner bill) would perpetuate discrimination against black children in the South. In this case Mrs. Kelley concluded that the defects outweighed the gains, so she decided to oppose the measure.[98] The NAACP did not object to federal aid to public education in principle; on the contrary, it expressly endorsed such assistance. But it strongly opposed any measure that would allow southern states to use funds in a racially discriminatory manner. "We have repeatedly asked for Federal aid for education," read a public statement of the NAACP in 1924, "and in answer we have a bill before Congress which is a travesty on justice and would perpetuate in local school systems these very discriminations against which we vigorously protest."[99] Although the education bill did not pass, its failure cannot be attributed primarily to the criticisms of the NAACP. Deep-seated fears about federal interference, not concerns for equal rights, were undoubtedly the most important obstacles at this time.

The Sheppard-Towner and the Sterling-Towner bills raised serious questions of racial injustice. But the issues were too remote to attract the fervent attention of many black Americans. The antilynching campaign, which went on during the same period, was a different matter. This struggle, the most important legislative effort of the decade in regard to Negro rights, must now be examined in order to delineate more clearly the limits of normalcy.

[98] "Minutes of the Meeting of the Board of Directors, February 14, 1923," NAACP Papers; Florence Kelley, "The Sterling Discrimination Bill," *Crisis*, 26 (Oct. 1923), 252–55. See also NAACP, *Annual Report: 1923*, p. 43.

[99] Resolution at annual meeting of the Board of Directors, Jan. 7, 1924, NAACP Papers; NAACP, *Annual Report: 1924*, p. 47. See also James W. Johnson to Mary R. Wellman, April 14, 1924, Moorfield Storey to Johnson, April 21, 1924, Johnson to Storey, May 1, 1924, NAACP Papers.

CHAPTER VII

The Antilynching Crusade

NEGROES confronted the gap between ideals and reality in American life in its most elemental form as the victims of lynching or other acts of mob violence. Here society failed to protect the most fundamental of all rights, that to life itself. Year after year the toll of dead and wounded testified to the fact that the failure was no temporary or isolated aberration. Moreover, lynchings or race riots affected not just immediate victims; they spread fear throughout whole communities and areas. Spurred on by the NAACP's antilynching drive, by 1920 Negroes were determined as never before that the federal government had to assume a responsibility for putting a stop to these crimes. With the return of the Republicans to power, many Negroes held that a major test of the GOP's good faith would be its willingness to take an effective stand against lynching.

Although the number of lynchings each year had declined fairly steadily since the 1890's, the death toll was still high. According to an NAACP report sixty-seven people were killed in 1918 alone. From 1889 to 1918 lynch mobs claimed some 3,224 victims. Of these, 2,522, or 78.2 percent, were Negroes, including 50 women. After 1900 the proportion of Negroes was considerably higher than before, and as the years went by lynching became more and more a crime committed against members of this race. It also became increasingly identified with one section as the number occurring in the North and West dropped sharply after the turn of the century. Between 1889 and 1918, 87.9 percent of all the recorded lynchings took place in the South and border regions.[1] These statistics actually understate the extent to which Negroes were the victims of interracial violence. Murders committed by one or two individuals, for example, were not included. Nor were the casualties of the great race riots usually counted in the total. Undoubtedly there were others whose deaths simply went unnoticed by the larger community.

There was something particularly terrible about lynching. Emboldened by the anonymity of a mob, the executioners all too frequently resorted to the most barbarous and ingenious acts of cruelty.

[1] National Association for the Advancement of Colored People, *Thirty Years of Lynching in the United States, 1889–1918* (New York, 1919), pp. 7–8, 29–30, 34–35.

Often the state itself, or one of its agents, was a partner in the crime, either by its failure to make a reasonable effort to prevent it or by actual participation. The states were even more negligent about taking serious steps to punish the lynchers. With a few exceptions, in the period up to the 1920's, the record shows that lynchers needed to have little fear of being punished for their crime. One student has estimated that conviction of lynchers followed only about .8 percent of all the lynchings in the United States from 1900 to 1933.[2]

A lynching was no casual act; the lynchers arrogated for themselves the function of the state. Lynching is not mere murder, observed James Weldon Johnson, "but a conspiracy by the mob which effectively substitutes the anarchy of mob action and mob justice for court trial and due process of law. It is a temporary overthrow of the State."[3] This feature in particular lay at the basis for the demand for federal antilynching legislation to guarantee that due process and equal protection of the law which the states were not providing.

The negligence of the states was encouraged by those southern politicians and community leaders who defended lynching, usually as a punishment made necessary by the crime of rape or the failure of the courts to punish crimes. To Congressman Frank Clark of Florida, those who were lynched were generally "brutes, both black and white," who had assaulted women. It was impossible to let the law take its course, he argued, for it would mean that innocent women would have to expose the details of rape in court. "I am quite sure that in the South they have always got the right man, and the swiftness and certainty of punishment has undoubtedly deterred other brutes from the commission of this crime."[4] Former Governor Coleman L. Blease of South Carolina held that "in the South the lynching of a man for the unmentionable crime is a protection to our civilization. . . . An aroused mob is an outraged community which carries out the law, but brushes aside the law's technicalities and delays."[5] Opponents pointed out again and again that accusation

[2] James H. Chadbourn, *Lynching and the Law* (Chapel Hill, N.C., 1933), p. 13.

[3] Johnson, "Lynching–America's National Disgrace," *Current History*, 19 (Jan. 1924), 600. There has never been perfect agreement as to what constitutes lynching, but the definition in the unsuccessful Dyer bill has the essential elements described by Johnson. In that bill a "mob of riotous assemblage" meant "an assemblage composed of three or more persons acting in concert for the purpose of depriving any person of his life without authority of law as a punishment for or to prevent the commission of some actual or supposed public offense."

[4] *Congressional Record*, 66th Cong., 1st sess., vol. 58, pt. 3, p. 2867 (July 19, 1919).

[5] New York *Times*, Aug. 27, 1915. The remark was from a speech delivered in Boston at a conference of governors.

of rape was the alleged cause of only a small proportion of the lynchings—19 percent for the period 1889 to 1918, according to the NAACP's figures. But men like Clark and Blease and others obsessed with the "rape complex" were impervious to argument. A second justification for lynching, the charge that the courts were likely to dismiss Negroes accused of crimes, was even more difficult to sustain. The facts showed that blacks indicted for capital crimes against whites, and these included rape in most southern states, received severe treatment by the courts.[6]

Lynching was a major reason for Negro discontent. As Robert R. Moton wrote in 1919, it was "the chief cause of unrest among Negroes. It was the cause most often given as a reason for wanting to migrate to the North."[7] The ultimate denial of due process, lynching was the final result of a social and political system that systematically deprived blacks of the rights of equal citizenship. Without political power, Negroes in the South were left to the uncertain mercy of the dominant whites. By 1920, however, the migrations had resulted in a considerable increase in the political strength of Negroes in the North, a fact that gave some impetus to a serious campaign for a federal antilynching law. With much of the country accepting the racial premises of the segregationist South, even though it did not condone lynching, the obstacles to success were still enormous.

In the past the Republican party had shown only slight concern over lynching. Its platform in 1896 and again in 1912 condemned lynching, but no serious efforts were made to do anything about it. The one exception concerned not American citizens but the treaty rights of aliens. In order to protect the latter, in December 1891 President Harrison recommended passage of an antilynching law. Several bills along this line were introduced in Congress in the 1890's and after. None was successful, although one got as far as passage by the House in December 1908. The first and only bill to make the lynching of an American citizen a federal crime was introduced by Negro Congressman George H. White of North Carolina in January 1900. It got nowhere.[8] One of the tasks of any group in-

[6] NAACP, *Lynching*, p. 36; Southern Commission on the Study of Lynching, *Lynchings and What They Mean* (Atlanta, 1931), pp. 18–19. The expression "rape complex" is W. J. Cash's; see his *The Mind of the South* (New York, 1941), pp. 113–17.

[7] Moton, "The South and the Lynching Evil," *South Atlantic Quarterly*, 18 (July 1919), 192.

[8] David O. Walter, "Proposals for a Federal Anti-Lynching Law," *American Political Science Review*, 28 (June 1934), 436–38; *Cong. Rec.*, 56th Cong., 1st sess., vol. 33, pt. 2, p. 1021, and pt. 3, p. 2153. See above, p. 15.

terested in obtaining federal action against lynching was to arouse the nation and its political leaders from this apathy.

The NAACP's campaign against lynching began in earnest in 1916. In February, Philip G. Peabody of Boston offered $10,000 to the association if it would develop an effective program against lynching. An antilynching committee was appointed which proposed a program emphasizing investigation and compilation of facts and the organization of southern businessmen and politicians who would publicly condemn lynching. Peabody was dissatisfied with this approach, which meant keeping the role of the NAACP in the background in the South. In July he changed his pledge to $1,000 on the condition that an additional $8,000 be raised by August 1. NAACP president Moorfield Storey encouraged the association to go ahead with its work and offered another $1,000 under the same conditions. After an extension of the deadline, by October more than $10,000 had been collected. Thereafter the fund continued to grow, eventually providing the means for investigations, publicity, legal actions, and political agitation. The NAACP considered that its "most striking achievement" in 1916 was its injection of "lynching into the public mind as something like a national problem."[9]

Nevertheless, public response came slowly. After the bloody riot at East St. Louis, the NAACP organized a great silent protest parade in New York City on July 28, 1917. Despite this demonstration and the continued outbreak of race riots and other forms of violence, President Wilson waited one year, until July 26, 1918, to issue a public statement condemning lynching and the mob spirit.[10] On May 5 and 6, 1919, the NAACP sponsored a national antilynching conference in New York City. Speakers included Charles Evans Hughes, who likened lynching to the "Hun spirit." The principles of the League covenant should begin at home, he said; the country owed Negroes justice and the rights guaranteed by the Constitution. An NAACP official, William Pickens of Morgan College, observed that general disregard for the Negro lay at the bottom of the lynching evil. "The man is in error who thinks he can indorse disfranchisement and segregation and 'Jim Crowism' and still oppose the mob."

9 New York *Times*, July 7, 1916, Jan. 3, 1917; "Minutes of the Meeting of the Board of Directors, December 11, 1916," NAACP Papers, Manuscript Division, Library of Congress; Charles F. Kellogg, *NAACP: A History of the National Association for the Advancement of Colored People,* vol. I: 1909–1920 (Baltimore, 1967), pp. 216–18; NAACP, *Annual Report: 1916.*

10 New York *Times*, July 29, 1917 and July 27, 1918; *Along This Way: The Autobiography of James Weldon Johnson* (New York: The Viking Press, Inc., 1933), pp. 320–21. See above, p. 123.

The conference adopted resolutions favoring an attempt to secure a federal antilynching law, requesting the NAACP to organize committees in each state to influence public opinion and to secure legislation as necessary, and requesting the NAACP's antilynching committee to continue its fund-raising and publicity campaigns.[11]

Investigations of specific lynchings and the collection of accurate statistics were essential for effective antilynching publicity. To assist in this process, in 1918 the NAACP brought Walter White, a twenty-four-year-old graduate of Atlanta University and secretary of its Atlanta branch, to its national office. Light-skinned and blond, White could pass as a white man, and his on-the-spot investigations served as the basis for numerous reports and protests. In April 1919 the NAACP published *Thirty Years of Lynching in the United States, 1889–1918,* which attempted, as a result of a search of newspapers and other records, to list all lynchings for those years and to classify them according to race, sex, location, and alleged cause. This book was the first significant study of the problem since the work by James E. Cutler in 1905.[12] The NAACP now had prepared the groundwork for more effective political agitation of the antilynching cause.

The next move was to press for federal legislation. Some steps had already been taken in Congress. On April 8, 1918, Republican Congressman Leonidas C. Dyer of St. Louis, Missouri, a representative with a considerable black constituency, introduced an antilynching bill. Several days later Merrill Moores, an Indiana Republican, submitted a somewhat similar measure. Dyer's bill held that the putting to death of a citizen of the United States by a mob or riotous assemblage of three or more persons was a denial of the equal protection of the laws and an offense against the United States. Any person participating in such a mob or riotous assemblage was guilty of murder, with jurisdiction of the case to be in the United States District Court in the area. The county in which a lynching occurred would for-

[11] New York *Times,* May 6–7, 1919; *Crisis,* 18 (May 1919), 23, and (June 1919), 92; Mary White Ovington, "The Anti-Lynching Conference," *Survey,* 42 (May 17, 1919), 292; *National Conference on Lynching,* pamphlet in James Weldon Johnson Papers, Yale University; Kellogg, 232–34; Robert L. Zangrando, "The Efforts of the National Association for the Advancement of Colored People to Secure Passage of a Federal Anti-Lynching Law, 1920–1940" (Ph.D. diss., University of Pennsylvania, 1963), pp. 46–48.

[12] Cutler, *Lynch Law: An Investigation into the History of Lynching in the United States* (New York, 1905); Walter White, *A Man Called White* (New York, 1948), pp. 35–43. White continued his investigations, and during the following years the NAACP published many of his reports; White later published a larger study, *Rope and Faggot: A Biography of Judge Lynch* (New York, 1929).

feit no less than $5,000 nor more than $10,000 to the dependent family of the victim, or if none, to the United States, and if the money was not paid the Circuit Court could levy a tax to obtain it. Any state or municipal officer who failed to make a reasonable effort to protect a prisoner and/or to prevent a lynching was guilty of an offense against the United States punishable by imprisonment up to five years or a fine up to $5,000, or both. Finally, it disqualified from jury duty any person convicted under the act.[13]

On April 6, two days before he introduced his bill in the House, Dyer sent a draft of his measure to NAACP secretary John R. Shillady. During the next few weeks Shillady and Walter White kept in close contact with Dyer, and to a lesser extent with Moores, over their proposed bills. On May 13 the NAACP board of directors approved a recommendation of its antilynching committee that it support actively a federal antilynching bill. White also told Dyer that representatives of the NAACP would testify at the House Judiciary Committee hearings on his bill and that the NAACP would launch a national campaign to create public sentiment for it.[14]

At the same time, Dyer's measure presented some difficulties for the NAACP. From the start Moorfield Storey had doubts about its constitutionality. Dyer wanted a preliminary hearing held in early June, but White objected that more time would be needed to prepare an argument on behalf of its constitutionality. He asked Storey to appear in August. By then, Storey had concluded that the Supreme Court would not uphold such a law, based as it was on the assumption that an individual, rather than the state, could be punished for denying a citizen the equal protection of the laws. He also found the Moores bill to be constitutionally unacceptable. Storey advised against NAACP participation in the committee hearings.[15] No more was heard of the two bills during that session of Congress.

13 *Cong. Rec.*, 65th Cong., 2d sess., vol. 56, pt. 5, p. 4821. For text of Dyer bill, see *ibid.*, pt. 6, p. 6177. For the Moores bill, see *ibid.*, pt. 6, p. 5362, and pt. 12, appendix, p. 338–40.

14 Dyer to Shillady, April 6, 1918, Shillady to Dyer, April 10, 1918, White to Dyer, May 15, 1918, NAACP Papers; "Memorandum to the Anti-Lynching Committee on Federal Anti-Lynching Bills, May 17, 1918," Moorfield Storey Papers, Manuscript Division, Library of Congress.

15 White to Storey, June 3, 1918, Storey Papers; Shillady to Dyer, Aug. 5, 1918, NAACP Papers. As president of the NAACP, Storey was deeply committed to the cause of civil rights for the Negro, but he agreed with prevailing legal opinion that the Fourteenth and Fifteenth Amendments did not grant authority to the federal government to prevent or punish private acts of violence. Within the next few years Storey's opinions on the constitutionality of federal antilynching legislation under-

In the meantime, Joel E. Spingarn, a member of the NAACP board of directors then on active duty in the intelligence branch of the army, proposed a possible substitute for the Dyer bill. This measure was based not on the Fourteenth Amendment but on the government's war powers. It held that the lynching of any person in the armed forces, a person subject to the draft, or relative of such a person, was a capital offense punishable as murder under the United States Code.[16] Such a bill was submitted as substitute for the Dyer bill in June during the hearings by the House Judiciary Committee. Its constitutionality was fairly clear, but the bill was applicable only in time of war, and after November 1918 it became irrelevant.

During the next two years Congress began to show more interest in the lynching problem, although the constitutional issue remained a significant obstacle. To avoid it Congressman Henry I. Emerson, an Ohio Republican, introduced in March 1919 a constitutional amendment granting Congress the power to enact legislation to prevent lynching.[17] Because this approach offered no immediate solution, Dyer continued to support the necessity and validity of a specific federal antilynching statute. On May 19, 1919, the first day of the new 66th Congress, he again introduced his bill. A few days later Congressman Frederick W. Dallinger, a Republican from Massachusetts, submitted another measure.[18] Dyer hoped to get the forthright support of the NAACP, but again it hesitated, mainly because of Storey's opinion that the bill was unconstitutional. Finally in November after discussions by its legal committee, the NAACP, including Storey, decided to back the bill.[19] A Boston member, Albert E. Pillsbury, agreed to argue on behalf of the bill's constitutionality. In January 1920 he went to Washington to confer with Dyer and several other congressmen. Pillsbury's report to James Weldon Johnson was not encouraging. Nothing, he said, was likely to be done by the

---

went a profound change (William B. Hixon, Jr., "Moorfield Storey and the Defense of the Dyer Anti-Lynching Bill," *New England Quarterly*, 42 [March 1969], 65–81.

16 Lt. Col. M. Churchill to Shillady, June 3, 1918, Spingarn to Storey, June 18, 1918, Storey Papers; brief of George S. Hornblower in U.S., Congress, House, Committee on the Judiciary, *To Protect Citizens against Lynching: Hearings on H.R. 11279*, 65th Cong., 2d sess. (June 6 and July 12, 1918), pp. 15–27.

17 *Cong. Rec.*, 65th Cong., 3d sess., vol. 57, pt. 5, p. 4966.

18 *Ibid.*, 66th Cong., 1st sess., vol. 58, pt. 1, p. 458. Congressman Moores also reintroduced his bill, but not until Jan. 19, 1920.

19 Dyer to Shillady, Nov. 7, 1919, Shillady to Dyer, Nov. 8, Nov. 13, 1919, NAACP Papers. Storey still had some doubts about the bill's constitutionality; so he did not testify at the hearings conducted by the House Committee on the Judiciary in Jan. 1920.

present Congress. Moreover, he doubted that Dyer would be an efficient leader of the antilynching cause.[20]

Johnson, Arthur B. Spingarn, and a few other representatives of the NAACP attended the hearings on the Dyer bill held by the House Judiciary Committee on January 29, 1920. Spingarn's statement showed that the group still had some doubts about the bill's constitutionality. Although he supported its passage, he also said that if it should be held unconstitutional an amendment should then be adopted to allow federal action. As before, the bill never emerged from the committee, even though this Congress now had a Republican majority. Hoping to overcome the committee's objections, Dyer introduced a slightly modified bill on May 17, 1920. This time the committee reported the measure favorably, and it was placed on the House calendar.[21] Democratic Congressman Thaddeus H. Caraway of Arkansas filed a stinging minority report. He attacked the majority's opinion as "merely a reprint of a brief filed with the committee by a society domiciled in New York which has for its sole object, not the securing of justice for negroes charged with a crime, but immunity from punishment for their crimes. . . . It is an appeal to the prejudices of that portion of the negro race that desires license and immunity and not law and justice."[22] Congress adjourned before the House had a chance to consider the bill.

During the 1920 campaign the Republican party took some note of lynching. The platform merely urged "Congress to consider the most effective means to end lynching," rather than forthrightly supporting the Dyer bill or some other measure, but this was further than the GOP had been willing to go in the past. Moreover, Harding stated in his acceptance speech of July 22, 1920, that "the Federal Government should stamp out lynching and remove that stain from the fair name of America."[23] With Harding's election, therefore, the prospects of congressional action improved.

At this time the NAACP finally decided to make the passage of a federal antilynching law its first order of business. Executive secretary Johnson took charge of the operation with the able assistance of White and the full backing of the association. For two years, 1921–22, Johnson spent the greater part of his time in Washington lobby-

20 Dyer to Johnson, Jan. 13, 1920, Pillsbury to Johnson, Jan. 22, 1920, Storey Papers.

21 New York *Times*, Jan. 30, 1920; NAACP, *Annual Report: 1920*, p. 44; *Cong. Rec.*, 66th Cong., 2d sess., vol. 59, pt. 7, pp. 7188, 7505; U.S., Congress, House, Committee on the Judiciary, *Antilynching Bill: Report to Accompany H.R. 14097*, 66th Cong., 2d sess., H. Rept. 1027, pt. 1 (May 22, 1920).

22 *Antilynching Bill*, H. Rept. 1027, pt. 2 (May 29, 1920), p. 1.

23 New York *Times*, July 23, 1920.

ing for the antilynching measure.[24] The congressional battle began shortly after Harding's inauguration. In his address at the opening of the special session of Congress on April 12, 1921, Harding urged the legislators "to wipe the stain of barbaric lynching" from America. The next day Dyer once again introduced his antilynching bill.[25]

The substance of Dyer's bill was about the same as his earlier ones.[26] Not all of its supporters were happy with the wording. Before it was introduced, for example, Mary White Ovington, a member of the NAACP's antilynching committee, complained that it had too "punitive a sound," and she doubted that it would pass. "It reads like a bill that a man would bring up to please his Negro constituents, going in for anything that sounds rousing, and expecting to have the bill turned down."[27] This comment indicates that some members of the NAACP doubted Dyer's sincerity, although his continuing endeavors on behalf of the antilynching campaign were unmatched by any other member of Congress.

Dyer was optimistic and said that he had no doubt that the House would pass his bill. "It will then go to the Senate and ought to pass there promptly. When it reaches the President I am sure he will sign it."[28] However, overcoming the constitutional qualms of many people remained a major problem. During the first part of 1921 Storey, who had resolved his own earlier doubts, Johnson, and White tried unsuccessfully to convince former Attorney General Wickersham, but he reluctantly concluded that past Supreme Court decisions indicated that such a measure would be held unconstitutional. Nevertheless, welcome support came from the Department of Justice when Attorney General Daugherty gave Congressman Andrew J.

[24] Johnson, *Along This Way*, pp. 361–74. See also White, *Rope and Faggot*, pp. 207–26.

[25] New York *Times*, April 13, 1921; *Cong. Rec.*, 67th Cong., 1st sess., vol. 61, pt. 1, p. 87. Dallinger of Massachusetts introduced another antilynching bill on April 13. On April 19 Martin C. Ansorge, a Republican from New York City, introduced a proposal to create a commission to study lynching and make recommendations. Later Ansorge agreed to subordinate his proposal to the Dyer bill, explaining that his was "a second line of attack, ready should the first line fail" (*Cong. Rec.*, 67th Cong., 1st sess., vol. 61, pt. 1, p. 461, and 2d sess., vol. 62, pt. 1, p. 547).

[26] For the text of the Dyer bill as finally revised and considered by the Senate, see Appendix B. Congressman Merrill Moores helped draft the 1921 Dyer bill, which also included in its coverage aliens entitled to treaty protection (see "Memorandum re Secretary's Trip to Washington, July 25–28, 1921" [NAACP], Storey Papers; Guy D. Goff to Albert E. Pillsbury, Aug. 29, 1921, File 158260, Record Group 60, National Archives).

[27] Ovington to Arthur B. Spingarn, Feb. 8, 1921, Arthur B. Spingarn Papers, Manuscript Division, Library of Congress.

[28] Dyer to NAACP, March 10, 1921, NAACP Papers.

Volstead, the chairman of the House Judiciary Committee, his unofficial opinion that the equal protection clause of the Fourteenth Amendment brought the problem within the jurisdiction of Congress.[29]

On October 20, 1921, the House Judiciary Committee reported favorably on the Dyer bill. For the second time within less than two years there was a chance that an antilynching proposal would be considered on the floor of the House. The dissenting minority report of the Judiciary Committee strongly expressed an argument that would be repeated often not only by southerners but by those from all sections who sought an excuse to prevent federal action. "This proposed intervention of the Federal Government directed against local power, supplanting and superseding the sovereignty of the States, would tend to destroy that sense of local responsibility for the protection of person and property and the administration of justice, from which sense of local responsibility alone protection and governmental efficiency can be secured among free peoples. . . . [It would] complete the reduction of the States to a condition of governmental vassalage."[30] Such reasoning, of course, ignored the fact that localities could avoid federal interference by putting a stop to lynchings.

Proponents of the bill had to find a way to force its prompt consideration. Dyer believed that their only hope was to get the Steering Committee to include the bill with others to be considered, and then to persuade the Rules Committee to adopt a special rule for it. Dyer urged Johnson to do his best to influence all the members of both committees. This he did. By letters, telephone calls, and personal conferences, Johnson worked diligently to win over all the congressmen he could, not only those on the two committees but others as well. Johnson warned the Republicans that raising the question of the bill's constitutionality would be regarded by Negroes "as a mere pretext" and failure to take prompt and favorable action "as a betrayal."[31] Johnson also urged Harding to assist by letting House members know he wanted the bill passed and by reiterating his stand in his forthcoming message to Congress. Although presidential secre-

[29] White to Storey, April 28, 1921, Storey Papers; George W. Wickersham to White, May 11, 1921, Louis Marshall to Wickersham, May 19, 1921, NAACP Papers; Hixson, pp. 71–73; Volstead to Harry M. Daugherty, July 26, 1921, Daugherty to Volmstead, Aug. 9, 1921, File 158260, Record Group 60, National Archives; the letter was reprinted in U.S., Congress, House, Committee on the Judiciary, *Antilynching Bill: Report to Accompany H.R. 13*, 67th Cong., 1st sess., H. Rept. 452 (Oct. 31, 1921), pp. 16–17.

[30] *Antilynching Bill*, H. Rept. 452, p. 18.

[31] Johnson, *Along This Way*, p. 364; Johnson to Martin B. Madden, Nov. 12, 1921, NAACP Papers.

tary Christian promised that Harding would refer to the subject, the December message was in fact silent on lynching and on any other matter of special concern to Negroes.[32]

Nevertheless, the prospects of favorable action after Congress reconvened in December 1921 were sufficient to arouse the concern of opponents. On December 17, Congressman James P. Buchanan of Texas delivered a bitter attack on the Dyer bill. Rape, he said, was the cause of lynching, and the Negro was "the race most addicted to the tragic infamy." This unconstitutional proposal was an act of "political demagoguery" and "malignant partisanship" in weeping with the spirit of the "bloody shirt days" and a crude attempt "to catch and to hold the deluded Negro vote." The Negro problem would have been solved long ago, Buchanan concluded, had not Republican partisans and white uplifters sent emissaries into the South preaching "the damnable doctrine of social equality" which incited the Negro criminal to rape.[33]

Two days later discussion began on the resolution presented by the Rules Committee providing for immediate consideration of the Dyer bill with debate limited to a total of ten hours. A number of southern opponents hurled acrimonious charges. Then they succeeded in delaying consideration of the resolution by absenting themselves and preventing a quorum. Only after Speaker Frederick H. Gillett of Massachusetts sent out special deputies to round up a number of the absentees, and after floor leader Frank W. Mondell of Wyoming agreed not to consider the bill until after Christmas, was a quorum obtained and the amended resolution passed. All the recorded opponents were from the South, plus one each from the border areas of Kentucky and Oklahoma.[34]

The Dyer bill was first taken up on the floor of the House on January 4, 1922. By this time Democratic opponents conceded that it would pass, but they still managed to sidetrack it several times. Dyer led the defense of the bill, joined by fellow Republicans Martin B. Madden of Illinois, Wells Goodykoontz of West Virginia, Andrew J. Volstead of Minnesota, and a few others. The southerners presented their usual opposing arguments. The bill was unconstitutional; it would mean federal government usurpation of the powers of the states; it would increase, not diminish, mob violence. The

[32] Johnson to Christian, Nov. 4, 1921, Johnson to Harding, Nov. 28, 1921, Johnson to Christian, Dec. 2, 1921, NAACP Papers; Christian to Johnson, Warren G. Harding Papers, Ohio Historical Society.

[33] *Cong. Rec.*, 67th Cong., 2d sess., vol. 62, pt. 1, pp. 458–68.

[34] *Ibid.*, pp. 541–58; New York *Times*, Dec. 20, 21, 1921; Johnson, *Along This Way*, p. 364.

threat of unchecked rape was frequently raised. "Girls and women in many sections of the South where criminal Negroes live are in constant danger of a fate a thousand times worse than death," cried John N. Tillman of Arkansas. "It will encourage the Negro brutes in their attacks on the defenseless white women of the country," argued John E. Rankin of Mississippi. William J. Driver of Arkansas rested his opposition on the grounds that the Negro simply had not evolved far enough. "We are the product of a civilization of thousands of years, while the Negro is comparatively a child in moral training. He is an emotional being without our mental processes and control of passion, and therefore with but little moral restraint. He is a slave to his appetite and will respond to a mere suggestion without thought of consequences."[35]

One of the strongest speeches against the bill came not from a southern Democrat but from a Republican, Ira G. Hersey, of Maine. First he pointed out that neither the 1920 Republican platform nor President Harding had specifically endorsed any bill against lynching. On that ground he argued that the Republicans had made no deal with the Negro. "We as a party owe the colored people nothing, and I for one refuse to be politically blackmailed." He denounced Storey as "an attorney for an organization of agitators" and concluded that "this is no time to enact this monstrous law that can have no other effect or result than to fan into flames the expiring embers of race and class hatred and bring back to the beautiful Southland the awful horrors of those days of darkness that followed the Civil War."[36] Hersey's was the most vehement Republican voice raised against the Dyer bill; but it was not the only one. For example, C. Frank Reavis of Nebraska claimed that although he would not object to all antilynching measures, he did to this particular bill. It put most Republicans "between the two horns of a dilemma," he said. "We must either do violence to our conscience and vote for it or lose many Negro votes at home by voting against it."[37] Harry B. Hawes, a Democrat from Missouri, praised these speakers for exposing the true motives of the bill's supporters.[38] Indeed, there can be no doubt that the willingness of northern Republicans to consider the passage of this antilynching bill, after so many years of indifference, was closely related to the increase in the black electorate in the North.

The climax of the debate was reached on January 25, 1922. Several hundred Negroes jammed the galleries and vocally demonstrated dur-

35 *Cong. Rec.*, 67th Cong., 2d sess., vol. 62, pt. 1, p. 1011, and pt. 2, pp. 1426, 1707.

36 *Ibid.*, pt. 1, pp. 1019–25.

37 *Ibid.*, pt. 2, p. 1286.

38 *Ibid.*, p. 1294.

ing a verbal clash between Congressmen Thomas U. Sisson of Mississippi and Henry A. Cooper of Wisconsin. The next day the House passed the Dyer bill by 231 to 119. On the whole the vote split on partisan lines. However, eight Democrats (three from New York, and one each from Pennsylvania, Massachusetts, New Jersey, Illinois, and Kentucky) went along with the majority, and seventeen Republicans joined the Democrats in opposition. Three of these Republicans, Joseph Brown and Wynne F. Clouse of Tennessee and C. Bascom Slemp of Virginia, came from southern states, and three others from the border areas of Delaware and Oklahoma. The other eleven represented northern constituencies from Maine to California.[39] An exhuberant NAACP statement announced that the passage of the bill in the House was "one of the most significant steps ever taken in the history of America."[40]

The struggle now moved to the Senate. Dyer warned Johnson that the senators would have to be convinced that there was great popular interest in an antilynching law. Johnson worked indefatigably. He conferred with and sent letters to all senators whom he thought he had a chance of influencing. To stimulate broader public interest, the NAACP sponsored a mass meeting at New York's Town Hall on the evening of March 1. Storey presided, and speakers included Du Bois and Dyer. A telegram from Senator William M. Calder of New York in support of the Dyer bill was read.[41]

Johnson was confident of the friendship of a number of senators. One was Arthur Capper, a Republican from Kansas, who was a member of the NAACP. After speaking to several of his colleagues on behalf of the bill, Capper told Johnson that Charles Curtis of Kansas would "do his level best" to assure passage and that they could count on James E. Watson of Indiana, Harry S. New of Indiana, Medill McCormick of Illinois, and Selden P. Spencer of Missouri, all Republicans.[42] In February majority leader Henry Cabot Lodge of Massachusetts informed Johnson that he expected to back the bill even though he had not then examined it in detail. Two months later he wrote: "I am in favor of the measure and shall be glad to give it my support."[43]

The immediate problem was to secure favorable action by the Ju-

39 *Ibid.*, p. 1795; New York *Times*, Jan. 26, Jan. 27, 1922; Johnson, *Along This Way*, pp. 365–66.

40 New York *Times*, Jan. 27, 1922.

41 Dyer to Johnson, Feb. 2, 1922, NAACP Papers; New York *Times*, March 2, 1922.

42 Johnson to the Branch Secretary, Feb. 8, 1922, Storey Papers; Capper to Johnson, Feb. 14, 1922, NAACP Papers; Johnson, *Along This Way*, p. 363.

43 Lodge to Johnson, Feb. 18, April 25, 1922, NAACP Papers.

diciary Committee. Johnson considered only two of the sixteen members, Richard P. Ernst of Kentucky and Samuel M. Shortridge of California, as probable friends. The views of chairman Knute Nelson of Minnesota were unknown. Another important figure, George W. Norris of Nebraska, gave rather disappointing responses to NAACP queries. At first he excused himself on the ground that he was chairman of the Committee on Agriculture and Forestry and had given little attention to the Judiciary Committee work. Later he explicitly denied the reports that he said were circulated among black voters claiming that he was opposed to legislation for the protection of Negro rights, and he promised that he would support any legislation that in his judgment would bring about such protection. Nevertheless, by April 1 he still had not examined the Dyer bill, and he merely emphasized that he would "maintain an open mind."[44]

The most important senator to win over was William E. Borah of Idaho, head of the subcommittee in charge of the bill. After a visit to Washington in March, Johnson reported that "Senator Borah is without doubt the most commanding figure in the United States Senate today, and if he undertakes the championing of the Bill, there is little doubt that he can put it through."[45] This assessment of Borah's power was probably excessive, but the hearty support by a man of his prestige and influence certainly would have improved the bill's chances. Unfortunately, Borah had doubts about its constitutionality. In February 1922 Storey, who had come to believe that the Dyer bill's passage would have a desirable effect even if it were later voided by the Supreme Court, wrote to Borah seeking support for the measure.[46] Borah admitted that he had not yet studied the constitutional issue, but he warned that should he conclude that it was unconstitutional, he would have to vote against it. "I have never voted for a bill which I thought was unconstitutional with a view to letting the court pass upon it later."[47]

For a while it seemed possible that Borah could be persuaded. Johnson did his best to help by showing that the bill had broad support. In March it got the backing of the Federal Council of Churches of Christ in America. In April, Johnson testified in Chicago at a meeting of the committee on law enforcement of the American Bar Association and received assurances that it would go on

44 Storey to Norris, Feb. 13, 1922, Norris to Storey, Feb. 20, 1922, Norris to Robert Smith, April 1, 1924, George W. Norris Papers, Manuscript Division, Library of Congress.

45 "Memorandum re Secretary's Washington Trip, March 7–11, 1922," Storey Papers.

46 Storey to James W. Johnson, Aug. 1, 1921, NAACP Papers; Hixson, pp. 72–73.

47 Borah to Storey, Feb. 9, 1922, Storey Papers.

record in favor of antilynching legislation.[48] The NAACP also prepared a "Memorial to the United States Senate" urging passage of the Dyer bill. By May the memorial had been endorsed by an impressive number of prominent men, including twenty-four state governors, thirty-eight mayors of principal cities, eighty-eight archbishops, bishops and leading churchmen, forty-seven jurists and lawyers including two former United States attorney generals (Palmer and Wickersham), nineteen judges on the highest state courts, and twenty-nine college presidents. On May 4 a committee for the NAACP led by Johnson met with Senator Lodge, who consented to present the petition to the Senate. The committee also talked to Borah. The senator readily conceded the infamy of lynching, but the memorial did nothing to remove his doubts about the Dyer bill's constitutionality.[49]

Former Attorney General Wickersham signed the petition, although he still entertained serious doubts about the bill's constitutionality.[50] Several senators took similar positions. Many said that they would vote for the bill if it actually got before the Senate, even if they questioned its constitutionality, and let the Supreme Court be the final arbiter.[51] The NAACP worked hard to put forth some strong constitutional arguments. One of the most effective was by a New York lawyer, Herbert K. Stockton, who later joined the legal committee of the NAACP. Stockton wrote to Borah on May 9, but the senator remained unconvinced, replying, "If you can cite me to a line of authorities which will sustain this present bill, so far as I am concerned, I shall be favorable to it."[52] On May 18 Johnson

48 Borah to Johnson, March 15, 1922, Johnson to Storey, March 28, 1922, *ibid.*; NAACP, *Annual Report: 1922*, p. 10. Later the American Bar Association unanimously passed a resolution at its annual meeting in San Francisco on Aug. 9, 1922, that stated: "We find that further legislation should be enacted by the Congress to punish and prevent lynching and mob violence."

49 "Memorial to the United States Senate" and the typed report of the committee presenting the memorial to Senator Lodge, NAACP Papers; *Cong. Rec.*, 67th Cong., 2d sess., vol. 62, pt. 6, p. 6480; Johnson, *Along This Way*, pp. 367–68. On May 10 Lodge also presented a resolution passed by the Massachusetts General Court urging passage of the Dyer bill, and on May 18 he presented a similar petition from the Boston branch of the National Equal Rights League (*Cong. Rec.*, 67th Cong., 2d sess., vol. 62, pt. 7, pp. 6627, 7158).

50 Wickersham to Walter White, April 18, 1922, Wickersham to Storey, April 21, 1922, Storey Papers.

51 From Feb. through July 1922 various senators sent letters to the NAACP in which they expressed such a position; see the files on congressional action in the NAACP Papers.

52 Borah to Stockton, May 10, 1922, Storey Papers; Stockton to Walter White, May 11, 1922, NAACP Papers.

sent him a copy of a detailed constitutional argument prepared by Storey, and a few days later Johnson went to Washington to go over the issues in person with the senator. Johnson "found him in no pleasant mood." Borah, who fancied himself an expert on constitutional law, complained that there was insufficient time to make a study of the constitutional points. But he did not slam the door. He told Johnson that "if there was anything he could do as a Senator to save the life of a single Negro from a lynching mob he would do it and that he would try to find a way to make this legislation adequate as well as constitutional."[53] This was on May 25. Shortly before, Borah's subcommittee had reported adversely on the Dyer bill to the full Judiciary Committee.[54]

Despite this setback, political pressure for a favorable report by the Judiciary Committee grew. Chairman Adams of the Republican national committee promised Johnson to get in touch with influential senators, and a number of them urged Harding to intervene. Johnson tried to make the senators realize that Negroes were deeply concerned. On June 1 he sent a letter to every senator pointing out that in the month of May alone twelve Negroes had been lynched. Five were burned alive.[55] In New York on June 3 and in Washington on June 14 Negroes paraded in silent protest against lynching and the delay over the Dyer bill.[56] Early in June, Republican leader Lodge virtually ordered the Judiciary Committee to report on the bill. This was an affront to Borah, who told Johnson angrily "that he would get out of the Senate before he would do anything to pull anybody's political chestnuts out of the fire."[57]

The constitutional issue was still a stumbling block. Senator Nelson, chairman of the Judiciary Committee, reported to Storey that

53 Johnson to Storey, May 18, 1922, and "Report of the Secretary, June 8, 1922," Storey Papers; Johnson, *Along This Way*, p. 368. For Storey's brief, see U.S., Congress, Senate, Committee on the Judiciary, *Antilynching Bill: Report to Accompany H.R. 13*, 67th Cong., 2d sess., Senate Rept. 837 (July 28, 1922), pp. 18–26.

54 The subcommittee had met in executive session, but Borah revealed to Johnson that it had voted 3 to 2 against the bill. Republicans William P. Dillingham of Vermont and Thomas Sterling of South Dakota were for it, while Borah and Democrats Lee S. Overman of North Carolina and John K. Shields of Tennessee were against ("Report of the Secretary, June 8, 1922," Storey Papers).

55 New York *Times*, May 24, June 1, 1922; "Report of the Secretary, June 8, 1922," Storey Papers; "Memorandum for the President, May 18, 1922," Harding Papers; Johnson, *Along This Way*, p. 368.

56 New York *Times*, June 4, 5, 1922.

57 "Report of the Secretary, June 8, 1922," Storey Papers. On the Borah-Lodge relationship, see Marian C. McKenna, *Borah* (Ann Arbor, Mich., 1961), pp. 172–88, 217–18; Zangrando, p. 121.

while there was a considerable diversity of opinion on the committee, a majority thought the bill was unconstitutional.[58] As for Borah, the more arguments he heard in its favor, the more adamantly opposed he became. Despite Storey's careful brief, he wrote to an NAACP official that he did not think there was "a single constitutional principle upon which to base the law."[59] In a long letter to Storey on June 1, he explained that he entertained "no doubt at all as to the unconstitutionality of this measure." Borah did promise not to use dilatory tactics to prevent others from voting on it, and he reiterated his dislike of mob violence. But he felt it was very unfair and dishonest to deal with Negroes by handing them "ineffective and inefficient remedies." He denounced strongly those who would shift judgment for the constitutionality of measures to the Supreme Court. "I think such miserable, cowardly shifting of responsibility is unworthy of a Senator of the United States."[60] On June 5 Stockton sent Borah another defense of the bill's constitutionality. He rested his case squarely on the equal protection clause of the Fourteenth Amendment, along with section 5 of the same amendment giving Congress the power of enforcement. As the bill was worded, Stockton saw no necessity to get involved in the troublesome question of what were the rights inherent in United States, as opposed to state, citizenship, and he felt that there was sound constitutional reasoning for the Supreme Court to uphold the antilynching bill.[61]

This argument won over one member of the Judiciary Committee, Albert B. Cummins of Iowa.[62] But nothing could move Borah, who became even more intemperate in his criticism of the bill and its sponsors. On June 11 he publicly announced his opposition, calling the Dyer bill ineffective and unconstitutional and accusing those who supported it of being "lawless brothers of lynchers" because of their desire to transfer to the federal government power vested by the Constitution in the states.[63] Proponents of the measure were appalled by Borah's blast. The charge that Congress had recklessly passed unconstitutional legislation was denounced by NAACP lawyer James A. Cobb as a "smoke screen" and a "red herring." In the

58 Nelson to Storey, May 27, 1922, Storey Papers.

59 Borah to W. Hayes McKinney, May 26, 1922, NAACP Papers.

60 Borah to Storey, June 1, 1922, Storey Papers.

61 Herbert K. Stockton to Borah, June 5, 1922, Harding Papers; for Stockton's brief, see *Antilynching Bill*, Senate Rept. 837, pp. 26–31.

62 Cummins to Stockton, June 10, 1922, Stockton to Cummins, June 14, 1922, Storey Papers.

63 New York *Times*, June 12, 1922; *Press Service of the NAACP*, June 12, 1922, Storey Papers.

whole life of the federal government, he pointed out to Lodge, only thirty-eight acts of Congress had been declared unconstitutional by the Supreme Court.[64] In a letter to the New York *Times,* Johnson defended the Dyer bill's constitutionality on the ground that the states were obviously failing to uphold equal protection of the law as required by the Fourteenth Amendment. Borah had seen the careful arguments of Storey, Stockton, and other experts. His charge that the bill's supporters wished to lynch the Constitution, said Johnson, was simply "disingenuous."[65] The break between Borah and the NAACP was complete.

In mid-June, while the Dyer bill lay bottled up in the Judiciary Committee, the NAACP held its thirteenth annual convention in Newark, New Jersey. The antilynching struggle dominated the discussion. NAACP leaders took the position that the Republicans, with a twenty-seat majority in the Senate could certainly pass the bill if they had the wish to do so. The question was how to encourage that desire. Using the threat of political reprisals was one approach. If the Dyer bill failed, "Republican Senators would be held responsible," Johnson announced. "We regard no man as our friend who opposes this bill," read another statement.[66] The convention also appealed to Harding to try to influence Congress. The president again refused to intervene. "Legislation dealing with the matter is pending," explained Christian, "and the President is disposed to doubt the propriety of an interposition of further counsel on his part for the present at least. You may be very sure of his continuing and very earnest interest in behalf of this cause."[67] In an answer to Christian, Johnson pointed out that the NAACP had felt confident in appealing to Harding because "he had been reported as recently urging upon Congress the enactment of other legislation."[68] Harding remained silent.

On June 30 the Judiciary Committee reported the bill favorably by a vote of eight to six. Except for Borah, who joined the Democratic opponents, the vote was along party lines; two committee members,

[64] Cobb to Arthur B. Spingarn, June 14, 1922; Spingarn to Cobb, June 15, 1922, Spingarn Papers; Cobb to Lodge, June 21, 1922, NAACP Papers. Cobb, a Negro, was a member of the NAACP's legal committee. In 1926 he was appointed judge of the Municipal Court of the District of Columbia.

[65] New York *Times,* July 2, 1922. The letter was dated June 15, 1922.

[66] New York *Times,* June 19, June 24, 1922; *Press Service of the NAACP* (Report on the 13th annual meeting of the NAACP, June 19–21, 1922), Storey Papers. See also Walter White to Herbert K. Stockton, April 7, 1922, NAACP Papers; *Crisis,* 23 (April 1922), 248.

[67] Christian to Johnson, June 23, 1922, Harding Papers.

[68] Johnson to Christian, July 6, 1922, *ibid.*

Norris and Henry F. Ashurst, a Democrat from Arizona, were absent.[69] Despite the close vote, Johnson was elated. Once the bill reached the floor of the Senate, he told Storey, "the chances for its final enactment are decidedly good." Johnson was pleased that Shortridge of California, who was preparing the committee's report, would lead the fight on the floor. He was "a fighter," said Johnson, and his "heart is in the legislation."[70]

Opponents of the bill felt that Lodge was mainly responsible for getting the committee to act favorably. They assumed that the Massachusetts senator, who faced reelection in 1922, was motivated by a cynical pursuit of black votes. He knew the Constitution, said the New York *World,* and thus he knew that if the bill was passed the court would throw it out. "But that will take time. Meanwhile the Negro vote is badly needed."[71] A political writer for the New York *Times* noted that Mayor John F. Hylan's large majority in the November 1921 New York City elections resulted in part from the massive defection of Negroes to the Democrats and concluded that the action on the Dyer bill was a move to stem such desertions.[72] The New York *Times* also denounced the bill not only as unconstitutional but as something that "was never intended to be passed. It was an inexpensive dotation [*sic*] to the 'colored vote.' Apparently Mr. Lodge needs all colors and all races in his business."[73]

Such criticism ignored the substance of the proposal; there was, after all, an urgent need for positive steps to stop lynching. It also was somewhat unfair to Lodge, for the security that black voters might have provided him in a close race was slight, coming as he did from a state in which Negroes comprised only 1.2 percent of the population as of the 1920 census. At the same time Lodge was a determined partisan politician who was certainly capable of lending his

69 New York *Times,* June 30, July 1, 1922; Henry C. Lodge to Johnson, June 23, 1922, NAACP Papers.

70 Johnson to Storey, July 1, 1922, Storey Papers.

71 New York *World,* July 8, 1922.

72 Ernest Harvier, "The Political Effect of the Dyer Bill," New York *Times,* July 9, 1922. A study of some election districts from the 19th and 21st Assembly Districts in New York City, having at least 90 percent Negro population, showed that in the 1921 mayorality election the Republican candidate received only 26.4 percent of the vote, compared to 73.6 for the Democratic (Gilbert Osofsky, *Harlem, the Making of a Ghetto: Negro New York, 1890–1930* [New York, 1966], pp. 242–43, nn. 36 and 38).

73 New York *Times,* July 31, 1922. Lodge was aware of the dissatisfaction of many black voters at that time (William M. Trotter to Lodge, July 30, 1922; Lodge to William Muller, Aug. 25, 1922, Henry Cabot Lodge, Sr., Papers, Massachusetts Historical Society).

support to the antilynching bill as a means of gaining votes for Republican party candidates elsewhere.

The attacks against Lodge were acknowledgments that the political power of blacks in the North had increased. The NAACP tried to make the most of this fact. "Our strongest weapon now is the threat of the Negro vote," Walter White wrote to Dyer in August, and he noted that the NAACP was carrying on an active campaign against three Republican congressmen who voted against the bill in the House, Patrick H. Kelley of Michigan, Caleb R. Layton of Delaware, and R. Wayne Parker of New Jersey.[74] Kelley was challenging incumbent Senator Charles E. Townsend, a supporter of the Dyer bill, for the Republican senatorial nomination. Townsend received NAACP backing. After he won the renomination in the summer of 1922, he expressed his "deep gratitude" to White for "the most valuable assistance of the colored voters of Michigan in the recent primary election."[75]

However important the NAACP's political activities might have been in some congressional districts, few senators at that time felt seriously endangered by a threatened loss of black votes. Even to get the Senate as a whole to take up the Dyer bill was a difficult matter, despite the favorable Judiciary Committee report. On August 22 White estimated that they could count on at least forty-three votes and probably ten or eleven more, thus giving them a clear majority. Lodge told Johnson that he would do all he could to forward action on it, although he warned that there would be vigorous opposition from the southern Democrats. Notwithstanding Borah's publicly announced opposition and the equivocal or negative statements of a few other senators, Lodge added disingenuously that "Republicans, so far as I know, all favor the bill."[76] On September 21 Shortridge, acting in conjunction with Lodge, attempted to place the bill on the floor. An involved parliamentary maneuver by Harrison of Mississippi delayed matters for a couple of hours, and after a short speech by Shortridge a quorum call failed to produce the required number. The second session of the 67th Congress then adjourned.[77] If Republican senators were playing for Negro votes they didn't get a chance to be counted in time for the November elections.

74 White to Dyer, Aug. 18, 1922, NAACP Papers.

75 "Report of the Secretary, September 7, 1922"; *Press Service of the NAACP*, Oct. 6, 1922, Storey Papers.

76 White to Herbert K. Stockton, Aug. 22, 1922, Lodge to Johnson, Aug. 25, 1922, NAACP Papers; see also Lodge to William Muller, Aug. 25, 1922, Lodge Papers.

77 New York *Times*, Sept. 22, 1922; Johnson, *Along This Way*, pp. 369–70.

During the fall the NAACP continued its campaign against certain congressmen who had opposed the Dyer bill. And it had some success. Layton and Parker were both defeated. Black voters also openly opposed Republican Congressman William H. Stafford of Wisconsin, who had voted against the bill, and Republican Senator T. Coleman du Pont of Delaware, who had expressed his opposition to the measure. Both of these men were also unseated.[78] Johnson counted upon such evidence of Negro political power to convince doubtful senators to support the bill. "For the last few months . . . ," he explained to Storey in mid-November, "we dropped all legal and ethical arguments and depended solely upon political pressure. This is what we need to do until the Bill is finally disposed of. . . . The Republicans will need to gather in every vote they possibly can for 1924."[79]

The antilynching bill was only one of several pieces of unfinished business. After the election Harding called Congress into special session on November 20. Three days later the NAACP ran a full-page advertisement, "The Shame of America," in the New York *Times* and seven other major dailies. "Do you know that the United States is the *Only Land on Earth* where human beings are *BURNED AT THE STAKE*?" it asked. Twenty-eight were so killed in the four years 1918 to 1921, and between 1889 and 1921 a total of 3,436 people had been lynched. "Telegraph your senators today [that] you want it enacted." Copies of the advertisement were sent to every senator.[80] On November 27 Shortridge tried to bring up the Dyer bill. Southern opponents immediately began obstructing every effort to conduct business by objections, quorum calls, and other dilatory tactics. The next day the filibuster began in earnest. Harrison refused his consent to dispense with the reading of the journal. He then found errors in the reporting and debated at length about corrections. Finally Oscar W. Underwood of Alabama cleared the air. "It must be apparent, not only to the Senate but to the country, that an effort is being made to prevent the consideration of . . . the Dyer bill. . . . I want to say right now to the Senate that if the majority party insists on this procedure they are not going to pass the bill,

78 NAACP, *Press Release,* Nov. 10, 1922, NAACP Papers; NAACP, *Annual Report: 1922,* p. 24; *Crisis,* 25 (Jan. 1923), 117–18; Stuart A. Rice, "What Do the Different Party Labels Mean?" *Current History,* 20 (Sept. 1924), 908.

79 Johnson to Storey, Nov. 15, 1922, Storey Papers.

80 According to Johnson (*Along This Way,* p. 370), this advertisement cost $5,136.93. Even before then the NAACP had spent almost $40,000 in six to seven years on its antilynching campaign (Arthur B. Spingarn to Roger Baldwin, Oct. 18, 1922, Spingarn Papers).

and they are not going to do any other business."[81] Later that day Senate Republicans held a caucus, attended by twenty-eight of their fifty-nine members, and voted 27 to 1 to continue the fight.[82]

November 29 was wasted by further filibustering. On November 30, Thanksgiving Day, Congress was not in session, and on the next day, December 1, it quickly adjourned because of the death of Congressman James R. Mann of Illinois. The only hope of bringing the Dyer bill to a vote was to end the filibuster by adopting a motion of cloture. This required a two-thirds majority of those voting. Even Johnson now admitted that they could not get that many votes, but he felt that it would be disastrous to capitulate to the souherners after so short a battle. Hoping that the Republicans would stick it out to March 4 if necessary, Johnson appealed to Harding to urge the senators not to yield. Johnson believed that if a long enough fight were made the bill might still get to a vote, and if that happened he was confident of passage. But simply to abandon the bill, he warned Harding, "would have incalcuable effect civilly and politically on the colored people of the whole country."[83]

When the Senate met again on Saturday, December 2, southerners once more prevented the transaction of any business. They were intractable and utterly confident of their ability to prevent the bill from coming to a vote. Underwood predicted that the Republicans would soon capitulate.[84] On that same day Johnson conferred with Senators Lodge, Curtis of Kansas, and Watson of Indiana and pleaded with them not to yield to the southern filibusterers. According to Johnson "each of them said to me that the bill would not be abandoned on any such terms."[85] That evening the Republican senators held another caucus and voted to drop the bill. Lodge issued a statement explaining that the Republicans felt that the bill ought to be passed, but that the Democrats could filibuster indefinitely. "Therefore, we had to choose between giving up the whole session to a protracted filibuster or going ahead with the regular business of the session, which includes the farm legislation, the shipping and

[81] *Cong. Rec.*, 67th Cong., 3d sess., vol. 63, pt. 1, p. 332. See also Johnson, *Along This Way*, pp. 370–71; Franklin L. Burdette, *Filibustering in the Senate* (Princeton, N.J., 1940), pp. 133–37.

[82] New York *Times*, Nov. 29, 1922; Henry Cabot Lodge to Bruce T. Bowens, Nov. 29, 1922, Lodge to William M. Trotter, Nov. 29, 1922, Lodge Papers.

[83] Johnson to Harding, Nov. 30, 1922, Harding Papers; Johnson to Walter White, Nov. 30, 1922, NAACP Papers.

[84] Underwood to John Sharp Williams, Dec. 2, 1922, John Sharp Williams Papers, Manuscript Division, Library of Congress.

[85] Johnson, *Along This Way*, p. 371.

the appropriation bills. The conference decided very reluctantly that it was our duty to set aside the Dyer bill and go on with the business of the session."[86] At the session on Monday, December 4, Lodge formally capitulated to Underwood. It was a humiliating moment. The leader of a party with a Senate majority of some two-dozen seats had been rendered powerless by the determined opposition of the minority. As the New York *Times* noted, "Never before has the Senate so openly advertised the impotence to which it is reduced by its antiquated rules of procedure."[87]

Johnson refused to accept the Republican action without a fight. Lodge's explanation of the caucus's decision seemed to him to be a complete betrayal of the promises the three senators had made earlier that day. On December 3 Johnson telegraphed these senators, asking if the newspaper reports of Lodge's statement were correct and reminding them of their conversation with him. Lodge's reply to Johnson gave a totally different version of that discussion. He claimed that he had said that there was no possibility of the bill passing and that a continued filibuster would only block all other business. He flatly denied telling Johnson that they would not abandon the bill on terms laid down by the filibusterers. "I never said anything of the kind. I never mentioned terms to you in any way. There was no question of terms. . . . The words you attribute to me were never uttered by me. Nothing of that sort was said."[88]

During these crucial days the White House provided no help at all. Johnson's telegram of November 30 and another on December 3 failed to convince Harding that he should try to prevent abandonment of the bill. Christian merely assured Johnson on December 5 that Harding had "made every effort on behalf of this legislation and still entertains the hope that, while the outlook at the moment appears unpromising, there may be a decided improvement in the situation in the not distant future."[89] The basis for that remark,

86 New York *Times*, Dec. 3, 1922.

87 *Ibid.*, Dec. 4, 1922; *Cong. Rec.*, 67th Cong., 3d sess., vol. 63, pt. 1, p. 450.

88 Lodge to Johnson, Dec. 4, 1922, Lodge Papers. Quoted by permission of the Massachusetts Historical Society. Senator Watson also replied to Johnson, but in a much more conciliatory, if cryptic, manner. "If you will come to my office, I will tell you what happened. There is too much about it to place within the limits of an ordinary letter" (Watson to Johnson, Dec. 4, 1922). Later Johnson did call on Watson, but the explanation he received was similar to Lodge's. The senators simply felt that it was impractical to abandon all congressional actions because of the Dyer bill, ("Report of the Secretary, December 11, 1922," Storey Papers. The Lodge and Watson letters are also printed in Johnson, *Along This Way*, pp. 372–73).

89 Johnson to Harding, Dec. 3, 1922, Christian to Johnson, Dec. 5, 1922, Harding Papers. See also Harry E. Davis to Harding, Dec. 2, 1922, E. Burtin Ceruti to

coming after the Republicans' capitulation, was not stated. In his message to Congress on December 8, Harding made no mention of antilynching legislation. The Dyer bill was dead.

Johnson was understandably bitter. "The Southern Democrats roared like a lion and the Republicans lay down like a scared 'possum,'" he stated on December 8. Except for Shortridge, Willis, New and Edge, "not a Republican Senator opened his mouth in actual support."[90] Harding's secretary, Christian, placed the blame squarely and solely on the Democrats. But Johnson would have none of that. In an emotional "Open Letter to Every Senator of the United States," dated December 13, 1922, Johnson pointed out that since December 4, the day the Senate abandoned the Dyer bill, there had been four lynchings, "one of the victims being publicly tortured and burned at the stake. This outbreak of barbarism, anarchy and degenerate bestiality and the blood of the victims rest upon the heads of three Southern senators who have obstructed even discussion of the measure designed to remedy this very condition. And the responsibility rests equally with the Republican majority who surrendered with hardly a struggle to the lynching tactics of the Democrats."[91] Johnson complained that the Republican leaders seemed to feel that all they had to do for Negroes was to put themselves on record as being in favor of the bill and then let the southerners take the blame if it failed. Passage itself became almost secondary. Negroes are "more than disappointed," wrote Johnson in another letter to Christian; they feel "chagrin and resentment. . . . This lukewarmness on the part of the Republicans is as much resented by the colored people as the aggressive tactics of the Southern Democrats."[92]

Many Negroes agreed with Johnson. The New York *Age* similarly condemned the "insincerity of the Republicans," and the Philadelphia *Public Ledger* called the surrender by the Senate a "betrayal

---

Harding, Dec. 4, 1922, Harding to Harry E. Davis, Dec. 4, 1922, *ibid.* Davis, a member of the Ohio House of Representatives, predicted that if the Dyer bill were not passed the defection of black voters would be so great as to ensure a Democratic victory in Ohio in 1924. He begged Harding to take a more than "passive interest in a measure promoting simple "justice." Harding replied that the Senate Republicans had honestly tried to pass the bill, but that there was nothing more that they or he could do.

90 *Press Service of the NAACP,* Dec. 8, 1922, Storey Papers. See also Johnson, *Along This Way,* p. 371.

91 Christian to Johnson, Dec. 8, 1922; NAACP Papers; *Press Service of the NAACP,* Dec. 13, 1922, Storey Papers.

92 Johnson to Christian, Dec. 21, 1922, Harding Papers. See also NAACP, *Annual Report: 1922,* pp. 19–23; *Crisis,* 25 (Feb. 1923), 171. For Christian's reply, see Christian to Johnson, Dec. 28, 1922, Harding Papers.

of the Negro cause that is not likely to be soon forgotten." The reaction of black people was one of "bitter cynicism," Ohio legislator Harry E. Davis wrote to Harding. At the very least, he said, the senators should have stood up to the filibuster for ten days.[93] Even a loyal GOP partisan like Cleveland Negro George A. Myers wrote that "the lay down of the Rep[ublican] majority in the Senate on the Dyer Bill has set the Negro to thinking as he never did before."[94] Oswald Garrison Villard warned Harding that Negroes had "lost their faith in both the old parties, as well they may, and are turning in other directions."[95]

The threat was not entirely an idle one. "We have lost a battle," explained Storey, "but we are winning a campaign. It is most encouraging to note the change in the attitude of the colored people all over the country. . . . We have also aroused people hitherto apathetic, and have elicited strong support, especially among the women. The goal is in sight."[96] Storey was trying hard to instill hope at a moment of defeat, but it was true that nothing in previous years had so aroused the black community as the NAACP's crusade against lynching. It also helped to teach Negroes to look more at results rather than promises, at actions rather than party labels. The November 1922 elections had already given concrete examples of the constructive use of political power. The campaign also helped the NAACP leaders gain useful experience in dealing with Congress and the public at large, and in so doing it had raised the prestige of the NAACP as an instrument of racial protest.

Another development that may have been related to the antilynching struggle was a marked decline in the number of lynchings. Some 121 people were killed in that manner during the two years between 1921 and 1922 while Congress wrangled over the Dyer bill. During the first six months of 1923 the number dropped to eleven. The NAACP attributed the reduction to the agitation for a federal antilynching law, along with the desire of southern states to retain Negro labor by reducing one of the causes for the northern migration.[97]

93 New York *Age*, Dec. 16, 1922; Philadelphia *Public Ledger*, Dec. 12, 1922; Davis to Harding, Dec. 15, 1922, Harding Papers.

94 Myers to Robert H. Terrell, Dec. 8, 1922, Robert H. Terrell Papers, Manuscript Division, Library of Congress.

95 Villard to Harding, Dec. 21, 1922, Oswald G. Villard Papers, Harvard College Library. Quoted by permission of the Harvard College Library.

96 Storey to Mary W. Ovington, Dec. 27, 1922, NAACP Papers.

97 New York *Times*, June 26, 1923. Dyer took a similar position in reporting on a new antilynching bill in the next Congress (U.S., Congress, House, Committee on the Judiciary, *Antilynching Bill: Report to Accompany H.R. 1*, 68th Cong., 1st sess., H. Rept. 71 [Jan. 19, 1924], p. 7).

The total number of lynching in 1923 was thirty-three, and it fell to sixteen in 1924.[98] These totals were the lowest on record up to that time. The reasons for the drop were doubtless complex, but it is conceivable that the anti-lynching campaign had prompted the southern states to exercise greater diligence in preventing the crime as a means of demonstrating that federal intervention was not necessary. To this extent the effort had by no means been wasted.

98 Arthur Raper, *The Tragedy of Lynching* (Chapel Hill, N.C., 1933), pp. 480–81.

CHAPTER VIII

The Silent Years

BLACK leaders had put more effort into the campaign against lynching than into any other project during the 1920's. Accordingly, they felt the Republican abandonment of the Dyer bill more deeply than the other disappointments of the period. But it should have come as no surprise. A determined GOP effort would have been inconsistent with its half-hearted gestures on most racial matters. By 1923 attention shifted to other problems. With Harding's death on August 2, 1923, Calvin Coolidge inherited the opportunity to plot a new and more enlightened course for his party in regard to Negro rights. Only the most irrepressible optimists, however, had much faith that this would happen.

Little was known about Coolidge's attitude toward Negroes. Except for a brief comment in his speech accepting the Republican nomination for vice-president in 1920, he had made no public statements on the subject, and there was no evidence that he had ever given any serious attention to racial problems. In mid-August 1923 representatives of the NAACP began an effort to educate him and, if possible, to secure his support for desired programs.[1] Coolidge made no commitments. Indeed, from August until December he issued no important policy statements of any kind. On November 12 James Weldon Johnson wrote to Coolidge about the acute disappointment of Negroes in the Republican party because of its failure to fight for the Dyer bill, and he urged the president to take a strong stand for an antilynching law in his forthcoming message to Congress. Johnson also asked for an investigation of Negro disfranchisement, the creation of an interracial commission, and the abolition of racial segregation in the government departments. In addition the National Equal Rights League petitioned Coolidge for action on government segregation, an antilynching bill, and pardons for the imprisoned members of the Twenty-fourth Infantry who had been involved in the 1917 Houston riots. Thus Coolidge, like Harding, had before him an agenda of at least some of the actions desired by black Americans.[2]

1 New York *Times*, Aug. 15, 1923.

2 Johnson to Coolidge, Nov. 12, 1923, NAACP Papers, Manuscript Division, Library of Congress; New York *Times*, Nov. 12, 1923.

In his first message to Congress on December 6, 1923, Coolidge included a fairly lengthy passage on Negroes.

Numbered among our population are 12,000,000 colored people. Under our Constitution their rights are just as sacred as those of any other citizen. It is both a public and a private duty to protect those rights. The Congress ought to exercise all its powers of prevention and punishment against the hideous crime of lynching, of which the negroes are by no means the sole sufferers, but for which they furnish a majority of its victims.

Already a considerable sum is appropriated to give the negroes vocational training in agriculture. About half a million dollars is recommended for medical courses at Howard University to help contribute to the education of 500 colored doctors needed each year.

On account of the migration of large numbers into industrial centers, it has been proposed that a commission be created composed of members from both races, to formulate a better policy for mutual understanding and confidence. Such an effort is to be commended. Every one would rejoice in the accomplishment of the results which it seeks. But it is well to recognize that these difficulties are to a large extent local problems which must be worked out by the mutual forbearance and human kindness of each community. Such a method gives much more promise of a real remedy than outside interference.[3]

Encouraged by this message, Johnson praised Coolidge for his words on behalf of "fair play, common justice and sympathetic interest for the race."[4] Much of the Negro press did not react so favorably.[5] This was not surprising. Most of Coolidge's statement was vague, and he did not refer to many of the problems, like disfranchisement, that immediately concerned Negroes. His comment about the local nature and solution of racial difficulties could become an excuse for federal inaction in the face of local discrimination. Indeed, one feature of Coolidge's approach to the presidency that came to have some attraction for many white southerners was his minimization of federal government responsibilities.[6]

His response to the lynching problem was a case in point. Despite his reference to it in his message to Congress, Coolidge refused to endorse the Dyer antilynching bill which had been reintroduced

[3] New York *Times*, Dec. 7, 1923.

[4] Johnson to Coolidge, Dec. 8, 1923, NAACP Papers.

[5] See *Negro Year Book: 1925/26*, p. 59.

[6] For a favorable comment by an influential southern politician on Coolidge's ideas about states' rights and the "return to local self-government," see *Selected Addresses of C. Bascom Slemp*, comp. J. Frederick Essary (Washington, D.C., 1938), p. 297. Se also Coolidge's address on "States' Rights and National Unity" delivered at the College of William and Mary, May 15, 1926, in Calvin Coolidge, *Foundations of the Republic: Speeches and Addresses* (New York, 1926), pp. 401–12.

on December 5. Johnson begged him to support the measure, for without administration backing it was doomed. But he pleaded in vain. The Rules Committee balked at preparing a special rule, which was needed to get the measure on the floor of the House in time for action during that session. On June 7, 1924, Congress adjourned without having considered the bill.[7]

In a number of other ways Coolidge failed to reassure black leaders during his first year in office. After some difficulty Johnson secured a conference with the president on February 7, 1924. It was not a happy meeting. Coolidge was obviously embarrassed and had nothing to say, not even questions about the problems or wants of Negroes. "It was clear that Mr. Coolidge knew absolutely nothing about the colored people," wrote Johnson. "I gathered that the only living Negro he had heard anything about was Major Moton. I was relieved when the audience was over, and I suppose Mr. Coolidge was too."[8]

Johnson's experience was not unique. Many people, of course, regardless of race, complained about Coolidge's frosty manner. Moreover, neither his personality nor his experience prepared him for an understanding of the lives and problems of black Americans; and he had little incentive or inclination to learn about them. During his presidency he occasionally recognized Negroes, pro forma, by sending greetings to the annual conventions of the NAACP or by regularly including in his messages to Congress a section praising their progress and upholding in general terms their constitutional rights. But Coolidge enjoyed no close relationships with any Negroes, nothing comparable to the association of Booker T. Washington with Theodore Roosevelt, or even Johnson with Harding during 1920–21.[9]

7 *Congressional Record,* 68th Cong., 1st sess., vol. 65, pt. 1, p. 25; *ibid.,* pt. 2, p. 1180; *ibid.,* pt. 10, pp. 10538–41; U.S., Congress, House, Committee on the Judiciary, *Antilynching Bill: Report to Accompany H.R. 1,* 68th Cong., 1st sess., H. Rept. 71 (Jan. 19, 1924); Johnson to Coolidge, March 21, 1924, Coolidge Papers, Manuscript Division, Library of Congress.

8 "Report of the Secretary's Trip to Washington, January 20–22, 1924," NAACP Papers; *Along This Way: The Autobiography of James Weldon Johnson* (New York: The Viking Press, Inc., 1933), p. 374.

9 Coolidge's most recent biographer, Donald R. McCoy, *Calvin Coolidge: The Quiet President* (New York, 1967), pp. 328–29, concludes that he did little to help Negroes and that he substituted "gestures where substantial improvements could have been made." Howard H. Quint and Robert H. Ferrell, eds., *The Talkative President: The Off-the-Record Press Conferences of Calvin Coolidge* (Amherst, Mass., 1964), pp. 1–4, attempt to revise the image of Coolidge as a dour and taciturn man. But see the very different portrayal by the White House chief usher, Irwin H. Hoover, in *Forty-Two Years in the White House* (Boston, 1934), pp. 131–32.

One of Coolidge's first official acts seemed to confirm the views of those who feared the worst about his attitude toward Negroes. On August 14, 1923, the White House announced the appointment of C. Bascom Slemp as presidential secretary, a move regarded as an indication that Coolidge was already preparing a campaign for nomination in 1924.[10] Slemp's reputation was clouded by charges that he had used his influence over southern patronage to traffic in political office, and the Democratic national committee issued a sharp criticism of the appointment.[11] Negroes were much more seriously alarmed because of Slemp's well-known lily-whitism and his opposition to antilynching legislation. "Twelve million negroes feel that they have received a slap in the face," complained one NAACP official.[12] On August 20 the NAACP put out a formal statement expressing its "surprise and shock," and the Harlem branch of the National Equal Rights League strongly protested the appointment of an "avowed political enemy of the race."[13] Even Robert L. Vann's Pittsburgh *Courier*, which only a few days before had hailed the new president as "the child of destiny, the instrument of God," warned that the action could cause even greater disaffection from the Republican party than already existed.[14] The adverse reaction seemed to have alarmed Coolidge, for he kept Slemp's activities out of the public eye as much as possible.

Coolidge's flirtations with the lily-whites and the New Republicanism in the South were generally less ardent than Harding's. His principal concern was to ensure his own nomination in 1924, and Slemp's job was to secure the necessary southern delegates. In December 1923 Coolidge oversaw the reversal by the national committee of its plan to change the basis of southern representation at national conventions. During the same month Coolidge took two other steps

[10] New York *Times*, Aug. 15, 1923; "The President's Secretary," *Outlook*, 134 (Aug. 29, 1923), 651; Henry L. Mencken, *A Carnival of Buncombe*, ed. Malcolm Moos (Baltimore, 1956), p. 65; Guy B. Hathorn, "The Political Career of C. Bascom Slemp" (Ph.D. diss., Duke University, 1950), pp. 193–98; William Allen White, *A Puritan in Babylon: The Story of Calvin Coolidge* (New York, 1958), p. 251.

[11] Slemp's activities had been brought up in Dec. 1922 in the course of a congressional investigation of a contested 1920 election in Virginia's Seventh Congressional District (*Cong. Rec.*, 67th Cong., 4th sess., vol. 64, pt. 1, pp. 529–47; see also New York *Times*, Aug. 15, Aug. 16, 1923; Hathorn, pp. 176–89).

[12] New York *Times*, Aug. 17, 1923. See also Walter White to J. Thomas Hewin, Aug. 16, 1923, Hewin to White, Aug. 21, 1923, John Mitchell, Jr., to White, Aug. 17, 1923, NAACP Papers.

[13] *Press Service of the NAACP*, Aug. 20, 1923, NAACP Papers; New York *Times*, Aug. 20, 1923.

[14] Aug. 11, 25, 1923.

that showed he did not wish either to offend black voters unnecessarily or to place too great an emphasis on lily-whitism. One was to nominate the Louisiana Negro political leader Walter L. Cohen to be comptroller of customs for the New Orleans District.[15] The other was to choose Senator William M. Butler of Massachusetts to head his preconvention organization. Slemp had little use for Butler, whom he considered an incompetent amateur, but he continued to work effectively in rounding up southern delegates to the national convention. Nevertheless, Slemp recognized that Butler's rise lessened his own influence, and on June 16 he offered to resign. Although Coolidge refused to accept the resignation, he obviously wished to avoid having Slemp become a campaign issue. After the convention Butler was made the new Republican national chairman and placed in charge of the campaign. Slemp continued as secretary to the president until January 1925, but his political influence had greatly declined.[16]

At the convention there were a few of the usual contests for southern seats involving rivalry between black-and-tans and lily-whites. The most important was that between two Georgia delegations. One led by J. Louis Phillips represented the reformed organization that had gained influence under Harding; the other was a faction that included Negro national committeeman Henry Lincoln Johnson. Friends of the latter group produced a letter that Harding had allegedly written to Slemp stating that a mistake had been made in recognizing the Phillips faction. On June 4 the credentials committee voted to seat the Johnson delegation. In the opinion of the Atlanta *Constitution* this rebuke of the "model" new Republican organization in Georgia ended all chance of building a new GOP in the South at that time.[17]

In other contests involving Negro delegates the issue was not entirely one of lily-whites versus black-and-tans. For example, the credentials committee seated a Mississippi delegation led by Perry Howard over one led by a white, M. J. Mulvihill. However, both delegations had Negro members. Howard's victory was largely a shift in the chief officers of a party structure that had been and continued to be predominantly black.[18]

15 New York *Times,* Dec. 11, 1923, Feb. 19, Feb. 26, March 18, 1924. Cohen was then serving as a recess appointee, having been rejected by the Senate after Harding's original nomination. His nomination was finally confirmed in March 1924.

16 Hathorn, pp. 200–231; McCoy, p. 252.

17 New York *Times,* June 2, June 5, 1924. A search of the Warren G. Harding Papers, Ohio Historical Society, failed to find this letter. The Atlanta *Constitution* was quoted in the Pittsburgh *Courier,* June 14, 1924.

18 New York *Times,* June 6, 1924; V. O. Key, Jr., *Southern Politics in State and*

Coolidge was anxious to avoid an open fight on the southern issue at the convention, and on the whole he succeeded. This did not mean that he had abandoned hopes of expanding Republicanism in the South. Political observers felt that the GOP had a good chance in both North Carolina and Tennessee. Coolidge honored the former state by asking its Republican nominee for governor to second his nomination. But, possibly on the advice of Chairman Butler and because of fears of the considerably increased black vote in a number of key northern states, Coolidge soft-pedaled his overtures to the white South much more than Republican leaders four years earlier had.

The 1924 Republican platform also reflected concern about the black voter by including the longest plank on the Negro since the one adopted in 1908. For the first time it explicitly urged Congress to enact an antilynching law. It also guardedly noted that the president had "recommended the creation of a commission for the investigation of social and economic conditions and the promotion of mutual understanding and confidence." This cautious plank suggested the Republican party's ambivalence: it did not feel safe in completely ignoring Negro demands, and it also feared making extensive commitments which would compromise its standing among white southerners.

The Republicans were even more circumspect in their handling of the highly inflammatory issue of the Ku Klux Klan. In some states, notably Colorado, Indiana, Maine, and Ohio, the Klan strongly influenced the selection of gubernatorial or other candidates. In Indiana it gave its full endorsement to Edward Jackson, who decisively won the Republican nomination for governor in the primary election. In Colorado, Judge Ben B. Lindsey claimed that the Klan was represented on the Republican ticket in practically every county.[19] Even the Republican national convention felt its influence. Led by Hiram W. Evans, the Klan set up headquarters in Cleveland and brazenly threatened to punish its opponents. The party leaders ob-

---

Nation (New York, 1949), p. 286. On the struggle between Howard and Mulvihill, see *Crisis,* 20 (Aug. 1920), 175; Ralph J. Bunche, "The Political Status of the Negro" (research memorandum prepared for the Carnegie-Myrdal study of the Negro in America, 1940), pp. 1212–14 (copy in Schomburg Collection of the New York Public Library).

19 "A Klan Shock in Indiana," *Literary Digest*, 81 (May 24, 1924), 14; Stanley Frost, "The Klan Shows Its Hand in Indiana," *Outlook*, 137 (June 4, 1924), 187–90; New York *Times,* May 13, Oct. 16, 1924; Emma L. Thornbrough, "Segregation in Indiana during the Klan Era of the 1920's," *Mississippi Valley Historical Review*, 47 (March 1961), 612–15; Ben B. Lindsey, "My Fight With the Ku Klux Klan," *Survey*, 54 (June 1, 1925), 272–73.

viously hoped to keep this divisive issue off the convention floor, and they were embarrassed when Rene B. Creager, a national committeeman from Texas, proposed a plank denouncing the Klan. The platform committee blocked this proposal and presented instead an innocuous resolution reaffirming the party's "unyielding devotion to the Constitution." On June 9 the Klan headquarters released a statement endorsing Senator James E. Watson of Indiana for vice-president. Watson's friends, fearing damage to his candidacy, rejected the endorsement. Evans in turn announced that the Klan had not authorized the statement, adding that he felt that both the Democratic and the Republican parties would nominate worthy candidates. Republicans were obviously uncertain about the best way to handle the Klan. Negroes demanded that the GOP repudiate it forthrightly, but instead a silent caution prevailed.[20]

At the Democratic convention later in June a much more open and bitter struggle occurred, and an anti-Klan plank was narrowly defeated. Some Negroes were then ready to write the Democrats off as hopelessly Klan-ridden, but the presidential candidate, John W. Davis, helped to modify such sentiments. In a speech delivered at Sea Girt, New Jersey, on August 22, he declared that "if any organization, no matter what it chooses to be called, whether Ku Klux Klan or by any other name, raises the standard of racial and religious prejudice . . . it does violence to the spirit of American institutions and must be condemned."[21] Davis also invited Coolidge to make a similar declaration and so remove the issue from the campaign.

Like the Democrats and the Republicans, the Progressives too failed to mention the Klan in their platform. This omission was rectified to some extent on August 8 when Senator Robert M. LaFollette made public a letter in which he stated that he was "unalterably opposed to the evident purpose of the secret organization known as the Ku Klux Klan."[22]

Only the Republican candidate had failed to take a stand on the Klan. Throughout the campaign many blacks and some whites implored Coolidge to disavow it.[23] They pleaded in vain. The most they

20 New York *Times*, June 8, 10, 12, 1924; Oswald G. Villard, "The Convention of the Fit-to-Rule," *Nation*, 118 (June 25, 1924), 730–32; Charles C. Alexander, *The Ku Klux Klan in the Southwest* (Lexington, Ky., 1965), p. 160; Arnold S. Rice, *The Ku Klux Klan in American Politics* (Washington, D.C., 1962), pp. 74–75.

21 New York *Times*, Aug. 23, 1924.

22 LaFollette to Robert P. Scripps, Aug. 5, 1924, in New York *Times*, Aug. 9, 1924; Bella Case LaFollette and Fola LaFollette, *Robert M. LaFollette, June 14, 1855–June 18, 1925* (New York, 1953), pp. 1119–20.

23 For many such requests, see Boxes 70, 71, Coolidge Papers. See also NAACP Papers, special correspondence file on Coolidge.

could get from the White House were letters from Slemp denying that the president was a Klan member or that he approved of its actions. Slemp urged Coolidge to join Davis in attacking the Klan; Chairman Butler held that silence was the best policy.[24] Coolidge's position certainly attracted some Klansmen. For example, the Klan leaders in Arkansas, who were alienated by Davis's Sea Girt speech, threw their support to him. During the first part of September, Arkansas national committeeman Harmon L. Remmel talked with J. A. Comer, the state's Grand Dragon, who told him that "the President's position on the Klan was exactly right." Comer predicted that "the Klan vote would go to him not only in the northern states, but largely in the southern states" as well.[25] Although Remmel urged Slemp to talk with Comer, Slemp declined. Coolidge had no direct contact with Klansmen, and their active support of him in the South was probably limited. But the fact remained that by his silence he alone of the three major candidates appeared to be the most acceptable to them.

Coolidge's position disappointed those concerned about civil rights. Even the conservative New York *Times* concluded that "either Mr. Coolidge holds his peace for mistaken reasons of policy and politics or he tolerates the Klan. . . . He has shown himself by his silence deficient in judgment and courage."[26] Vice-presidential candidate Charles G. Dawes made matters worse during a visit to Augusta, Maine on August 23. The Klan had shown a considerable strength in that state, having successfully backed Ralph O. Brewster in the primaries for the Republican gubernatorial nomination. Against the wishes of Butler, Everett Sanders, head of the national committee's speakers' bureau, and local Republican leaders, Dawes decided to discuss the Klan. His comments, cast as a reproof, were regarded by many as a near apology.[27] Dawes's performance aroused

24 New York *Times*, Aug. 23, 1924; Charles G. Dawes, *Notes as Vice-President, 1928–1929* (Boston, 1935), p. 23.

25 Remmel to Slemp, Sept. 15, 1924, Coolidge Papers; Alexander, pp. 172–74

26 Sept. 7, 1924.

27 New York *Times*, Aug. 24, 1924; Dawes, pp. 23–27; Bascom N. Timmons, *Portrait of an American: Charles G. Dawes* (New York, 1953), pp. 234–35. Dawes's speech included the following comments on the Klan: "Let me say at once that I recognize that the Ku Klux Klan in many localities and among many peoples represents only an instinctive groping for leadership, moving in the interest of law enforcement, which they do not find in many cowardly politicians and office holders. But it is not the right way to forward law enforcement. . . .

"There is much in the Ku Klux Klan which appeals to the adventurous youth . . . but, my friends, government cannot last if that is the right way to enforce law in this country. Lawlessness cannot be met with lawlessness and civilization be maintained. . . .

the ire of Klan opponents. For Norman Thomas the speech came "close to being a left-handed defense of the Klan; appearing to accuse, he really excuses." Fiery New York Congressman Fiorello LaGuardia exclaimed disgustedly that "General Dawes praised the Klan with faint damn."[28] The *New Republic* was even harsher. "He virtually condoned mob violence if only the participants believe they are acting in a righteous cause. . . . Any Klansman who reads the General's speech carefully will come away from it with the conviction that Dawes is at worst a half-hearted enemy and is probably a half-hearted friend. . . . Unless Mr. Coolidge wants to be labeled as the Ku Klux Kandidate, he must either repudiate the Dawes statement or wipe it out with an unequivocal declaration of his own."[29] Coolidge remained silent.

To many blacks such timidity was just another indication of the unreliability of the Republican leadership since its return to power in 1921. Their dissatisfaction with the GOP was the product of a series of disappointments. Basic was the fact that the anticipated improvements over the Wilson administration had not come about. Although most Negroes, including radicals, had been kindly disposed toward Harding, their attitude began to change in the face of his overtures to the lily-whites, his reluctance to appoint Negroes, his decision to continue the American occupation of Haiti, his failure to abolish segregation in government departments, and his party's position on disfranchisement, antilynching legislation, the Klan, and other matters.

As a result political restlessness had been increasing long before Coolidge became involved in the 1924 election. As early as September 24, 1921, a member of the Harlem Republican Club warned George B. Christian, Jr., that "my people all over the country are very angry and are discussing plans for forming a party of their own."[30] By February 1922 even a conservative like Emmett J. Scott pleaded that something had to be done to counter the unfavorable publicity directed against the administration. Scott talked with John T. Adams, Republican national chairman, but without results. "In my opinion," said Scott, "it is definitely important, if the Administration cares anything at all for the good will of the colored voters of the country, that measures be taken to set in motion a more favor-

---

"Appeals to racial, religious, or class prejudice by minority organizations are opposed to the welfare of all peaceful and civilized communities. Our Constitution stands for religious tolerance and freedom."

28 New York *Times*, Aug. 24, 25, 1924.

29 *New Republic*, 40 (Sept. 3, 1924), 3.

30 Guildford M. Crawford to Christian, Sept. 24, 1921, Harding Papers.

able public opinion."[31] Another conservative Negro and loyal Republican, George A. Myers, reported in May 1922 that "the Ohio Negro is up in arms, but has not decided which way to turn."[32] W. E. B. Du Bois thought that he knew the proper direction: a third party. "May God write us down as asses if ever again we are found putting our trust in either the Republican or the Democratic Parties."[33]

Most Negroes were still too attached to the Republican party either to switch to the Democrats or to follow Du Bois into some third party. As for the former, the bitter experience of the Wilson administration was all too recent to encourage another such experiment, at least on the national level. A third party seemed a somewhat stronger possibility. In July 1923, black Republicans from eighteen states held a convention at Atlantic City, New Jersey. They were angry, and many talked of bolting the party unless Negroes got better treatment. Senator Walter E. Edge of New Jersey received a cool reception when he attempted to defend the Harding administration. The convention adopted an ultimatum calling for "equality of membership in the Republican Party, both North and South, and for the abolition of the lily white policy."[34] A few weeks later the NAACP took a clear stand for independence. In a "Message to Colored Americans," adopted at its fourteenth annual conference on September 4, 1923, it recommended scrapping "allegiance to any party on historical grounds" and proposed "a new political emancipation."[35] At its next annual conference in June 1924, just after the Republican national convention, the NAACP passed a resolution urging Negroes to disregard party labels and assailed the Republicans for their numerous failures. "Nothing" it concluded, "will more quickly bring the old parties to a clear realization of their obligations to us and the nation than a vigorous third party movement."[36]

When the Progressives met in Cleveland in July 1924, the NAACP appealed for them to take "enlightened and far-sighted steps against

31 Scott to Judson C. Welliver, Feb. 24, 1922, *ibid.*

32 Myers to James Ford Rhodes, May 22, 1922, in John A. Garraty, ed., *The Barber and the Historian: The Correspondence of George A. Myers and James Ford Rhodes, 1910–1923* (Columbus, Ohio, 1956), p. 144. After the Nov. 1922 elections, a Negro city councilman in Cleveland wrote to Harding: "Never in my long experience in party politics have I seen such a condition toward the party by the colored people, as now" (Thomas W. Fleming to Harding, Nov. 11, 1922, Harding Papers).

33 *Crisis,* 24 (May 1922), 11.

34 New York *Times,* July 21, July 22, 1923; Pittsburgh *Courier,* July 28, 1923.

35 NAACP, *Annual Report: 1923,* pp. 40–41.

36 NAACP, *Annual Report: 1924,* pp. 46–47; New York *Times,* July 1, 1924; Pittsburgh *Courier,* July 5, 1924.

race and color discrimination."[37] But neither the platform of the Conference for Progressive Political Action, which was the backbone of the new party, nor the personal platform of its candidate, Senator LaFollette, specifically mentioned the Negro or the problem of civil rights. His program is otherwise so good, said Du Bois, that "it is most disheartening to find Mr. LaFollette deliberately dodging two tremendous issues—the Ku Klux Klan and the Negro. This is inexcusable."[38] A number of NAACP leaders, like Villard, Johnson, and William Pickens, urged LaFollette to speak out on these matters, assuring him that it could bring in thousands of Negro votes.[39] His letter denouncing the Klan, made public on August 8, helped somewhat, but the Progressive candidate attracted the support of only a few black leaders or of whites connected with the struggle for Negro rights. Villard was one who worked hard for LaFollette.[40] Another was Pickens, who asserted that LaFollette was "about the only self-respecting choice for any colored voter."[41] In mid-October, Du Bois finally gave him his rather reluctant endorsement. Many other Negroes, including some who had previously welcomed a third party, agreed with Walter White in refusing to support LaFollette on the ground that he had been evasive on issues of greatest importance to them.[42]

Well aware of the Negro dissatisfaction with the Republican party, the Democratic leaders, at least in the North, made a somewhat greater effort than usual to attract black voters. The defeat of the anti-Klan plank at the national convention hurt, but Davis's subsequent anti-Klan statement, the most forthright on the subject of any of the three major candidates, made up for this deficiency to a considerable degree. In his acceptance speech Davis strongly denounced "bigotry, intolerance and race prejudice as alien to the spirit of America" and promised that if elected he would "set up no standard of religious faith or racial origin as a qualification for any office."

37 NAACP, *Annual Report: 1924*, p. 48.

38 *Crisis*, 28 (Aug. 1924), 154. The editorial was written before LaFollette's anti-Klan letter was published.

39 Villard to LaFollette, July 11, 1924, Johnson to LaFollette, July 23, 1924, Pickens to LaFollette, July 25, 1924, Oswald G. Villard Papers, Harvard College Library.

40 See Villard, *Fighting Years: Memoirs of a Liberal Editor* (New York, 1939), pp. 502–3; and Villard Papers, File 2158.

41 Pickens to G. Victor Cools, Oct. 2, 1924, NAACP Papers.

42 White to G. Victor Cools, Aug. 14, 1924, White to Ernest Gruening, Sept. 17, 1924, *ibid.* White said that he would vote for Davis because of his forthright statement on the Klan. On Du Bois's position, see New York *Times*, Oct. 21, 1924; Elliott M. Rudwick, *W. E. B. Du Bois: A Study in Minority Group Leadership* (Philadelphia, 1960), p. 260.

Later in the campaign Davis made a strong bid for the Negro vote in his home state of West Virginia, and at the end of October he spoke to a Negro audience in Harlem.[43]

The largest concentration of Negroes was in New York City, and there they had already given the Democrats a considerable amount of support in local elections. In 1921 a majority of the black voters deserted the Republicans and helped reelect Mayor John P. Hylan. The next year many backed the Democratic candidate for Congress from the Twenty-first District, Royal H. Weller, in his successful campaign to unseat Republican incumbent Martin S. Ansorge.[44] With an eye toward this important block of votes in 1924, the Democratic organization placed Ferdinand Q. Morton, the head of Tammany Hall United Colored Democracy, in charge of the Colored Division of eastern Democratic headquarters. Lester A. Walton was made secretary and director of publicity, and Alice Dunbar Nelson became the Director of Colored Women.[45] The Democrats were further assisted by the defection of a number of prominent Negro Republicans to their side. The most important was William H. Lewis of Boston, the former United States assistant attorney general. On August 30 he renounced the GOP as "the party of Little America and Ku Kluxism" and offered to go on the stump for Davis.[46] Another was Roscoe Conklin Bruce, son of the former United States senator from Mississippi, Blanche K. Bruce, and assistant superintendent of public schools in the District of Columbia, who on September 14 announced his support for Davis because of the Klan issue.[47]

43 New York *Times,* Aug. 12, Aug. 21, Oct. 15, Oct. 29, 1924.

44 The growth of Democratic strength in Harlem alarmed Negro Republican leaders. In 1922 they made an unsuccessful attempt to replace Ansorge with a Negro as the GOP candidate for Congress. Ansorge finally agreed to step down in 1924, and a Negro, Dr. Charles Roberts, got the Republican nomination. He did not, however, win the support of most Negro voters. The NAACP also disapproved of Roberts as a reactionary. Weller, the white Democrat, was thus reelected (New York *Times,* July 13, 1922, Aug. 11, 1925; *Crisis,* 29 [Dec. 1924], 55; John G. Vann Deusen, "The Negro in Politics," *Journal of Negro History,* 21 [July 1936], 269; Lester A. Walton, "The Negro in Politics," *Outlook,* 137 [July 23, 1924], 472; Gilbert Osofsky, *Harlem, the Making of a Ghetto: Negro New York, 1890–1930* [New York, 1966], pp. 171–77, 242–43 nn. 36–38; Martin C. Ansorge, "Reminiscences," p. 66, Oral History Research Office, Butler Library, Columbia University).

45 New York *Times,* Aug. 24, 1924; William F. Nowlin, *The Negro in American National Politics* (Boston, 1931), p. 91; Subject File on Politics, NAACP Papers. Morton had been recognized by Mayor Hylan in Jan. 1922 with an appointment as a municipal civil service commissioner. Walton was a well-known journalist. Mrs. Nelson, the former wife of the late poet Paul Lawrence Dunbar, was a writer who was active in many Negro organizations.

46 New York *Times,* Aug. 31, 1924.

47 New York *Times,* Sept. 15, 1924.

Coolidge, refusing to speak out on the Klan, did make one forthright comment on Negro rights during the campaign in a letter made public on August 12. A New York resident had written to him to protest the nomination of Dr. Charles Roberts, a Negro, as the Republican candidate in the Twenty-first New York Congressional District. In reply Coolidge stated that one could not uphold the principles of the Republican party and deny full political rights to Negroes. "Our Constitution guarantees equal rights to all our citizens, without discrimination on account of race or color. I have taken my oath to support that Constitution. . . . A colored man is precisely as much entitled to submit his candidacy in a party primary as is any other citizen. The decision must be made by the constituents to whom he offers himself, and by nobody else."[48]

Even Villard's *Nation,* no admirer of the president on most matters, found this statement highly praiseworthy. So did a number of Negro newspapers. But other critics pointed out that Coolidge had done little to uphold equal rights in those parts of the country where violations of the constitutional guarantees had become the rule. One Democratic paper, the Brooklyn *Eagle,* was even unwilling to give Coolidge credit for goodwill. His letter, it argued, was an effort to dodge the necessity of a real attack on the Klan. He seemed "to imagine that without denouncing the Klan he can avoid loss of votes by saying nice things about the classes that are victims of the Klan's hostility."[49]

Coolidge made another gesture in his acceptance speech of August 14. The Negro, he said, is entitled "to the protection of the Constitution and the law." Law and justice must apply to all.[50] But these words were quite inadequate as a means of stilling the Negro dissatisfaction with the GOP. Many prominent Negroes who had at one time or another been associated with the Republican party were unconvinced. The NAACP refused to go on record in favor of any candidate, although a number of its officials backed either Davis or LaFollette. Johnson argued that the best strategy was to keep the politicians guessing how the Negroes would vote. No vote should be taken for granted; it should be earned. Negroes should emancipate themselves from a blind loyalty to the Republican party. Du Bois, who finally supported LaFollette, saw little to choose between the

[48] Coolidge to Charles F. Gardner, Aug. 9, 1924, in New York *Times,* Aug. 12, 1924 (reprinted in C. Bascom Slemp, ed., *The Mind of the President as Revealed by Himself in His Own Words* [Garden City, N.Y., 1926], pp. 247–48).

[49] "Coolidge on Colored Candidates," *Literary Digest,* 82 Aug. 30, 1924), 13; *Nation,* 119 (Sept. 10, 1924), 248; Pittsburgh *Courier,* Aug. 16, 1924.

[50] *Republican Campaign Text-Book: 1924,* p. 33.

three presidential candidates and argued that Negroes should concentrate their efforts on congressional and local elections where they had some hope of influencing the results.[51] Some Negroes tried to impress the GOP with the claim that in several doubtful states—ten according to Kelly Miller—Negroes could hold the balance of power.[52]

The belief that the black voter had to develop independent voting habits, concentrating his efforts in favor of his friends regardless of party affiliation, was clearly spreading among thoughtful Negroes, and it foreshadowed a general abandonment of the Republican party by the rank and file. But in the 1924 election it made little difference. Coolidge was returned with a margin of landslide proportions, although he did not do as well as Harding in 1920. Even if the Negro defection had been substantial, and it probably was not in terms of the total number of black voters, it would not have changed the results. At the same time, the election was a disappointment to those who thought that the GOP would continue to make gains in the South. In every one of the eleven southern states except Texas, the Republican vote fell off from what it had been in 1920, and Tennessee returned to the Democratic fold. The decline cannot be entirely explained by the presence of a strong third-party candidate, for the Democratic percentage of the popular vote increased in every one of these eleven states except Florida. After 1924 there was less talk of the New Republicanism than there had been four years earlier. Rather, the dull campaign suggested a widespread indifference to public issues. These were not propitious times to expect action on disturbing questions of racial injustices.

This did not mean that Coolidge completely ignored black Americans. In his annual message to Congress, for example, he regularly indulged his penchant for platitudes on the race question. On December 3, 1924, he noted that there had been "a very remarkable improvement in the condition of the negro race" and that the "colored people" enjoyed the "almost universal sympathy" of their neighbors. He concluded that it was "better for all concerned that they should be cheerfully accorded their full constitutional rights" and that they should especially be protected from the crime of lynching.[53] On a number of other occasions he expressed similar sentiments. In a speech to the American Legion convention at Omaha on Oc-

[51] New York *Times*, Sept. 21, 1924; *Crisis*, 28 (Oct. 1924), 247; *ibid.*, 29 (Jan. 1925), 103; Rudwick, p. 260.

[52] See Miller's article in New York *Times*, Aug. 24, 1924, and his letter, *ibid.*, Aug. 31, 1924.

[53] *Ibid.*, Dec. 4, 1924.

tober 6, 1925, he deplored intolerance and "narrowness of outlook" and praised the contributions of the diverse national, racial, and religious elements that made up America.[54] His December 8, 1925, message to Congress slightly expanded these themes. "Bigotry is only another name for slavery," he warned. "It reduces to serfdom not only those against whom it is directed, but also those who seek to apply it."[55]

However, when the opportunity arose to support specific programs needed by black Americans, Coolidge failed to act. Such, for example, was his response to the renewed attempts to enact a federal antilynching law. Obviously neither the president nor most congressmen believed that there was any political necessity to fight for an antilynching law. Their indifference was also supported by the fact that the number of reported lynchings declined considerably in 1923, 1924, and 1925. In his address accepting the 1924 Republican presidential nomination, Coolidge expressed satisfaction with that downward trend. He added his hope "that any further continuation of this national shame may be prevented by law,"[56] but this comment was perfunctory, for he refused to support any specific measure to achieve that end.

Meanwhile lynch mobs continued their deadly work. Johnson brought some of the more hideous cases to Coolidge's attention and again pleaded the case for federal intervention.[57] Dyer decided to try once more to get his bill passed. In December 1925 he reintroduced a measure that had been revised and strengthened with the assistance of Herbert K. Stockton. William B. McKinley of Illinois also introduced the bill in the Senate, and on February 16, 1926, the Senate Judiciary Committee held short hearings. Johnson testified on the facts of lynching and submitted a brief prepared by Stockton in defense of the bill's constitutionality.[58] As before, however, the president and most members of Congress were uninterested. When a delegation of Negro Republicans asked about his stand on the Dyer-McKinley bill, Coolidge merely referred them to his last mes-

54 *Ibid.*, Oct. 7, 1925.

55 *Ibid.*, Dec. 9, 1925.

56 Slemp, ed., *Mind of the President,* p. 247.

57 Johnson to Coolidge, Sept. 21, Sept. 22, 1925, Coolidge Papers. In addition numerous letters of complaint were sent by Negroes to the president or the Department of Justice; see File 158260, Record Group 60, National Archives.

58 NAACP, *Annual Report: 1925,* p. 21; *Cong. Rec.*, 69th Cong., 1st sess., vol. 67, pt. 1, pp. 447, 475; U.S., Congress, Senate, Committee on the Judiciary, *To Prevent and Punish the Crime of Lynching: Hearings on S. 121,* 69th Cong., 1st sess. (Feb. 16, 1926). See also Special Correspondence File, Dyer, NAACP Papers.

sage to Congress, in which he had said that Negroes "should be protected from all violence," without suggesting how that was to be done.[59] After talking to Republican leaders early in 1926, even Dyer became discouraged. He concluded that there was no reasonable chance for his bill in the Senate, and thus that little was to be gained by pressing for House action. He was probably correct. Shortly afterwards the Senate Judiciary Committee voted against the antilynching bill. It had the support of only three of the nine Republicans on the committee.[60]

After a three-year decline the number of lynchings increased again in 1926. The NAACP attributed this development to the decreasing fear of federal intervention that followed from Congress's repeated failure to act.[61] In October 1926 a triple lynching near Aiken, South Carolina, dramatically pointed out this lack of effective deterrent. Three Negroes, Bertha Lowman, her brother and her cousin, had been falsely charged with murder, convicted, and sentenced to death. The state supreme court reversed the conviction and ordered a new trial. The case against one of the defendants was dismissed, but he was promptly rearrested on a petty charge. A mob then broke into the jail, removed the three Negroes, and shot them. Walter White investigated the case for the NAACP and discovered that the lynchers were well known in the area. He accumulated evidence, including sworn affidavits naming the individuals involved, and submitted the material to Governor Thomas G. McLeod. On January 28, 1927, the Aiken County grand jury reported that it had insufficient evidence to bring any indictments in the case. The new governor, John G. Richards, attacked the grand jury findings as "a miserable miscarriage of justice." But the lynchers still went unpunished.[62] Johnson sent an impassioned letter to Coolidge citing the Lowman case as proof of the need for federal action. All he received in return was a letter from presidential secretary Everett Sanders, referring

[59] New York *Times*, March 17, 1926. See also Baltimore *Afro-American*, Feb. 26, 1926.

[60] Dyer to James W. Johnson, March 3, 1926, NAACP Papers; NAACP, *Annual Report: 1926*, p. 32.

[61] New York *Times*, Sept. 1, 1926; James W. Johnson, "The Practice of Lynching," *Century Magazine*, 115 (Nov. 1927), 69. According to Arthur Raper, *The Tragedy of Lynching* (Chapel Hill, N.C., 1933), p. 481, there were 17 lynchings in 1925 but 30 in 1926. However, all of the victims were Negroes in 1925; 7 were whites in 1926.

[62] White, *A Man Called White* (New York, 1948), pp. 56–59; *Press Service of the NAACP*, Jan. 29, 1927, in Schomburg Collection of New York Public Library; New York *Times*, Jan. 3, 4, 29, 30, 1927.

to some remarks against lynching in Coolidge's last message to Congress.[63]

Although Dyer was discouraged by the administration's lack of concern, he believed that it would be wrong to abandon all attempts at legislation. He reintroduced his bill in December 1927 at the beginning of the 70th Congress, and again in May 1929 at the beginning of the 71st Congress.[64] "We must keep up an active interest," he explained to Johnson, "otherwise lynchings will drop back to where they were before we started our fight against this crime."[65] But Dyer found few people who seriously cared. In a speech to a Negro audience in May, 1929, he complained that even they had become indifferent to the passage of an antilynching bill. He singled out ministers in particular for their lack of enthusiasm.[66] One probable reason for this was the fact that the number of lynchings sharply declined after 1926. Sixteen were reported for 1927, ten in 1929. Not until 1930, with the onset of the depression, did the lynching rate start to rise again, and then the yearly total never became as high as it had been before 1923.[67]

Nevertheless, there was still a long way to go before lynchings ceased to be a tragic fact of life for many black Americans or before states took seriously their obligation to uphold the equal protection of the laws. Until such a day arrived there was no cause for rejoicing. In their struggle against lynching, Negroes certainly had little reason to praise the actions of the President or Congress during the 1920's.

Confidence in the Republicans during the Coolidge years was further lessened by their failure to abolish segregation and other forms of racial discrimination in federal government employment. Harding had failed to carry out promised reforms; Coolidge did little better.

With Harding's death came many rumors of change. A Negro newspaper in Washington reported in mid-September 1923 that an order

63 Johnson and Mary W. Ovington to Coolidge, Jan. 29, 1927, Sanders to Johnson, Jan. 29, 1927, Coolidge Papers. On Dec. 7, 1926, Coolidge had said: "Our claim that we are an enlightened people requires us to use all our power to protect them [Negroes] from the crime of lynching. Although violence of this kind has very much decreased, while any of it remains we cannot justify neglecting to make every effort to eradicate it by law" (New York *Times,* Dec. 8, 1926).

64 *Cong. Rec.,* 70th Cong., 1st sess., vol. 69, pt. 1, p. 92; *ibid.,* 71st Cong., 1st sess., vol. 71, pt. 1, p. 762. See also Dyer to George W. Norris, Jan. 19, 1927, NAACP Papers.

65 Dyer to Johnson, Jan. 22, 1927, NAACP Papers.

66 New York *Amsterdam News,* May 29, 1929.

67 Raper, p. 481; Commission on Interracial Cooperation, *The Mob Still Rides: A Review of the Lynching Record, 1931–1935* (Atlanta, 1936), pp. 5–7. The worst year of the decade of the 1930's was 1933 when 28 were killed. Between 1930 and 1935 there were 105 reported lynchings, an average of 17.5 a year.

had been sent to all government departments forbidding discrimination on account of race. The report proved to be false. Slemp explained to Johnson that no such order had been issued, and he added that "it has not been felt that there was necessity for such action."[68] Johnson and many others disagreed. During the next few years numerous protests were made to the government about the continued instances of segregation and discrimination. Johnson wrote to Coolidge in December 1924 that "colored people feel that under your administration they have a right to expect that such practices, expressive of the Jim Crow spirit and a relic of slavery days, will receive the rebuke which they deserve."[69]

In January 1925 the NAACP sent a woman investigator to Washington to look into the numerous complaints. She found that Negro employees were often reluctant to make explicit statements because they feared losing their jobs. Although such caution made its work more difficult, the NAACP continued its efforts.[70] The National Equal Rights League also appealed to Coolidge. In October 1925 it claimed there was segregation in offices of the register of the Treasury, the Navy Department, the Census Bureau, the Bonus Section and the Transportation Division of the War Department, the Department of Justice, the Internal Revenue Service, the Treasury Department, and the Forest Service; segregated lunchrooms in the Post Office Department and the Government Printing Office; and a segregated washroom in the auditor's office.[71] Other reports added to the list.

In May 1926 the board of directors of the NAACP agreed to make governmental segregation an issue in the next election. At its annual conference a month later, the NAACP passed a resolution which noted with astonishment the continuation of segregation under a Republican administration. "We have repeatedly appealed for redress of this grievance and we appeal again to the sense of decency and honor which should exist at the Capital of the nation and which should save from insult persons who are serving their country in the organized civil service."[72] In July 1926 Coolidge met with a delegation from the National Equal Rights League and led them to believe that he would abolish departmental segregation. But as one member

[68] Johnson to Coolidge, Sept. 25, 1923, Slemp to Johnson, Sept. 27, 1923, NAACP Papers.

[69] Johnson to Coolidge, Dec. 7, 1924, *ibid.* For numerous protests, see File on Discrimination in Federal Service, *ibid.*, and File 93, Coolidge Papers.

[70] Johnson to A. S. Pinkett, April 3, 1925, NAACP Papers.

[71] Petition of National Equal Rights League to Coolidge, Oct. 17, 1925, Coolidge Papers.

[72] "Minutes of the Meeting of the Board of Directors, May 10, 1926," NAACP Papers; NAACP, *Annual Report: 1926*, pp. 31–32; New York *Times*, June 30, 1926.

of the group, Kelly Miller, later complained, they waited twenty months and nothing happened.[73]

Actually some changes did occur, usually only after vigorous protests had been lodged in specific cases. For example, on August 1, 1927, a reorganization of the Pension Bureau of the Interior Department resulted in the segregation of four Negro examiners. Acting Secretary of the Interior E. C. Finney defended it on the ground that the reorganization had for the first time raised a Negro to be chief of a division, the new consolidated file division. William Monroe Trotter complained to Coolidge that the segregation of the examiners was a violation of the pledge he had made to the delegation from the National Equal Rights League, and he demanded that it be stopped. The next day the White House issued an order revoking the segregation of the examiners.[74] Negroes continued to complain about conditions in the file division, and Neval H. Thomas, president of the District of Columbia branch of the NAACP, brought the matter to Coolidge's attention. Finally in October 1927 forty-two employees were ordered back to their unsegregated posts.[75] Shortly afterward, however, similar objections to the segregation of seven clerks in the General Land Office failed to induce either Coolidge or Secretary of the Interior Hubert Work to order the needed changes.[76]

On the basis of investigations made in the fall and winter of 1927–28, Thomas claimed that segregation existed "in every department where there . . . [were] enough Negroes to fill a room or other segregated area."[77] When a department head was challenged about such segregation, his response was often negative. The attitude of Ulysses S. Grant, 3rd, the director of public buildings and public parks, well illustrated this difficulty. In April and again in May 1928 the NAACP questioned him about segregation in the government restaurants, which were under his supervision. Grant did not deny that segregation was practiced; he excused it on the ground that the res-

[73] William M. Trotter to Coolidge, June 26, 1926; Maurice W. Spencer to Edward Clark, July 3, 1926, Coolidge Papers; Miller, "Segregation Hit by Hoover," undated article in Gumby Collection of Negroiana, Butler Library, Columbia University.

[74] Trotter to Coolidge, Aug. 1, 1927, Everett Sanders to Winfield Scott, Aug. 2, 1927, Finney to Sanders, Aug. 2, Aug. 3, 1927, Coolidge Papers.

[75] Thomas to Coolidge, Aug. 8, 1927, *ibid.*; *Press Service of the NAACP*, Aug. 19, Sept. 30, Oct. 14, 1927, NAACP Papers.

[76] *Press Service of the NAACP*, Oct. 28, Nov. 25, Dec. 9, 1927, Jan. 27, March 2, 1928, NAACP Papers; Neval H. Thomas to Herbert Seligmann, May 29, 1928, Robert W. Bagnall to Roy West, Sept. 27, 1928, E. K. Burlew to Bagnall, Oct. 16, 1928, Gretchen McRae to West, Oct. 22, Oct. 23, 1928, and undated letter (Feb. 1929), Gretchen McRae to Seligmann, Feb. 15, 1929, *ibid.*

[77] Thomas to James W. Johnson, March 22, 1928, NAACP Papers.

taurants were run by private concessionaires and not directly by the government. He added that every effort was made to maintain the same quality of food and service for blacks as for whites and that in his opinion the Negro employees who ate there were well satisfied. "As a very sincere friend of the colored race," Grant wrote to Johnson, "I can not but deplore the effort of your Association, as indicated in your letters, to stir up ill-will and race prejudice at this time."[78] Johnson replied, to no avail, that the NAACP was attempting to eradicate the causes of bad feeling, not to stir it up.[79]

Complaints to Secretary of Commerce Herbert Hoover about conditions in the Census Bureau were more successful. In late March 1928, Hoover ordered an end to racial segregation and discrimination in the Department of Commerce. The action caused a small flurry in Congress when Hoover was bitterly attacked by Senators Coleman L. Blease of South Carolina, J. Thomas Heflin of Alabama, and Hubert D. Stephens of Mississippi. Hoover had disturbed "the splendid arrangement established in the Commerce Department by the Democratic Party," complained Heflin. "Will the white Republicans of the country tamely submit to this dangerous political play and humiliating action on the part of Mr. Hoover?"[80] Although Hoover's order was widely regarded as a bid for Negro support for his presidential aspirations, he had at least responded positively to a legitimate complaint.[81]

In the spring of 1928 the NAACP sent letters to the heads of all federal government departments where segregation was reported to exist. The letters called attention to the reforms instituted by Hoover and urged similar action. Most of the replies denied that there was segregation. Secretary of the Treasury Andrew W. Mellon not only described the accusation as "unwarranted" but added that Negro employees in his department were well satisfied with their condition and had no complaints.[82] The NAACP was unconvinced. At Mellon's invitation it sent two staff members to examine conditions for themselves. They found that thirty clerks were segregated in room 308 in the register's office and that others were segregated in the

78 Grant to Johnson, June 4, 1928, *ibid.*

79 Johnson to Grant, June 19, 1928, Grant to Johnson, July 3, 1928, *ibid.*

80 *Press Service of the NAACP*, March 23, April 6, 1928, *ibid. Cong. Rec.*, 70th Cong., 1st sess., vol. 69, pt. 6, pp. 6145–75, 6486; *ibid.*, pt. 7, pp. 7701–3; *ibid.*; pt. 10, pp. 10657–58.

81 Kelly Miller to Editor, *New Republic*, 56 (Oct. 3, 1928), 180; Duff Gilfond, "Notes from Washington," *Nation*, 127 (Nov. 14, 1928), 519.

82 Mellon to James W. Johnson, May 16, 1928, *ibid.* See also sworn affidavits dated Aug. 17, 1928, by two Negro clerks claiming that five Negro clerks were segregated in room 341 of the United States Treasury (*ibid.*)

Stamp Book and Engraving Divisions of the Bureau of Printing and Engraving. Negroes were also required to eat at a separate end of the lunchroom in the bureau. The NAACP investigators claimed that the Negro employees, who were willing to complain to them about these conditions, were afraid to go to their department superiors because "their economic status was at stake."[83]

Investigations made by the NAACP in August 1928 also uncovered many complaints about unfairness in rating and promotion as well as instances of segregated working or rest-room facilities in the Government Printing Office and in the Washington city post office. Segregation in the lunchrooms was one of the most frequent grievances. In the Navy Department this practice had begun after the Republicans had returned to power in 1921. These investigations also revealed that some improvements had been made. W. T. Andrews, a special legal assistant for the NAACP, reported no indication of segregation in the Departments of Agriculture, Labor, and State, and except for the cafeteria, no glaring instances in the Department of the Interior.[84] Another report prepared by Walter White was surprisingly favorable, considering the nearly eight years of continued complaints. White concluded "that segregation is not as widespread nor as flagrant as some people believe. Whether this is due to the activities of the Washington Branch and its President or whether the sum total of discrimination has been somewhat exaggerated, this observer has been unable to say. It is probable that both are true."[85] White's investigations were completed in only three days, and the reluctance of Negro employees to talk about their problems may have left some instances of segregation unobserved. Moreover, his report was not without criticism, particularly over the related issue of discrimination in hiring. No one had ever claimed that segregation was practiced in every government department. But there was ample evidence that it was widespread during the period of the Harding

[83] Robert W. Bagnall to Mellon, Sept. 26, 1928, *ibid.* Mellon's reply denied that any segregation existed in the Bureau of Printing and Engraving and claimed that there was no rule requiring segregation in the lunchroom. As for the other instances of segregation, Mellon argued that these few cases merely showed that the department did not wish to segregate its 2,200 Negro employees, for if it did the practice would have been universal (Mellon to Bagnall, Oct. 18, 1928, *ibid.*)

[84] "Segregation in Government Departments," report by Andrews of an investigation made Aug. 10–17, 1928, Arthur B. Spingarn Papers, Manuscript Division, Library of Congress.

[85] "Segregation in Government Departments," report by White of an investigation made Aug. 27–30, 1928, *ibid.* See also the summary of the NAACP's investigations in "Color Discrimination in Government Service," *Crisis*, 35 (Nov. 1928), 369, 387–90.

and Coolidge presidencies. Any improvement hardly exonerated the Republicans for their long failure to live up to either their promises or their presumed ideals.

The administration's record on other aspects of Negro employment was not much better. Like Harding, Coolidge was reluctant to return to the pre-Wilsonian level of Negro presidential appointments. He made a few well-received Negro appointments, notably his selection of James A. Cobb in February 1926 to succeed Robert H. Terrell as judge of the Municipal Court of the District of Columbia. But many of the old political plums, such as the ministerships in Nicaragua, Venezuela, Haiti, and Santo Domingo, remained in white hands. When Coolidge had the opportunity to appoint a register of the Treasury in 1927, he disappointed blacks by selecting another white for this position which had once been reserved for Negroes.[86] During the Coolidge years the total number of Negroes holding responsible positions in the federal government remained far short of what it had been during Roosevelt's presidency.[87]

Much more serious was the Republicans' failure to attempt to protect the right of Negroes to vote. Nothing had been done since the collapse in 1921 of Congressman George H. Tinkham's efforts to investigate disfranchisement and to enforce the Fourteenth Amendment by reducing southern representation. On December 5, 1927, Tinkham introduced another resolution with similar objectives.[88] It was a hopeless task. "Let us admit frankly," Tinkham finally lamented, "that the negro has been abandoned to his political fate and will remain abandoned unless he organizes politically and asserts his power in those states where he may freely vote."[89]

In June 1929, Tinkham came somewhat closer to success. To a census and reapportionment bill, which had already passed the Senate, he offered two amendments. One called for a census of all people twenty-one years of age or older whose right to vote in a presidential or congressional election had been denied; the other

86 Pittsburgh *Courier*, July 16, 1927. Coolidge appointed Walter O. Wood to succeed Harley V. Speelman, a white originally appointed by Wilson and retained by the Harding-Coolidge administrations.

87 Pittsburg *Courier*, Feb. 20, 1926; William C. Matthews, "The Negro Bloc," *Opportunity*, 5 (Feb. 1927), 49. On Coolidge's Negro appointments, see *Negro Year Book: 1925/26*, pp. 58, 244; "Appointments of Colored Men," undated (1926?) memorandum; statement released by the Department of Labor, Sept. 1, 1928; chart prepared by Emmett J. Scott on presidential positions held by Negroes, File 93 Coolidge Papers.

88 *Cong. Rec.*, 70th Cong., 1st sess., vol. 69, pt. 1, p. 100; New York *Times*, Dec. 5, 1927.

89 *Cong. Rec.*, 70th Cong., 1st sess., vol. 69, pt. 4, p. 3731.

provided that the population used as the basis for legislative apportionment should exclude those enumerated in the special census. In a move directed against the northern urban states, southern Democrats and farm-belt Republicans changed the wording of the second amendment so that it would also exclude aliens twenty-one years or older. In a surprise action, the House adopted this second amendment by a vote of 145 to 118. Fearing the defeat of the whole census-reapportionment bill, floor leader John Q. Tilson of Connecticut and Speaker Nicholas Longworth of Ohio then maneuvered through a revised version of the section in question that cut out all the offensive proposals.[90]

Congress matched this failure to act on the matter of Negro suffrage with a related dereliction of duty, letting the decade go by without enacting a reapportionment measure based on the 1920 census, despite its constitutional obligation. With the rapid growth of cities, a process in which the black migration had begun to play a significant part, most new seats allotted under a reapportionment would go to the urban centers at the expense of the rural areas. Therefore, the farm bloc joined with southern Democrats and others in resisting a change.[91]

During the 1920's serious attempts to protect the right of Negroes to vote were unlikely, not only because they conflicted with lily-white Republican aspirations in the South but also because they continued to run counter to critical opinions about the actual concept of the extended franchise. The attitude of many Republicans tended to range from apathy to positive hostility. Former President Taft, for example, asserted that granting the vote to a "mass of densely ignorant people" had been a mistake, and he still naively argued, as he had earlier, that as Negroes became better educated they would be given the vote in the South.[92] President Nicholas Murray Butler of Columbia University, long an influential figure in the GOP, not only lamented the passage of the Fourteenth and Fifteenth Amendments but implied that it might be well to repeal the latter and enforce the section of the former reducing representation rather than have Negroes voting.[93] The powerful Senator Borah expressed

90 *Ibid.*, 71st Cong., 1st sess., vol. 71, pt. 3, pp. 2348, 2364, 2448–58; New York *Times*, June 5–7, 1929.

91 Ray T. Tucker, "Our Delinquent Congress," *New Republic*, 47 (May 26, 1926), 11–13; *Nation*, 123 (July 7, 1926), 1; "Congress Evades Reapportionment," *Literary Digest*, 92 (Feb. 19, 1927), 13.

92 Taft, "The Negro Problem in America," *Southern Workman*, 50 (Jan. 1921), 13.

93 Butler, *The Faith of a Liberal: Essays and Addresses on Political Principles and Public Policies* (New York, 1924), pp. 117–19; see also pp. 297–98.

doubts about Negro suffrage on several occasions. "I think that the enfranchisement of the slaves at the time it was brought about was one of the greatest mistakes ever made in this country," he said on June 13, 1926, in a commencement address to the National Law School. Questioned on his opinions by Du Bois, Borah identified his views with those of Lincoln.[94] In a subsequent article on Negro suffrage published in the *Crisis* he argued that "the South is in good faith seeking to work out this problem and in accordance with the Constitution. I do not find any spirit of nullification."[95] As long as such opinions were commonly held it was little wonder that disfranchised southern Negroes got no help from the Republicans.

During the Coolidge years race relations and the conditions of black Americans were matters of only minor concern to most Republican leaders. In this regard they reflected the attitude of most white Americans, but in so doing they failed to assume the responsibilities or take advantage of some of the opportunities that their leadership entailed. For the most part the neglect of the Negro was less the result of a deliberate policy than it was the product of lack of concern. The results were much the same in either case: throughout most of the 1920's little was attempted and even less was done by the federal government to improve the conditions of life for black Americans.

94 New York *Herald Tribune*, June 14, 1926; *Crisis*, 32 (Aug. 1926), 166.

95 Borah, "Negro Suffrage," *Crisis*, 33 (Jan. 1927), 132. For another statement by Borah, see *Cong. Rec.*, 70th Cong., 1st sess., vol. 69, pt. 2, pp. 1861–62 (Jan. 23, 1928).

CHAPTER IX

Hoover and the End of an Era

DURING the 1920's Republican leaders seemed increasingly out of touch with many of the changing realities of American life. Their lack of understanding and sympathy for the problems of black Americans, as well as those of the cities and of recent immigrants and workingmen, suggested a loss of both democratic ideals and political foresight. It was a loss for which they would pay a heavy price. As for black leaders and their allies, their sense of alienation from the GOP grew inexorably during the years of Republican ascendancy. A resolution adopted by the NAACP at its 1926 annual convention forcefully asserted that: "Our political salvation and our social survival lie in our *absolute independence of party allegiance in politics* and the casting of our vote for our friends and against our enemies whoever they may be and whatever party labels they carry."[1] The ties of the Negro rank and file with the Republican party remained strong, but as the decade advanced the number who were willing to assert their independence, especially in local elections in several northern states, notably increased.[2] In retrospect it seems clear that the presidential election of 1928 and the subsequent Hoover administration were the Republicans' last major opportunities to reverse this development.

Hoover's upbringing and career had done little to prepare him to understand the plight of black Americans. Throughout his childhood in West Branch, Iowa, his years with his uncle in Oregon, and his education at Stanford University, he lived in a world remote from that of the southern rural Negro or the resident of the newly developing black ghettos. His own successful career reinforced the values of rural, Protestant, white America and fostered in him the illusion that achievement could be explained largely in terms of personal merit, given the equality of opportunity which he believed

[1] NAACP, *Annual Report: 1926*, p. 32.

[2] E. Franklin Frazier, "The American Negro's New Leaders," *Current History*, 28 (April 1928), 59; Ira De A. Reid, "Mirrors of Harlem: Investigations and Problems of America's Largest Colored Community," *Social Forces*, 5 (June 1927), 631; Herbert Seligmann, "The Negro's Influence as a Voter," *Current History*, 28 (May 1928), 230–31.

was a reality in the United States.[3] With such an attitude it was unlikely that he could readily comprehend the problems of the poor. In addition, his cold, austere personality made it difficult for anyone, least of all Negroes, to develop a warm, personal relationship with him. Hoover's early experience as a mining engineer in many parts of the world had also led him to draw unflattering conclusions about the intelligence and working capacity of nonwhites, Asians or Negroes, whom he described as the "lower races" in his 1909 work on the *Principles of Mining*.[4] Later he achieved a brilliant success as administrator of relief to a wartorn Europe; his role then, as it had been in business, was that of a superior overseeing the labor and needs of the less fortunate. Until his tenure as secretary of Commerce from 1921 to 1928, Hoover had spent most of his adult life outside of the United States. A man who became a virtual symbol of the American way, he was, paradoxically, a stranger to much of his own country.

As far as Negroes were concerned, Hoover was largely an unknown quantity until 1927. Then his handling of the Mississippi flood relief raised many questions about his racial attitudes. During the spring of 1927 the Mississippi River went on a rampage, causing the most terrible floods in its history. The greatest damage and loss of life was in the flat bottom lands of the lower Mississippi valley covering parts of Arkansas, Louisiana, and Mississippi. There the levees broke and thousands of sufferers, especially poor black and white sharecroppers, were driven from the land. Hoover was appointed to head a cabinet committee to aid the Red Cross and the relief agencies that were assisting the victims. He made his first inspection of the stricken areas in late April and early May and a second in June.

3 For example, in his address accepting the presidential nomination on Aug. 11, 1928, he said: "We, through free and universal education, provide in the government the umpire of fairness in the race. The winner is he who shows the most conscientious training, the greatest ability and the greatest character" (Hoover, *The New Day: Campaign Speeches of Herbert Hoover* [Stanford, Calif., 1928], p. 42).

4 Hoover, *Principles of Mining* (New York, 1909), chap. 16, esp. pp. 161–65. See also Richard Hofstadter, *The American Political Tradition and the Men Who Made It* (New York, 1948), p. 289. In 1920 Hoover argued against the importation of Chinese labor on both economic and social grounds. The Chinese, he said, could not be Americanized, and there certainly should not be a "mixture of Asiatic and white races. Their common product is degenerate." In parts of Asia, he noted, Eurasians have been born for 150 years, but they have added nothing good to the world ("Stabilization of Bituminous Coal Industry," *Mining and Metallurgy*, no. 159 [March 1920],4, copy in Master Speech File, II, Hoover Papers, Hoover Presidential Library, West Branch Iowa; and *Sacramento Union*, Aug. 19, 1920, copy in *ibid.*, IV).

Meanwhile reports began to circulate that Negro refugees were being made to perform forced labor, were treated unequally by the Red Cross, and were subjected to other abuses. On May 9 the NAACP directed Walter White to investigate these charges. The intervention by the NAACP displeased Hoover, and his first response was to deny that Negroes had been mistreated. Nevertheless, he agreed to sponsor an investigation of his own and asked Dr. Robert R. Moton of Tuskegee to name and head a committee of "representative colored citizens" to undertake the task.[5]

Despite Hoover's fears, White reported that he found less unfairness than he had expected in the administration of flood relief. The refugee camps were another matter. Negroes were penned in like prisoners and only released to the landlord from whose plantation they had come, or temporarily to local industries where they were sometimes subjected to "cursing, beating and other brutalities."[6] "The greatest and most significant injustice," White wrote in the *Nation*, "is in the denial to Negroes of the right of free movement and of the privilege of selling their services to the highest bidder. That, if persisted in, would recreate and crystallize a new slavery almost as miserable as the old."[7]

On June 14 White wrote to Hoover about the conditions in the camps at Vicksburg and Memphis. In reply, Hoover pointed out that because of the emergency there had to be quick action under highly adverse conditions. Hundreds of thousands of people had been assisted, and after the national organization of the Red Cross stepped in on April 20, only three lives had been lost, none Negro. But he sidestepped White's specific complaints and failed to address himself to some of the immediate human problems. "The National agencies," he asserted, "have no responsibility for the economic system which exists in the South or for matters which have taken place in previous years. . . . The Red Cross cannot undertake either social or economic reforms."[8] Unsatisfied with this explanation, White asked James L. Fieser, vice chairman of the American Red

[5] "Minutes of the Meeting of the Board of Directors, May 9, 1927," NAACP Papers, Manuscript Division, Library of Congress; New York *Times*, May 28, May 29, 1927; Arthur Capper to Hoover, May 10, 1927, Hoover to Capper, May 13, 1927, Lawrence Richey to George Akerson, June 9, 1927, Hoover to Moton, May 24, May 28, 1927, Moton to Hoover, May 26, 1927, "Mississippi Valley Flood–1927," Commerce, Official File, Hoover Papers.

[6] White to Hoover, June 14, 1927, "Mississippi Valley Flood–1927," Commerce, Official File, Hoover Papers.

[7] White, "The Negro and the Flood," *Nation*, 124 (June 22, 1927), 689.

[8] Hoover to White, June 21, 1927, "Mississippi Valley Flood–1927," Commerce, Official File, Hoover Papers.

Cross, to make certain that landlords, planters, or others were not using any camp directly or indirectly under Red Cross control to hold Negro refugees improperly. White also requested that armed guards be removed from any camp where they were being used to prevent the freedom of movement of the refugees and that the Red Cross see that landlords did not charge Negroes for supplies that it furnished.[9]

Meanwhile, the advisory committee headed by Moton began its investigation. As no members of the NAACP had been appointed to the committee, the NAACP feared that it would attempt to whitewash all evidence of wrongdoing. But, as White later wrote, "to Hoover's great disappointment the absolution he manifestly expected did not materialize."[10] The committee delivered its first report to Hoover at a meeting in Baton Rouge on June 11. Moderately worded, it found much to condemn in the conditions in most of the refugee camps, and it made a number of specific recommendations concerning the distribution of needed supplies, the removal of armed white guardsmen, and the appointment of Negro advisors.[11]

Some of the committee's recommendations were carried out, but at the end of the summer the plight of many refugees was still very bad. "Continued vigilance" was essential, Moton told Hoover in reporting the findings of a Tuskegee investigator who visited the flood region in September. Hoover asked Moton's committee to make another survey.[12] This was done in November, and the results were reported to Hoover on December 13 at a conference in Washington. Half a year had passed since the first complaints had been voiced; yet Moton's committee found that many conditions were still "totally unsatisfactory." The program as laid down by the Red Cross was "totally just and fair," but in practice there were many irregularities. In violation of Red Cross instructions, relief sometimes went to the landlords rather than directly to the tenants and sharecroppers. Negroes were still being forced to return to their old plantations from the camps. Those who were caught attempting to leave "were whipped and at times threatened with death." Many lived in fear and "semi-peonage." "The policy of the national Red Cross is still subject to the interpretation of local white people and the treatment

9 White to Fieser, July 12, 1927, *ibid.*

10 White, *A Man Called White* (New York, 1948), p. 81.

11 Moton to Hoover, June 13, 1927, "Mississippi Valley Flood–1927," Commerce, Official File, Hoover Papers. See also the editorial in *Opportunity*, 5 (Aug. 1927), 222.

12 Moton to Hoover, Oct. 1, 1927, Hoover to Moton, Oct. 17, 1927, Hoover to De Witt Smith, Nov. 3, 1927, Hoover and James L. Fieser to Moton, Nov. 6, 1927, "Mississippi Valley Flood–1927," Commerce, Official File, Hoover Papers.

of Negroes is reflected very largely in the personal attitude of local men and women in charge of the Red Cross affairs." As the report showed, this attitude was frequently hostile to the interests of the black refugees.[13]

Moton's findings had largely supported the charges made by White and the NAACP. But the texts of these reports were not made public, creating the impression, or so the NAACP charged, that the advisory committee had no complaints and that the NAACP accusations were unfounded. At the beginning of 1928 the NAACP tried to rectify this by publishing in the *Crisis* a series of detailed reports on its own investigations made in May and October 1927.[14] These revelations had little apparent impact on the country generally or on Hoover's standing as a presidential candidate.

All the investigations showed conclusively that Negroes had suffered more than others during the disaster and that they had been the victims of numerous injustices. What was less clear was the degree to which Hoover could be legitimately held responsible. Moton refused to blame him. "The Secretary of Commerce did everything that the Advisory Commission . . . asked." Moreover, Moton claimed that "Hoover is a man who disregards differences in race, color, creed, and condition. He sees and serves humanity in terms of equality, justice, and absolute fairness." The charge that he had been unfair to Negroes was "a gross misrepresentation of the facts." Moton insisted that Hoover took what steps he could to correct the abuses that were uncovered.[15] Another member of the committee, Jesse O. Thomas, the field secretary of the National Urban League, acknowledged that they had found "many manifestations of cruelty and injustice," including "violent measures" used to force Negro men and boys to work on the levees against their will. But he, too, believed that Hoover "did not countenance any discrimination or injustice that was brought to his attention."[16]

13 Moton to Hoover, undated report [Dec. 1927], *ibid.*

14 "An Open Letter to the Colored Flood Rehabilitation Commission," undated [1928], Arthur B. Spingarn Papers, Manuscript Division, Library of Congress; "The Flood, the Red Cross and the National Guard," *Crisis*, 35 (Jan.–March 1928), 5–7, 26, 28, 41–43, 64, 80–81, 100, 102.

15 Moton to Sidney B. Thompson, March 26, 1928, quoted in William H. Hughes and Frederick D. Patterson, eds., *Robert Russa Moton of Hampton and Tuskegee* (Chapel Hill: University of North Carolina Press, 1956), p. 201. See also Moton to John Barton Payne, May 14, 1928, "Mississippi Valley Flood–1927," Commerce, Official File, Hoover Papers; Moton to C. C. Goines, Oct. 1, 1928, in Hughes and Patterson, pp. 201–2.

16 Thomas, "Large Scale Interracial Cooperation," *Southern Workman*, 58 (July 1928), 278–80.

The NAACP leaders came to a different conclusion. Admitting that some problems had been corrected, they remained highly critical of Hoover's handling of the flood relief. Certainly they could not agree with Moton's assessment of Hoover's equalitarian attitude on race. Although they recognized that he was not responsible for all the discriminations committed by the Red Cross workers and National Guardsmen in the stricken areas, they believed that he was slow to take corrective action, and they noted that his public statements showed neither indignation over the deplorable conditions nor sympathy for the victims. The episode was thus an important factor in creating the negative attitude among NAACP leaders toward Hoover's presidential candidacy.

When the Republican national convention assembled at Kansas City, Missouri, in June 1928, Hoover seemed virtually assured of the nomination. Among many Negroes his reputation was already suspect, partly because of his role in the flood relief, but also because of the favoritism his managers had shown to lily-whites in their quest for the support of a large bloc of southern delegates. On June 4 the national committee began hearings on contested delegations. Eight southern states were involved. In nearly every instance the committee's decision favored Hoover, often to the disadvantage of Negro politicians. For example, the pro-Hoover delegation from Texas, led by R. B. Creager, was seated in place of a racially mixed group, with the result that the Texas delegation to the national convention was for the first time entirely white. Although the lily-whites were not awarded every contested seat, the decisions tended to put the black-and-tan regulars on the defensive.[17]

With the exception of these disputes, the Republicans showed very little interest in racial problems at the convention. The platform contained only one sentence specifically devoted to the Negro, a recommendation for the enactment of a federal antilynching law, and they selected a candidate whose ideas on matters of special interest to black Americans were largely unknown. After his nomination Hoover was asked by some Negroes to clarify his position in his August 11 acceptance speech. But in that address he merely asserted his belief that "equality of opportunity is the right of every American—rich or poor, foreign or native-born, irrespective of faith

[17] New York *Times*, June 5–16, 1928; *Official Report of the Proceedings of the Nineteenth Republican National Convention Held in Kansas City, Missouri, June 12, 13, 14, and 15, 1928*, pp. 50–65, 72, 77, 92–3; Paul Casdorph, *A History of the Republican Party in Texas, 1865–1965* (Austin, Tex., 1965), pp. 134–35; Paul Lewinson, *Race, Class and Party: A History of Negro Suffrage and White Politics in the South* (New York, 1932), pp. 172–73.

or color."[18] Neither then nor later did he make specific recommendations about what the government could do to promote such equality.

During the campaign Hoover's sympathies increasingly appeared to be with the lily-whites in the South. One indication of this was the prosecution of Perry Howard and some other Mississippi Negroes for the sale of federal offices, an action that apparently had Hoover's approval. Howard, who was not only a national committeeman but also an assistant United States attorney general, was indicted by a federal grand jury in mid-July. Critics of his prosecution readily admitted that the southern organizations had been involved in many scandalous activities, but as for trafficking in offices and appointments, they claimed that Howard had merely acted like a traditional southern Republican. "When it became politically expedient for the Republican Party to dissociate itself from the Negroes in the South," argued the *Nation*, "Perry Howard was suddenly prosecuted for doing what he had been paid to do."[19] Du Bois, no admirer of Howard, pointed out that Howard's conduct had been no worse than that of C. Bascom Slemp, who some years earlier had been accused of selling offices. Now Slemp, the lily-white, was in charge of Hoover's southern campaign, and Howard was being prosecuted. When the pinch came, concluded Du Bois, it was only the black politicians who got condemned.[20] In December 1928 Howard and four other defendants were tried and acquitted. Reindicted on similar charges, he was again acquitted in April 1929. Despite these difficulties he retained his seat on the national committee; apparently Republican leaders finally decided that the frank espousal of Negro disfranchisement by Howard's lily-white opponent in Mississippi, George B. Sheldon, was a little too dangerous to accept as long as they had any interest at all in the Negro vote in the North.[21]

Another indication of Hoover's willingness to play up to the southern whites was seen in a speech he delivered at Elizabethtown, Tennessee, on October 6 during his first campaign trip south. "I

[18] *Republican Campaign Text-Book: 1928*, p. 34; Elbert L. Tatum, *The Changed Political Thought of the Negro, 1915–1940* (New York, 1951), pp. 100–101.

[19] "The Roots of Corruption," *Nation*, 127 (Sept. 19, 1928), 258; New York *Times*, July 17, 1928.

[20] *Crisis*, 35 (Sept. 1928), 312. See also Du Bois, "Is Al Smith Afraid of the South?", *Nation*, 127 (Oct. 17, 1928), 392.

[21] *Nation*, 127 (Dec. 26, 1928), 700; New York *Times*, April 27, 1929; Louis M. Jiggitts, "Post Offices and Politics," *Independent*, 121 (Aug. 11, 1928), 135–36; Samuel Taylor Moore, "Mississippi Auction Block–New Style," *ibid.*, 118 (Feb. 26, 1927), 231–34.

believe in the merit system of the civil service," he said, "and I believe further that appointive offices must be filled by those who deserve the confidence and respect of the communities they serve."[22] A southern white audience could regard this as a promise not to appoint Negroes to office in the South. Such an interpretation was consistent with other reports of Hoover's thinking at that time. For example, after talking with him in late October, Chief Justice Taft wrote that Hoover had condemned southern Negro politicians for "blackmailing" Republican administrations into giving them offices to sell (an apparent reference to the Perry Howard case). Taft also noted that Hoover had been "intensely interested in his purpose to break up the solid south and to drive the negroes out of Republican politics."[23] Hoover would not express such frank intentions publicly, but he did enough to convince many Negroes that they were not welcome in the Republican party.

Black voters still had to decide whether Al Smith and the Democrats presented a worthwhile alternative to Hoover. In New York City they had earlier shown a considerable liking for Smith during his campaigns for governor, but this support fell off after 1922.[24] Outside of New York many Negroes viewed him with suspicion. As a Democrat he would necessarily be tied to some extent to southern anti-Negro politicians, and the experience with Wilson was a painful reminder of what such associations could mean. Moreover, the religious preference of most Negroes had traditionally been Protestant, and at least some of them shared the anti-Catholic prejudices of many white Americans.[25]

The Democrats made a stronger bid than usual for the black vote in the North. Smith's publicity director, Mrs. Belle Moskowitz, asked Walter White to take a leave of absence from the NAACP in order to assume direction of the Negro division of the Democratic party. White refused, in part because he opposed the whole idea of a racially segregated campaign bureau. However, he did ask Smith to issue a strong statement to the effect that if elected he would be president of all the people, and not be dominated by an anti-Negro South. But no such statement was published. As the campaign progressed, it appeared that Smith's fears of antagonizing the white

22 New York *Times*, Oct. 7, 1928.

23 William H. Taft to H. D. Taft, Oct. 31, 1928, quoted in Alpheus T. Mason, *William Howard Taft: Chief Justice* (New York, 1964), p. 152.

24 New York *Times*, Oct. 29, 1926; Gilbert Osofsky, *Harlem, the Making of a Ghetto: Negro New York, 1890–1930* (New York, 1966), p. 243 n. 37.

25 For example, note the anti-Catholic views expressed by Rev. Francis J. Grimké in "Stray Thoughts and Meditations," dated Nov. 7, 1928, in *The Works of Francis J. Grimké* (Washington, D.C., 1942), III, 292–93.

South overcame his desire to reassure blacks.[26] Despite the party's Negro division, neither the Democratic platform nor Smith himself took any stand directly in favor of Negro rights.

Nevertheless, many Negroes defected from the Republican party in 1928, probably more than ever before in a national election. Several influential Negro newspapers, like the Chicago *Defender*, the Baltimore *Afro-American*, the Boston *Guardian*, and the Norfolk *Journal and Guide*, supported Smith. An important Negro politician, Robert R. Church, Jr., of Tennessee, refused for the first time to serve on the GOP's Colored Voters Division. Other Negroes felt it was better to stick with the Republicans. William H. Lewis returned to the fold, after his bolt in 1924, and such leading newspapers as the Pittsburgh *Courier* and the Amsterdam *News* favored Hoover.[27] Many thoughtful Negroes seem to have agreed with Du Bois's caustic conclusion that "in our humble opinion, it does not matter a tinker's damn which of these gentlemen succeed. With minor exceptions, they stand for exactly the same thing: oligarchy in the South, color caste in national office holding, and recognition of the rule of organized wealth."[28]

Not all aspects of the 1928 campaign were discouraging to black Americans. The most promising developments were in the elections for lesser offices. By far the most important example was the election of Oscar DePriest of Chicago as a Republican congressman from the First Illinois District. The first Negro to be elected to Congress since the retirement of George H. White of North Carolina in 1901, DePriest won the seat vacated by the sudden death of Martin B. Madden in April. A ward committeeman and former member of the Chicago City Council, DePriest had the support of Mayor William H. Thompson, whose organization had long held the allegiance of Negro voters in Chicago.[29] DePriest's election to Congress, then possible only in a

[26] White, *A Man Called White*, pp. 99–101; DuBois, "Is Al Smith Afraid of the South?" p. 393.

[27] John Hope Franklin, *From Slavery to Freedom* (3d ed., New York, 1967), p. 524; Du Bois, "Is Al Smith Afraid of the South?" p. 392; Pittsburgh *Courier*, Sept. 22, 1928; "Confidential Comments on Loyalty," prepared by the Republican party's Publicity Committee, Colored Voters Division, 1928 campaign, in "Colored Question," Presidential, Subject File, Hoover Papers.

[28] *Crisis*, 35 (Nov. 1928), 381.

[29] Harold F. Gosnell, *Negro Politicians: The Rise of Negro Politics in Chicago* (Chicago, 1935), pp. 29, 163–85. DePriest's victory did not mean, however, that there had been a Republican upswing among Negro voters. In the Chicago black belt Hoover's 1928 vote was about 15 percent less than that of Coolidge in 1924. In New York City there was a similar loss for the GOP in Negro districts (Osofsky, p. 242, n. 36; see also John M. Allswang, *A House for All Peoples: Ethnic Politics in Chicago, 1890–1936* [Lexington, Ky., 1971], pp. 42, 145–48, 187; David Burner,

northern city, showed that under certain conditions, as when a large, concentrated population united behind a candidate, black voters could wield significant political power. It was an important lesson. As Du Bois pointed out after the election, only when Negroes learned that such power was a necessary basis of permanent freedom could there be hope of lasting reform.[30]

In 1928 Republicans were much more interested in Hoover's impressive victory than in the changes DePriest's election foreshadowed. Later analysts have noted Hoover's weakness in the urban centers of the North, in parts of the farm belt, and in areas of the South with high Negro concentration, as well as the special factors—prohibition, Smith's Catholicism, and his ethnic background—that have to be weighed in evaluating the significance of Hoover's overwhelming triumph.[31] But in 1928 Republican elation was understandable. Hoover had won more electoral votes than any previous Republican candidate. His percentage of the popular vote had been exceeded only by that received by Harding in 1920. And, at the presidential level the solid South had been broken, with Florida, North Carolina, Tennessee, Texas, and Virginia in the Republican column. Hoover had not needed the black vote, and his courting of southern whites had apparently paid off. The election returns provided no incentive for Republicans to attempt to strengthen the ties of Negroes to the party.

After Hoover became president his understanding of the problems of black Americans did not noticeably improve. His inaugural address contained no specific references to racial matters, and during his administration he made fewer public statements on racial issues than any other president in the twentieth century.

The Negro with whom Hoover worked most closely was Dr. Moton. Their contacts received relatively little notice, and it is doubtful that Moton significantly altered the president's feelings. Hoover's record on Negro appointments was a case in point. Throughout 1929 not one Negro's name appeared among the nominees he sent to the Senate for confirmation. On January 15, 1930, Moton conferred with

The Politics of Provincialism: The Democratic Party in Transition, 1918–1932 [New York, 1968], pp. 237, 241).

30 Du Bois, "The Negro Citizen," in Charles S. Johnson, *The Negro in American Civilization* (New York, 1930), p. 464.

31 See John D. Hicks, *Republican Ascendancy, 1921–1933* (New York, 1960), pp. 212–14; Richard Hofstadter, "Could a Protestant Have Beaten Hoover in 1928?" *Reporter*, 22 (March 17, 1960), 33; Samuel Lubell, *The Future of American Politics* (New York, 1952), pp. 34–41; Ruth Silva, *Rum, Religion and Votes: 1928 Re-Examined* (University Park, Pa., 1962), passim, esp. pp. 1–15; V. O. Key, Jr., *Southern Politics in State and Nation* (New York, 1949), pp. 318–29. Cf. Burner, pp. 217–43.

Hoover about this problem and recommended candidates for a number of positions.[32] The first action was not taken until March, and it was merely the reappointment of James A. Cobb as judge of the Municipal Court of the District of Columbia. Other appointments eventually followed, but not enough to allay the fears of many Negroes. In November 1931 a survey of the executive departments made at the request of the White House showed that since Hoover had taken office only two important Negro appointments had been made in the State Department. The record was better in the Departments of Agriculture, Interior, Justice, and Labor, where several Negroes served in positions of some responsibility. Larger numbers served at lower levels, such as county agents in the Extension Service of the Department of Agriculture or nurses at the Freedmen's Hospital under the administration of the Department of the Interior. When expedient, as in the report sent in November 1931 to the National Negro Republican League, it was possible to compile a lengthy list of Negroes employed in government service. But not many were presidential appointees, and with a few exceptions, Hoover, like Harding and Coolidge, failed to restore Negroes to the number of positions in the Executive Departments that they had held before Wilson's presidency.[33]

Negro spokesmen eventually began to complain about the administration's attitude. "President Hoover has a national program, but no negro policy," wrote Kelly Miller in October 1929. "During his whole public career he has never uttered one word concerning the negro as a separate entity, nor engaged to deal with his separate problems as such."[34] A few weeks later Robert R. Church, Jr., sent a strong letter of protest to Hoover. Church asserted that the president's attitude was alarming and that Negroes had suffered a "grievous disappointment." "Where their hopes had been fondest their sorrow is keenest now and where they had been led to expect the bread of encouragement they have received the stones of contempt. Their disappointment can be measured only by their surprise and

[32] Moton to Hoover, Jan. 15, Feb. 5, 1930, "Colored Question," Presidential, Subject File, Hoover Papers. For examples of Negro complaints on this matter, see Eugene McIntosh to Hoover, July 15, 1929, Robert R. Church to Hoover, Nov. 6, 1929, *ibid.*; New York *World*, May 1, 1929; *Along This Way: The Autobiography of James Weldon Johnson* (New York: The Viking Press, Inc., 1933), p. 239.

[33] See the reports submitted by the various departments on Nov. 4, Nov. 5, and Nov. 6, 1931, to Lawrence Richey, secretary to Hoover, in "Colored Question," Presidential, Subject File, Hoover Papers; John R. Hawkins, "The National Negro Republican League–What It Is and What It Stands For," Nov. 25, 1931, copy in *ibid.*

[34] Miller to the editor, New York *Times*, Oct. 6, 1929.

their resentment is universal. . . . They were not prepared to believe that any Republican president would adopt and embrace the principle of disfranchisement and from his advantage encourage attacks upon their nationality."[35] Church's chief concern seemed to have been Hoover's southern policy and his failure to appoint Negroes to office. Even allowing for any personal interest, the letter was a powerful indictment. But it had no apparent results. When the NAACP met for its annual convention in June 1930, for the first time since Wilson it received no greeting from the president. Du Bois was disgusted with Hoover. "Any Negro who hereafter regards him as a friend of his race or as having even reasonable human respect for it, must have proof which is not in the possession of *The Crisis,*" he wrote in July 1930. Hoover "can only be regarded as Walter White says, as 'The Man in the Lily White House!' "[36]

Although his policies angered blacks, Hoover was also attacked at times by racially sensitive southern whites. The unaccustomed presence in Washington of a Negro congressman, Oscar DePriest of Chicago, accounted for the best known instance. In the spring of 1929 Mrs. Hoover held a series of teas for the wives of congressmen and cabinet officers. Mrs. DePriest was not included in any of the first four, but she had to be invited sooner or later. After considerable discussion among the White House staff it was decided to hold a special party, to which a carefully selected list of guests was invited, each having been warned in advance about the nature of the occasion. A few of these refused to attend, and some at the tea were apparently under a strain, but the affair went off with no untoward incident.[37]

The story was not released to the press, but somehow the newspapers got hold of it and published an account of the tea the next day, June 13.[38] Cries of outrage went up throughout the South. Indeed the reaction was almost as vehement as it had been nearly three decades before when President Roosevelt entertained Booker T.

35 Church to Hoover, June 24, 1929, "Colored Question," Presidential, Subject File, Hoover Papers. For similar criticisms, see James W. Johnson, "A Negro Looks at Politics," *American Mercury,* 18 (Sept. 1929), 88–94; Thomas L. Dabney, "Southern Negroes and Politics," *Opportunity,* 8 (Sept. 1930), 272–74.

36 *Crisis,* 37 (July 1930), 244. In 1931 and 1932 Hoover sent cautious greetings to the NAACP conventions.

37 Irwin H. Hoover, *Forty-Two Years in the White House* (Boston, 1934), pp. 301–3.

38 Senator Thaddeus H. Caraway of Arkansas immediately had the article from the Washington *Daily News,* June 13, 1929, printed in the *Congressional Record,* 71st Cong., 1st sess., vol. 71, pt. 3, p. 2781. The New York *Times* carried the story on June 14, 1929.

Washington at dinner. On June 17 Senator Blease of South Carolina introduced a resolution "To Request the Chief Executive to Respect the White House." He accompanied it with an obscene doggerel entitled "Niggers in the White House." This drew such criticism that Blease finally agreed to expunge it from the record. In a short while one or both houses of the legislatures of Florida, Georgia, Mississippi, Oklahoma, and Texas passed resolutions of censure. "It was a terrible mistake on Mr. Hoover's part," said Governor Dan Moody of Texas, "and an affront to a large part of the people of the nation."[39] Many citizens wrote directly to Hoover to express their disapproval. " 'With one fell swoop' you have destroyed every atom of respect and possible loyalty that the Democrats of this state may have felt toward you," wrote one irate critic from North Carolina. "The folks down this way wouldn't vote for you again, even in the capacity of a city dog catcher."[40]

In response, the White House explained that "the incident was official and not social" and that it had thus nothing to do with the matter of social equality. Congressman DePriest took the same position in a public statement issued on June 20.[41] The State Department's Division of Protocol scurried about to find earlier instances when Negroes were entertained at the White House and announced that there had been two occasions under Taft, five under Wilson, one under Harding, and three under Coolidge. These all involved foreign diplomats or visiting heads of state. Secretary of Labor James J. Davis also made public a report that claimed that as early as 1886 President Cleveland, a Democrat, had entertained the minister to Haiti, and that in 1864 Frederick Douglass had dined at the White House with Lincoln. This appeal to precedent did little to calm the tempest. The incident was highly embarrassing to Hoover and to the white Republicans of the South, and southern Democrats seized upon it as proof that southerners had made a mistake when they voted for Hoover in 1928.[42]

39 New York *Times*, June 18, 26, 28, July 3, 1929; *Literary Digest*, 101 (June 29, 1929), 10.

40 H. I. Crumpler to Hoover, June 17, 1929, "Colored Question–DePriest Incident," Presidential, Subject File, Hoover Papers.

41 Walter H. Newton to Henry W. Anderson, June 16, 1929, *ibid.*; New York *Times*, June 21, 1929.

42 Copy of the State Department's report is in "Colored Question–DePriest Incident," Presidential, Subject File, Hoover Papers. See also New York *Times*, July 4, 1929. On the southern Democrats' position, see the Memphis *Commercial Appeal*, June 30, 1929, clipping in Hoover Papers; speech by Congressman Hamilton Fish, Jr., of New York delivered at the NAACP annual meeting, in New York *Times*, July 1, 1929; Julian Harris, "De Priest Incident Still Stirs South," New York *Times*, July 7, 1929; "Mrs. De Priest Drinks Tea," *Crisis*, 36 (Sept. 1929), 298.

Hoover was more or less an innocent bystander in the DePriest affair, and it did not offset the generally adverse impression that many Negroes had of him. It certainly did not signify a change in his southern strategy. Encouraged by the big increase in Republican presidential votes in the South in 1928, Hoover and his advisers were more determined than ever to reconstruct the GOP along lily-white lines. "The solid South was not only broken, it was demolished, and I believe that the effects will be permanent," exclaimed Earle Kinsley, the national committeeman from Vermont and an aide to Republican Chairman Work, immediately after the election.[43] In line with this strategy the attack on the black-and-tan regulars was intensified. One indication of this was the decision to prosecute Perry Howard again, after his first acquittal in December 1928. Another was the support given to the opponents of Benjamin J. Davis, the Negro politician who had been struggling to regain control of the Georgia organization after losing his seat on the national committee in June 1928. On November 17, 1928, Davis admitted his defeat by announcing that he would not be a candidate for reelection to the still unfilled position as Georgia national committeeman and that thereafter Republican affairs in his state would be conducted by whites.[44] In the early part of 1929 Hoover spent a considerable amount of time in discussions of this southern strategy with such advisers as Horace A. Mann of Tennessee, the organizer of the independent white voters in the South during the campaign, Henry W. Anderson, a lily-white leader from Virginia, and Stuart W. Cramer, a textile manufacturer from Charlotte, North Carolina. After one of these meetings with Hoover, Anderson was quoted as promising that "a big housecleaning" was at hand.[45]

Such indeed appeared to be the case. At a press conference on March 26 Hoover announced what was probably the most forthright lily-white policy ever set forth by a Republican president. Praising the virtues of a two-party system, he asserted that a "sound Republican organization" must be built up in the South that would be "of such character as would commend itself to the citizens of those states." More specifically, and with evident reference to the lily-whites, Hoover added: "I highly approve and welcome the movement of the leaders of Texas, Alabama, Florida and other states to broaden the basis of party organization by the establishment of ad-

43 New York *Times*, Nov. 8, 1928. See also Lewinson, pp. 172–73; Tatum, p. 131.

44 New York *Times*, July 28, Nov. 18, 1928.

45 New York *Times*, Feb. 4, 1929. See also New York *Times*, Jan. 24, 29, 30, 1929; Andrew Buni, *The Negro in Virginia Politics, 1902–1965* (Charlottesville, Va., 1967), p. 107.

visory committees of the highest type of citizenship to deal with administrative questions and who will cooperate with independent Democrats. . . . Recent exposures of abuse in recommendations for Federal office, particularly in some parts of the States of South Carolina, Georgia, and Mississippi, under which some of the Federal departments, mainly the Post Office, were misled in appointments, obviously render it impossible for the old organizations in these states to command the confidence of the administration."[46] Hoover was saying, in effect, that in the South Negroes, at least those associated with the old black-and-tan parties, were not wanted.

Hoover's statement put Negro politicians and officeholders squarely on the defensive. "The Republican party is no longer the party of The People, but the party of the white people," complained the Chicago *Defender*.[47] This conclusion was slightly exaggerated, but it was close to the truth. Ultimately, however, the results of Hoover's southern strategy were limited. Opposition by the South's Democratic leaders was one reason for this. They had nothing to gain and much to lose if the Republicans succeeded in creating a viable party, whereas the older black-and-tans were no threat to their supremacy and often were useful in channeling federal patronage into Democratic hands. Thus Mississippi Democrats worked to clear Perry Howard, and his acquittal for the second time on April 26, 1929, represented a notable defeat for Hoover's attempt to cleanse the southern GOP. Although Howard still faced lily-white opposition, he retained control of the organization in Mississippi. In most other states the lily-whites also failed to take over the Republican party. For example, in South Carolina, Joseph W. Tolbert, the white leader of the black-and-tans, remained in charge, and such Negroes as Walter L. Cohen and Robert R. Church, Jr., held on to their positions in Louisiana and Tennessee. By 1930 only in Virginia, North Carolina, and to some extent Texas had the lily-whites shown sufficient strength to endanger the regular black-and-tan organizations.[48]

This limited success in reforming the southern GOP was due in

[46] Press Conference, March 26, 1929, Hoover Papers. The statement was published in the New York *Times*, March 27, 1929. Hoover was obviously referring to Perry Howard in Mississippi, Ben Davis in Georgia, and Joseph W. Tolbert in South Carolina.

[47] Quoted in *Literary Digest*, 101 (April 13, 1929), 7.

[48] Lewinson, pp. 175–85; Key, pp. 288–90. On Tolbert, see Samuel Taylor Moore, "Republican Patronage in South Carolina," *Independent*, 118 (Feb. 5, 1927), 149–52. For material on the Republican party in the South, see also Ralph J. Bunche, "The Political Status of the Negro" (research memorandum prepared for the Carnegie-Myrdal study of the Negro in America, 1940), chap. 13, pp. 1175–1226 (copy in Schomburg Collection of the New York Public Library).

part to the administration's own lack of determination. Some of Hoover's advisers feared that his southern strategy would backfire and that as a consequence he would be unable to control the delegates from the South at the 1932 national convention. Obviously he could not count upon the allegiance of those black-and-tans regulars who remained in power if he continued to support their lily-white opponents. Unless the housecleaning was complete, with a whole new political cadre taking charge of state organizations that were loyal to the administration, Hoover's standing with the southern politicians would be very uncertain. This problem became the particular concern of Postmaster General Walter Brown, whose quarrel with Mann over the distribution of patronage led to Mann's retirement from active leadership of the administration's effort to organize southern whites. After a year and a half of observing the postmaster general's activities, the *New Republic*'s T. R. B. noted sarcastically that "Mr. Brown has not permitted the plane to soar so high that he may have difficulty in ensuring administration control of the delegates at the next national convention. On the contrary, all of Mr. Brown's new leaders in the South were selected with the notion that one of the logical consequences of raising things to a 'higher plane' in states heretofore given over to patronage debauchery was cooperation in the noble movement to continue the present administration in power for a second term."[49] As it became increasingly clear that Hoover was not able to replace all the old black-and-tan parties with clean and viable lily-white organizations, Brown began to court some of the very men whom Hoover supposedly had repudiated. "President Hoover has now found out," commented the New York *Times*, in April 1931, "that the old rules of the Republican machine in the South are still binding. He must still abide by them, however distasteful they may be to him personally, if he desires to win."[50] Once again the Republicans backed away from an unequivocal commitment to change in their policy toward the South. They had gone far enough to alarm Negro politicians and voters, but they had stopped far short of what might have resulted in permanent two-party South.

While struggling with the complexities of the lily-white movement, the administration discovered in an unexpected way how it could be affected by the vagaries of southern Republicanism. On March 8, 1930, Associate Justice Edward T. Sanford, the only southerner on the United States Supreme Court, unexpectedly died. It was gen-

[49] *New Republic*, 64 (Sept. 10, 1930), 100; New York *Times*, March 11, May 4, 1929.

[50] April 19, 1931.

erally assumed that Hoover would select another southerner to fill this vacancy, and in many ways the credentials of Judge John J. Parker of North Carolina were admirable. Long active in Republican state politics, he had run unsuccessfully for congressman in 1910, attorney general in 1916, and governor in 1920. Since 1925 he had earned a reputation as a competent, if undistinguished, judge of the Fourth Circuit Court. His service on behalf of the Republican party in a state that had cast its electoral vote for Hoover in 1928 strengthened his qualifications as a person whose nomination was likely to promote the administration's political aspirations in the South.

Hoover submitted Parker's name to the Senate on March 21, 1930. Within a few days two different organizations, the American Federation of Labor and the NAACP, launched vigorous campaigns to block his confirmation.[51] The AFL's effort was quite separate from that of the NAACP and was occasioned by what it considered to be Parker's unsympathetic attitude to the problems of modern labor, most specifically his decision in a 1927 case (*United Mine Workers v. Red Jacket Coal and Coke Company*) upholding a lower court's injunction issued against the United Mine Workers to prevent a unionization drive in a mine with a yellow dog contract. The NAACP's objections were on entirely different grounds. As soon as Parker's name was announced, the NAACP began an inquiry into his past position on the race issue. Shortly afterwards it was reported to the NAACP that in 1920 he had advocated the continued disfranchisement of Negroes in his speech accepting the gubernatorial nomination at the North Carolina Republican state convention. As proof an informant submitted a clipping from the Greensboro *Daily News* of April 19, 1920, in which the speech was quoted. The story claimed that Parker stood by the letter and spirit of the North Carolina disfranchising amendment and that he believed that Negroes accepted it also. Parker was quoted as saying:

> The negro as a class does not desire to enter politics. The Republican party of North Carolina does not desire him to do so. We recognize the fact that he has not yet reached that stage in his development when he can share the burdens and responsibilities of government. This being true, and every intelligent man in North Carolina knows that it is true, the attempt of certain petty Democratic politicians to inject the race issue into every campaign is most reprehensible. I say it deliberately, there is no more dangerous or contemptible enemy of the state than the man who for personal

[51] The best account of this battle is Richard L. Watson, Jr., "The Defeat of Judge Parker: A Study in Pressure Groups and Politics," *Mississippi Valley Historical Review*, 50 (Sept. 1963), 213–34.

or political advantage will attempt to kindle the flame of racial prejudice or hatred.[52]

On March 26 the NAACP telegraphed Parker asking if he had been quoted correctly and if he still held those views. Receiving no answer, it decided upon a campaign to prevent his confirmation.

A subcommittee of the Senate Judiciary Committee held hearings on April 5; representatives of both the AFL and the NAACP testified against Parker. Neither group showed any interest in the other's particular concern, and they worked quite separately. Walter White led the fight for the NAACP. In his testimony before the subcommittee he insisted that the NAACP had no personal animosity toward Parker, but "that no man who entertains such ideas of utter disregard of integral parts of the Federal Constitution [the Fourteenth and Fifteenth Amendments] is fitted to occupy a place on the bench of the United States Supreme Court."[53] Senator Lee S. Overman of North Carolina tried to counter White's arguments by claiming "that most of the intelligent, educated, colored people vote in North Carolina," that they had supported Parker for governor in 1920, and that there were prominent Negroes who favored his appointment. As proof Overman introduced a letter endorsing Parker that had been written by James E. Shepard, president of the North Carolina College for Negroes. A few other Negroes, encouraged by the Parker forces, also supported him, but Shepard seems to have been the only one of any standing to do so.[54]

On April 14 the subcommittee recommended Parker's approval by a vote of two to one, with Senators Overman and Felix Hebert of Rhode Island in favor and Senator Borah opposed. Borah's decision was based on the labor, not the race, issue. Indeed, at the subcommittee hearings and elsewhere he showed no sympathy for the NAACP's position and, according to White, was incensed that Negroes would even protest.[55]

Despite the subcommittee vote, opposition to Parker was growing. His backers attempted to organize support and to answer both his labor and his black critics. In a letter to David H. Blair, a North Carolina Republican, Parker explained that his stand in 1920 was

52 A copy of the clipping is in "Judiciary–Endorsements: Parker," Presidential, Subject File, Hoover Papers.

53 U.S., Congress, Senate, Committee on the Judiciary, *Hearings before the Subcommittee of the Committee on the Judiciary on the Confirmation of Hon. John J. Parker*, 71st Cong., 2d sess. (April 5, 1930), p. 75.

54 *Ibid.*, pp. 76–78; Walter White, "The Negro and the Supreme Court," *Harper's Magazine*, 162 (Jan. 1931), 241.

55 White, *A Man Called White*, p. 106.

intended to help, not hurt, Negroes. "Instead of appealing to race prejudice, I deplored the attempt to raise the race issue. A campaign of racial prejudice is always most harmful to the state and its citizens; and I felt that I was rendering a service to the state and to the colored people as well as the white people in doing what I could to avoid such a campaign."[56] This explanation did not specifically answer the question of whether he still believed that Negroes should not participate in politics.

In mid-April the NAACP gained an ally, the Committee on Race Relations of the Society of Friends of Philadelphia. On April 17 this committee sent letters of protest to Parker and to Hoover, with copies to each senator, with the understanding that the protest would be withdrawn if Parker answered satisfactorily to three questions: Did he make the statement in 1920? Did he still hold to it? Would he support it letter and spirit the Fourteenth and Fifteenth Amendments to the Constitution? There is no evidence of a reply from Hoover. Only a few days earlier, however, the White House had announced its continued support of Parker. It was obvious that Hoover was in no mood to back down.[57]

Nevertheless, Parker was concerned, so much so in fact that he spent the entire day of April 19 discussing the problem with Robert Gray Taylor of the Society of Friends at a meeting in the John Marshall Hotel in Richmond, Virginia. Parker gave Taylor a letter of explanation which he had written to Senator Henry D. Hatfield of West Virginia, but Taylor dismissed it as "very weak." The judge admitted that he had made the statements that were under attack and, according to Taylor, said that he still believed in them. On the basis of their discussion Taylor concluded that Parker would uphold the letter of the Fourteenth and Fifteenth Amendments but not the spirit. Nevertheless, when Taylor left the Richmond meeting he was inclined to recommend a qualified acceptance of Parker and a withdrawal of the protest. After a discussion on the following day with other members of the Committee on Race Relations, however, Taylor changed his mind. The committee unanimously agreed that Parker's responses were unsatisfactory.[58]

56 Parker to Blair, April 9, 1930, "Judiciary–Endorsements: Parker," Presidential, Subject File, Hoover Papers. A similar statement by Blair was introduced at the hearings on April 5 (*Parker Hearings*, pp. 9–10).

57 Robert Gray Taylor to Ludwell Denny, May 9, 1930, Ruth Verlenden Foley and Taylor to Hoover, April 17, 1930, Oswald G. Villard Papers, Harvard College Library; New York *Times*, April 13, 1930.

58 Parker to Hatfield, April 19, 1930, "Judiciary–Endorsements: Parker," Presidential, Subject File, Hoover Papers; Taylor to Ludwell Denny, May 9, 1930, Villard Papers.

On April 24 Parker sent a detailed defense of his position on both the labor and racial issues to Senator Overman. Four days later Senate debate on the nomination began, and Overman made Parker's letter public. Its content was almost identical to that of his letter to Hatfield. Parker termed the fear that he would not enforce the Constitution as "entirely groundless." Furthermore, he argued that in 1920 his objective had been to keep racial controversy out of the gubernatorial campaign and to promote the best interests of both races. "I have no prejudice whatever against the Colored People and no disposition to deny them any of their rights or privileges under the Constitution and the laws." In defense of his attitude toward labor he held that in the Red Jacket case he had simply "followed the law as laid down by the Supreme Court," that he was bound by previous decisions, and that he "had no latitude or discretion in expressing any opinion or views" of his own.[59]

At the conclusion of the subcommittee hearings the NAACP requested all its local branches to write to their senators expressing opposition to the nomination, and before long a considerable amount of protest material began to flow into Washington.[60] On April 21 the full Senate Judiciary Committee voted ten to six against Parker's confirmation. When Senate debate began on April 28, the final outcome was very much in doubt. With the exception of Democratic Senator Robert F. Wagner of New York, who made a few remarks on the race issue in the course of a speech devoted mainly to the labor problem, the senators who spoke in opposition to Parker—Republicans Borah of Idaho, George W. Norris of Nebraska, Hiram Johnson of California, and Farmer-Laborite Henrik Shipstead of Minnesota—based their case on the nominee's attitude toward labor.[61] Parker's defenders, however, frequently commented on the Negro's attitude. Senator Overman argued that despite the NAACP a large majority of black people were in favor of Parker. Senator Frederick H. Gillett, a Republican from Massachusetts, said that although he differed "absolutely" from Parker in the matter of the Negro in politics, it would be virtually impossible to find a fit candidate for the Supreme Court from the South who did not entertain similar views.

[59] Parker to Overman, April 24, 1930, "Judiciary–Endorsements: Parker," Presidential, Subject File, Hoover Papers (copy in the Villard Papers, and printed in *Cong. Rec.*, 71st Cong., 2d sess., vol. 72, pt. 7, pp. 7793–94 [April 28, 1930]).

[60] White, *A Man Called White*, pp. 106–7. For examples, see the petitions of William M. Trotter for the National Equal Rights League to Hoover, April [28?] 1930, "Judiciary–Endorsements: Parker," Presidential, Subject File, Hoover Papers, and the folders on the Parker case in the NAACP Papers.

[61] *Cong. Rec.*, 71st Cong., 2d sess., vol. 72, pts. 7 and 8, pp. 7807–8487. For Wagner's speech, delivered on April 30, 1930, see *ibid.*, pt. 8, pp. 8033–37.

Therefore, he concluded that to oppose a person on such grounds would mean depriving "a large section of the country [of] representation on the court."[62] Republican Senators Hebert of Rhode Island, Hatfield of West Virginia, and Henry J. Allen of Kansas all pointed out that as recently as January 14, 1930, Parker had held unconstitutional a Richmond ordinance requiring segregated residential areas. The NAACP considered this decision inadequate evidence of an acceptable racial attitude, however, as Parker had merely followed a clear precedent established by the Supreme Court.[63]

The nomination was put to a vote on May 7. The result was extremely close, with 41 against and 39 in favor of confirmation. The sixteen senators not voting were all evenly paired.[64] Several issues were responsible for Parker's defeat. Quite possibly the most important was "the determination of the part of a substantial number of Democratic and Republican senators that the appointee should have liberal leanings."[65] Parker did not meet these specifications. The specific labor and racial issues considerably strengthened the hand of those who saw Parker as illiberal. Undoubtedly the fear of losing black votes influenced some senators and may have been the determining factor in several cases.[66] Finally, Parker failed to win the support of half the southern senators. They had no desire to reward North Carolina for its support of Hoover in 1928 and thus possibly to strengthen Republicanism in the South. As the Atlanta *Journal* said, these southern Democrats opposed Parker because his nomination had been determined not by basic fitness but by "political motives of a very devious character."[67]

The defeat of Parker had an exhilarating effect on many Negroes. In a statement issued after the Senate vote, White declared that they "felt stirred on the issue of the Parker nomination as on no issue in recent years. . . . Negroes have delivered an effective blow against

[62] *Ibid.*, pt. 8, p. 7943. For Overman's remarks, see *ibid.*, pt. 7, pp. 7810–14.

[63] *Ibid.*, pt. 8, pp. 8105, 8114, 8434.

[64] *Ibid.*, p. 8487. The Republicans split with 29 voting for confirmation and 17 against. For the Democrats the vote was 10 for and 23 against. One Farmer-Labor Senator voted against confirmation. The Democrats from the eleven southern states divided evenly: 9 for and 9 against with 2 paired for and 2 paired against.

[65] Watson, p. 231. The Baltimore *Sun*, May 8, 1930, called the rejection part of a revolt against the ultraconservative views that predominated on the Supreme Court (quoted in *Cong. Rec.*, 71st Cong., 2d sess., vol. 72, pt. 8, p. 9054).

[66] See Frank R. Kent's article in the Baltimore *Sun*, April 28, 1930, quoted in *Cong. Rec.*, 71st Cong., 2d sess., vol. 72, pt. 8, p. 8348; Washington *Post*, May 8, 1930, quoted in *ibid.*, p. 8567; W. E. B. Du Bois, "The Defeat of Judge Parker," *Crisis*, 37 (July 1930), 225; Watson, p. 232.

[67] Atlanta *Journal*, May 11, 1930, quoted in *Cong. Rec.*, 71st Cong., 2d sess., vol. 72, pt. 8, p. 8847.

the Republican party's lily white policy. . . . [They] have had a striking object lesson in the use of organized effort to defend their fundamental rights."[68] The successful battle also boosted the prestige of the NAACP. But that organization was not content to rest on its laurels. As Du Bois argued, the case "must be followed up by the unflinching determination of Negroes to defeat the Senators who defied their vote and supported Parker. Nothing else will convince the United States that our gesture was not mere braggadocio and bluff."[69]

A campaign against the pro-Parker senators was soon underway. Seven of them, six Republicans and one Democrat, came up for reelection in 1930. The NAACP directed particular attention to Senator Roscoe C. McCullock of Ohio, described by White "as a symbol of the growing disregard by the Republican Party of the Negro's interests."[70] White estimated that there were 150,000 black voters in Ohio. Not numerous enough to have been decisive in recent elections, in 1930 they might hold the balance of power because of the impact of prohibition and the economic decline.[71] Outside of Ohio the NAACP used its influence to oppose the reelection of Republican Senators Allen of Kansas, Jesse H. Metcalf of Rhode Island, and Daniel O. Hastings of Delaware.

The results were mixed. McCullock and Allen were defeated; Metcalf and Hastings won reelection. The influence of other significant issues, notably prohibition in the Ohio contest, makes it difficult to prove that the NAACP's campaign was the decisive factor in the two defeats, although both candidates did badly in certain Negro districts. At the same time, Allen's Republican colleague in Kansas, Arthur Capper, was also up for reelection. Possibly it was significant that, supported by the NAACP, he was returned to the Senate.[72] Encouraged by these successes, the NAACP waged a campaign against Republican Senator David Baird, Jr., when he ran for governor of New Jersey in the fall of 1931. According to White's

68 New York *Times*, May 8, 1930.

69 *Crisis*, 37 (July 1930), 244.

70 Walter White, "The Test in Ohio," *ibid.* (Nov. 1930), p. 374.

71 White to Harry E. Davis, Sept. 22, 1930; "Report of Trip to Cleveland, September 19, 20, 21, by Acting Secretary [White] for Interview with Robert J. Bulkley," NAACP Papers.

72 NAACP, *Annual Report: 1930*, p. 15; New York *Times*, April 13, 1931; *Crisis*, 37 (Dec. 1930), 425; White, *A Man Called White*, pp. 111–13; Mary White Ovington, *The Walls Came Tumbling Down* (New York, 1947), pp. 256–57. Capper claimed that the Negro vote was solidly behind him (Capper to White, Nov. 5, 1930, NAACP Papers). Allen had been appointed to the Senate to fill the vacancy caused when Charles Curtis became vice-president in 1929, but he had to stand for election in 1930 in order to win the remainder of Curtis's term.

estimate, in that contest Negroes cast more than 80 percent of their votes against Baird, who lost to his Democratic opponent, A. Harry Moore.[73]

Even if the black vote was not decisive in any of these elections, the willingness of Negroes to ignore the Republican label was important. It could at least be argued that they had exerted more political influence in the fight against Parker and his supporters than at any time since Reconstruction. By ignoring the deeply felt anxiety of Negroes over Parker's elevation to the Supreme Court, Hoover gave Negroes an additional reason to suspect him; by campaigning actively and to some extent successfully against Parker's supporters, Negroes gained a new sense of the meaning of organized political power.

The controversy over the Parker nomination had not been settled when the Hoover administration added to its troubles with the black community by its inept handling of a very different problem, the European pilgrimage of gold star mothers and widows. In December 1927 Congressman Thomas S. Butler of Pennsylvania introduced a bill to enable the mothers and widows of American service men interred in Europe to visit the graves of the deceased. This sentimental proposal attracted considerable support, and in February 1928 the House voted its approval. The Senate delayed until the next session, but in late February 1929 it passed the bill, which was signed by President Coolidge shortly before Hoover's inauguration.[74] According to the measure the women were to be furnished first-class accommodations on government owned or chartered vessels. The first group was scheduled to depart from New York City on May 6, 1930.

Several months before that date, the news leaked out that the War Department, which was in charge of the arrangements, intended to send the black mothers and widows on separate ships from the whites. The NAACP wrote letters to the Negroes who had been invited to sail asking them to sign a petition of protest which stated that they would refuse to go if such segregation was not abolished. The petition was sent to Hoover, but it went unacknowledged, as did two more letters from the NAACP asking for a reversal of the War Department's ruling. On May 29, 1930, Assistant Secretary of War F. Trubee Davison finally issued a statement upholding the decision to put all Negroes together, although he claimed that "no discrimination whatever will be made as between the various groups. Each

73 White to Robert L. Vann, Nov. 5, 1931, NAACP Papers.

74 *Cong. Rec.*, 70th Cong., 1st sess., vol. 69, pt. 1, p. 1, pt. 3, pp. 2399, 3286–87; *ibid.*, 2d sess., vol. 70, pt. 2, p. 1612, pt. 5, pp. 4721, 4723, 4954, 5224. Coverage was extended by other bills passed by the 71st Congress.

will receive equal accommodations, care and consideration."[75] On July 10 Secretary of War Patrick J. Hurley put out a more detailed defense of the policy. He not only denied that there would be any discrimination in the quality of the accommodations; he also criticized the NAACP for stirring up the protest. Reviewing in detail the reasons for the segregation, Hurley concluded that "the formation of white and colored groups of mothers and widows would best assure the contentment and comfort of the pilgrims themselves. . . . It would seem natural to assume that these mothers and widows would prefer to seek solace in their grief from companions of their own people." Hurley added, however, that if the NAACP could furnish evidence that any member of one group wished to join another, and if she were welcome by that group, his department would grant this arrangement.[76]

These explanations were all unacceptable to the NAACP and to other concerned Negroes. The Philadelphia *Tribune* carried the story under the headline "National Government Fosters, Condones, and Supports Discrimination."[77] The Chicago *Defender* pointed out that nothing in the legislation required such segregation; it was all planned by Hurley and Hoover. "The great wave of intolerance that is sweeping the country has its source in the White House, presided over by one Herbert Clark Hoover, Republican."[78] A considerable number of Negroes refused to go on the pilgrimage under the conditions set by Hurley. The first ship carrying Negroes, the *American Merchant*, sailed from New York on July 12, 1930, with only fifty-eight pilgrims, far fewer than the approximately 450 originally scheduled.[79] Other groups of Negroes went in 1931 and 1932, but the total was not large.

The War Department insisted that all the accommodations it provided were equal. But Roy Wilkins of the NAACP noted that the whites traveled on big, fast liners like the *Leviathan, George Washington,* and *Roosevelt,* while blacks went on slower and smaller ships that were primarily freight carriers like the *American Merchant* and *American Banker*. This difference may have been, as the govern-

75 New York *Times*, May 30, 1930; M. W. Spencer and W. M. Trotter to Hoover, Feb. 19, 1930, "Gold Star Mothers," Presidential, Subject File, Hoover Papers; "Report of the Acting Secretary, June 4, 1930," Spingarn Papers; NAACP, *Annual Report: 1930*, p. 32.

76 New York *Times*, July 11, 1930; "Report of the Acting Secretary, July 14, 1930," Spingarn Papers.

77 July 17, 1930, clipping in Hoover Papers.

78 July 19, 1930.

79 New York *Times*, July 11–13, 1930.

ment explained, simply a result of the small size of the Negro groups; in 1932, when there were only thirty-seven whites, they too were sent on a merchant ship, the *American Importer,* similar to the ones that had carried Negroes.[80] However, the main issue was not the quality of the accommodations, but the enforced segregation itself. "Surely there was no time in the history of our country," observed the *Nation,* "when segregation was less necessary and more cruel."[81] The inability of the Hoover administration to grasp this point turned a well-meaning gesture into a painful insult.

Another sort of racial discrimination, the unfair treatment of black federal government employees, was a problem that the Hoover administration inherited. The extent that Negroes were segregated on the job or treated unequally in hirings and promotions cannot be readily ascertained, as no outside group made a systematic study of the situation during these years. But protests continued to be lodged, for example, against the Civil Service Commission's practice of requiring job applicants to submit photographs, a procedure that Negroes believed was used to eliminate them from certain positions.[82] In another instance an employee of the Veterans Bureau claimed that it was the policy of that department not to hire any Negro clerks, and as evidence of her charge she reported that papers of applicants coming from the personnel office had "col" marked beside the name where appropriate.[83] Reports of various forms of segregation within the departments turned up from time to time, but there appear to have been fewer complaints than earlier in the decade.[84]

The administration's handling of several other matters did little to bolster the declining reputation of the Republican party among black Americans. At the beginning of Hoover's presidency it became known that he intended to appoint a commission to study the problem of the widespread disrespect for law in America. The difficulties over prohibition prompted the original idea for such a commission, but its work did not have to be limited to that subject. The NAACP

80 Wilkins to W. J. Rice, Sept. 29, 1932, NAACP Papers; F. H. Payne to Lawrence Richey, Oct. 25, 1932, "Gold Star Mothers," Presidential, Subject File, Hoover Papers.

81 "Black and Gold Stars," *Nation,* 131 (July 23, 1930), 86.

82 H. E. Barnett to Hoover, July 7, 1931, "Colored Question–Segregation," Presidential, Subject File, Hoover Papers.

83 Harriet A. Lee to Mary C. Terrell, July 1, 1932, Mary C. Terrell Papers, Manuscript Division, Library of Congress.

84 Black leaders pointed out that employees often failed to register valid complaints for fear of endangering their jobs. See William M. Trotter to Hoover, March 7, July 1, Nov. 11, 1929, July 3, 1931, Feb. 15, Sept. 28, 1932, Walter White to Hoover, Dec. 10, 1931, Hoover Papers.

tried unsuccessfully to have a Negro appointed to the commission and to have an investigation into the violation of the rights of Negroes put on its agenda. The government, however, showed no interest in requiring the commission to look into such problems as lynching and mob violence, peonage, segregation, or disfranchisement.[85]

The NAACP made no major effort to obtain federal antilynching legislation during the years of the Hoover presidency. But when the number of lynchings began to increase again in 1930 it did appeal to him "to make a public pronouncement calling upon all law-abiding citizens to engage themselves in meeting this challenge of the mob."[86] Hoover's secretary finally sent a letter to the NAACP in which the president was quoted as asking "every decent citizen" to "condemn the lynching evil as an undermining of the very essence of both justice and democracy."[87] This condemnation did not mean that Hoover intended to take any positive steps to end the problem. In October 1930, for example, he refused to meet with White, who wanted to present his idea for summoning a conference of southern governors to consider means of dealing with lynching.[88] Others who attempted to get Hoover to act—the Northeastern Federation of Women's Clubs, the General Conference of the Religious Society of Friends, numerous individual churches, and Negro organizations such as the National Equal Rights League—had no more success.[89] The harried president had no intention of adding to his troubles at that time by assuming leadership of an antilynching campaign.[90]

Hoover could not avoid dealing with another problem involving the abuse of southern Negroes. After the 1927 disaster along the

85 James W. Johnson to A. S. Pinkett, March 19, 1929, NAACP Papers, New York *Times*, June 24, 1921; "This Lawless Nation," *Nation*, 129 (Aug. 7, 1929), 134.

86 Walter White to Hoover, August 15, 1930, "Colored Question–Lynching," Presidential, Subject File, Hoover Papers.

87 Quoted by Walter H. Newton in letter to Walter White, Aug. 20, 1930, *ibid.* Hoover's statement first appeared in a letter to Sam H. Reading of Philadelphia, Aug. 13, 1930, *ibid.*

88 White to Hoover, Oct. 3, Oct. 20, 1930, George Akerson to White, Oct. 21, 1930, White to Hoover, Nov. 13, 1930, *ibid.*; NAACP to Hoover, Oct. 30, 1930; White to Hoover, Dec. 12, 1930, Spingarn Papers.

89 There are numerous such requests in "Colored Question–Lynching," Presidential, Subject File, Hoover Papers. A year later on Nov. 30, 1931, Hoover did meet with a delegation from the National Equal Rights League led by William M. Trotter. Although Hoover appeared to be sympathetic, nothing came of the meeting (New York *Times*, Dec. 1, 1931; William M. Trotter to Hoover, Dec. 7, 1931, Hoover Papers).

90 His attorney general, William D. Mitchell, specifically advised against any such step (Mitchell to Hoover, Jan. 6, 1932, "Colored Question–Lynching," Presidential, Subject File, Hoover Papers.

lower Mississippi River, the federal government began a major flood control project. By 1932 numerous charges had been made that private contractors were exploiting Negro workers through low wages, excessive hours, commissary overcharges, and violence. In December 1931 two investigators for the AFL visited the region and prepared a damning report that was published in the March 1932 issue of the *American Federationist*.[91] An NAACP investigation undertaken in the summer of 1932, whose findings were made public on August 30, 1932, confirmed the existence of such abuses. Hours of labor were excessive, seven days a week with no holidays being typical. Wages averaged about 10 cents an hour. Commissaries in labor camps so overcharged that Negroes paid from 50 to 75 percent of their earnings for their supplies. Living conditions were often unsanitary. The attitude of many of the contractors toward the workers was "reminiscent of slavery at its worst. Men . . . [were] beaten on the slightest pretext and fired without pay on the slightest provocation."[92]

On August 22, 1932, the NAACP sent a copy of its report to President Hoover, Secretary of War Hurley, Attorney General Mitchell, and several senators. In response Major General Lytle Brown, chief of Army Engineers, defended the low pay and the long hours and angrily belittled the reports of brutality. At Hurley's request the Mississippi River Commission held a brief inquiry, but it too failed to convince the army authorities that there had been any mistreatment.[93] After Senator Wagner indicated his intention to press for a congressional investigation, Hoover finally acted. On October 26 he announced the appointment of a commission of investigation headed by Dr. Moton and including Judge James A. Cobb, Eugene Kinckle Jones of the Urban League, and Ulysses S. Grant, 3rd. The presence of Grant, a man with little understanding of racial problems, was not encouraging, especially when it became apparent to the Negro members that they were expected to take their instructions from him and to clear all information through him. Moreover, the government failed to provide the commission with funds to undertake its work. White concluded that Hoover had appointed the commission merely as an attempt to forestall a Senate investigation.[94]

91 Holt Ross and Thomas E. Carroll, "Levees, Labor and Liberty," *American Federationist*, 39 (March 1932), 291–96.

92 "Report of the Secretary, June 7, 1932," "Investigations of Labor Camps in Federal Control Operations, August 1932," "Report of the Secretary, September 8, 1932," Spingarn Papers; New York *Times*, Aug. 31, 1932.

93 "Report of the Secretary, September 8, 1932," Spingarn Papers; New York *Times*, Sept. 25, 1932; NAACP, *Annual Report: 1932*, p. 10.

94 "Report of the Secretary, September 8, 1932," "Report of the Secretary, November 10, 1932," "Report of the Secretary, December 8, 1932," Spingarn Pa-

On December 12 Wagner presented a resolution for an investigation by the Senate Committee on Commerce. A revised version, providing for an inquiry by a select committee of three senators appointed by the vice-president, was passed on February 22, 1933.[95] Its inquiries began later in 1933 under Wagner's chairmanship. Eventually some improvements in working conditions were made. In October 1933 the new secretary of War, George H. Dern, announced that the flood control workers would be subject to PWA labor regulations, which provided for a 34-hour week and a 40-cent minimum wage for the unskilled. When White toured the flood control camps in July 1934 he found that the working conditions were much improved.[96] To that extent the NAACP's effort had been successful. However, the changes occurred only after the Democrats had come to power in Washington.

On one issue, the prolonged American involvement in Haiti, the Hoover administration won qualified praise from some black Americans. By 1932 Hoover had taken significant steps toward bringing it to an end. There is no evidence that this action was taken in response to the persistent protests by the NAACP and various Negro critics. Moreover, the administration's Haitian policy, in contrast to the actions and attitudes shown in numerous domestic issues, was a matter of relatively minor concern to Negroes in the United States. As the 1932 election approached much more than this was needed to counterbalance the mistrust, if not positive contempt, that many Negroes had for Hoover's administration and for the party he represented.

---

pers. A copy of the White House announcement is in "Colored Question," Presidential, Subject File, Hoover Papers.

95 *Cong. Rec.*, 72d Cong., 2d sess., vol. 76, pt. 1, p. 305, and pt. 5, p. 4692. The authorized expenses were cut from the original $10,000 to a mere $1,000, so that the committee could hardly undertake a sweeping investigation.

96 "Report of the Secretary, April 6, 1933," Report of the Secretary, October 5, 1933," "Report of the Secretary, July 11, 1934," Spingarn Papers.

CHAPTER X

Background to Revolt

BY THE EARLY 1930's the allegiance of most blacks to the Republican party was an anachronism that was more a result of legend and habit than a response to constructive programs designed to protect and advance their special interests. From the 1890's, when the GOP first became the majority party, through the 1920's, Republican leaders had repeatedly shown how little their actions were guided by their party's supposed equalitarian ideals. It became increasingly difficult to argue that it made any difference to Negroes, at the national level anyway, whether Republicans or Democrats held office. The economic collapse of the 1930's was the final blow. As the depression worsened no group suffered more than black Americans, and they, like so many others, discovered that they could count on little help from the floundering Hoover administration. When a meaningful Democratic alternative was at last presented they too were ready to shift their allegiance.

Meeting in Chicago in mid-June, the 1932 Republican national convention aroused little enthusiasm and produced no real surprises. Few Negroes seemed excited about Hoover's candidacy, except some of the most dedicated party functionaries like Roscoe Conklin Simmons of Illinois, who delivered a fulsome speech seconding the president's renomination.[1] Hoover's sympathy with the lily-whites was one of the specific causes of the Negroes' resentment, even though he had given relatively little attention to the reform of the southern GOP after the 1930 election.[2] The mixed results of the lily-white movement were apparent at the convention. Such Negro regulars as Ben Davis of Georgia, Perry Howard of Mississippi, and Robert R. Church, Jr., of Tennessee were all members of their states' delegations. Joseph W. Tolbert's black-and-tan delegation from South Carolina was placed on the temporary roll by the national committee, but the committee on credentials voted to unseat it in favor of the

[1] *Official Report of the Proceedings of the Twentieth Republican National Convention Held in Chicago, Illinois, July 14, 15 and 16, 1932*, pp. 189–91.

[2] In 1930 only five southern Republicans were elected to Congress, compared to nineteen in 1928 (George F. Tindall, *The Emergence of the New South, 1913–1945* [Baton Rouge, La., 1967], p. 253).

lily-white faction led by J. C. Hambright.[3] In the final roll the percentage of Negroes among southern delegates was smaller than at any previous convention.[4] Lily-whitism had failed to remake the southern GOP into a party with broad popular support; nevertheless it had left its mark and foreshadowed a future in which blacks would play an ever diminishing role in the Republican party.

The very minor place that racial issues had in the thinking of the party leaders was well illustrated by the vague and meaningless Negro plank that the convention adopted without question. The NAACP had made a number of concrete proposals, including denunciation of the lily-white movement, opposition to any form of racial discrimination, especially in unemployment relief, support for antilynching legislation, and a guarantee of the independence of Haiti. The platform carefully avoided making any specific pledges on these issues.[5] Instead it relied upon a claim that the Republican party had been a friend of black Americans for seventy years. In the face of the party's recent record it was little short of mockery to assert that "vindication of the rights of the Negro citizen to enjoy the full benefits of life, liberty and the pursuit of happiness is traditional in the Republican Party." The plank, said Walter White, was mere "flapdoodle." It was a "catch-penny device to get the votes from the unthinking."[6]

Little else in the 1932 campaign suggested that the Republicans gave more than perfunctory attention to the black voter. Hoover's overwhelming concern was with the depression. The national committee set up some of the usual apparatus, such as the Colored Bureau headed by Francis E. Rivers, but less effort seems to have been expended than in previous campaigns.[7] The White House said little

3 Hambright's so-called lily-white delegation actually contained four Negroes, the same number as in Tolbert's. In Georgia the state convention replaced Mrs. George N. Williams, a black national committeewoman, with a white woman. Mrs. Williams had been one of two black committeewomen, and despite her objections the national committee upheld the change (*Proc. 20th Rep. Nat. Conv.*, pp. 49, 165; New York *Times*, March 27, April 27, June 14, June 15, 1932).

4 Alexander Heard, *A Two-Party South?* (Chapel Hill, N.C., 1952), p. 314, n. 17. The decline in Negro percentage was related to the fact that the South had been awarded more seats at the 1932 convention (as a result of the strong showing in 1928), and all of the new seats were taken by whites.

5 *Press Service of the NAACP*, June 14, 1932, NAACP Papers, Manuscript Division, Library of Congress; "Report of the Secretary, July 7, 1932," Arthur B. Spingarn Papers, Manuscript Division, Library of Congress; Walter White, *A Man Called White* (New York, 1948), pp. 139–40.

6 *Press Service of the NAACP*, June 17, 1932, NAACP Papers.

7 See Mary Church Terrell Papers, Box 6, Library of Congress. Mrs. Terrell served as the assistant advisor to women.

about racial problems in reply to the various critics who presented the Negroes' case against Hoover. When presidential secretary Walter H. Newton learned that the NAACP was preparing a set of questions for submission to Hoover and to the Democratic candidate Franklin D. Roosevelt, he immediately criticized the project. Hoover's record was an "open book," Newton explained to Judge James A. Cobb. "We are all part of one great country. . . . I think it is a mistake for a group to single themselves out the way some members of some groups do from time to time."[8] Neither Hoover nor Roosevelt answered the questionnaire, but the NAACP felt that the publicity that had been stirred up over it was useful in calling attention to Negro demands.[9]

On October 1 some 200 prominent Negroes came to Washington in response to an invitation by the Republican national committee. A delegation led by Roscoe Conklin Simmons met Hoover on the south lawn of the White House and begged him to speak out firmly on the racial issue. In response the president cited the Republican platform, noted the recent advances made by Negroes in education and welfare, and assured them that "the Republican party would not abandon its traditional duty to the American Negro, given in the first instance by the immortal Lincoln and transmitted to those who followed as a sacred trust." This was Hoover's one published statement on the subject during the 1932 campaign. The loyal Negroes present seemed to have accepted these remarks as constituting an adequate statement of the racial issue.[10] But they were party functionaries. More significant was the fact that the number of Negroes willing to speak out for the Republican candidate was smaller than usual, and the number who defected from the party was impressive. This was well illustrated by the position of the Negro press. The majority of the black newspapers and journals continued to be Republican; at the same time, many of the most influential, like the Baltimore *Afro-American*, the Boston *Guardian*, the New York *Age*, the Norfolk *Journal and Guide*, and the Pittsburgh *Courier*, either actively supported Roosevelt or attacked Hoover. Several others, including the Chicago *Defender*, declined to endorse the president. The NAACP's *Crisis* made no specific commitment, al-

[8] Newton to Cobb, Aug. 16, 1932, "Colored Question," Presidential, Subject File, Herbert Hoover Papers, Hoover Presidential Library.

[9] Walter White to Hoover, Sept. 14, 1932, *ibid.*; *Press Service of the NAACP*, Sept. 16, 1932, NAACP Papers; NAACP, *Annual Report: 1932*, pp. 31–32.

[10] New York *Times*, Oct. 1, 1932; Lester A. Walton, "Vote for Roosevelt," *Crisis*, 39 (Nov. 1932), 343.

though Du Bois, its editor, opposed Hoover. Even *Opportunity*, the far more conservative journal of the National Urban League, leaned toward the Democrats without making an actual endorsement.[11]

That many Negroes who were unhappy with Hoover were reluctant to support Roosevelt is easily understandable. There was nothing in his record to indicate that he had any special concern for or understanding of America's racial problems. Some doubters remembered that he had been assistant secretary of the Navy under Wilson when American troops occupied Haiti and that when he was a candidate for the vice-presidency in 1920 he had made an unfortunate remark about having written Haiti's new constitution. As governor of New York, Roosevelt had paid no particular attention to blacks. The Democratic platform in 1932 was entirely silent on racial problems. In addition, any national Democratic leader was encumbered to some extent by his party's southern wing, a fact that had always limited its attractiveness to Negroes regardless of the candidate. In 1932 the apparent debt that Roosevelt owed to the South, shown by his acceptance of John Nance Garner of Texas as the vice-presidential candidate, was a special liability.

Thus it is not surprising that a majority of the black voters in 1932 stayed with the Republicans. In Chicago, for example, the Republican percentage of the presidential vote in predominantly Negro districts remained about what it had been in 1928, as it did in Philadelphia, Cincinnati, Baltimore, and Columbus.[12] In Cleveland the Republican percentage of Negro voters actually increased over what it had been in 1928.[13] In Detroit, however, the Democrats registered significant gains among Negro voters, and in Manhattan a majority of the vote in black districts went Democratic for the first

[11] For a listing of Negro newspapers and their political leanings, see the report prepared by John R. Hawkins, the head of the Colored Voters Division during the 1928 campaign, in "Colored Question," Presidential, Subject File, Hoover Papers. See also Hawkins to Everett S. Sanders, Aug. 4, 1932, *ibid.*; *Crisis*, 39 (Nov. 1932), 362–63; Allen Francis Kifer, "The Negro under the New Deal, 1933–1941" (Ph.D. diss., University of Wisconsin, 1961), pp. vii–ix.

[12] John M. Allswang, *A House for All Peoples: Ethnic Politics in Chicago, 1890–1936* (Lexington, Ky., 1971), pp. 42, 187; Allswang, "The Chicago Voter and the Democratic Consensus: A Case Study, 1918–1936," *Journal of the Illinois State Historical Society*, 60 (Summer 1967), 170–71; David Burner, *The Politics of Provincialism: The Democratic Party in Transition, 1918–1932* (New York, 1968), p. 241; Harold F. Gosnell, *Negro Politicians: The Rise of Negro Politics in Chicago* (Chicago, 1935), p. 31; Gunnar Myrdal, *An American Dilemma: The Negro Problem and Modern Democracy* (New York, 1944), p. 494.

[13] Henry Lee Moon, *Balance of Power: The Negro Vote* (Garden City, N.Y., 1949), p. 18.

time in a presidential election.[14] As in previous elections the defections from the Republican party were far greater among Negro leaders than among the masses of voters.

The results of the 1932 presidential election showed the failure of the long-term Republican aspirations in the South. The GOP's percentage of the total popular vote in the eleven states of the former Confederacy dropped to 18.55, the lowest since the Civil War. All the gains made in decades of effort had disappeared. The celebrations in 1928 about cracking the solid South had been premature. Not until 1952 was the Republican presidential vote in the South restored to the approximate proportions that it had been in 1928.

The failure of the southern policy was particularly ironic in view of the party's neglect of Negroes. The reconciliation of the needs of black Americans with the immediate goals of practical politics was a problem that had plagued the GOP from its inception. Republicans could not escape their special relationship to Negroes, even when it had ceased to pay dividends on election day. They also had never abandoned their hope of building a truly national party, and from Hayes to Hoover they had tried, with varying degrees of enthusiasm, to strengthen the GOP in the South. In the early years this goal was not always seen as something that had to be done at the expense of Negroes, but by the 1890's it had become obvious that there could be no two-party South without winning over large numbers of whites to the Republican side. To the extent that Republican leaders sought the votes of these whites, they found that more and more they had to ignore the needs of the black community. Equalitarian ideals had to be sacrificed to the exigencies of practical politics. Under McKinley and his successors this increasingly meant the acceptance of the southern "solution" to the racial problem. As Republicans became ever more attentive to the southern whites, they acquiesced in, or gave support to, Jim Crow practices, disfranchisement, and all the appurtenances of the subordinate status to which Negroes were relegated. This rejection of the Negro was thus accepted as a necessary first step if the Republican machinery in the South was to be "cleased" and "reorganized."

Even if the Republicans had desired to alter the South's racially proscriptive practices significantly, it would have been enormously difficult, if not impossible. How little the Republicans cared, however, was shown by their attitude toward racial problems well beyond the immediate limits or control of the South. The GOP record was clearly deficient in areas where it had the power to act, as in Negro

[14] Edward H. Litchfield, "A Case Study of Negro Political Behavior in Detroit," *Public Opinion Quarterly*, 5 (June 1941), 271; Burner, p. 237.

appointments or in the problem of segregation and discrimination in federal government employment. When legislation was called for, most notably against lynching, Republicans showed little will to fight. When it came to taking action against the Ku Klux Klan, they were even more hesitant. And when they had an opportunity to change a foreign policy that reflected a racial bias, as in the occupation of Haiti, the Republicans of the 1920's were little better than the Wilsonian Democrats. It was small wonder that black leaders began to argue that it made no difference which party was in power in Washington. By 1932 the Republicans had not only failed in the South; they had also gone a long way toward driving Negroes from their party.

It was not that the Republicans had not been warned. For years black leaders cautioned the GOP about the possible consequences of its racial policies. But it was to no avail, primarily because there was no immediate political necessity for most Republicans to listen to the Negroes' complaints. To be heard, Negroes had to show that they had political power, the ability to reward or punish their friends and enemies at the polls. For this reason, Negro leaders often overrated the strength of black voters; they did not hold the balance of power in presidential elections as some claimed. At the same time, they were wise to preach the necessity of political independence. Negroes had to abandon their automatic loyalty to the Republican party if politicians were to cease taking their votes for granted. In some of the emerging urban districts of the North, this power had already become effective in local elections, although apathy, traditional loyalty to the party of Lincoln, and gerrymandering all limited the immediate importance of the black vote. But as more Negroes moved to the city, and as they gained experience in the political process, their power would inevitably increase. In turn, it would have been politically wise, as well as consistent with the heritage of their party, for Republicans to have cultivated these northern urban black voters.

But they did not. This fact was related to a basic weakness in the Republicans' approach to American politics during the years of their ascendancy, a weakness that helped to explain the length and the degree of their eclipse in the years after 1932. It was not simply a loss of idealism, although this was part of the problem. It was, more fundamentally, a lack of political good sense, as too many Republicans clung to an outmoded concept of America. In the first half of the twentieth century a predominantly urban society was emerging, with large, multiethnic populations. A political party could not continue to be successful if it failed to respond to the needs of these people. As Negroes moved to the North and to the cities, they became a part of this new urban constituency. Just as America had ceased to be predominantly Anglo-Saxon, so had black-white relations ceased to be primarily a problem for the South. Yet there is little evidence that Republican leaders had adjusted to these changes by trying to make their party more inclusive, not only of Negroes, but of the other urban ethnic minorities as well. The shibboleths of Republican leaders about rugged individualism and their solicitude for business and financial interests did little to attract the urban workingmen. Similarly, their invocation of Lincoln and emancipation ceased to satisfy the needs of the black community. In short, Republicans had failed to develop a program which would attract major elements of the new, urban America, elements that formed an important part of the coalition that gave the Democratic party majority status from the 1930's through the 1960's.

Since the Hoover years some Republicans from the party's northern liberal wing have tried to reorient the GOP to make it more acceptable to a diversified, urban America. These attempts have enjoyed limited success. Distrust of the city, especially of the increasingly black centers, runs very deep in the party and was strengthened by the urban disorders of the 1960's. When Republican politicians looked to the city it was most often to the predominantly white suburbs, not the central areas that formed the basis of Democratic strength. Moreover, their attitude toward Negroes, even during the years of the civil rights movement of the 1950's and 1960's, showed that few were as advanced or constant supporters of the drive for equality as their northern Democratic opponents. Thus the historic roles of the two parties were reversed. With the victories of Eisenhower and Nixon the solid South was broken, in presidential elections at least, and that section became more and more important in the planning of Republican politicians. The southern strategy of Goldwater in 1964 and of Nixon since 1968 has been frankly directed toward white southerners. The language of recent Republican politicians has been more guarded than that of the lily-whites earlier in the century, but it is apparent that the support of black voters is frequently neither assumed nor sought. Some Republican strategists would write off the urban Northeast as well, because they no longer consider it essential for winning a popular majority. The once-solid South, coupled with the so-called Republican heartland and parts of the Pacific coast, are seen as the bastions of GOP strength.[15]

[15] For a presentation of this strategy by a Nixon assistant during the 1968 campaign, see Kevin P. Phillips, *The Emerging Republican Majority* (New Rochelle, N.Y., 1969).

Whether this strategy will result in a new cycle of Republican ascendancy, as some predict, remains to be seen. What is certain is that Negroes play a small part, if any part at all, in these calculations. During the long years of Republican dominance from the 1890's to the early 1930's, GOP politicians appealed to the myth of Lincoln and to their party's equalitarian ideals, even when their practices belied their words. Unless Republicans discover compelling political reasons to alter their present course, the ambiguities and equivocations of the past may have been finally resolved.

Appendixes

Bibliographical Note

Index

APPENDIX A

Republican Presidential Vote in the South, 1876-1940

Year	Republican presidential vote in South	Republican presidential vote in South as percentage of total Republican presidential vote	Republican presidential vote in South as percentage of total presidential vote, all parties, in South
1876	739,623	18.33%	40.40%
1880	673,423	15.12	37.47
1884	780,364	16.08	40.15
1888	772,319	14.18	36.67
1892	542,754	10.45	25.34
	(Populist: 339,908)		(Populist: 15.87)
1896	807,975	11.36	35.30
1900	669,321	9.27	35.54
1904	399,711	5.24	29.00
1908	503,229	6.55	31.71
1912	189,628	5.44	12.22
	(Progressive: 259,974)		(Progressive: 16.76)
1916	465,628	5.45	24.89
1920	942,176	5.83	35.09
1924	706,858	4.43	27.94
	(Progressive: 121,363)		(Progressive: 4.80)
1928	1,602,221	7.48	47.41
1932	700,932	4.45	18.55
1936	797,476	4.78	19.09
1940	1,012,343	4.53	21.65

Source: The figures are derived from Svend Petersen, *A Statistical History of the American Presidential Elections* (New York, 1963).
Note: South is defined as the eleven states of the former Confederacy: Alabama, Arkansas, Florida, Georgia, Louisiana, Mississippi, North Carolina, South Carolina, Tennessee, Texas and Virginia.

APPENDIX B

Dyer Antilynching Bill, 1922

AN ACT To assure to persons within the jurisdiction of every State the equal protection of the laws, and to punish the crime of lynching.

Be it enacted by the Senate and House of Representatives of the United States of America in Congress assembled, That the phrase "mob or riotous assemblage," when used in this act, shall mean an assemblage composed of three or more persons acting in concert for the purpose of depriving any person of his life without authority of law as a punishment for or to prevent the commission of some actual or supposed public offense.

SEC. 2. That if any State or governmental subdivision thereof fails, neglects, or refuses to provide and maintain protection to the life of any person within its jurisdiction against a mob or riotous assemblage, such State shall by reason of such failure, neglect, or refusal be deemed to have denied to such person the equal protection of the laws of the State, and to the end that such protection as is guaranteed to the citizens of the United States by its Constitution may be secured it is provided:

SEC. 3. That any State or municipal officer charged with the duty or who possesses the power or authority as such officer to protect the life of any person that may be put to death by any mob or riotous assemblage, or who has any such person in his charge as a prisoner, who fails, neglects, or refuses to make all reasonable efforts to prevent such person from being so put to death, or any State or municipal officer charged with the duty of apprehending or prosecuting any person participating in such mob or riotous assemblage who fails, neglects, or refuses to make all reasonable efforts to perform his duty in apprehending or prosecuting to final judgment under the laws of such State all persons so participating except such, if any, as are or have been held to answer for such participation in any district court of the United States, as herein provided, shall be guilty of a felony, and upon conviction thereof shall be punished by imprisonment not

As amended by the Senate Committee on the Judiciary. From U.S., Congress, Senate, Committee on the Judiciary, *Antilynching Bill: Report to Accompany H.R. 13*, 67th Cong., 2d sess., Senate Report 837 (July 28, 1922), pp. 1–3.

exceeding five years or by a fine of not exceeding $5,000, or by both such fine and imprisonment.

Any State or municipal officer, acting as such officer under authority of State law, having in his custody or control a prisoner, who shall conspire, combine, or confederate with any person to put such prisoner to death without authority of law as a punishment for some alleged public offense, or who shall conspire, combine, or confederate with any person to suffer such prisoner to be taken or obtained from his custody or control for the purpose of being put to death without authority of law as a punishment for an alleged public offense, shall be guilty of a felony, and those who so conspire, combine, or confederate with such officer shall likewise be guilty of a felony. On conviction the parties participating therein shall be punished by imprisonment for life or not less than five years.

SEC. 4. That the district court of the judicial district wherein a person is put to death by a mob or riotous assemblage shall have jurisdiction to try and punish, in accordance with the laws of the State where the homocide is committed, those who participate therein: *Provided,* That it shall be charged in the indictment that by reason of the failure, neglect, or refusal of the officer of the State charged with the duty of prosecuting such offense under the laws of the State to proceed with due diligence to apprehend and prosecute such participants the State has denied to its citizens the equal protection of the laws. It shall not be necessary that the jurisdictional allegations herein required shall be proven beyond a reasonable doubt, and it shall be sufficient if such allegations are sustained by a preponderance of the evidence.

SEC. 5. That any county in which a person is put to death by a mob or riotous assemblage shall, if it is alleged and proven that the officers of the State charged with the duty of prosecuting criminally such offense under the laws of the State have failed, neglected, or refused to proceed with due diligence to apprehend and prosecute the participants in the mob or riotous assemblage, forfeit $10,000, which sum may be recovered by an action therefor in the name of the United States against such county for the use of the family, if any, of the person so put to death; if he had no family, then to his dependent parents, if any; otherwise for the use of the United States. Such action shall be brought and prosecuted by the district attorney of the United States of the district in which such county is situated in any court of the United States having jurisdiction therein. If such forfeiture is not paid upon recovery of a judgment therefor, such court shall have jurisdiction to enforce payment thereof by levy of execution upon any property of the county, or may compel the levy and collection of a tax therefor, or may otherwise compel payment thereof by mandamus or other appropriate process; and any officer of such county or other person who disobeys or fails to comply with any lawful order of the court in the premises shall be liable to punishment as for contempt and to any other penalty provided by law therefor.

SEC. 6. That in the event that any person so put to death shall have been transported by such mob or riotous assemblage from one county to another county during the time intervening between his capture and putting to death, the county in which he is seized and the county in which he is put to death shall be jointly and severally liable to pay the forfeiture herein provided.

SEC. 7. That any act committed in any State or Territory of the United States in violation of the rights of a citizen or subject of a foreign country secured to such citizens or subject by treaty between the United States and such foreign country, which act constitutes a crime under the laws of such State or Territory, shall constitute a like crime against the peace and dignity of the United States, punishable in like manner as in the courts of said State or Territory, and within the period limited by the laws of such State or Territory, and may be prosecuted in the courts of the United States, and upon conviction the sentence executed in like manner as sentences upon convictions for crimes under the laws of the United States.

SEC. 8. That in construing and applying this act the District of Columbia shall be deemed a county, as shall also each of the parishes of the State of Louisiana.

That if any section or provision of this act shall be held by any court to be invalid, the balance of the act shall not for that reason be held invalid.

Bibliographical Note

A COMPLETE list of all the books, articles, reports, and other materials consulted in the preparation of this book would be unnecessarily long. The principal sources used are indicated in the footnotes. The papers of all the Republican presidents from McKinley to Hoover were basic. Nevertheless, these, as well as the papers of other major Republican leaders, when available, were of uneven value for the study of attitudes and policies toward Negroes. Materials were seldom arranged in a manner that was directly applicable to this subject, although there are some important exceptions, especially in the Hoover Papers. The papers of a number of prominent Republican leaders contained little or no useful information for the purpose of this study. Several other manuscript collections, however, have a wealth of relevant material. Especially noteworthy in this respect are the Booker T. Washington Papers, the Moorfield Storey Papers, and the papers of the National Association for the Advancement of Colored People, all in the Manuscript Division of the Library of Congress.

Negro newspapers often contained much material ignored by the white press. The Washington *Bee* was particularly useful for information on federal government activities. Unfortunately, copies of many Negro newspapers are often difficult to obtain, and in some instances there are large gaps in existing holdings. Hence, the extensive collection of newspaper clippings, conveniently arranged by topic and preserved in numerous scrapbooks, in the George Foster Peabody Collection, Collis P. Huntington Memorial Library, Hampton Institute, Hampton, Virginia, proved to be extremely valuable. In addition to the Peabody Collection, special mention should also be made of the following collections of books, pamphlets, clippings of Negro newspapers, and other related materials of Afro-American history: the Gumby Collection of Negroiana, Butler Library, Columbia University; the Moorland Collection, Howard University Library; the Schomburg Collection, Harlem Branch, New York Public Library; and the James Weldon Johnson Memorial Collection of Negro Arts and Letters, Beinecke Library, Yale University.

Index